Implicit Meanings

This new edition of a classic work provides an indispensable introduction to the thought of Mary Douglas.

First published to great acclaim in 1975, this second edition of *Implicit Meanings* includes a new introduction with Mary Douglas's reflections on how her ideas have been taken up and how her own thinking has developed over the last forty years.

Implicit Meanings includes writing on the key themes which are associated with Mary Douglas's work and which have had a major influence on anthropological thought. Essays on animals, food, pollution, risk, joking, sorcery and myth derive from initial fieldwork experiences in Africa. In different ways, the essays probe beneath the surface meanings and seek to expose the implicit understandings which tend to be taken as unchallengeable. Mary Douglas has shown that anthropology can make a central contribution to debates in many academic disciplines, and can also illuminate everyday life.

Mary Douglas is a distinguished international anthropologist. She retired as Professor of Anthropology at University College London, and taught in the USA until 1988. Her books include *Purity and Danger* (1966), *Natural Symbols* (1970), *The World of Goods* (1979), *How Institutions Think* (1986), and *Risk and Blame* (1992).

Implicit Meanings

Selected Essays in Anthropology
Second Edition

Mary Douglas

London and New York

First published 1999 by Routledge
11 New Fetter Lane, London EC4P 4EE

Simultaneously published in the USA and Canada
by Routledge
29 West 35th Street, New York, NY 10001

Routledge is an imprint of the Taylor & Francis Group

© 1975, 1978, 1999 Mary Douglas

Figures 3.1, 3.2, 19.1 and 19.2 were drawn by Pat Novy.

Typeset in Galliard by
J&L Composition Ltd, Filey, North Yorkshire
Printed and bound in Great Britain by
Biddles Ltd, Guildford & King's Lynn

British Library Cataloguing in Publication Data
A catalogue record for this book is available from the British Library

Library of Congress Cataloging in Publication Data
Douglas, Mary.
  Implicit meanings: selected essays in anthropology/Mary Douglas. – 2nd ed.
  p. cm.
  Includes bibliographical references.
  1. Ethnology. I. Title.
  GN304.D68   1999
  301–dc21   99–19937
                CIP

ISBN 0–415–20553–0 (hbk)
ISBN 0–415–20554–9 (pbk)

Contents

Preface, 1999

Starting to do anthropology, no one knows in advance where it is going. These essays mark where the first twenty years of that voyage took me. Anyone interested in belief, religion, and symbols looks to anthropology for insight. These essays are all either saying the same message, or providing some necessary background. The message is that it is useless to look for the meaning of a symbol, useless to take meanings one at a time, item by item, expecting to find something that will translate into our language. Meaning is part of a constructed world, the problem of understanding symbols is how to take a grip on a whole world. What is actually said in words is only the tip of the iceberg. The unspoken understandings are essential. How do we reach the implicit? By studying the classifications by which people decide if an action has been done well or badly, whether it is right or wrong. This is what these essays are saying.

There are two main justifications for anthropology. First is the imperative to make a full record of human society. That has little to do with disappearing cultures and much to do with the huge variety of ways of being human. Those who take on that project usually adopt an area, say the South Pacific, or India, China, or Japan, or the arctic circle, or west, south, east or central Africa, America, or wherever. They become regional experts and with like-minded colleagues they study the varieties of languages, agriculture, religion, and so on within their region.

Second, anthropology feeds the ambition to understand ourselves better by making comparisons with the rest of human kind – call it the project to find meaning. The combination of the two projects gives anthropology its distinctive outlook. Accepting the peculiar stress entailed by that vocation, the major challenge is for the regional specialists to deal with their own prejudice and bias. Somehow they must avoid interpreting everything through local Western lenses. The vast compass of comparisons creates the strain. It is never good enough to say that these other people think differently from us because they are different. Instead of exempting ourselves from the scrutiny, anthropology puts ourselves under it and turns local questions into universal ones. By the comparisons we put ourselves on the line. The anthropologist has to be daring. There must be empathy.

This book follows the second project. Its object is to find meanings. Its method is to universalise foreign and strange beliefs until what seemed at first to be inexplicable is eventually absorbed into our own enlarged experience. To examine the implicit it is necessary to go below beliefs that can be made explicit and to watch how submerged ideas determine action. For example, the idea that dirt is dangerous is mostly implicit. Taboo, for example, has a place in a general idea about forbidden behaviour as the cause of illness. Sink it back into a wider set of ideas and you find a common theory that moral failure causes bodily afflictions. Anthropologists sometimes talk about 'the problem of belief', but beliefs only generate problems when there is disbelief. It is no easier to suspend the one or the other. Belief is a matter of how worlds are constructed, not a matter of personal idiosyncrasy. Consider, for example, the conflict between African belief in the dangerousness of sorcerers, and English disbelief. How can people communicate at all when their worlds are built upon such grave discrepancies?

The book has three parts. The first approaches the idea of the implicit by examining ideas which underprop action. The essays in the first section are about the Lele of the Kasai, a people in the Congo among whom I did my fieldwork training. Outsiders to the profession are often witty at the expense of anthropologists' fieldwork, as if it were a ritual requirement, an entry fee. They speak of it as a traditional ceremony of initiation which has taken this form fortuitously; strictly speaking it is unnecessary, anyone who wants to do anthropology without fieldwork will be none the worse. But whoever has the patience to read this first part and go on further will recognise how strongly the Lele themselves have shaped my professional judgment. A writer or traveller who has not been through it, may find it hard to imagine fieldwork as the source of creative understanding. But I think that this effect of prolonged and intense experience is common to most anthropologists.

The second part lets the esoteric African case histories lead into discussing other anthropologists' interpretations. So this is where essays on the structuralist interpretation of myth and ritual belong. Familiar problems of interpretation get their universalising and systematising treatment. Laughter, for example: is it the same thing from one period or place to another? Everyone thinks they know why they laugh and most can recognise a joke. But it is more difficult to say what makes a joke funny. Why do people insult each other and then laugh? Do animals laugh, or is laughter a uniquely human gift? To all these miscellaneous questions I find myself preparing the same general answer. The questions should not be asked as if individuals are non-social beings who laugh and worry on their own: they are social beings who live together, and who collectively shape each others' fears and laughter in standard ways. They act on beliefs they have collectively made. A theory of bodily behaviour is implicit here. The body turns out to be responding sensitively to the society, even the amount of movement that it can use, and the amount of signalling it is supposed to do is regulated. Therefore, if we want to understand symbols, we have to work out some way of comparing collective behaviour.

The main preoccupation which shows in all the essays is communication. The practical problem of belief is how to be believed. Also how to give readable signals. If I do not believe in the power of sorcerers, why is it so difficult to convince the people who are desperately worried about them? Certain symbols calm the anxiety of the sick and even cure barrenness (but which ones?). The strictures of the second part make a jumping off point for the third. The thread that links them is the question of how to interpret claims that moral defects have spoilt the course of nature. The Lele thought that quarrelling spoilt the hunting, the Hadza thought that the presence of a man whose wife was menstruating would spoil the hunting. In both cases the hunting is being used to enforce claims against the neighbours. The collective production of the world has made an environment equipped with set punishments which it will invariably apply so long as everyone wants to believe in its responsiveness to moral failure. With this we are into the basic issue of belief, its relation to society. We have the choice of treating the politicising of nature as something that far-off exotic peoples do, something utterly remote from our own behaviour. Or we can use anthropology to universalise the insights and apply them to the study of risk and environmental protection.

When in 1966 I chose the title *Purity and Danger* with a subtitle referring to theories of pollution I did not imagine that both purity and danger would be linked in a world-wide anxiety about pollution of water and air, and the environment. But by 1970, the topic of 'Environments at risk' (Chapter 16 at the beginning of the third section) had become prominent, and has been ever since. This is why there has to be a special anthropological branch of the theory of knowledge. Thinking about reason and knowledge as they appear within any one society is not so exacting as thinking about knowledge in general with libraries of discordant examples to take into account.

Innatism is a theory of mind which sets the psychologists on the search for universal categories hardwired in the human psyche. Various forms of innatism can be espoused without serious challenge when they surface in Western culture because the counter-evidence can be brushed aside. But anthropologists cannot support supposed universal phobias against snakes, or universal disgust at blood or dirt. I wrote *Purity and Danger* with the express intention of replacing psychologistic ideas about such universal tendencies. Disgust and fear are taught, they are put into the mind by culture and have to be understood in a cultural (not a psychologistic) theory of classification and anomaly.[1]

One of the most important things that anthropology can do is to qualify contemporary theorising about mind and emotion. And from here it can bring sustained criticism to the reading of ancient texts. For example, it has been assumed for two millennia that the animals which the Bible forbids the people of Israel to eat are revolting, disgusting, abominable in one way or another. But over that long period no agreement has been reached about what it is about them that deserves such aversion. Over the last twelve years I have been study-ing the Book of Numbers[2] and the Book of Leviticus. I have come to the conclusion that the emphasis, as between forbidden and permitted animals, should be reversed. It is always assumed that the forbidden animals are more worthy of scholarly interest and much attention has been devoted to trying to identify what was so abominable about them. The intriguing problem was the banning of a few creatures, the pig, the camel, the hare and the rockbadger, and certain water creatures, whereas it now seems clear that the interest should have been fastened on to the permitted animals, the few allowed to be eaten.[3]

The last sentence of the original Preface has been misunderstood and re-reading it, I can see why, and need to explain. I was writing about how knowledge is founded, that is, about the confidence to believe and trust interpretation. I was reproaching Durkheim for attempting a sociology of knowledge that made a fundamental distinction between post- and pre-scientific knowledge, and for arrogantly supposing that the questions that undermine the bases of knowledge in foreign parts can never raise problems about the foundations of our own knowledge. In a grand rhetorical flourish I declared: 'Surely now it is an anachronism to believe that our world is more securely founded in knowledge than one that is driven by pangolin power.' Some readers thought I had gone off my rocker with a wild claim that something called 'pangolin power' was just as effective as a source of energy for heat and light and communications as modern industrial technology. No! Not at all, far from it – I only meant that knowledge of the world is always founded in trust and faith. The confidence that the Lele had in their cult-based knowledge was secured in the same ways as our confidence in scientific knowledge. The confidence depends on the fact that the system actually works.

There are several obvious weaknesses of essays written thirty or forty years ago. One is due to the change in vocabulary, itself due to changes in public attitudes which anthropologists helped to bring about. I now get a shock to read of 'primitive peoples', 'primitive religion', 'primitive society', 'tribal religions' and 'tribes', terms which have practically disappeared. In those days anthropologists were struggling against a general assumption that moderns were different from 'primitives' and for that argument they needed contrasting terms in order to deny any difference.

NOTES

1 Due no doubt to careless writing I seemed to be proposing a theory of universal fear of or dislike of anomaly, the exact opposite of my central thesis. Edmund Leach subsequently developed an innatist and psychologistic theory of pollution which locates the sacred in anomaly. This was naïve insofar as he allowed his own culture to provide principles for detecting anomaly. E.R. Leach, *Culture and Communication, the Logic by which Symbols are Connected*, Cambridge, 1976. Leach, Introduction to Herbert Hoffman, *Sexual and Asexual Pursuit, a structuralist approach to Greek vase painting*, Royal Anthropological Institute, Occasional Paper 34, 1977, p. 5.
2 Mary Douglas, *In the Wilderness, the Doctrine of Defilement in the Book of Numbers*, Sheffield, 1993.
3 Mary Douglas, *Leviticus as Literature*, Oxford University Press, forthcoming 1999.

Preface, 1975

By piecing together, context to context, the references the Lele made to animals in their daily life, I reached some understanding of their main fertility cult, centred on the pangolin. If my fieldwork had been more thorough I would have been able to understand better the meaning this scaly ant-eater had for them. Their knowledge was not explicit; it was based on shared, unspoken assumptions. At the grass-roots level of daily behaviour the sense that emerged from their rituals and beliefs posed the problems about implicit forms of communication that I have been pondering ever since, as these essays show. Re-reading them, I see how confused and timid presentation has disguised the unity of theme. I also realise that with better fieldwork this theme would certainly have been shelved. For thanks to the work of others in Central Africa I am even more aware of rich layers of context I left unexplored. Above all, Luc de Heusch's study of the traditions of Luba royalty has made me see the gap between the daily-bread, common-sense world that I recorded and the high tradition of Central African cosmology in which the Lele beliefs fit so well. Disengaging certain recurring threads and identifying them as the warp of the different local cosmologies, he has greatly advanced the analysis of implicit forms of communication. If only the material and the theory had been available earlier.

The Lele cult of the pangolin was performed by a few initiates who alone could eat its flesh and were sworn not to reveal its secrets. It was one of many cults, each vested with its communal property of esoteric knowledge. I was never made privy to those secrets. Apart from the aristocratic clan, no women were admitted to knowledge of the cult. If I had stayed longer, and if I had known what theoretical uses the unveiling of their secrets would have served, I could have learnt much from a formidably clever and witty princess from the Eastern Lele. But structural analysis had not at that time redeemed myth and ritual from folklorism. Only now do I glimpse, in the pages of *Le Roi ivre* (de Heusch, 1973), the possible sources of the pangolin's power. For, though I knew that this fish-like tree-dweller was the potent sign for a union of heaven and earth, I did not know that just such a union was celebrated in different ways by other tribes of the region. The pangolin was said to be a chief. The sacral kingship of the Lunda, Luba, and Bushong was also instituted in a marriage between celestial and earthly powers and in the rituals and myths about it are many echoes of Lele custom. De Heusch's book makes me see in very different light the brief, mysterious little tales of the origin of the Lele, which I dismissed as truncated and defective. Rather as the synoptic gospels need the structural analyses of John and the Pauline epistles for their exegesis, so the miracles of the pangolin need, for their full meaning to emerge, to be related to the cosmic themes of divine kingship and to the constitution of human nature and the planetary system. All that is too late for me now. Access to that implicit public language (Bernstein, 1972) from which the sacred canopy was woven would have given me enough work for the rest of my days, simply to analyse it. Moreover, the question of why the pangolin had so much power over human destiny would have been satisfactorily answered within the terms of the culture itself. Because my material was poor, I was driven to consider the matter under its more general aspect. In a comparative perspective, the question of implicit knowledge confronts the question of cognitive relativity so that they come to form only one single problem, as I shall try to explain below.

Among the Lele I found that rules of hygiene and etiquette, rules of sex and edibility fed into or were derived from submerged assumptions about how the universe works. It was evident that a very satisfactory fit, between the structure of thought and the structure of nature as they thought it, was given in the way that their thought was rooted in community life. Further, the latter was furnished with an armoury of support by this intellectually impressive fit. If we can understand how the inarticulate, implicit areas of Lele consciousness are constituted, we should be able to apply the lesson to ourselves. If they use appeals to the a priori in nature as weapons of coercion or as fences around communal property, it is probable that we do likewise. The anthropologist is inclined to respect the intellectual capacities of the tribe he studies. There is a built-in professional bias to believe that our own implicit knowledge is likely to be of the same order as theirs. Consequently the anthropologist who realises that their idea of nature is the product of their relations with one another finds it of critical importance to know just where and why our own ideas about the world are exempt from sociological analysis.

Around the beginning of this century Durkheim demonstrated the social factors controlling thought. He demonstrated it for one portion of humanity only, those tribes whose members were united by mechanical solidarity. Somehow he managed to be satisfied that his critique did not apply to modern industrial man or to the findings of science. One may ask why his original insights were never fully exploited in philosophical circles. Nowadays they are being joyously rediscovered by phenomenologists on the one hand, and ethnomethodologists on the other. Neither scarcely pauses to ask how their project differs from his, or why his remained so little used. If Durkheim did not push his thoughts on the social determination of knowledge to their full and radical conclusion, the barrier that inhibited him may well have been the same that has stopped others from carrying his programme through. It seems that he cherished two unquestioned assumptions that blocked him. One was that he really believed that primitives are utterly different from us. A week's fieldwork would have brought correction. For him, primitive groups are organised by similarities; their members are committed to a common symbolic life. We by contrast are diversified individuals, united by exchange of specialised services. The contrast is a very interesting one, full of value, but it does not distinguish between primitives and moderns. It cuts across both categories. However, believing in this sharp difference encouraged him to harbour the idea of another difference between us and primitives. Their knowledge of the world could readily be understood as unanchored to any fixed material points, and secured only by the stability of the social relations which generated it and which it legitimised. For them he evolved a brilliant epistemology which set no limits to the organising power of mind. He could not say the same for ourselves. His other assumption allowed him to reserve part of our knowledge from his own sociological theory. This was his belief in objective scientific truth, itself the product of our own kind of society, with its scope for individual diversity of thought. His concern to protect his own cognitive commitment from his own scrutiny prevented him from developing his sociology of knowledge. His biographer, Steven Lukes (1973: 495), says:

> Durkheim was really maintaining two different theses which he failed to separate from one another because he did not distinguish between the truth of a belief and the acceptance of a belief as true. The first was the important philosophical thesis that there is a non-context-dependent or non-culture-dependent sense of truth (as correspondence to reality) such that, for example, primitive magical beliefs could be called 'false', mythological ideas could be characterised as 'false in relation to things', scientific truths could be said to 'express the world as it is' and the Pragmatists' claim that the truth is essentially variable could be denied.

With one arm he was brandishing the sabre of sociological determinism, and with the other he was protecting from any such criticism the intellectual achievements of his own culture. He believed in things, in 'the world as it is', in an unvarying reality and truth. The social construction of reality applied fully to them, the primitives, and only partially to us. And so, for this contradiction, his central thesis deserved to remain obscure and his programme unrealised.

Anyone who takes on the biography of a famous thinker is in a dilemma if he finds he is obliged to toss overboard as useless and wrong his subject's most cherished theory. Normally the would-be historian would have to choose either to look for a worthier subject or to spend the next ten years of research explaining how the thinker acquired an undeserved reputation. Steven Lukes's massive biography of Durkheim makes him a great expert on the man. He must have felt this dilemma when he decided that the contrast of sacred–profane was an empirically inadequate dichotomy which vitiates Durkheim's analysis in important ways (1973: 24–8). This judgment attaints also the distinguished group of Durkheim's colleagues who made central use of the contrast in their work. Durkheim himself thought the dichotomy was central to his theoretical position. Even if he was mistaken here as well, it is cavalier to dismiss an idea which closely parallels Marx's important remarks on fetishism. I shall argue below that the latter become a more powerful instrument of social criticism if added to Durkheim's analysis, once that is purged of the reserves he made on behalf of modern science.

Durkheim's work was all focused upon the relation of the individual to the group. The excitement he aroused among his close associates came from his claim to have discovered how the individual internalises the prescriptions of the group. The discovery is about the process of categorisation. He claimed to reveal the social factors which bound the categories and relate them to one another. When the process has worked through, the so-called individual is shown using a set of conceptual tools generated from outside himself and exerting over him the authority of an external, objective power. For Durkheim, sacred and profane are the two poles of the religious life on which the relation between individual and society is worked out. The sacred is that which the individual recognises as having ultimate authority, as being other than himself and greater than himself. The dichotomy profane and sacred is not isomorphic with that between individual and society. It is not correct to interpret the individual as profane and society as sacred, for each individual recognises in himself something of the sacred. Sacredness inheres in the moral law erected by consensus to which each individual himself subscribes. The sacred is constructed by the efforts of individuals to live together in society and to bind themselves to their agreed rules. It is characterised by the dangers alleged to follow upon breach of the rules. Belief in these dangers acts as a deterrent. It defends society in its work of self-creation and self-maintenance. Because of the dangers attributed to breach of the rules, the sacred is treated as if it were contagious and can be recognised by the insulating behaviour of its devotees. This is roughly fair to what Durkheim says of the sacred in his *Elementary Forms of Religious Life* and how it is used by Hertz and Mauss.

To reject the concept of sacred contagion is to reject everything Durkheim contributed to comparative religion. From a present-day perspective, after fifty years of social anthropology (Kuper, 1973), it is hard to see how such a fruitful approach to religion should cause so much difficulty. One might reject it indeed if one were unable to separate the insight itself from the moral and political conclusions Durkheim and others drew. But this is the elementary exercise of scholarly judgment. Let us address the matter afresh, since so many streams of thought are now ready to converge just here.

Durkheim's theory of the sacred is a theory about how knowledge of the universe is socially constructed. The known universe is the product of human conventions and so is the idea of God, as its ultimate point of appeal. Durkheim saw that all religious beliefs are pulled this way and that in men's haggling and justifying of ways to live together. He could see that in all small, isolated tribal societies men create their entire knowledge of their universe in this manner. They covenant implicitly to breed a host of imaginary powers, all dangerous, to watch over their agreed morality and to punish defectors. But having tacitly colluded to set up their awesome cosmos, the initial convention is buried. Delusion is necessary. For unless the sacred beings are credited with autonomous existence, their coercive power is weakened and with it the fragile social agreement which gave them being. A good part of the human predicament is always to be unaware of the mind's own generative powers and to be limited by concepts of the mind's own fashioning.

For any fundamentalist who would not wish to allow that men's ideas of God have to be refracted through a social dimension, the theory of sacred contagion is straight impiety. One can fully sympathise with the sense of threat and blasphemy. The religious believer normally uses a theory of cognitive precariousness within the framework of his doctrine; his theology provides areas of illusion and scepticism which are clearly bounded so that his own faith is secure while everything else is vanity and flux. But here is an attack on all religious cognition and therefore one to be resisted. One can well understand the initial religious hostility to Durkheim's rationalism. But hostility breeds the wrong atmosphere for philosophising. A little more calm and open reflection on this theme could have shown the devout that what Durkheim claimed for the social construction of reality in primitive society was no more destructive of fundamentalist Christianity than it was of secular theories of knowledge. It is no more easy to defend non-context-dependent, non-culture-dependent beliefs in things or objective scientific truth than beliefs in gods and demons. Clearly Durkheim intended to challenge existing theories of knowledge, for he meant to offer his account of social determinants to qualify or supplement Kant's subjective determinants of perception. Surely Steven Lukes is right to insist that the 1914 war broke the developing thread of that idea. The challenge remained incomplete and few have taken it seriously.

When an important thinker presents two intellectual positions which contradict one another, a sensible procedure is to choose the most original and push it to its logical conclusion. If it is a good theory it will end by transforming the more established one. Durkheim used the sacred–profane dichotomy to develop a completely sociological theory of knowledge. The theory comes to a halt in his thinking when it reaches objective scientific truth. It peters out when it seems about to conflict with the most widely held beliefs of his own day. Therefore we should take the sacred–profane dichotomy and see if in its most extreme application it does not engulf fundamentalist theories of knowledge as well as fundamentalist religious doctrines.

The first essential character by which the sacred is recognisable is its dangerousness. Because of the contagion it emanates the sacred is hedged by protective rules. The universe is so constituted that all its energies are transformed into dangers and powers which are diverted from or tapped by humans in their dealings with the sacred. The sacred is the universe in its dynamic aspect. The second essential character of the sacred is that its boundaries are inexplicable, since the reasons for any particular way of defining the sacred are embedded in the social consensus which it protects. The ultimate explanation of the sacred is that this is how the universe is constituted; it is dangerous because that is what reality is like. The only person who holds nothing sacred is the one who has not internalised the norms of any community. With this definition in hand one should divest oneself of any preconceived ideas of what is going to be discovered to be sacred in any given cognitive scheme. If there are sprites and goblins which do not protect their sanctuaries with sanctions unleashing mysterious dangers, then they have nothing to do with the sacredness we are investigating. The definition quickly identifies the sacred which in Durkheim's universe is not to be profaned: it is scientific truth. In Steven Lukes's universe it would seem to be commitment to a non-context-dependent sense of truth (as correspondence to reality). Each of them risks a big sacrifice to his deity: both risk professional success and the acclaim of posterity by protecting their sacred thing from profanation. Both demonstrate in their work itself the validity of the sacred–profane dichotomy. It is entirely understandable that Durkheim should have internalised unquestioningly the categories of nineteenth-century scientific debate since he strove to have an honourable place in that very community from which the standards of conduct emanated. His blind spot, for all the theoretical weakness it brought him, at least vindicates once and for all the value of his central theory of the sacred. At that time science itself was unselfconscious about how its edicts were formulated and followed. But science has now diversified. It has moved from the primitive mythological state of a small isolated community to an international body of highly specialised individuals among whom consensus is hard to achieve. According to his theory, such a new kind of scientific community would be hard put to identify anything we could have recognised as sacred fifty years ago. So he is vindicated again by the passage of time which has made 'correspondence-to-reality' a fuzzier concept than it used to be.

In his Inaugural Lecture to the Collège de France, Michel Foucault focuses on the procedural rules which control discourse, including those which separate true from false (1971). He observes that humanity's long drive to establish truth in discourse has gone through many historical transformations. First, starting with the Greek poets of the sixth century, true discourse was the prophecy which announced what would happen, helped to bring it about and commanded men's assent to its justice. True discourse then was ritual action in which destiny was seen and justified. A century later, by a shift from action to speech, the truth of discourse was to be found in the correspondence between the form of the statement and the object to which it referred. Since then, while correspondence between word and reality has remained important, a new concern for a new kind of truth developed from the sixteenth century, with the scientific revolution. Its peculiar characteristic is its vast investment in specialised techniques of measurement and testing and in authoritative institutions for proclaiming its truths. Each of these phases he treats as systems of exclusion which impose on discourse their prohibitions and privileges. Foucault speaks of discourse as a continuing social process setting up controls and boundaries and shrines of worship in a way that recalls Durkheim. But whereas Durkheim venerates the system of controls, Foucault savagely denounces it. His work celebrates a current phase in the evolution of the ways in which discourse requires a division between truth and falsehood. The present concern is focused on subjective truth; this is the day of consciousness. A sophisticated doubt dogs other forms of truth when they are presented as god-given objective facts with the right to exclude from and to control the discourse. This is a generation deeply interested in the liberation of consciousness from control. It is normal radical criticism to enjoy unveiling the fetishes of past generations. But a philosophy intending to be radical could well sift Durkheim more thoroughly and make use of his theory of sacredness as a tool for relativising the sacred shibboleths of others who would limit and transform the current discourse.

This is why it is timely to inquire again about the philosopher's bogy of relativism. Bracket aside Durkheim's wish to protect from defilement the values of his own community as a distracting illustration of the value of his theory – then follow his thought through to the bitter end: we seem to have a thoroughly relativised theory of knowledge. The boundaries which philosophers rally instinctively to protect themselves from the threat of relativism would seem to hedge something very sacred. The volumes which are written to defend that thing testify to its obscurity and difficulty of access. Relativity would seem to sum up all the threats to our cognitive security. Were truth and reality to be made context-dependent and culture-dependent by relativising philosophy, then the truth status of that philosophy is itself automatically destroyed. Therefore, anyone who would follow Durkheim must give up the comfort of stable anchorage for his cognitive efforts. His only security lies in the evolution of the cognitive scheme, unashamedly and openly culture-bound, and accepting all the challenges of that culture. It is part of our culture to recognise at last our cognitive precariousness. It is part of our culture to be sophisticated about fundamentalist claims to secure knowledge. It is part of our culture to be forced to take aboard the idea that other cultures are rational in the same way as ours. Their organisation of experience is different, their objectives different, their successes and weak points different too. The refusal to privilege one bit of reality as more absolutely real, one kind of truth more true, one intellectual process more valid, allows the original comparative project dear to Durkheim to go forward at last. In the last essay in this collection I try to show how, when relativism is less feared, new questions can be asked about cognition. This project has waited very long to be launched. I venture a Durkheimian speculation on its tardiness.

Relativism is the common enemy of philosophers who are otherwise very much at odds with one another. To avoid its threat of cognitive precariousness, they shore up their theory of knowledge by investing some part of it with certain authority. For some there is fundamental reality in the propositions of logic or in mathematics. For others, the physical world is real and thought is a process of coming to know that real external reality – as if there could be any way of talking about it without preconceiving its constitutive boundaries. Whatever position is taken, the philosopher can be charged by his opponents with committing his theory to an arbitrarily selected and impossible-to-defend fundamental reality. The disestablishing anthropologist finds in W.V.O. Quine a sympathetic philosopher. Quine's whole 'ontic commitment' is to the evolving cognitive scheme itself (1960). This implies a theory of knowledge in which the mind is admitted to be actively creating its universe. An active theory of knowledge fits the needs of a radicalised Durkheimian theory. But active theories of knowledge seem to be especially vulnerable to seduction. Either the thinker in his old age endows a bit of his scheme with priviledged concreteness or his followers do. Instead of being seen as a process of active organisation, knowledge is then taken to be a matter of stubbing a toe on or being bombarded by solid reality or being passively processed by the power of real ideas, a matter of discovering what is there rather than of inventing it.

An active theory of knowledge allows full weight to historical and sociological factors. Herein, I suggest, lies the reason for its fragility. It eschews a solid anchorage; it is committed to movement and revision. By definition it runs counter to all the common-sense theories of knowledge which support separate intellectual disciplines using lower orders of abstraction. In these, the bit of the cosmos under specialised scrutiny is being busily furnished with indisputable hardware. Each discipline turns its fundamental knowledge into a piece of professional property. The click between its concepts and the real nature they discover validates the practitioner's status. There are some examples below of how contemporary anthropology tends to endow bits of its data arbitrarily with extra reality. Consequently at every lower level of theorising, fundamentalists theories of knowledge are continually winning the day, until a new theoretical revolution grades their discovered realities as so much junk. No wonder, on such a contrary base, an unanchored, unpropertied theory of knowledge is vulnerable. But it suffers a worse disability. It has no hard core to use as weapon in arguments of a political or moral kind. It can only patiently expound the whole of its coherent scheme. Bludgeonless, such a theory of mind seems doomed to be remote and trivial in relation to human affairs. For, as Durkheim saw for the world of the primitive, and as Wittgenstein for all worlds, the known cosmos is constructed for helping arguments of a practical kind.

Jean-Jacques Rousseau has described an evening he spent with David Hume (Guébenno, 1966: 169). At first he had been suspicious of the latter's good will. Hume's contribution to their conversation seems to have consisted mostly of long silences, interspersed with 'Tut, tut!' or 'My dear Sir!' But such was the reassurance conveyed along these restricted verbal channels, that Rousseau's heart overflowed with affection and Hume recalled a 'tender scene'. If

Durkheim and Wittgenstein could have spent such an inspired evening, how few words would they have needed to reach agreement. With a few tut, tuts Wittgenstein could soon have shattered Durkheim's faith in objective scientific truth. He would have put it to him that even the truths of mathematics are established by social process and protected by convention (Bloor, 1973, Wittgenstein, 1956). He would have shown him how much more elegant and forceful his theory of the sacred would be, stripped of exceptions made in honour of science. Thus encouraged, for his part Durkheim would have guaranteed to cognitive relativism the vigorous, questioning framework that would redeem it from triviality. A new epistemology would have been launched, anchored to ongoing social reality, and dedicated to developing a unified theory of consciousness.

Marx and Freud were not sanguine when they unveiled the secret places of the mind. Marx, when he showed ideology for a flimsy justification of control, shook the great chancelleries. The scene of anguished hate and fear which Freud exposed to view was just as alarming at a more intimate level. The first looked to a long-span historical determination of political forms and the second to a short-span determination of the emotions in family life. Between these two, another intermediate span is necessary that Durkheim's insights were ready to supply: the social determination of culture. It should have become the central critical task of philosophy in this century to integrate these three approaches. If Durkheim's contribution was accepted only in a narrow circle, his friends have to admit frankly that it was his own fault. When he entered that great debate, he muffed his cue. He could have thrown upon the screen X-ray pictures just as disturbing as either of the others. He could have been telling us that our colonisation of each other's minds is the price we pay for thought. He could have been warning us that our home is bugged; that though we try to build our Jerusalem, others must tear up our bridges and run roads through our temple, the paths we use will lead in directions we have not chosen. Woe! he should have cried, to those who never read the small print, who listen only to the spoken word and naïvely believe its promises. Bane to those who claim that their sacred mysteries are true and that other people's sacred is false; bane to those who claim that it is within the nature of humans to be free of each other. Begging us to turn round and listen urgently to ourselves, his speech would have disturbed the complacency of Europe as deeply as the other two. But instead of showing us the social structuring of our minds, he showed us the minds of feathered Indians and painted aborigines. With unforgivable optimism he declared that his discoveries applied to them only. He taught that we have a more genial destiny. For this mistake our knowledge of ourselves has been delayed by half a century. Time has passed. Marx and Freud have been heard. Wittgenstein has had his say. Surely now it is an anachronism to believe that our world is more securely founded in knowledge than one that is driven by pangolin power.

BIBLIOGRAPHY

BERNSTEIN, BASIL (1972), *Class, Codes and Control, Vol. I*, London, Routledge & Kegan Paul.

BLOOR, DAVID (1973), 'Wittgenstein and Mannheim on the sociology of mathematics', *Studies in History and Philosophy of Science*.

DE HEUSCH, LUC (1973), *Le Roi ivre: ou l'origine de l'état*, Paris, Gallimard.

DURKHEIM, ÉMILE. (1912), *The Elementary Forms of the Religious Life*, London, Allen & Unwin.

FOUCAULT, MICHEL (1971), *L'Ordre du discours*, Paris, Gallimard.

GUÉBENNO, JEAN (1966), *Jean-Jacques Rousseau, 1758–78*, vol. II, London, Routledge & Kegan Paul (trans. J. and D. Weightman).

HERTZ, R. (1960), *Death and the Right Hand*, London, Routledge & Kegan Paul.

KUPER, ADAM (1973), *British Anthropology, 1922–72*, Harmondsworth, Penguin.

LUKES, STEVEN (1973), *Émile Durkheim, his Life and Work*, Harmondsworth, Penguin.

QUINE, W.V.O. (1960), *Word and Object*, Cambridge, Mass., MIT.

WITTGENSTEIN, L. (1956), *Remarks on the Foundations of Mathematics*, Oxford, Blackwell.

Part I

Essays on the implicit

Introduction
1975

It seems hardly worth noting that some matters are deemed more worthy of scholarship than others. If there is any one idea on which the present currents of thought are agreed it is that at any given moment of time the state of received knowledge is backgrounded by a clutter of suppressed information. It is also agreed that the information is not suppressed by reason of its inherent worth-lessness, nor by any passive process of forgetting: it is actively thrust out of the way because of difficulties in making it fit whatever happens to be in hand. The process of 'foregrounding' or 'relevating' now receives attention from many different quarters. But for obvious reasons the process of 'backgrounding' is less accessible. The chapters in this section focus on 'backgrounding'. They identify a number of different situations in which information is pushed out of sight. At one extreme it is automatically destroyed by reason of its conflict with other information. For example, the continuity of human with animal life is a piece of information which is consistently relegated to oblivion by all the social criteria which allow humans to use a discontinuity between nature and culture for judging good behaviour. The history of the behavioural sciences has been to reclaim bit by bit and make significant to us our common animal nature.

By a less extreme process of relegation, some information is treated as self-evident. The logical steps by which other knowledge has to be justified are not required. This kind of information, never being made explicit, furnishes the stable background on which more coherent meanings are based. It is referred to obliquely as a set of known truths about the earth, the weight and powers of objects, the physiology of humans, and so on. This is a completely different pigeonhole of oblivion from the first. Whereas the former knowledge is destroyed by being labelled untrue, the latter is regarded as too true to warrant discussion. It provides the necessary unexamined assumptions upon which ordinary discourse takes place. Its stability is an illusion, for a large part of discourse is dedicated to creating, revising, and obliquely affirming this implicit background, without ever directing explicit attention upon it. When the back-ground of assumptions upholds what is verbally explicit, meanings come across loud and clear. Through these implicit channels of meaning, human society itself is achieved, clarity, and speed of clue-reading ensured. In the elusive exchange between explicit and implicit meanings a perceived-to-be-regular universe establishes itself precariously, shifts, topples, and sets itself up again.

A third kind of backgrounding stems from the first two. This is the creation of dirt, rubbish, and defilement. Humble rules of hygiene turn out to be rationally connected with the way that the Lele cosmos is constructed. Rejection of body dirt and rejection of inedible animals is an indivisible part of the foregrounding processes by which the universe is classified and known. For example, there cannot be any possibility of truth, in a cognitive system such as that of the Lele, for the notion that menstrual blood is harmless or that its contagion is not conveyed through food cooked on a fire tended by a menstruating woman. The whole cosmos would topple if such a piece of tendentious and obviously false information were accepted.

The essay on 'Pollution' (Chapter 7) opens the topic in a strictly anthropological vein. Defilement and magic were not thought to be worthy of a nineteenth-century scholar's attention and to poke into the processes of thought which attached the label of impurity was suspect in the same way as the investigation of sex or death in our day. In consequence, a lot of unexplained assumptions have lumbered the study of primitive religion. This paper was being editorially processed before *Purity and Danger* was drafted, though it was published two years later – producing an encyclopaedia is necessarily a stately business. The central theme of *Purity and Danger* is stated here: each tribe actively construes its particular universe in the course of an internal dialogue about law and order. The currently accepted tribal wisdom invests the physical world it knows with a powerful backlash on moral disorder. Peter Berger and Thomas Luckmann say much that is valuable about the social construction of reality (1961). But, like other followers of Alfred Schutz, they make an unnecessary and misleading distinction between two kinds of reality, one social and one not social. This prevents them from being able to appreciate the social uses of the environment as a weapon of mutual coercion. If they could be more radical in their thought, if they could admit that the environment is for enlisting support, and therefore that all reality is social reality, then they could embark on the comparative project. How many kinds of appeals to the objective environment can be used to drum up support? What sort of typology of morality-sustaining universes could be made that would embrace ours and those of primitive societies? It is easier to see that tribesmen project the moral order upon their universe than to recognise the same process working among ourselves. Therefore the two essays, one on 'Environments at risk' (Chapter 16) and one on 'Couvade and menstruation' (Chapter 12), take the argument of *Purity and Danger* out of its secluded anthropological context. They challenge us to discover how we ourselves have constructed in collusion the constraints which we find in our universe. Our fears about the perils of global over-population or destruction of resources or the evil effects of thoughtless procreation, pornography, and a failure of parental love, match those of a tribal society worrying about epidemics unleashed by incest or game animals disappearing from the forest because of human quarrelling. Our consciousness has so internalised these fears that we are fascinated by the symptoms and unable to look dispassionately at the social relations that generate them.

But the alternative, true consciousness, scarcely bears contemplation. The implicit is the necessary foundation of social intercourse. For men to speak with one another with perfect explicitness, uttering no threats of a backlash from nature – science fiction would be hard put to make such a society convincing. Ethnomethodologists, who disparage the assumed environment for its political inertia, cannot tell us what society would be like with all communication fully verbalised and none oblique. But if that is unimaginable, there are many problems about the implicit that can be discussed. Once we agree that the idea of nature is put to social uses, the challenge is to examine the social relations it masks.

The next two essays consider how and why some information has to be discounted. Information that forms an intelligible pattern in that very process destroys competing information. How the notion of primitive man is presented at any one time is a case in point. 'Heathen Darkness' shows the idea of primitive man being chopped to this or that shape to fit the dialectical needs of parties to a political debate. It was modern man they were talking about when they hotly argued that primitives were deeply religious or deeply superstitious. Realising that primitive man includes the whole gamut of human possibility, and realising that how he worships is part of how he lives and has little comfort one way or another for theology, we can remove the filters that showed him in any preordained light. Suddenly masses of suppressed information surface about thoroughly secular, pragmatic primitives. The screening out process is switched off, but not before we have caught it at work.

'Do Dogs Laugh?' (Chapter 11) considers the screening of information from another angle. It asks the reader to take a standpoint from within any verbal debate and note how much information is given and received through non-verbal channels. It is an attempt to reverse the usual organic analogy by which society is seen as a body. Instead the body is seen as an information coding and transmitting machine, a communication system which can be wired to carry a number of different loads. The heavier the load of messages, the more economical the use of available space and time. The total load and the total pressure of control are determined by the expected density of significant interactions, by something, that is to say, in the social system as it affects the communicating individuals. In a heavily loaded system each signal has to register its effect with less use of the resources of the bodily system as a whole. Vice versa, with light loading, each signal can use more of the communication resources. The underlying assumption reverses a common one in the social sciences, that loss of control is the exception needing to be explained. Here it is assumed that more control is more improbable and needs more explaining than less control. The narrower upshot is to suggest that the screening out of irrelevant bodily information is one of the distinctively human capacities. Animals are presumed to take account of involuntary smells and eructations: we select according to a screening and assessing principle which submits free bodily expression to the demand to be informed about the social situation. By means of such a systemic approach, problems can be solved which cannot even be formulated by a piecemeal interpretation of discrete signals and responses.

It is all very well to repeat that foregrounding and backgrounding are necessary for creating form. When the whole social process is taken integrally as the production of meaning, the next sets of questions to be tackled have to do with the relation between different channels of expression.

In 'Jokes' (Chapter 10) we suppose that in communication the conveyor of information seeks to achieve some harmony between all possible sources of information. It is not exactly a daring assumption. We have seen that the cognitive drive to demand coherence and regularity in experience requires the destruction of some information for the sake of a more regular processing of the rest. At the same time, for the same reasons, it musters agreement from the different channels of communication. Senders of information seek to convince their would-be receivers. Under the threat of refusing to ratify the credibility of information given in contradictory styles, the very situation of communication forces the different channels to strive to match their separate performances. This article uses joke-perception as an example of concordances between different channels. In its structure the verbal joke replicates the situation in which it is uttered and so it can be perceived to be a joke. The laugh is a bodily response which mimes both the verbal and social structures. Freud's analysis of wit suggests further miming at a psychological level. By such mimesis, when one area of experience figured upon another is rendered intelligible, all domains, the social, the physical, the emotional, snap into alignment. This set of correspondences, which results from the subject's organising effort, is the subjective recognition of truth. Intelligibility organises the subject as well as the object of knowledge. If this description holds good for jokes, it ought to be demonstrable from other formally patterned experience.

Where does the energy for foregrounding some information and destroying or backgrounding some other information derive? In case the point is missed, I emphasise again that this vast energy is not an undirected, random intellectual force. It can only be generated directly in and as part of social interaction. Most forms of social life call somewhere for coherence and clear definition. The same energy that constrains disruptive passions and creates a certain pattern of society also organises knowledge in a compatible, workable, usable form.

Since the whole social process is too large and unwieldy for dissection, there are great problems of method in trying to study how related channels of communication agree so well that they tend to deliver the same message each in its different way. One solution is to study units of behaviour whose limits are formally recognised within the flow of communications. Like an illness, a rite or a meal, a joke's beginning and end are established. This is because the social roles which sickness, ritual, meals, and jokes permit are also bounded. As a delimited enactment the joke lends itself to our study. By noting the multi-layered repetition of formal patterns that deliver the joke we can see that it is anchored in a social situation. Particular meanings are parts of larger ones and these refer ultimately to a whole in which all the available knowledge is related. But the largest whole into which all minor meanings fit can only be a metaphysical scheme. This itself has to be traced to the particular way of life which is realised within it and which generates the meanings. In the end, all meanings are social meanings.

Though all the essays in this section deal with rituals and symbolic systems, they all transcend the distinction between sacred and secular, mystical and real, expressive and instrumental. They approach the so-called expressive order full of wariness against the misleading implications of the verb 'to express'. That word establishes a distinction between the expression and that which is expressed. The object of our study discloses no such cleavage. Knowledge is a continuous process of realisation involving both the implicit and the explicit.

Chapter 1

The Lele of the Kasai

First published in D. Forde (ed.) (1954), *African Worlds*, Oxford, International African Institute

The Lele[1] are the western neighbours of the Bushongo[2] in the southwest of the Belgian Congo. The population of 20,000 has a density of about four to the square mile, but the total density of the district they inhabit is doubled by recent immigrants of the Luba and Cokwe tribes. The region is bounded on the north and east by the Kasai river, whose tributary, the Lumbundji, divides it into eastern and western sub-regions, each a separate chiefdom. It is with the western sub-region, lying between the Loange and the Lumbundji, that I am familiar and from which my observations are drawn. However, what I have learnt in the west is probably true also of the easterly chiefdom, which shares similar ecological conditions. There is a third group of Lele living to the south, whose country is predominantly savannah, instead of mixed savannah and forest. It is unlikely that my observations about the western Lele apply also to these southerners.

Lele country is at the extreme edge of the equatorial forest belt,[3] hence the great change of scene in the 150 miles from north to south. The Nkutu, their northern neighbours on the other bank of the Kasai, inhabit dense forest. Their southern neighbours, the Njembe, live in rolling grassland. Lele country has thickly forested valleys separated by barren grass-topped hills.

It is useless to discuss any aspect of Lele religion without first summarising the material conditions of their life. This is not because these seem to have determined the bias of their religious thinking. On the contrary, the manner in which they have chosen to exploit their environment may well be due to the ritual categories through which they apprehend it.

MATERIAL ENVIRONMENT AND ECONOMY

A straightforward account of Lele material culture would not give the impression that hunting is their most important activity. By comparison with the Cokwe hunters, who have immigrated from the Kwango district into Lele country, they even seem inefficient in this pursuit. On the contrary, the culture of the raffia palm would seem to be their most vital economic activity, and if their ritual values were derived from their social and economic values, then we would expect the Lele religion to be centred round the cultivation of the raffia palm. Yet this is not so. Again, assuming that a people long settled[4] in their environment normally exploit it to the full, it is difficult to see why the Lele refuse to breed goats and pigs (which thrive locally), and why the cultivation of groundnuts is left entirely to the women. These problems find some solution, however, when they are seen in the context of their metaphysical assumptions and religious practice.

The Lele village, a compact square of 20 to 100 huts, is always set in the grassland. From each corner of the village, paths run down to the nearest part of the forest. They wind first through groves of palms which ring the village round, and then through the grass and scrub. The palm groves give shade to the men working at their weaving-looms. Each corner of the village belongs to one of the four men's age-sets, which has its own groves adjacent to its row of huts. Alternating with the men's groves are other groves used by their women-folk for pounding grain. Farther away still is another ring of groves where the women prepare palm-oil. The layout of the village shows a deliberate separation of sexes. In all their work, feeding, and leisure, the women are set apart from the men. This separation of the sexes is a formality which they observe, a rule of social etiquette, not a natural principle derived from the nature of the work they perform, for in many of their economic activities there is a close collaboration between men and women. The separation and interdependence of the sexes is a basic theme of their social organisation and ritual, and one which is reiterated in almost every possible context.

Their staple food is maize, cultivated in the forest by slash and burn methods. With such a scattered population no land shortage is recognised and no crop rotation is practised. Maize is only planted once in a forest clearing, and fresh clearings are made each year for the new crop.[5] The original clearing is kept open for several years, until the other crops planted in it have matured. The most important of these is raffia palm, and in recent years manioc has become nearly as important as maize. Small quantities of pineapples, red peppers, and hill rice are also cultivated.

The palm takes four or five years to mature, and is very carefully cultivated. All its products are used; its main ribs for hut wall and roof supports, its fibres as string in hut building and basketry, its smaller ribs as arrow shafts, its outside leaves as thatching for the walls and roofs of huts. The inner cuticle of the young leaf is the material from which they weave their raffia cloths. Finally, one of the most valued products of the palm is the fermented wine, which forms the second staple article of diet. When the wine is all drawn off and the palm dead, its rotting stem harbours grubs which are a highly prized delicacy. When they have grown fat, and can be heard moving inside the stem, it is chopped open, and made to yield its last product.

This list of the uses of the raffia palm does not yet give an idea of its full importance in Lele culture. The Lele pride themselves on their skill in weaving, and despise their neighbouring Cokwe, Nkutu, and Dinga who are ignorant of the art, and who exchange their products for woven squares. The Dinga give fish, the Nkutu give lengths of red camwood, the Cokwe give meat in exchange. Although every Lele man can weave, they also use the woven squares among themselves as a kind of currency. There is no object which has not its fixed price in raffia squares – two for an arrow-head, two for a basket, one for a standard lump of salt. Moreover, they are required as marriage gifts, fifty to the father and forty to the mother of the bride. They are expected as mourning gifts, demanded in initiation fees, apprenticeship dues, fines, and payment for medical services. For diet, clothes, huts, and ceremonial gifts this is a culture heavily dependent on the raffia palm.

The palm and the banana are the only crops which, although they grow best in the forest's rich soil, are also planted around the village. Apart from these, and the groundnut, all good things come out of the forest: water, firewood, salt, maize, manioc, oil,[6] fish, and animal flesh.

The division of labour is based mainly on two principles. The first is that work which relates to cookery and the preparation of food is performed by women. They draw water, gather firewood, cultivate fish-ponds in the marshy streams, cultivate salt-yielding plants, and prepare salt from the ashes. They are excluded from certain other tasks for which they are held to lack the necessary skill, strength, or courage. On these grounds hunting and everything to do with the weapons and medicines of the hunt are men's work, although women cook the meat. Women cannot climb trees, so cutting oil-palm fruits and drawing palm wine, and preparing all the products of the raffia palm are men's tasks. All the complicated process of preparing raffia and setting up the looms, weaving, and sewing is performed by men, although there is no prejudice against a man's wife or sister helping if she is able. The men cut down the trees for the maize clearings, and are aided by their women-folk who clear away the undergrowth, and later take on most of the work of keeping the crops clear of weeds. Women help with the planting and undertake all the harvesting of crops.

From this it is clear that the division of labour is based on practical considerations, men and women taking their appropriate share of the burden. Both are required to spend the major part of their time in the forest. Apart from the clearing and planting of crops there, which men and women share together, the time the men spend hunting and seeing to the raffia palms is paralleled by the time the women spend tending their salt and fish-ponds, chopping firewood, fetching water, and washing their manioc. If the women did not work in the forest the economic life of the village would collapse. Yet the Lele regard the forest as almost exclusively a male sphere, and women are frequently prohibited from entering it. On every third day they are excluded from the forest and must lay in their supplies of food, firewood, and water the day before. On all important religious occasions, such as mourning, birth of twins, appearance of the new moon, departure of a chief, in menstruation and childbirth, they are similarly excluded from the forest until proper rites have been performed by the men.

This exclusion of women from the forest is one of the principal recurring themes of their religious practice.

THE FOREST

The prestige of the forest is immense. The Lele speak of it with almost poetic enthusiasm. God gave it to them as the source of all good things. They often contrast the forest with the village. In the heat of the day, when the dusty village is unpleasantly hot, they like to escape to the cool and dark of the forest. Work there is full of interest and pleasure, work elsewhere is drudgery. They say, 'Time goes slowly in the village, quickly in the forest.' Men boast that in the forest they can work all day without feeling hunger, but in the village they are always thinking about food. For going into the forest they use the verb *nyingena*, to enter, as one might speak of entering a hut, or plunging into water, giving the impression that they regard the forest as a separate element.

But as well as being the source of all good things the forest is a place of danger, not only for women at the specified times but often for men. No mourner may enter the forest, nor one who has had a nightmare. A bad dream is interpreted as a warning not to enter the forest on the next day. All kinds of natural dangers may hurt the man who disregards it. A tree may fall on his head, he may twist his ankle, cut himself with a knife, fall off a palm-tree, or otherwise suffer a fatal accident. These hazards exist at all times, but the risk on certain occasions is that inimical powers may direct them against him. The danger for a man is one of personal mishap, but a woman who breaks the injunction against entering the forest may endanger the whole village.

These risks, personal or general, can be warded off, or afterwards remedied, by means of sacred medicines, which give men power to dominate their environment, heal sickness, make barren women conceive, and make hunting successful. There seem therefore to be three distinct reasons for the great prestige of the forest: it is the source of all good and necessary things, food, drink, huts, clothes; it is the source of the sacred medicines; and, thirdly, it is the scene of the hunt, which in Lele eyes is the supremely important activity. At this stage of description it would seem that two of these reasons are economic, not religious, but further examination shows that in reality the immense import-ance of the forest is derived from its role in Lele religion.

The attitude to hunting cannot be entirely ascribed to the importance of meat in Lele diet, although it is true that they have a craving for meat. Cooked maize, or manioc dough, would be unpalatable unless served with the appetising sauces prepared daily by the women from vegetables, red pepper, salt, and oil. A purely vegetable diet is so much disliked that unless meat or fish can be served as well, people often prefer to drink palm wine and sleep unfed. Mushrooms, cater-pillars, grubs, and so on are poor substitutes for fish, and even fish is second in their esteem to meat. In their ideal life the men would set traps and hunt regularly to provide their families with a daily supply of meat. To offer a vegetable meal to a guest is regarded as a grave insult. Much of their conversation about social events dwells on the amount and kind of meat provided.

The craving for meat has never led the Lele to breed goats and pigs, as do their southern neighbours, the Njembe. They profess to be revolted at the notion of eating animals reared in the village. Good food, they say, should come out of the forest, clean and wholesome, like antelope and wild pig. They consider rats and dogs to be unclean food, to which they apply the word *hama*, used also for the uncleanness of bodily dirt, suppurating wounds, and excreta. The same uncleanness attaches to the flesh of goats and pigs, just because they are bred in the village. Even plants which are used in sauces when gathered in the forest are left untouched if they grow near the village. This attitude does not seem to apply to poultry. Between men various social conventions cluster around the giving and receiving of chickens, but women are forbidden to eat their flesh or eggs. This prohibition, like most food taboos, is unexplained, but there may be greater danger to women from eating unclean food than for men, as in many contexts women are treated as if they were more vulnerable to pollution than men are.

Knowing of their craving for meat, and knowing that recent hunts had been unsuccessful, I was puzzled early in my visit to see a large pig carcass being carved up and carried some miles for sale to Luba and Dinga tribesmen. The Lele would not eat it. A few go-ahead men keep goats or pigs, but not for food. They rear them for sale to the rich Luba lorry drivers and mechanics of the oil company at Brabanta. The Lele owners make no attempt to feed or control their livestock, which does much damage to the palms and bananas near the village. This carelessness does not result from total ignorance of rearing animals, for the Lele keep poultry and dogs successfully. In particular, the dogs are objects of an elaborate veterinary theory and practice. It seems that if they wished to make a success of goat herding they could do so.

Livestock is not the only source of meat which the Lele overlook when they declare that the forest is the source of all good things, for the grassland around the village harbours quantities of game. These duikers are eaten with relish when they are killed, but the Lele hunt them only at one season of the year – the short dry season when the grass is burnt, and the animals are slaughtered as they rush out of the fire. Their normal hunting techniques are not adapted to the pursuit of grassland game.

The way in which the Lele, in speaking of the forest, disregard other important sources of meat and food can be explained only in terms of the coherence of their religious concepts. To admit an alternative supply of meat, independent of the forest game, would be inconsistent with their attitude to the forest as the source of all the best things of life. Their view of the village as totally dependent on the forest is fundamental to their perception of the relation between human life and the natural and spiritual powers on which they depend. Ultimately, it appears that the prestige of the forest is entirely due to its place in Lele religion.

It is the source of sacred medicines, but it need not be the only source of the material things of life. It is the scene of the hunt, but Lele hunting has primary religious functions which outweigh its economic importance.

The distinction of the village from the forest is one of the principal themes of their ritual, which is constantly emphasised and elaborated. There is also a subtle interplay between this theme and that of the separation of the sexes mentioned above. The separation of women from men, of forest from village, the dependence of village on forest, and the exclusion of women from the forest are the principal recurring elements of their ritual, on which minor variations are embroidered.

THE GRASSLAND

The appropriation of the forest by the men is balanced by treatment of the grassland as the exclusive sphere of women. The grassland has no prestige like the forest. It is dry and barren. The only crop which thrives there, the ground-nut, is exclusively cultivated by the women. Ritual sanctions forbid a woman who has lifted the first sod of grass on her groundnut plot to have sexual intercourse until a month or six weeks later, when the seedlings are well established. No man must even set eyes on the work in progress, to say nothing of helping in the heavy work of cutting down the bushy trees on the plot. This is the only crop which women tend from start to finish, and the only crop which does not grow in the forest.

Most activities which custom allocates entirely to one or the other sex are similarly protected by sexual taboos, some lasting even longer than this example. No hunting expedition is undertaken without one night of continence being imposed first on the whole village. A man making pit traps may have to abstain from sexual relations for several months until certain specified animals have been caught. Most situations of ritual danger affecting the village as a whole are treated in the same way. The refrain 'Tonight each woman her mat alone, each man his mat alone' is a regular announcement preceding important rites.

The groundnut crop is the most striking example of the appropriation of the grassland by the women as their sphere. They often manage to find in the grassland some substitutes for what they cannot get on days when they are excluded from the forest. When they may not go fishing, other delicacies may be gathered in the grassland: grasshoppers in the dry season, caterpillars in the wet, or grubs from decaying palms planted near the village. A woman who has run short of firewood may collect in the grassland enough brushwood for the day's cooking. There are no ritual prohibitions connected with the grassland. As a neutral sphere between the two it is used again and again in the prohibitions which separate the village from the forest.

At first view I was tempted to find a natural explanation of the allocation of male and female spheres, the forest to the men, the grassland to the women. It is obvious that women, in spite of their economic tasks there, are at a disadvantage in the forest. Unarmed, and loaded with baskets, they are defenceless against strange men or wild animals. They are afraid of the dark. They do not understand the medicines which men find there and administer to the village. Hunting is a man's task. On the face of it there is something appropriate in regarding the forest as primarily the sphere of men, particularly if we associate the prestige and danger of the forest with male domination. But these considerations in themselves do not adequately explain the strict ritual exclusion of women on so many occasions.

A more satisfactory explanation can be given in terms of their religious concepts, according to which women hold a very complex status. Child-bearing, their most vital function, is regarded as highly vulnerable. On the other hand, sexual intercourse and menstruation are dangerous to all male activities. These contrasted themes are handled with elaborate subtlety in the treatment of marital and extra-marital relations, which do not concern us here. It is enough to remember the complex ritual status of women when trying to understand the separation of the sexes and the exclusion of women from the forest. As women are both highly vulnerable and highly polluting some separation of male and female spheres is indicated, and the very neutrality of the grassland makes its allocation to the women more appropriate.

MEDICINE

In Lele religion nearly all important rites are associated with the practice of medicine. The idiom of medical healing has so dominated their religious forms that it is often hard to distinguish two separate spheres of action. This is consistent with Lele speculations about life and death, which they consider to be controlled exclusively by God, *Njambi*. Such power of healing and curing barrenness as may be exercised by humans is derived only from God. Hence, the diviners must be at the same time healers and religious experts. Whether they are trying to cure a fever, or to set right the relation of a village to spiritual powers, the same vocabulary is used to describe the treatment, and the same personnel and resources are employed. To find the cause of the disorder they first use divination; then they prescribe and apply some herbal remedy with the proper formula, and impose a number of restrictions on the patient.

Although up to this point the vocabulary is the same, beneath the general similarity two categories are distinguished. The words used by the sick man to describe his symptoms are not used to describe the state of the village needing medical treatment. The man says he is feverish, sick, or weak, but of the village they say that it is bad (*bube*) or spoilt (*wonyi*). If the man is cured he says that he is strong (*bunono*) or that he has gained vigour (*manyin*). But a village in a sound condition is said to be soft (*bolabolu*) or peaceful, quiet (*polo*). The word for curing a sick man is *belu*; for setting right a disordered village, *ponga*, to mend, set straight, arrange in order. These important verbal differences show that there is a distinction between the two situations, and it may be only by analogy that they draw on the same vocabulary in describing the treatment given to a sick person or to a village.

The word for rites and medicines is *nengu*, which applies equally to healing and to village ritual. The practitioner who applies the medicine or performs the rite is in either case *ngang*, which in its widest application means only 'expert'; in its narrowest it refers to members of the group of diviners. As individuals they have each their own practice. As a body they have a public responsibility towards their village. They administer its *nengu* for it.

I prefer to translate *nengu* as sacred medicine, whether in its medical or its mainly religious sense, because the Lele themselves consistently identify rite and medicine. I should point out a distinction which they make between these sacred medicines and a range of simple remedies called *bilumbela*, which are used to treat minor ailments. The latter work by virtue of their natural properties, as wine intoxicates or food nourishes. They may be applied for headaches, constipation, coughs, and colds. Knowledge of them carries no prestige, for they are not worth a diviner's serious attention. Consistently with what has been said so far, these simple remedies are applied mainly by the women, not by the men, and significantly, they are to be found in the grassland. Sacred medicines, by contrast with women's remedies, are found in the forest. Diviners asking for a high fee remind their clients that their calling imposes on them arduous expeditions through the damp undergrowth.

Unlike simples, all sacred medicines, to be effective, require prohibitions to be imposed on the patient. Their power depends largely on the control the diviner has over them: according to whether he has undergone the correct initiation and paid for the power to apply them and followed the proper restrictions himself. It depends also on the recital of an address which adjures the medicine to do its work, and on the goodwill between the diviner and his client.

A man under medical treatment must accept restrictions on his way of living. He may be forbidden to drink palm wine, to eat certain kinds of fish, to enter the forest, and so on. If a village is undergoing a course of medicines, it is similarly put under restrictions. The character of these gives us some further insight into Lele religious ideas. The favourite themes which are used over and over again have already been indicated: the separation of the two spheres, forest and village, the separation of the sexes, women's exclusion from the forest, the association of the forest with spiritual power, the neutrality of the grassland. To the Lele their rites do not appear as a series of disconnected and meaningless acts. The very economy and repetition of the themes they draw upon produces a kind of pattern which is intelligible in terms of their assumptions about the relation of God to men and animals.

SPIRITUAL BEINGS: GOD

In writing about God and the spirits, and the sacred medicines which draw their power from them, it is convenient to use the word 'spiritual', although I do not know of a Lele word to cover this single category of things which are not human and not animal. They frequently dwell on the distinction between humans and animals, emphasising the superiority of the former and their right to exploit the latter. When they feel that too much is being required of them by the Administration, they like to exclaim; '*Cung bahutu i?*' 'Are we animals then?' But there is no suggestion in their speech that God and the spirits belong to either of these categories.

Of God, *Njambi,* they say that he has created men and animals, rivers, and all things. The relation of God to men is like that of their owner to his slaves. He orders them, protects them, sets their affairs straight, and avenges injustice. Animals of the forest are also under God's power, though they have been given to the Lele for their food. Game protection laws enforced by the Administration strike the Lele as an impious contravening of God's act, since he originally gave all the animals in the forest to their ancestors to hunt and kill.

The third class of beings under the power of God are the spirits, *mingehe.* In talking about them the Lele are careful not to speak in anthropomorphic terms. They insist that spirits are not and never have been men. They have never been seen by men. If one were to set eyes on a spirit he would be struck blind, and die of sores. If pressed for more details they are forced to give analogies from human behaviour, but they do not like talking of the spirits. It is obvious that they are held in fear in spite of their benevolent powers.

The spirits inhabit the deep forest, especially the sources of streams. They sleep in the day, but roam about at night. Hence the need to avoid loud noises in the village at night, lest a spirit walking in the fringe of the forest hear, and be tempted to come near. The day of rest is the one time when the spirits roam abroad in daylight. Spirits suffer no death or illness. They control fertility of women and prosper men's hunting. Or they may withhold the game, and turn aside the hunter's arrow. They may prevent women from conceiving. They can strike a village with sickness. In all their acts they do not behave capriciously. The study of their ways is the diviner's secret lore.

This is the official view of the spirits, held by the diviners, and which influences their practice of medicine. There are also popular fancies about them, told to children, or believed by the uninitiated. The thin wreaths of mist twisting up from the forest in the early morning are said to be smoke from the night fires of the spirits. A man walking alone in a strange forest at night may find his hair stiffening, his body pouring with cold sweat, his heart beating madly. He suddenly comes on a clearing, where there was a bright light. He sees a smouldering fire, but no one there . . . a fire of the spirits.

The diviners regard the water pigs as the animals most highly charged with spiritual power, because they spend their days wallowing in the stream sources, which are the favourite haunt of the spirits. The ordinary man thinks of the pig as a sort of dog, owned by the spirits; he lives in his master's home, sleeps and feeds with him, obeys him like a hunter's dog. The spirits punish and reward hunters by giving or withholding game, but in the single act they control opposite destinies. For while they are rewarding a hunter with game, they are punishing the animal for some disobedience to their commands.

NATURAL OBJECTS ASSOCIATED WITH SPIRITS

Certain animals and plants show signs that they are associated with the spirits in a particularly close way; the pig, as I have said, because he frequents the sources of streams. Certain bush bucks, because, like the spirits, they sleep all day and move at night, are spirit animals, and for that reason their flesh is forbidden to women. Fish also, because they live in streams, are associated with spirits, and are therefore prescribed or prohibited in different medicines. A pregnant woman must not eat fish. Crocodiles are the subject of some controversy among the experts. In the south they are classed with fish, because they live in water, and are therefore forbidden to pregnant women. In the north the fact that they inhabit water does not make them fish, and so here, crocodile flesh, since it can be bought and dried, is considered to be the food *par excellence* for pregnant women forbidden to eat fish.

Certain plants are either forbidden or recommended in medical treatment, because they are associated with the spirits. The banana, for example, is a plant of the spirits because, when it has been cut down, it does not die, as would a palm, but sprouts and lives again. Only spirits do not die, so this characteristic marks the banana as the proper ritual food on certain occasions. These few examples show how the animal and vegetable worlds are studied and classified according to religious categories.

Spring water and rain water are spirit things, because they are essential to life. The moon is called a spirit for two reasons. First, it seems to die, and to disappear completely, but always reappears. Second, it is associated with fertility, because by it a woman reckons the nine months of her pregnancy. They say, 'The moon brings children.' The moon therefore shares with the spirits their immortality and their control over fertility. The appearance of the new moon is treated with characteristic rites. Sexual relations are forbidden, women are not allowed to pound grain, nor to enter the forest. No one may make loud noises in the forest, such as chopping trees. The next day the men go hunting and shed the blood of an animal. The hunt may be a pure formality, the death of one squirrel suffices. Then the restrictions are lifted. This rite is performed in order that the maize crop may thrive. It is highly characteristic of the bias of the Lele culture that the only rite which they perform to prosper their staple crop is a hunting rite. The taboos accompanying it are also characteristic: taboos on sexual relations, on women entering the forest, on noisy work. Further examples will make clear how the medical prescriptions draw constantly on the simple familiar themes which have been outlined above.

Fish, when freshly taken from the stream, are treated as if charged with spiritual power, or as if there were danger in their improper handling. They figure frequently in medical advice for this reason. There is a significant rite which must be observed before any fish can be brought into the village. A woman returning from her fishing expedition in the forest first sends a child ahead into the village to fetch a firebrand. The fish touched with the fire may then be carried into the village. Her fishing-baskets may not be brought in until they have been left for a night in the grassland outside the village. Special stakes are set up at the paths leading to the forest, on which fishing-baskets are always to be seen hanging. Similar rules apply to some other forest products, creeper-ropes and withies used in basket-making, but not to meat, nor to planted products, maize, manioc, or palm wine. I do not know the basis of the distinction which treats fish and certain natural forest products as dangerous in this way, while exempting meat and planted products, but Lele ritual seems to be so consistent that deeper research would probably explain the distinction.

These are rules of everyday behaviour, but particular medicines also treat the grassland as if it were a ritually neutralising element. For example, a woman in childbirth who confesses her adultery is held to be in mortal danger. The appropriate medicine for her case prescribes among other things that she be first carried out of the village, so that the difficult delivery takes place in grassland. When medicines are being used to establish a new village, there is a period between the setting up of the huts and the killing of certain game in the hunt, during which it is forbidden for villagers to eat in the village. They carry their food to be eaten in the grassland just outside. Examples could be multiplied.

RULES OF BEHAVIOUR TOWARDS GOD AND SPIRITS

Some of the stock prohibitions concern noise. Noise associated with the day are always forbidden at night: for instance, women may not pound grain after dusk. Drumming, on the other hand, is a legitimate night-time noise, and dancing does not usually take place in the day. On all important religious occasions, such as the day of rest, at the new moon, in mourning, and in villages undergoing certain medicines, pounding is completely forbidden. A mourning village goes hungry for three days, and the closest relatives of the dead may not pound grain for two or three months. Medicines sometimes forbid pounding to be done in the village, so the mortars are carried to the grassland outside. Other medicines forbid any kind of loud noise in the village at night. In such a case, were a man to let out a loud, yodelling call in the dark in the village, he would have to pay the maximum fine for spoiling the medicine. In one village a medicine required that the women should not carry their full load of firewood into their compounds, lest they drop it with a loud crash. They were obliged to drop the load in the grassland outside the village, then bring in the logs in armfuls, a few at a time.

Dance drums may not be beaten in periods of mourning. If a man dies his village does not dance for three months. On days of rest and other religious occasions, all work in the forest which involves what they call a drum-like noise is forbidden to men and women. No trees may be cut, no clearing of the forest, no chopping of wood, no opening of dead palm-trees to extract the grubs. Noisy work seems to bring the village into a dangerous relation with the forest, except on specified occasions. On ordinary days the spirits are sleeping in the farthest depths of the forest, and would not be disturbed, but on the day of rest they come out, and may be near the village. They would be angry to hear chopping sounds in the forest, or pounding in the village. On the day of rest the rules are in part reversed where drums are concerned. The spirits are then abroad in daylight as it if were night, so no workaday noise of pounding or chopping is allowed; but this is the only day when the drums may be beaten in full daylight, and everyone dances.

These examples sufficiently illustrate the themes on which the ritual idiom is based. The prohibitions are acceptable to the Lele because they relate in an intelligible way to what they know of the spiritual and natural worlds. They provide a code of behaviour for men towards God and the spirits. They introduce order into the universe; regulations distinguish the day from night, one month from another, the day of rest from working days, forest from the village, males from females. They place the whole environment in intelligible categories. These categories have unquestionable validity, because they have been proved, from the beginning of Lele times to the present day, by the working of the sacred medicines. Any particular medicine may fail, for a number of possible reasons, but the whole theory and practice of medicine is not thereby jeopardised. On the other hand, any little cure, any successful hunt, testifies to the soundness of the basic hypotheses. The rites contain in them-selves the proof of their own efficacy and of the truth of the assumption on which they are based.

The various medicines bring before the mind the kind of good relations which ought to exist between the spiritual, the human, and the natural worlds. But they do more than this. As well as demonstrating order in the universe, they also provide for order in social relations. They insist on a high degree of harmony between the persons undergoing and performing the treatment.

HARMONY IN HUMAN RELATIONS

I have not said so far what kind of interest the spirits in the forest are thought to take in the affairs of men, what acts are meritorious, and what are transgressions to be punished. They uphold all the regulations which I have mentioned concerning men's relation to the spiritual: observance of the day of rest, of the food privileges of cult groups, the taboos on workaday noise at night-time, the distinction of the sexes, and of the forest from village. In the second place, they require all persons living in a village to be at peace with each other. The village faces its own forest, and through it the spiritual world, as a single whole. In this the ritual corresponds to the political situation, in which each village is autonomous and potentially at war with other villages. In religion the solidarity of each village is such that an offence by one member affects adversely the whole village, and the barrenness of a woman or the failure of an individual hunter may be attributed to the general condition of the village in which they live. This spiritual condition is constantly discussed in terms I have given: the village is either *polo*, soft and quiet, or *bube*, bad. The exchange of greetings with a visitor usually includes a question; 'Is your village quiet?', to which the answer may be that they are in mourning for a dead person, or that they are undergoing hunting medicine, or that all is well and quiet, wild pig having recently been killed.

Good hunting is the clearest sign that all is well with the village. The small amount of meat which each man, woman, and child may receive when a wild pig is killed cannot explain the joy which is shown in talking about it for weeks afterwards. The hunt is a kind of spiritual barometer whose rise and fall is eagerly watched by the entire village. This is one of the reasons why hunting carries more prestige than any other activity.

It is impossible not to be struck by the way in which child-bearing and hunting are coupled together, as if they were equivalent male and female functions. A village which has had a long series of bad hunts will begin soon to remark how few pregnancies there have been lately, or a village suffering from an epidemic or frightened by a recent series of deaths will send for a diviner to do medicines for them, saying that the village is spoilt, hunting has failed, women are barren, everyone is dying. Diviners themselves do not confuse the two symptoms. They perform distinct medicines for the separate disorders, but the grateful village whose hunting has been set on a sound basis will praise the medicine, saying, for example, 'Our village is soft and good now. Since the diviner went home we have killed three wild pigs and many antelopes, four women have conceived, we are all healthy and strong.' These are the accepted signs of a generally prosperous condition.

In a small village changes in the fertility of women are not easily observed. It is by watching the hunt, in the way that the Lele do, that we can see what kind of harmony between its members is rewarded by the spirits, and what dissensions are punished by hunting failure.

The concept of peace within the village receives a profound interpretation. The success of the hunt requires that internal solidarity be real in the fullest sense. Bloodshed, striking of blows, tearing of hair, scratching, or any violence spoils the village, but so also do hard words and insults. Whether the offender is a resident or a temporary visitor makes no difference. Villagers naturally resent violent behaviour by outsiders more acutely than they mind quarrels between residents. On the other hand, within the village itself the higher the ritual status of the persons quarrelling, the more fatal their ill will may be. The officially appointed diviner of the village may spoil it by a rebuke to his wife, whereas a more open show of anger from an ordinary man might escape notice. The village seems to be specially sensitive to any breach of marital peace. A wife who runs away in anger, even if she returns penitent the same evening, has spoilt the village, and both she and her husband owe a fine before hunting can be resumed. The anger of an old man, whether just or unprovoked, is highly dangerous. A simple rite performed usually before any hunt illustrates their interpretation of ritual peace. Each man, as he sets out, takes the matchet or knife from his girdle and gives it silently to his neighbour, who completes the exchange with his own knife. The meaning of this action is explained as if one were saying: 'My age-mate, you take the matchet with which I may have been hitting my wife', and the other replying: 'And you take my knife, in case I have struck my children with it.' At the end of the hunt the weapons are returned to their owners, for the need for covering all secret breaches of peace is over.

ORGANISATION OF VILLAGES

Village solidarity is evidently a major preoccupation. This is intelligible in view of the lack of strong internal village organisation. Although the village is united politically against all other villages, and although it acts as a single unit in face of the supernatural, yet, apart from their religious institutions, it is difficult to see any underlying principle which is capable of producing this unity.

The men of the village belong to age-sets, but these do not perform any obvious function in regulating village life. They are the basis of a form of gerontocracy. Old men of the senior sets enjoy considerable prestige, but they only dominate the village in subtle, unformalised ways, through esoteric knowledge, and reputation as sorcerers. The principle of seniority is carried so far that it even prevents any strong leadership emerging in the person of the village chief. The man who carries this title is qualified by being the oldest man in the village. Since by definition he is approaching senility, he has little real power.

There is no centre of authority in the village and, moreover, it is customary to avoid public responsibility. Most men shun conspicuous roles for fear of exciting jealousy. The Lele ideal of a man fitted to hold public office is not a dominating personality, but one who is modest, gentle, self-effacing. There are several posts in the village to which young men of this character are appointed, by the old men in some cases, by their age-mates in others, but they are junior executives of the village and not in any way its leaders.

To make internal cohesion more unlikely the population of the village fluctuates constantly. Of twenty or more men in the oldest age-sets, only two or three will have been born in the village. Every ten or fifteen years the village itself changes its site. There is no closely knit kin group forming the core of the village. The matrilineal clans are weak and scattered, and a man's tie with his father's people generally lasts only during the father's lifetime. From the standpoint of social organisation alone it is surprising that such a heterogeneous collection of people can form a village highly conscious of its identity, and capable of carrying on historic feuds with other villages. Their very real corporate unity evidently derives from their religious institutions, and from the way these are related to the communal hunt.

HUNTING: A COMMUNAL ACTIVITY

It is the communal hunt, and not the private hunter's or trapper's success, which is the anxiously scanned indication of spiritual health. The method is to set a cordon of men armed with bows and arrows around a section of the forest, which is then combed by beaters and their dogs. Young boys and old men who can barely walk try to join the hunt, but the most valued members are the dog-owners, who have the heavy work of scrambling through the undergrowth, shouting to control and encourage their dogs. The game startled by them rushes out on to the arrows of the waiting hunters. This is probably the most effective method of hunting in dense forest. It depends on surprising the game and on quick shooting at very short range.

What is strange in a people proud of their hunting is the general lack of individual skills. A man going into the forest for any purpose carries his bow and a few arrows, but these are intended for birds or squirrels. He does not expect to take large game by himself. They know none of the specialised techniques of the single hunter. They do not stalk, do not know how to imitate the calls of animals, do not camouflage or use decoys, seldom penetrate into deep forest alone. All their interest is centred on the communal hunt. I was often struck by the lack of confidence an individual hunter would have in his own aim. A range of 40 feet or more is outside their power, and they expect to hit at 10 or 15 feet. A man walking in the forest might come on a herd of pig wallowing in a marsh, creep up to them so close as to hear their breathing, then, rather than risk a long shot, he will tiptoe away agog to call out the village.

These weaknesses of the Lele style of hunting I attribute to their having specialised in techniques suited to the dense forest. Their inefficiency is noticeable by comparison with the Cokwe hunters, who are immigrants from true savannah country, and have what I suppose must be the characteristic skills of savannah hunting. They hunt in pairs or singly, stalk and call their game, and have such success that they decimate the animals of the forest in a few months. Admittedly, the Cokwe have for many generations been used to firearms, since the Portuguese used them as slave raiders, whereas very few Lele villages possess more than two or three guns.

The Lele have specialised in the communal hunt of the forest to such a degree that they only hunt the grassland when the same techniques are applicable, that is, in the dry season when they fire the grass. On this annual occasion several villages combine to ring around the burning countryside. This is the time when young boys expect to make their first kill, for the slaughter, I am told, is terrific.[7] This is the only occasion when the hunting unit is more than the male population of one village, as it is in all forest hunting. Ultimately the village is a political and a ritual unit because it is a single hunting unit. It is not surprising that the Lele think of theirs as a hunting culture first and foremost.

An account of a month's wet season hunting in one village will illustrate the points which have been discussed so far. Unfortunately, the period covered by the hunting journal gives a poor impression both of their skill in the hunt and of the efficacy of their medicine. It is only fair to mention that a party of Cokwe hunters had been for the previous three months staying in the village, killing the animals and selling the meat to the villagers at exorbitant prices. Finally, their funds of cash were as depleted as the game in the forest, and they chased the Cokwe away from the village when bargaining for lower prices had failed. However, for the purpose of illustrating an account of their ritual, a series of bad hunts is more illuminating than successful ones.

A village has sometimes to undergo a long course of medicine, extending over several months. At various stages of the performance a specified kill may be required. Until the pig or the right type of antelope is brought home and the dedicated parts eaten by the appropriate cult group, the medicines cannot be continued. An example of such a series of medicines is the one called *Kinda*, which is usually set up in a village after it has been moved to a new site. It ensures fertility for the women and good hunting. In these medicines the hunt becomes an essential part of the ritual which makes for the prosperity of the village.

Hunting journal[8] of Yenga-Yenga[9]
February – March 1950

18 February. Fruitless hunt. The failure was generally attributed to the refusal on the eve of the hunt of one of the diviners, Ngondu, a fiery tempered man, to cooperate with his colleagues. In the middle of their consultation he had suddenly burst out complaining that his wife's groundnuts had been stolen, and that when the Administration came to inspect the crop he would be sent to prison, though it was no fault of his that an enemy had stolen them. He flung out of the meeting and someone whispered: 'See the diviner is spoiling the village.' The hunt was fruitless, in spite of the medicines prepared.

19 February. The whole day was taken up in discussing the cause of failure. Ngondu's sister's son, who had overheard the whisper against his uncle, told him that he was suspected of having spoilt the hunt. Quarrelling went on in the centre of the village about this, Ngondu shouting with tears of rage that he was the injured party. He brought up all his old grievances: one of his wives had died the year before, allegedly killed by the poison of the catechist. Ngondu had actually been building her a new hut, and its unfinished framework still stood in the village. He declared that every time he saw it he felt bitter in his heart, for no food cooked by his remaining wives tasted so sweet to him as hers. This brought up all his concentrated dislike of the catechist. Now his other wife was in distress because her child had been beaten for playing truant from the catechism class. If this were reported to the missionary he, Ngondu, would be sent to prison, and for none of his own fault. And not for the first time. He could not speak the language of the white men, and did not understand their ways, so it was he, and no others who got sent to prison for avoiding road-corvée work, when others had been slacker than he. And so on. He brought up complicated histories reaching far back into the past. His friends tried to calm him, his enemies insisted that none of this was a reason for spoiling the hunting medicines; a diviner should feel more responsibility for his village. Finally, the matter was settled by a summing-up from a visitor, Bikwak, a famous diviner, who had been invited from another village to set up the *Kinda*, the fertility medicine which every new village should have. He suggested that the matter be dropped; Ngondu was in the wrong in having left the diviners' meeting in a rage, but he had been sorely provoked by the theft of his wife's groundnuts. No one knew who had stolen them. Perhaps it was some unthinking child. Let the matter rest there.

20 February. Bikwak, the visiting diviner, together with two important local diviners, Ngondu and Nyama, prepared the medicine for the next day's hunt. In the night Bikwak sang in a trance, during which he was visited by spirits, who told him where game would be found the next day.

21 February. The medicines were finished at dawn. Bikwak, as superintending diviner, directed the hunters where to go, but he had to stay in the village all day. Women were forbidden to pound grain or to cut wood until he gave the all-clear.

The kill was disappointing: one little blue duiker and one red duiker. In all, seven antelopes had been put up by the dogs, so the spirits had not deceived Bikwak. The village was undoubtedly spoilt, as they had only killed two instead of seven.

At night Bikwak sang again, and divined in his singing the cause of the failure to kill seven animals. The spirits were protesting at the prolonged absence of the *Kinda* medicine in the village. The village was over two years old, but after the *Kinda* had originally been set up with full rites by Nyama, it had been maliciously stolen by an unknown thief. The catechists and the young Christians of the village had been suspect. Bikwak learnt in the night's trance that it had been stolen by the men of Hanga, a rival village, which had been defeated in war many years ago by Yenga-Yenga and which, ever since, had been trying to be revenged by underhand means. Hunting would continue to fail so long as the *Kinda* was not set up. So they began at once to make preparations for it.

24 February. Bikwak sang again in the night, after announcing that men and women should sleep apart, as next day there would be hunting.

25 February. In the morning he streaked each man's leg with charcoal and white clay. But it rained, and the hunt was postponed. As the medicine for the new *Kinda* had been started, no visitors were allowed to eat in the village. A man and his wife from Mbombe were turned away, as, if they had taken food, they would have had to spend the night in the village. Taking food in the village brings the stranger under the full ritual prohibition affecting residents. Were he to eat, then go away, and have sexual relations while the village was still under the ban, he would be charged with having spoilt the medicine and be obliged to pay a heavy fine.

26 February. The hunt was successful. One blue duiker, one red duiker, and one big yellow-backed duiker. Bikwak ordered that the backs, heads, feet, and intestines should be set aside to be eaten by the cult groups of the village.

28 February. Bikwak still needed wild pig before he could proceed with the next step in the *Kinda* medicines. He announced that today everyone must get on with their usual work, for tomorrow he would send the men off on a hunt.

In the afternoon a bloody fight broke out between two road-menders and their wives. As the villagers gathered to watch the fight, the scratching and tearing of women's hair and head-wounds, nose-bleeding and insults, they were unanimous in their indignation: 'Fancy spoiling the village for other people! Disgusting! They are ruining tomorrow's hunt.' After the fight Bikwak, with the other diviners, ordered a fine of two raffia cloths and a chicken from the initiators of hostilities. They pleaded for time to pay. In order not to delay the hunt the village went bail for them, notching the ears of a goat in token of their payment. Bikwak did new medicine to cancel the effects of the fight, and announced in the evening: 'Tonight each woman her mat, each man his mat. Tomorrow we hunt.'

1 March. Rain. No hunt. The fighters were reported to the Tribunal, and taken away by the police. At night, Bikwak again announced: 'Woman, her mat, man, his mat', and so on.

2 March. Rain. No Hunt. Announced: 'Woman, her mat, man, his mat', and so on.

3 March. Hunt: killed three: one red duiker, one blue duiker, one bay duiker. No pig killed. At this hunt they drew cover four times:

1st draw. Blank. Consultation held. Agreed that the village must still be spoilt by the road-menders' fight. The fine asked could not have been heavy enough for so much violence. In token of a bigger fine, one man gave his matchet to another.

2nd draw. Blank again.

3rd draw. They put up an antelope, one man shot and wounded it, another fired his gun and killed it.

4th draw. One blue duiker killed, one bay duiker.

End of hunt. Still no pig. At this stage, Bikwak, the diviner in charge, went away temporarily, and the medicines were suspended until his return.

5 March. A hunt without medicines, undertaken because they wanted to taste meat. One red duiker only killed. This time failure to kill more was not ascribed to moral or religious conditions. The two best dog-owners were absent, and neither of their two juniors knew the forest so well. Several animals had been put up by the dogs, but had slipped between the waiting hunters. Too many were missing for the communal hunt to be effective. A thunderstorm finally broke up the hunt, and they decided to postpone further attempts until the leading dog-owner returned.

10 March. The leading dog-owner returned, so they went hunting. Nothing to do with medicine, just to chase up some little blue duikers for food. No game.

16 March. Wild pig spoor reported very near the village. The men went off quickly. A fruitless expedition, the pig had passed by in the night. A few young men were in favour of going on in the hope of rounding up some little blue duikers. Then one of the dogs fell suddenly sick, and the owner had to prepare medicines for it. As the dog looked like dying, the hunt was abandoned.

18 March. Another impromptu hunt. A man reported fresh wild pig tracks. The men were called in from their work. They met at the grove of one of the chief diviners, Ngondu. The plan of the hunt was decided upon. Then a matter was raised by one of the other diviners. He mentioned the rumour that when Bikwak, the visiting diviner, had been at work, he had not been given the help of his colleagues of the village. Was it right that he should have been left to collect medicines by himself? Was it true? In reply Ngondu asked scornfully, when was a visiting diviner ever left unaided? Of course they had all collaborated. Another diviner suggested that the rumour might have arisen because Bikwak had sent one of them to look for herbs in one direction, the other in another direction, and had set off himself in a third, so giving the impression of working alone. This settled the matter, and the man who had raised it took one of the dog bells, and breathed over it, in sign of goodwill. He then swopped his matchet with that of Ngondu and the hunt moved off.

No kill, as the herd of pig had escaped behind the place where the dogs were sent in.

23 March. Bikwak still absent. A local diviner, Nyama, prepared hunting medicines in the evening. He shouted his orders: no one was to sleep on Cokwe woven mats, but only on traditional Lele beds; no one to sleep in European blankets; no one to smoke European cigarettes or to wear European clothes, only Lele raffia loin-cloths; each man to sleep on his mat alone, each woman alone. Next morning at dawn, before the hunt, they were all to meet and to bring up their grievances, lest any secret grudge should spoil the hunt.

24 March. At the meeting, the first man called upon to speak was the village chief. A few days ago, on the morning of the impromptu hunt (18th), the tax-collectors and policemen were going away, and ordered him to provide men to carry their boxes. Just before the hunt the village chief went round pathetically pleading for volunteers. The young men laughed at his anxiety, and promised that after the hunt they would carry the luggage. But when they got back they said they were too tired, and would first sit down and rest. The village chief, though goaded by the police, could persuade no one. Finally, in despair, though so weak in the knees that he could hardly walk, he and his nearest age-mate (nearly as decrepit as himself, and even more a by-word for senility) prepared to lift the load themselves. Loudly complaining of aching backs, they staggered a few feet, and two young men were shamed into taking the load. This disrespect and indignity was felt to be very disgraceful to the village, so the chief was asked to breathe out a blessing on the hunt, to show that he harboured no ill will.

The next to be asked for a blessing was Nyama, one of the principal diviners, and he who had prepared the medicines for that day. He said that he felt very bitter because, two years ago, he had made the *Kinda* medicine for the new village, and it had worked well: seven women in all had conceived, hunting had been good. Then someone had come in the night and stolen it away. It was useless their asking him to make it anew. Someone else could, but he felt too angry in his heart. However, he would not let his grief spoil the day's hunt, and he breathed out a blessing.

Then someone brought up the question of Nyama's wives who had been bickering for some time. On the previous day one of them, Ihowa, had been so stung by the taunts of her co-wife that she had run away to her mother's village. Was not this likely to spoil the medicine of the hunt? Nyama replied that the quarrel had not been serious, and Ihowa had not left in anger, she had merely paid a normal visit to her mother.

This completed the agenda, the meeting ended, and the hunters moved off. The first two coverts they drew were blank. They consulted and decided to swop matchets. In the next draw the dogs put up a duiker but it got away with a surface scratch. They consulted again, and decided that something should be done at once about Nyama's wife, in case her running off to her mother's village had been in anger after all. Nyama's sister's son, representing him, gave a knife to a man representing the village elders. At the next draw they put up a duiker again, but the arrow missed it altogether. The fifth draw was a blank. Decided it was useless to pursue the hunt. Someone must have been fighting secretly in the village. They would have to have an inquiry to find out what was wrong. No good hunting until it was set right.

24 March. Oracles were consulted. Nyama's wife was convicted of running away in anger. She was ordered to pay two raffia cloths and a chicken, and to destroy the skirt she had worn while running away. That evening all the diviners co-operated in a medicine for the next hunt.

25 March. They went hunting and killed two antelopes. Nyama's wife paid the fine, protesting her innocence.

30 March. Bikwak, the visiting diviner, came back at last, and took up again the series of medicines he had begun in order to replace the stolen *Kinda* medicine. Orders were given for men and women to sleep apart and to stay in their huts next morning until the all-clear was given. At dawn next day all the men, lined up in a single file, went slowly out of the village, the women behind them bent double sweeping the ground. At the diviner's grove he gave medicines to the men, smearing their chests with it. The women were sent back to their huts and told not to pound grain until the word was given. The hunt went off.

It was quite fruitless. The three gun-owners fired and missed. Three arrows were shot, and three blue duikers escaped unhurt. All that was brought home in the evening was one half-grown duiker, which was reserved entirely for the cult group whose privilege it is to eat the young of animals. The rest of the village prepared to go to bed meatless again. Talking over the reason for the failure, Nyama was almost jubilant. He felt that the blank day proved that it had never been the quarrel between his wives which had spoilt the village in the first place. He kept saying: 'Look, we paid a chicken and two raffia cloths, and Ihowa's skirt has been burnt. All in vain. They accused us falsely. Someone else has been fighting and has hidden it.'

One theory was that Bikwak himself had been at fault. Medical convention required that after he had done the medicine he ought to have stayed in the village all day, ensuring by his presence there that the medicine worked success-fully. But he had gone to set his wife and children on their homeward journey, about an hour's absence.

Another theory was soon circulated: that the official diviner of the village, who had been on bad terms with his wife for some time, had, on the day before the hunt, refused to eat what she had cooked for him. When her friends reproached her, she denied there had been a quarrel. Her husband had merely refused to eat because he could not stomach another vegetable meal. In spite of her denials she seemed to welcome the attention drawn to her domestic affairs. While she was sitting with her friends in the compound of the senior official diviner of the village, her husband came in. Without a word he gave a raffia cloth and two chickens to his colleague, who took them in silence. An official diviner cannot be even mildly annoyed with his wife without spoiling the village.

The journal ends at this point as I had to leave. Bikwak told me frequently that when he had finished the course of medicines and set up the *Kinda*, he would ask no payment for his services, but would simply take with him a haunch of meat to give to his wife. He had been born in the village, but had left it after his father's death. Now he belonged to a village to the north of Yenga-Yenga which had the same traditional name, Homba, and which recognised a common origin with it. As he counted himself a son of the village, and as he was resident in a 'brother village', he felt he could not charge the usual fee for his medicines.

DIVINERS

The lending and borrowing of diviners is a very important aspect of inter-village relations, particularly when it takes place between villages which do not acknowledge a common origin. One of the obligations to each other accepted by 'brother-villages' (i.e. those which have at some time split off from each other or from another parent village) is the supply of expert help in religious matters for a fee smaller than would be demanded from an unrelated village. But the borrowing of a diviner from a 'brother village' is a much less interesting affair than a visit from a stranger village.

Any diviner imposes a ban on fighting in a village undergoing his medicines. But if he is only a local expert the village itself exacts fines for breaches of the peace and takes the proceeds into its own treasury. If fighting breaks out while a visiting diviner is at work it is he and his village which will demand payment for the spoilt medicine, and the fine will be much greater. He is temporarily a 'chief' in the village which has invited him. A village which lends its official diviner or one of its Pangolin men to another village does not allow him to appropriate the whole of the fees paid. He should show his colleagues at home what he has been given, and a certain amount is taken from him as 'things of the village'. As few important village medicines can be completed in less than three months, the visiting expert is put to much inconvenience, and a fee of 100 raffia cloths and a bar of red camwood is not thought to be excessive.

If he brings the rites to a successful conclusion, after the last hunt, say when wild pig has been killed the specified number of times, his grateful clients send all their young men, dressed in finery and playing drums, to escort him to his home. He first sends word to his wife that on the day of rest after the next moon he will be returning. She then should spend all her spare time catching and drying fish against his arrival. The whole village is warned to expect the visitors, and the young men practise wrestling and summon their age-mates from other 'brother-villages' of the same cluster. When the diviner's escort arrives, the two villages contest with each other in a wrestling match, the home team supported by all its 'brother-villages'. This wrestling match does not take place when the diviner has been lent by a 'brother-village', for villages which have a common name and origin are not allowed to wrestle against each other. Then the visitors are feasted on fish provided by the diviner's wife, and he, to thank them for escorting him home, gives them a present of say twenty or thirty raffia cloths. If, however, something has gone wrong in the course of the expert's visit, if he is judged for some reason to have failed to achieve the results he promised, then he is sent home without pay, without escort, and is ridiculed by songs invented to mock his name. Some diviners acquire a country-wide fame and can list ten or more villages to which they have been called. Without doubt, this feature of Lele religious organisation exercises a strong unifying influence on the scattered villages, for it is the most important form of friendly intercourse between them.

CULT GROUPS

The full role of the hunt in Lele religion is not made clear without a description of the cult groups. There are three of these, the Begetters, the Pangolin men, and the Diviners. The second and third have important duties in preparing medicines for the village, but the first seems to have no function more important than that of defending and enjoying its food privileges. Membership of all Lele cult groups is defined by a food privilege enjoyed by initiates, and forbidden to outsiders on pain of grave illness. The Begetters are entitled to eat the chest of game and the meat of all young animals. The Pangolin men are so called because only they are allowed to eat the flesh of the pangolin. The Diviners as a group may eat the head of wild pig and its intestines. The fact that in each case the cult privilege relates to the division of game gives the final clue to the religious importance of the hunt.

The Begetters' group is composed of men who have qualified by begetting a child, of either sex, and who have undergone a painful and expensive initiation. Within this group there is a subdivision of men who have begotten a male and a female child. From the latter are selected the candidates for the Pangolin group, the leading religious experts of the village, who are also diviners. Initiation into the Diviners' guild depends on other criteria altogether. They are supposed to be called to their status by spirit-possession or by a dream summons. A candidate has to undergo a novitiate of a year or more of restrictions on his life, and to pay crushing fees to his future colleagues. Once initiated he is bound to share the councils of the other diviners on village matters. One of the group is selected by the village to be its official diviner, a post to which various special functions are attached. He, together with the Pangolin men and the Diviners, performs all the rites of the village.

Nearly all major rites, such as those for setting up the *Kinda* for a new village, or for installing the official diviner, or for initiating a new diviner, require that the whole of the game taken in the hunt be reserved to the Diviners, or to the Begetters, or that certain additional parts be eaten by one of the cult groups. This very common practice could be regarded as simply derived from the interest of the cult groups in extending their gastronomic advantages. It is not clearly stated that these extensions of normal privilege are in themselves effective for the future of good hunting, and the enthusiasm with which breaches are punished could perhaps be attributed to the natural desire to protect privileged status. But similar practices in the field of gun- and trap-medicines show more clearly the general implications of food taboos in Lele hunting rites.

HUNTING MEDICINE

A man who buys a medicine to make a trap more effective undergoes various restrictions on his life. He may have to refrain from sexual intercourse, avoid various foods, and so on, until a certain number of animals have been killed in the trap. These restrictions are in the same spirit as those accompanying any medicine, but trap-medicines generally specify a particular treatment for the first three or five animals caught in the trap. In some cases certain parts, such as the head, liver, and feet, must be eaten by the trapper himself alone. In others these parts must be eaten by the trapper and his wives. After the given number of animals has been killed and eaten in this way, the medicine is completed, and the trap fully established to take game to which no further restrictions apply. But if any other person were to steal and eat the parts indicated by the medicine, he would spoil the trap, and be made to pay a fine to the trapper for interfering with his medicine. In this case it is quite clear that the trap will not perform its work unless the food privileges are enjoyed by the owner of the medicine. The eating of the first meat, alone or with his wives, is itself a rite which completes the action of the medicine.

Guns are a relatively new weapon in Lele hunting. They replace bows and arrows, but no traditional medicine exists for rendering these more effective. They were assumed to profit from the general effects of the village medicines. The gun, therefore, has been treated as if it were in the same category as the trap. Trap-medicines have been adapted to guns, suitably enough in one way, as the gun is like the trap in being primarily the weapon of the individual hunter. However, unlike the trap, the gun is taken on the communal hunt, and hence arises a conflict of medicines. An uninitiated man who trapped a big animal would always give the chest to be eaten by an uncle or other relative belonging to the Begetters' group. No trap-medicine would require him to eat the chest of game, only the head, liver, or other parts not usually reserved to the Begetters except on special communal hunts. But the gun-owner, having bought a similar medicine for his gun, may find that the specified part of the game he has killed on a communal hunt has been reserved by village medicines to a cult group to which he does not belong. In such a case of conflicting medicines the gun-owner must give way to the village, but his medicine can be saved by payment of a fee to him by the village.

This is the situation which arose on 26 February in the hunt described above. A man who had bought a medicine for his new gun shot on the communal hunt the big yellow-backed duiker. The parts of the kill which the medicine pre-scribed should be eaten by himself alone, were reserved, by the village *Kinda* medicine, to the cult group of Begetters of which he was not a member. He was not paid for forgoing his rights. On 3 March he joined the hunt again, and a bay duiker was put up by the dogs. It came towards him, but not within what he considered to be the range of his gun. After it escaped the hunters consulted, and asked why he, usually so successful, was not shooting on that day; he replied that his gun-medicine had evidently been spoilt. After he had shot the yellow-backed duiker he had not eaten the meat reserved to him by his gun-medicine, nor had any of those who had eaten it paid him. His friends admitted the justice of his complaint, and then and there one gave him a franc in token for the part of the head which he had eaten. In the next draw they put up an antelope; one man shot and wounded it with his arrow, and the gun-owner fired the final shot that brought it down. He killed nothing else that day, and remarked that if only everyone had paid a fine to satisfy his gun-medicine he would undoubtedly have killed a whole beast by himself.

FOOD PRIVILEGES OF CULT GROUPS

The food privileges of the cult group demonstrate the same spirit as that shown in the eating of special parts of game prescribed by gun- or trap-medicines. The shared feast of cult initiates is in itself spiritually efficacious for the hunting of the village. It is not an object in itself, but a rite which brings to a climax the series of preparatory medicines and taboos which are undergone to ensure a variety of ends. Sometimes the object is good hunting, at other times the fertility of women, at others to establish a new village site, or to initiate a diviner. The dedication of certain parts of game has an aspect which completes the analogy between healing medicines and village rites. In the former case the private practitioner imposes on his patient food restrictions necessary for the working of the medicine. In the latter the body of diviners imposes on the uninitiated in favour of the cult members sacrifices which are necessary to the efficacy of the rites.

At first it seemed difficult to understand how a cult group so important as that of the Begetters should exist solely in order to enjoy its privilege of eating the chest of game and young animals. But as all cult privileges relate to the division of game, the result is that no big animal can be killed without being the object of a religious act. Only birds, squirrels, and monkeys are not counted as game and can be eaten by any man, woman, or boy. Of all animals the wild pig has most significance. The head and entrails are reserved to the Diviners, the chest to the Begetters, the shoulders go to the men who carried it home, the throat to the dog-owners, the back, one haunch, and one foreleg belong to the man who shot it, the stomach goes to the group of village-smiths who forge the arrows. This division is made for all animals except that the Diviners only claim the head of the pig.

RELIGIOUS SIGNIFICANCE OF THE HUNT

It is because it provides the feast of the cult groups that the hunt is the supreme religious activity, around which all the paraphernalia of medicines, divination, and taboos cluster. And it is to these religious aspects of the hunt that the forest owes its pre-eminent place in the Lele estimation of their environment. Without its central religious functions the hunt would not be able to sanction as effec-tively as it does the social solidarity of the village.

It is not difficult to account for the Lele tendency to regard hunting as the supreme male activity, more vital to the general prosperity than the equivalent female role of child-bearing. It provides the field in which Lele traditions are constantly validated. For when it is successful, and equally, as we have seen, when it fails, it shows that the relations of God and spirits to men and animals are in fact what the Lele ancestors have taught. It is the sign of the spiritual condition of the village, the test or orderliness in human relations, and in the relations of the village to God. It is itself an essential act in the rites which establish the desired religious condition in which the forest yields its products, and the fertility of women is assured.

NOTES

1 The fieldwork on which this chapter is based was carried out under the auspices of the International African Institute and the Institut de la Recherche Scientifique en Afrique Centrale in 1949–50. For choice of tribe and much valuable advice I am indebted to Mr G. Brausch, Administrateur Territorial in the Congo Belge.

2 Described by Torday, *Les Bushongo*, 1908.

3 J.P. Harroy, *Afrique, terre qui meurt*, 1944, p. 119.

4 Torday considered the Bushongo and Lele to have been settled in their present homes for many centuries and I found no evidence to conflict with his view in the ethnographic literature on the area, except in Dekerken, *Ethnie Mongo*, pp. 210, 261. See also Verhulpen, *Baluba et Balubaïsés*, pp. 51, 52. According to Dekerken the Bushongo and Lele chiefdoms were founded 150 years ago by conquerors from the northeast related to the Dekese and other Mongo. If this were so one would expect close political and cultural links to be still maintained between the Lele and their northern neighbours, but they regard the latter, whom they term collectively 'Nkutu', with mixed fear and contempt as having an alien and savage culture. It is more likely that their environment itself has changed in the last 100 years as there is evidence that the savannah has encroached considerably on the forest. See Harroy, 1944.

5 I speak of traditional methods only. The Administration now encourages two yearly sowings of maize in each clearing.

6 The Elaïs palm from which oil is made grows in natural plantations in the forest. The Lele do nothing to cultivate it.

7 This form of hunt has now been ended by the Administration, in an effort to stop erosion of the land and extinction of the game.

8 For translating the Lele names for animals I am much indebted to Mr J. Jobaert, who has been for many years game-warden in the Kasai region, and to Mr H. Hoofd, Administrator of Basongo, who obtained Luba translations for most of the Lele words. As the result depends on translation through three languages, there is a wide margin of uncertainty for which they are not in any way responsible.

9 Yenga-Yenga is the name given by the Administration to the southernmost of three villages called Homba.

Chapter 2

Social and religious symbolism of the Lele[1]

First published in *Zaïre*, 9 April 1955

Like many other primitive peoples the Lele have no systematic theology, nor even any half-systematised body of doctrines through which their religion can be studied. As practised by them, it appears to be no more than a bewildering variety of prohibitions, falling on certain people all the time, or on everybody at certain times. For the people who obey them, there is presumably some context in which these prohibitions make sense. But what is intelligible in them is not extracted from the rituals and presented in the form of myths or doctrines. Like all ritual, they are symbolic, but their meaning must remain obscure to the student who confines his interest to the rites themselves. The clues lie in everyday situations in which the same sets of symbols are used. It is like a religion whose liturgical language, by metaphor and poetic allusion stirs a profound response, but never defines its terms, because it draws on a vocabulary which is well-understood in nonliturgical writings.

By learning the symbols in their secular context we can find a kind of back-door approach to Lele religion. We need to appreciate their idea of propriety, their ideals of womanhood and manhood, and of personal cleanliness, in order to interpret their rites.

The Lele inhabit the southern margin of the tropical forest of the Kasai District. They grow maize, hunt, weave raffia, and draw palm wine. Of all their activities, hunting is the highest in their own esteem. It is not surprising that the richest vein of symbolism is derived from reflections on the animal world, on its relation to the human sphere, and on the relations between the different breeds of birds and beasts. They are keenly interested in the natural history of their region and their attitude to animals is fraught with ambivalence. They are hunters, yet at the same time they feel a certain sympathy with the other living inhabitants of their land. Animal symbolism in their religion is a whole subject in itself. The point I wish to emphasise here is the constant reiteration in daily social intercourse of the basic distinction, the opposition between mankind and animal kind.

This idea, central to Lele culture, is expressed most usually by relating it to one dominant value, the virtue of *buhonyi*, which is shame, shyness, or modesty. Animals are thought of essentially as being without *buhonyi*. They urinate publicly, snatch without asking, are not embarrassed by refusal, they eat filth, and mate incestuously. Some animals intrigue the Lele because they seem to act with a measure of *buhonyi*. Animals which show a dislike of dirt, and frequent water to wash, are in a class of their own in Lele religious practice. Animals which shyly hide in holes or curl up into little balls at the approach of the hunter, instead of rudely making off (such as porcupines and pangolins), are also in a special class of animals associated with spirits for this reason. The most shameless animal is the dog. Dogs share their masters' domestic life, but never acquire the human virtue of *buhonyi*.

Buhonyi is the sense of propriety. It is nothing less than the reaction of the nicely cultivated person to any improper behaviour. It provides the standard for all social relations. Every kind of claim that a man or woman can make against another is backed by an appeal to their feelings of *buhonyi*. It is the product of culture, not natural virtue. Infants are not expected to feel it, but the informal training of childhood is directed to awakening a lively sense of *buhonyi*. If a whole moral code can be summed up in one word, such as honour, or charity, for the Lele it would be *buhonyi*.

All recognition of status is expressed in terms of this concept. Respect for elders is a matter for embarrassment, shyness. To see an old man insulted should fill bystanders with shame. A father feels constrained in the presence of his son, and the son stands silent and respectful before his father or elder brother. Only between equals (age-mates) is there no embarrassment. Any loss of face causes *buhonyi*.

Relative status is capable of being worked out in terms of this attitude. As all bodily dirt is *hama*, disgusting, it is a matter of *buhonyi* shame, to have contact with the hair-shavings or nail-clippings of a man of different status. A man will dress the hair of his social equal, age-mate or classificatory grandfather or grandson, but *buhonyi* would be too great for him to perform this service for his father, mother's brother, or father-in-law. Anal injections, the commonest method of administering purges, are given subject to similar rules, by age-mates and equals to each other, but never by persons between whom social distance is recognised.

As the relations of women to each other are less governed by considerations of status than are those of men, it is consistent that women are at times less sensitive to *buhonyi* of this kind. Adult men should avoid seeing the loins of their fathers, mother's brothers and fathers-in-law. When they go to the stream to wash, they shout to warn any of these relatives to clothe themselves. But mother and daughter go together to the stream, and standing naked, scrub each other's backs without the least embarrassment. Nor do they hesitate to administer anal injections to each other. Men express disgust at such insensibility on the part of women and remark that they are no better than animals.

The idea that other people's dirt is more disgusting that one's own is so well recognised that a piece of magical therapy is based on this principle. Hens normally roost in their owner's hut, and the latter sweeps out their droppings in the morning. Sometimes a hen will decide to nest and lay in another hut. Then it is the custom to leave her to hatch her brood there, the bird's owner giving one of the hatched chickens to the owner of the hut which sheltered them. This gift is sanctioned by the belief that a man who sweeps up the droppings of another man's bird is exposed to the risk of developing a water-filled cyst unless one of the chickens can be called his own. Sweeping the droppings of one's own hen is not supposed to have any ill effects.

At its strongest *buhonyi* is sexual shame. All sexual intercourse is embarrassing and should be hidden. The strict avoidance by a man of his mother-in-law, by a women of her father-in-law, is an expression of *buhonyi*. All natural functions are embarrassing and should be performed in private. Eating is embarrassing, so men and women eat apart. If an infant defecates in the presence of its elders, its father will call a child to remove the dirt, commenting on his own confusion and *buhonyi*.

Revulsion from dirt is of course an important part of the general sensibility of the man, of *buhonyi*. The word *hama* refers to rotten, smelly things: corpses, excreta, suppurating wounds, clotted blood, and maggots. In use the word is extended to apply to anything which produces a feeling of disgust. Vermin, frogs, toads, snakes, bodily dirt, and used clothing are *hama*. So are foods, the thought of eating which would be revolting. For example, the European habit of drinking milk of cows, and of eating the eggs of birds is revolting to the Lele and these things are called *hama*. The flesh of cats and dogs, and even of goats and pigs is abhorred, and called *hama*, on the grounds that it would be disgusting to eat tame or domesticated animals.

I avoid translating the word as unclean, partly because unclean is the negative of clean, whereas the Lele word *hama* is positive. Also, unclean has a specialised meaning in Semitic and European traditions. The full list of things regarded as *hama*, as inspiring disgust, reveals an arbitrary and conventional application of the concept. The list differs for men, for women, for children. There is no need to consider whether any individual Lele ever does experience revulsion at the thought of eating foods prescribed by his culture. It is enough to know that they say they do, are expected to do so, and gain prestige by exhibiting susceptibility of this kind.

The importance of *hama* as a dominant theme in Lele culture can hardly be exaggerated. The avoidance of dirt is the earliest lesson of childhood and forms the constant preoccupation of women in their work in the home, and in cooking. It is natural that it should provide the culture with vivid intelligible symbols. The emotional power of the contrast between human and animal is largely based on the idea of *hama*, animals, particularly the dog, being unaware of it.

In any culture insulting terms are the most illuminating indication of accepted values. In the heat of a dispute a man has recourse to standardised expressions which are hurtful just because they carry the strongest implications of contempt which the symbolism of the culture is capable of concentrating into a word or phrase. In other societies the deepest insults may be based on obscenities of a sexual kind. By contrast, the Lele when quarrelling does not try to insult his enemy by asserting that he was born of incestuous or extra-marital union. The effective insult is *ipondela hama* or *iponji*, that is, putrid, rotten thing. Or a man may reproach his rival for not washing, or for not paring his nails. This is almost as good as calling him an animal to his face. Proverbially, animals do not wash or manicure.[2] To call him a dog and tell him to go and eat excrement like a dog, that is the deadly insult, for which a man will try to kill his defamer. This is, of course, between men. A man can with impunity, and regularly does, call his wives 'beasts, dogs'.

The word *tebe* (excrement) is constantly flung in quarrels. They say that to insult a man is like rubbing *tebe* in his face. To submit to such treatment would be to admit lack of manliness. Another common taunt is to say 'You are not a man'. Women may literally rub each other's faces in *tebe*. This was the conventional form for expressing disgust and anger with a woman who had been the cause of fighting and loss of life. The female relatives of the dead man, distraught by grief and rage, would tear off their loin clothes and, insulting her with their nakedness, dance up to the offending woman, rub her face in the dirty cloth, forcing her to inhale smells of *tebe*.

Rules of cleanliness largely amount to an attempt to separate food from dirt. Cleaning of food vessels, washing of hands before eating, before cooking, before drawing palmwine, are insisted upon. Personal cleanliness requires the Lele to use the left hand for dirty work, the right for noble work and for taking food. The left is therefore associated with *hama*, and it is an insult to offer anything with the left hand. Lefthandedness in children is punished. The symbolism of male and female is also associated with left and right symbolism by a habit of language which refers to the left side as the woman's, and the right as the man's. In sexual intercourse the man holds the woman in his left arm, and afterwards she is required to clean him with her left hand. The constant dissociation of right from filth, and its association with male, builds up the positive value of the male symbol.

In their general attitude to food the Lele show their awareness of the two cultural themes, man's superiority to animals, and the need to avoid dirt. Essentially they might say that 'man is a culinary animal', or rather that he is a man, not an animal, because he exercises discrimination in eating. A conventional expression of anger or of mourning is to refuse cooked food for a period. The mourner or the angry man will eat groundnuts and pieces of manioc roasted in the embers. This is a recognised gesture of abandoning the arts of civilisation. Ordinarily, food, when possible, should be pounded and cooked, not eaten in its natural state. Vegetables, groundnuts, even mushrooms, are pounded before being cooked and served. Pineapple is not offered 'natural', but in a pepper and salt dressing. Cooked maize or manioc meal should be hard and stodgy, not mushy. Mushy foods suggest to them excreta, *tebe*. Bananas are eaten before they are fully ripe, and if they should chance to soften and blacken on the outside, they are thrown away. One must think of the Lele as hungry, but always discriminating.

Animal foods offer a particularly rich field for discernment. Certain animals are abhorrent to all the Lele, men and women, and not considered as edible: rats, dogs and cats, snakes, and smelly animals such as jackals. Other animals are avoided by adults, but children, if they have not reached the age of discernment, may eat them. For example, if little boys can catch bats, they roast and eat them. Hunters, if they should kill a Nile monitor, though they feel revolted at the idea of eating anything so like a snake, will bring it home for their children. A little girl may eat eggs, hard-baked in their shells of course, before she is married, but after marriage will disdain them as food. Discernment in eating is made the basis of status-evaluation, not only between men and women, adults and children within the tribe, but between tribes. The Cokwe are thought of as rat-eaters, the Luba as winged-termite eaters, or goat-eaters, the Nkutshu as snake-eaters, and consequently despised.

There are numerous foods which men relish, but which women avoid. No automatic or other sanctions attach to these observances. Few women can give any explanation of why they avoid certain animals. Some may say, 'We avoid them because our ancestors did.' Others that 'If we eat them we will come out in spots.' Others, 'We don't eat carnivorous animals because they are men's food.' Or, 'If I were to eat a long-nosed rat my next child might have a long nose.' The most usual answer is simply to reiterate blankly: 'Women never eat them.' When I found women voluntarily imposing further restrictions on themselves, and boasting of their susceptibility, I realised that the last was the true explanation: the eating of certain animals conflicts with the Lele ideal of womanhood.

Fastidiousness in feeding is part of the definition of womanhood. As soon as the importance of this theme struck me, I collected what information I could about Lele natural history, and found an interesting classification of fauna.

One whole class of animals is set aside for avoidance by women, as 'spirit animals'. I do not consider them here, as the rules applying to them are part of religious symbolism, whereas at this stage I want to discuss the underlying secular symbolism which provides the raw material for religious symbols.

All the other animals which women avoid are labelled by them as *hama* for one reason or another: carnivorous animals, smelly animals, dirty feeders, and rat-like animals. Women usually eat monkeys; but one, which I have not been able to identify, is avoided by them. It feeds on the secretions of palm trees, and as the Lele word *tebe* is the same for vegetable secretions as for animal excreta, the animal naturally counts as a dirty feeder and so is unfit for women.

There are a number of little animals which are not classed as rats by the Lele, but are admitted to be rat-like, a little tree mouse and a long-nosed rat, for example. These can be eaten by men under the stress of hunger, but never by women. The cane-rat[3] which lives in the grassland outside the village is highly prized as meat by men and women, yet one woman told me that it looked so like a rat that she herself could never stomach it. She told me this with evident pride.

There is an animal, half-bird, half-animal, the flying squirrel or scaly tail,[4] which seems to the Lele uncanny because it defies normal classification, and so this too is avoided by women. Poultry is unsuitable food for women, for the same kind of reason as makes all Lele abhor flesh of dogs and goats. Whereas men confine their discrimination to animals, women carry it on to bird-life, and so a womanly woman is expected to feel disgust at the thought of eating chicken.[5] Feminine tenderness seems to be involved: the wife feeds the hens, and calls them into her hut at night. She should feel too strong a sympathy to be capable of eating them.

The idea of eating that which is *hama*, disgusting, often implies that there would be danger in doing so. The Lele recognise that to eat putrefying matter would cause illness. Anything labelled in their culture as *hama* would produce a feeling of revulsion and nausea if offered as food. So it is that aesthetic rules are also rules of hygiene. A man who felt hopelessly surrounded by enemies told me that he no longer cared to live: he would eat foul rotten things and die. Another man accounted for his superb health by his care in not eating *hama* things.

Certain animal meats would seem to pose a cultural dilemma for the Lele, in being highly delicious, and yet, on the face of it, liable to be classed as disgusting. It is significant that a cult group exists whose members can enjoy these meats because an initiation rite has made it safe for them.

Cult groups are a central feature of Lele social organisation. Men gain entry to them by payment of heavy fees, and by a painful initiation. To join the outer group, that of Begetters, *Baboci*, a man must first beget a child in wedlock. A special title, *Bina Pengu*, is given to members who have gone on to beget a male and a female child by the same wife, and from their ranks are elected the members of the most influential cult group of all, *Bina Luwawa*, or the Pangolin Men. They are men qualified to officiate in important public rites for the village.

Nearly all the male population belongs to the group of Begetters. No man who had begotten a child would fail to join. They enjoy three privileges. Only initiates may eat the chest of game, carnivorous animals, and the young of animals. Non-members who infringe their privileges are held to incur an automatic sanction, pulmonary disease which will be fatal unless the initiates intervene and do magic for them. The Begetters have no function, no respon-sibilities, no special ceremonies other than the initiation of their members. They seem to exist to enjoy their own privileges, to perform magic to save the lives of penitent transgressors. They are scarcely deserving to be called a cult group. Yet the Lele recognise the Begetters as the foremost of their several cult societies.

Like any important institution in a closely integrated society, the Begetters' group has multiple functions. Its initiation is a typical *rite de passage* which must be understood in relation to the whole society. Full manhood is attained only when proof of sexual potency has been given. The couple who are honoured as *Bina Pengu*, for having male and female offspring, have, demographically speaking, reproduced themselves. By limiting membership to those who have begotten in wedlock, since the age of marriage used to be late, privilege was retained in the hands of the old men, and wealth as well, for the entrance fees were heavy. In addition to these various sociological functions, the society also satisfies other less evident requirements of a culture which is preoccupied with a certain number of contradictory ideas. The opposition of mankind to animal-kind is basic to Lele ways of thinking about humans. Man is defined by contrast with animal. At the same time, they cultivate a sensibility in regard to animals, which causes a man to mourn for his dog as he might mourn a wife, to go away and hide if he has arranged for one of his goats to be slaughtered, and to express horror at the idea of eating 'baby animals' (*bana bahutu*). The cult group enables its initiates to suppress feelings of squeamishness which, in the general context of their attitude to different meats, we can see might be evoked by the foods reserved to them. The creation of a sacred privilege entails at the same time that the eating of the meats by non-initiates should be regarded as dangerous, even fatal . . . a belief which is easy to accept in terms of the usual attitude to foods classed as *hama*. And at the same time, the whole complex of notions regarding food fit for humans is further entrenched in their culture.

The cult group is always called *Baboci*, the Begetters. A fuller designation runs as follows: 'The Begetters are those who can eat the chest of game.' This privilege is connected with Lele theory of physiotherapy and sympathetic magic. Ribs are, according to them, liable to get twisted, or to rub against each other. A bad fit of coughing may displace them, and bronchial wheezing, the noise made by the rubbing together of the rib bones, is taken as proof that the displacement has occurred. If they are not put back into place, the sufferer will die of a pain in his chest. In all dangerous conditions Lele avoid eating animal parts corresponding to the afflicted part. A man with a bad headache would avoid the head of animals, a man with intestine trouble would avoid eating intestines. Since all humans are held to be prone to rib trouble, it is understandable that ribs should be dangerous meat, only eaten safely by initiates. The belief emphasises the basic opposition between men and animals, since men, weakened by certain diseases, are held to be endangered by contact with the corresponding animal organ, whereas, in another cultural context, where sympathy with the animal world is emphasised, one might expect to find that such a contact might strengthen. In his preface to *Androcles and the Lion*, Bernard Shaw discussed the English faith in the value of beef-eating as a simple example of sympathetic magic.

The second privilege of the Begetters is to eat the young of animals. The symbolism here would seem to be that only men who have given proof of their own sexual potency, who are complete in their manhood, can make this possibly dangerous contact with the animal world with impunity. Without what I have said about Lele fastidiousness in feeding, the implications of the Begetters' right to eat the young of animals would appear fanciful. We can enter into their feelings if we feel disgust at the sight of grotesque, transparent-skinned nestlings, or at the thought of eating the antelope foetus from the womb of its dam. The Lele never speak of these as *hama*, only as forbidden and fatal to the uninitiated; but significantly, they never speak of the Begetters as those who can eat young animals, only as those entitled to eat ribs, as if there were something embarrassing about eating 'baby animals', which would make this an unflattering description.

Men who have begotten twins are held to have an intimate connection with animals (who also reproduce by multiple births). For this reason they have special hunting magic, and also special avoidances. By reason of their peculiar connection with the animal world twin-Begetters, alone of all initiated Begetters, are not allowed to eat, or even to see, on pain of illness, the unborn young of animals. When the division of the meat is being made for the Begetters, the carver shouts a warning to twin-Begetters when he sees that he is going to expose foetus in the womb, and they must turn aside their heads, shielding their eyes with their hands in the conventional expression of *buhonyi*.

The third privilege of the Begetters is to eat carnivorous animals. These are in a special category for two reasons. For one they prey on the human sphere. Unlike other wild animals, which keep to the forest, they enter the village and steal goats and chickens. Carnivorous animals which do not keep to the normal animal sphere are thought to be sorcerers' familiars, or sorcerers in disguise, or the unhappy ghosts of sorcerers' victims. To eat of them is to run the risk of indirect anthropophagy. Secondly, an animal which fights and kills its fellow creatures is obviously a symbol of men as warriors. Their meat is described as unfit for women: 'men's food'. There is evidently something universally repellant about an animal which preys on its fellows. As far as I know the fox does not figure in the diet of any European country. Lele women are prohibited anyway (with all non-initiates) from eating carnivorous animals, but they also abstain from carnivorous birds, which men eat freely. They say simply that they would not eat, say, a kite[6] because it kills the chickens of the village.

The first two privileges of the Begetters, ribs and young of animals, are sanctioned by the threat of rib trouble. Pulmonary complaints provide the greatest single cause of mortality among the natives of the Congo. Any uninitiated man who falls ill with coughing wonders whether he can have infringed the privilege of the Begetters, and asks them to do healing magic for him. The third privilege, to eat the meat of carnivores, is not sanctioned by any automatic danger. It is a prerogative which the initiates insist upon, and which they will sanction with sorcery if they hear of a case of breach.

In discussing the food privileges of the cult groups I have had to broach already symbolism which operates in a ritual, not simply in a secular context. I started to show that the opposition of men and animals, which inspires much of their etiquette (the presentation of food, the care of the body, the symbolism of right and left, and the definition of cleanliness and propriety), produces a body of what can be called secular symbolism. Of this, discrimination between various animal foods leads us straight into the domain of religious symbolism. Just as safety for a sick man lies in avoiding certain animal foods, for the ritual specialist ritual power is procured by avoiding the meat of certain animals. Diviners have to observe prohibitions on numerous meats, and one class of diviner practises near-vegetarian austerity as part of the vocation which gives powerful hunting magic.

Here I want to show how the crude symbolism of everyday life provides a basic vocabulary on which religious symbolism draws. I do not at all mean to imply that religious notions are simply derived from everyday experience. It would be consistent with my theme even to conclude the contrary, that ordinary life is experienced through categories which are essentially religious. Everyday experience provides a welter of words, and religion selects from these to produce a number of themes which are regulative in everyday life just because they express religious values. The secular and the religious are two aspects of the same collective representations which give the society its distinctive structure.

The distinction between man and animal is largely based on the reaction to *hama*, the feeling for propriety in humans, its absence in animals. *Hama* and *buhonyi* provide a standard of values against which a certain number of contrasted pairs of ideas are immediately judged. The superiority of human to animal, food to excreta, right to left, male to female, is self-evident, because of the stock associations made with *hama* and *buhonyi* in each case.

These sets of contrasted ideas in various combinations provide some of the main ingredients for religious ceremonies. For example, the distinction between forest and grassland is important in religious practice. The fertility of the forest contrasts with the barrenness of the grassland. The forest is seen as the place of God, the haunt of powerful spiritual beings, the source of all the necessities of life, maize, raffia, wine, meat, fish, water, and firewood. Various rites emphasise the distinction between the two, and the superiority of the forest to the grassland, by associating the forest with males, the grassland with females.

In the first place, women are prohibited from entering the forest on religious occasions, the Lele day of rest, and after the new moon and as a regular part of numerous rituals. The day of rest is not a day of abstention from work, but of separation of women from the forest. On these days they cannot draw water, go fishing, prepare salt from water-plants, cultivate forest clearings, sow or harvest crops. There is an appropriateness about the association of men with the forest, since men are hunters, go through the forest armed, are not afraid of the dark, and control magic which protects them against malign spiritual forces. Women are nervous, defenceless, and burdened with baskets.

There is a compensatory association of women with the grassland, in the practical and the ritual spheres. Work which can only be pursued there is regarded as proper to women. Groundnuts, which are cultivated in the grassland, are from first to last a woman's crop, and from the first hoeing of the ground until the plants are established, women avoid male contact.

At their times of periodic uncleanness women are excluded from the forest, though they may work in the grassland. Men like to blame their failures in hunting on women whom they suspect of infringing the taboo.

Although the forest is not normally thought to be ritually polluted by sexual intercourse taking place in it, on the day following the new moon such inter-course is forbidden under sanction of 'spoiling the forest' for hunting and for palmwine, two male activities. Other important ritual injunctions separate the forest sphere of spirits and animals from the village sphere of humans. This separation fully allows of human dependence on the forest.[7] It is like the separation of male and female, which is necessary for an orderly social life, and which yet recognises the interdependence of the sexes. Without knowing the secular association of the contrasts which are made in ritual, the numerous ritual prohibitions would be difficult to interpret. Knowing something of the implications in social life of the ideas of propriety, manhood, womanhood, etc., it is possible to recognise the rites as a set of dramatised analogies.[8] They use symbols which are already established in, and rich with the associations of daily life. Without this element the ritual injunctions would have no power over the imagination, no force to compel assent. They are symbolic. They make analogies between the relations of male to female, man to animal, forest to grassland, and through these analogies a further relation between man and God and the spirits is indicated. The analogies are not statements about the nature, only about the relations of things. It would be grotesque to conclude that the forest is thought of as male, or the grassland as female, clean or unclean. Nor are there persons, or actions or spheres that are in themselves either sacred or profane. Only in certain contexts, on certain occasions, do these categories apply in a strictly relative sense.

To illustrate the fruitfulness of these dramatised analogies for religious symbolism, I must introduce another contrast, that between upstream and downstream, *tende* and *angele*. These terms are used for position and direction in various contexts. *Tende*, upstream, has all the prestige. It is also used for the back, interior part of the hut, contrasted with the entrance side, and for the head of the bed, as contrasted with the foot. A bed is supposed to be placed so that is head, *tende*, is in alignment with the *tende* of the hut, that is, with its head near the entrance. *Angele* is the brim, as contrasted with the bottom of the mug. *Angele* is also used as a euphemism for sexual organs, the lower part of the body as contrasted with the head.

Every year at the opening of the dry season, a rite used to be performed to ward off coughs and illness from the village. The official diviner, *ilumbi*, would prepare a magic brew of which every man, woman and child took a little. Some would be drunk, some given as an anal injection. When the purge began to have its effect everyone had to defecate on one of the paths leading from the village. To separate the women from the men it would be arranged that the men should soil the upstream path, *tende*, and the women the downstream path, *angele*. Then these paths would be abandoned, strangers could carry off the dirt of the village on their feet, or the rains would wash it away. The symbolism is obvious.

The coherence and force of the ideas I have discussed, of *buhonyi*, shame, *hama*, filth, and of the contrasted ideas of food and excreta, human and animal, appear when we consider the persons whom the Lele consider to be without shame: chiefs and sorcerers. The idea of the sorcerer, as the epitome of badness, is contrasted with the idea of the good man who is sensitive to *buhonyi*. The sensibilities of the sorcerer are blunted and his ingrained malice drives him to heap grief and shame on his fellow men. The concept is based on the full range of paired contrasts. His lethal charms are supposed to be concocted with faecal matter. Disgusting things arouse no revulsion in him, and are the hallmark of his trade. Given the associations of the contrast of food with excreta, it is intelligible that the faeces used by the sorcerer are considered as potent to destroy life as food is to nourish it. He is, for Lele culture, the type of the complete pervert. He is thought to have turned against his own flesh and blood, human-kind, and to have made an unholy alliance with the animal world. He kills humans and strikes women with barrenness, yet protects animals, runs with the hunted, uses his magic to turn aside arrows, and springs traps. A denatured man, he uses animals as his familiars to carry out his nefarious work. Even his supposed lack of interest in the hunt, incomprehensible to the normal Lele, is explained by the association of sorcery with *hama* disgusting things. The ordinary healthy-minded man has a craving for meat, and would not wish for the hunt to be anything but successful. But as the sorcerer is supposed to be thoroughly corrupt, it is intelligible to the Lele that he should even abhor fresh animal meats, and should lust for the putrefying flesh of his human victims.

Of course no man would ever admit to being a sorcerer. But there is no doubt that individual Lele try to satisfy their jealousies and get vengeance by recourse to magic, and others exploit the current ideas about sorcery to achieve their private ends. Several times I heard of people who found *tebe*, human excreta, in their huts, at the climax of some quarrel, and had taken it as frightening proof that sorcery was being employed against them.

In one case, an old widow was disputing the right to draw palmwine from a palm which had been planted by her late husband. The latter's sisters' sons ignored her claim, and started to draw the wine for themselves, arguing with her every time they met. One day one of the young men passing her hut on the way to draw the wine, was surprised to find her standing at the doorway, watching him in grim silence. He climbed the palm, and came down quickly in horror and disgust, reporting that he had put his hand into a mess of *tebe*. All the villagers were interested in the case; several climbed the palm to verify for themselves, and all agreed that it was indeed *tebe*, and that the palm would have to be abandoned. The widow was accused of sorcery, and was eventually driven away from the village, a number of cases of recent deaths being laid to her charge. Her own kinsman in her defence asked how anyone supposed that a woman would be physically capable of climbing a tall palm and defecating on the top of it, but her enemies replied that the extraordinary feat was further proof of her mastery of the black arts of sorcery. The problem which mystified the villagers seems to me also to be insoluble, unless the woman or someone else had placed the offending matter on a long pole and so lifted it into the palm.

Other pairs of contrasts are also used to build up the idea of the sorcerer. He is supposed to meet his colleagues at night, in the grassland, to carry out bargaining for the lives of men. A convicted sorcerer is buried, without honours, like a dog, in the grassland, whereas ordinary men are buried near the village, and diviners are buried in a secret place in the forest.

Chiefs are the other class of persons said to be wanting in *buhonyi*. This is regarded as an inevitable aspect of the exercise of authority. Feelings of compassion, respect for age, recognition of the claims of hunger and fatigue, these aspects of *buhonyi* are incompatible with chiefship as the Lele think of it, arbitrary, irregular, and predatory in the enjoyment of its prerogatives. Significantly, the chiefs are supposed to be the arch-sorcerers. They say that sorcery came originally to the Lele from God, who gave it first to a chief who wanted to punish his subjects for associating with his wives. If a chief is without shame, it is because he is not completely in the same category as other human beings. Chiefs are 'with God'; when they speak, God hears. Sometimes they say that chiefs are spirits, *ngehe*. A chief can break the ordinary rules of social life, without being classed with animals. Ritual incest is an essential part of the accession rites. A young chief is supposed to kill a sibling at each of the transition rites of his adolescence. These transgressions against the normal code are, for chiefs, a source of magic power, though for ordinary humans they would bring down divine retribution. The normal symbolism is here inverted, giving sinister power to the idea of chiefship. To kill a fellow clansman, and to commit incest with a clanswoman are the two major crimes against the solidarity of the clan. Both are regarded as bestial behaviour. For chiefs to flout these norms is to assert the gulf that separates them from commoners. They say: '*Biitu Bakumu, kacuapa malunji, bo. Ilunji diitu, bukumu.*' 'We chiefs, we have no clans. Our clan is chiefship.'

The idea of chiefship thus symbolised for the Lele is hardly warranted by their actual experience of the chiefs, who are ineffectual and weakened by rivalry with each other. Like much else of their culture the idea is probably taken from their neighbours, the Bushongo, whose Nyimi is the most powerful chief west of the Mwatiamvo of the Lunda. However, the symbolism is not without its relevance to the actual Lele political scene. Village organisation is characterised by an absence of authority, or rather by such an elaborate system of checks and balances that there is no seat of influence. There is little scope for personal leadership; pressure is exerted in devious and hidden ways. The Lele obviously have very little experience of authority in any form. It is perhaps understandable that in circumstances such as these the idea of strong government should be a frightening one, and that chiefship should be symbolised by inhuman behaviour.

NOTES

1 The fieldwork on which this article is based was undertaken under the auspices of the International African Institute, and with generous assistance from IRSAC. The first draft was read as a paper to the Royal Anthropological Institute, 6 May 1954. I am grateful to Dr Louis Dumont for his criticism and suggestions.

2 Native riddle – *To! ibamba! Teteti? Mbwa, kaha tet biala bo.* Scrape, scrape? A dog, he does not scrape his nails.

3 *Thryonomys swinderianus angola.* I am grateful to M. Jobaerts for the identification of these animals.

4 *Anomalurus beecrofti citrinus.*

5 This explanation is the only one which holds good for Lele culture but there is little doubt that they are influenced more than they know by their neighbours the Bushongo. There, according to Professor J. Vansina, the chicken is reserved as food of initiated men, as it is a symbol of the sun, and therefore of God. See his article 'Initiation rituals of the Bushong', *Africa,* April 1955.

6 *Miluus aegyptius.*

7 See Chapter 1 for greater detail about the contrast of forest and grassland, and its working out in terms of the distinction between male and female.

8 I am indebted to Professor Evans-Pritchard's discussion of the use of analogy in the religious thought of the Nuer. See 'A problem of Nuer religious thought', *Sociologus,* *1*, 23–41, 1954.

Chapter 3

Animals in Lele religious symbolism

First published in *Africa*, *27*, 1 January 1957

Lele religious life is organised by a number of cult groups. For a long time they seemed to me to be a collection of quite heterogeneous cults, uncoordinated except for a certain overlap in membership. In one of them, the Diviners' Group, entry is by initiation only, though the candidate is supposed to give evidence of a dream summons. In another, the Twin Parents, there is no initiation. Parents of twins have no choice but to pay the fees and become Twin Diviners. In another, the Begetters, candidates must have begotten a child, pay fees and undergo initiation. Members of this group who have begotten children of both sexes are qualified for entrance into another group, which makes a cult of the pangolin (*Manis tricuspis*).[1] Lastly there are Diviners of God (*Bangang banjambi*) who are supposed to acquire their power not by initiation, but by direct communication with supernatural beings, the spirits. The primary objects of all these cults[2] are fertility and good hunting.

The Pangolin cult is the only one in which an animal is the cult object. In the other cults parts of certain animals are reserved to initiates: the head and stomach of the bush pig to Diviners, the chest and young of all animals to the Begetters. Or parts of animals or whole animals may be prohibited to them as a condition of their calling: Twin Parents must not eat the back of any animal; so many animals are prohibited to the Diviners of God that they practise an almost vegetarian austerity.

Regarding these practices the Lele offer very little explanation of the symbolism involved. The different animals are associated traditionally with the different cults. The symbolism of the bush pig is relatively explicit. It is the Diviners' animal, they will say, because it frequents the marshy sources of streams where the spirits abide, and because it produces the largest litters in the animal world. In very few other instances is the symbolism so clearly recognised. In most cases one would be justified in assuming that no symbolism whatever is involved, and that the prohibitions concerning different animals are observed simply as diacritical badges of cult membership.

If this be the correct interpretation of the different observations, one must equally accept the view that there is no single system of thought integrating the various fertility cults. At first I felt obliged to adopt this point of view. Believing the Lele culture to be highly eclectic and capable of assimilating into itself any number of cults of neighbouring tribes, I concluded that the connection between the various cults was probably only an historical one, and that in the absence of historical or ethnographic data from surrounding areas, it was impossible to take the problem any further.

Although I could never get a direct answer that satisfied me as to why the pangolin should be the object of a fertility cult, I kept receiving odd scraps of disconnected information about it and about other animals in different religious and secular contexts. Gradually I was able to relate these ideas within a broad framework of assumptions about animals and humans. These assumptions are so fundamental to Lele thought that one could almost describe them as unformulated categories through which they unconsciously organise their experience. They could never emerge in reply to direct questions because it was impossible for Lele to suppose that the questioner might take his standpoint on another set of assumptions. Only when I was able to appreciate the kind of implicit connections they made between one set of facts and another, did a framework of metaphysical ideas emerge. Within this it was not difficult to understand the central role of the pangolin, and significance of other animals in Lele religion. The different cult groups no longer seemed to be disconnected and overlapping, but appeared rather as complementary developments of the same basic theme.

ANIMALS IN THE NATURAL ORDER

The Lele have a clear concept of order in their universe which is based on a few simple categories. The first is the distinction between humans and animals.[3] Humans are mannerly. They observe polite conventions in their dealings with each other and hide themselves when performing their natural functions. Animals satisfy their natural appetites uncontrolled. They are regarded as the 'brute beasts which have no understanding' of the Anglican marriage service. This governing distinction between men and animals testifies to the superiority of mankind. It gives men a kind of moral licence to hunt and kill wild animals without shame or pity.

A subsidiary characteristic of animals is held to be their immense fecundity. In this, animals have the advantage of humans. They give birth to two, three, six or seven of their young at a time. Barrenness in humans is attributed to sorcery: barrenness in animals is not normally envisaged in Lele ideas about them. The set incantation in fertility rites refers to the fecundity of the animals in the forest, and asks why humans should not be so prolific.

The third defining characteristic of animals is their acceptance of their own sphere in the natural order. Most animals run away from the hunter and shun all human contact. Sometimes there are individual animals which, contrary to the habit of their kind, disregard the boundary between humans and themselves.

Such a deviation from characteristically animal behaviour shows them to be not entirely animal, but partly human.[4] Two sets of beliefs account for the fact that some wild animals occasionally attack humans, loiter near villages, even enter them and steal chickens and goats: sorcery and metempsychosis. I do not propose to describe them here.

Apart from these individual deviants, there are whole deviant species. Breeding habits, sleeping, watering, and feeding habits give the Lele categories in which there is consistency among the secondary characteristics, so that different species can be recognised. Carnivorous[5] animals have fur and claws as distinct from vegetarian animals, such as the antelopes with their smooth hides and hoofs. Egg-laying creatures tend to fly with wings. Mammals are four-footed and walk or climb, and so on. But some species defy classification by the usual means. There are four-footed animals which lay eggs, and mammals which fly like birds, land animals which live in the water, aquatic animals which live on the land.

AVOIDANCES IN CONNECTION WITH ANIMALS

These problems in animal taxonomy struck me first when I inquired into the food prohibitions observed by women. Some animals they avoid simply because they are anomalous, no ritual sanction being involved. For example, there is a 'flying squirrel', the scaly tail, which women avoid, because they are not sure what it is, bird or animal.[6] I have described elsewhere[7] their self-imposed prohibitions on foods which they consider disgusting apart from any religious symbolism. Here I am concerned with the provisions made in Lele religion for regulating human contact with animals. Restrictions on the contact of women with one species or another is the most usual ritual rule.

A wide diversity of animals are classed as 'spirit animals' (*hut a ngehe*). I could not clarify in what sense these creatures are spirits. In some contexts they are spoken of as if they were spirits or manifestations of spirits. In others they are animals closely associated with spirits. They can be divided according to the restrictions which are imposed on women's contact with them.

Women may never touch the Nile monitor (*Varanus niloticus*) or the small pangolin (*Manis tricuspis*). Concerning the pangolin I shall say more below. The Nile monitor is a large aquatic lizard. The Lele describe it as a cousin of the crocodile, but without scales; like a snake with little legs; a lizard, but bigger, swifter, and more vicious than any lizard. Like the crocodile, it is a large, potentially dangerous amphibian.

Women may touch, but never eat, the tortoise and the yellow baboon (*Papio cynocephalus kindae*). The tortoise is a curious beast. Its shell distinguishes it from other reptiles but, as a four-footed creature, it is anomalous in that it lays eggs. The baboon is interesting in several ways. Unlike other monkeys it is reputed not to be afraid of men, but will stand up to a hunter, strike him, talk, and throw sticks at him. When the troop of baboons goes off from the grassland to the water, the females pick up their young in their arms, and those which are childless hitch a stone or stick into the crook of their arms, pretending that they too have babies. They go to the water, not merely to drink, but to wash. Moreover, they shelter in deep erosion gullies which are associated by the Lele with spirits who are thought to dig them for their own inscrutable purposes. Some of these gullies are very deep and become rushing torrents in the rains. As one of the ordeals of initiation, Diviners have to climb down into one of these gullies and carry back mud from the bottom. Baboons, then, are unlike other animals in that they will stand up to a man, they experience barrenness, they wash, and they undergo one of the ordeals of initiation.

There is one animal which women never eat unless they are pregnant. It is the giant rat (*Cricetomys dissimilis proparator*) which has a white tail and burrows underground. It is associated with the ghosts of the dead, perhaps because of the holes in the ground. The ghosts of the dead are often referred to as *bina hin*, the people down below. The habit of sleeping in a hole seems to be associated with the spirits. Several of the spirit animals which women have to avoid are characterised as sleeping in holes, but I am not confident about this category, as there are other burrowing animals which are not classed as spirit animals. The porcupine (*Hystrix galatea*) and the giant pangolin (*Manis gigantea*) are spirit animals which women may not eat if they are pregnant. The ant-bear (*Orycteropus afer*), which digs holes to escape from its pursuers, may be eaten by women except during the four months immediately following a certain fertility rite.

Water creatures are all associated with spirits and pregnant women must avoid them. The wild bush pig (*Potamochaerus koiropotamus*), as I have already said, is a spirit animal because it frequents the streams and breeds prolifically. Pregnant women avoid it. There are two antelopes associated with spirits, which women must avoid during pregnancy. One is the water-chevrotain (*Hyemoschus aquaticus*) which hides itself by sinking down into the water until only its nostrils appear above the surface. The other is *Cephalophus grimmi*, whose idiosyncrasy is to sleep in daylight with its eyes wide open, so soundly asleep that a hunter can grab it by the leg. This habit associates it with the spirits, who are supposed to be active at night and asleep in the day. The little antelope is thought to be a servant of the spirits, resting in the day from its labours of the night.

So far as I know, this is the complete list of the animals whose contact with women is normally restricted. There are local variations. In the north crocodiles may be eaten by pregnant women; in the far south, women's postnatal food includes squirrels and birds, i.e. animals of above (*hutadiku*) as opposed to ground animals (*hutahin*). In reply to my queries, Lele would merely reiterate the characteristics of the animal in question, as if its oddity would be instantly appreciated by me and would provide sufficient answer to my question.

No doubt the first essential procedure for understanding one's environment is to introduce order into apparent chaos by classifying. But, under any very simple scheme of classification, certain creatures seem to be anomalous. Their irregular behaviour is not merely puzzling but even offensive to the dignity of human reason. We find this attitude in our own spontaneous reaction to 'monstrosities' of all kinds. Paul Claudel understood it well, in depicting the disgust of a seventeenth-century grammarian confronted with a female whale suckling her young in mid-Atlantic:[8]

> *Vous trouvez ça convenable? C'est simplement révoltant! J'appelle ça de la bouffonnerie! Et pense que la nature est toute remplie de ces choses absurdes, révoltantes, exagérées! Nul bon sens! Nul sentiment de la proportion, de la mesure et de l'honnêteté! On ne sait où mettre les yeux!*

The Lele do not turn away their eyes in disgust, but they react to 'unnatural behaviour' in animals in somewhat the same way as did the author of Deuteronomy – by prescribing avoidance.[9]

> Every beast that divideth the hoof into two parts, and cheweth the cud, you shall eat. But of them that chew the cud, but divide not the hoof, you shall not eat, such as the camel, the hare and the rock-badger . . . these shall you eat of all that abide in the waters, all that have fins and scales you shall eat. Such as are without fins and scales, you shall not eat.

The baboon, the scaly tail, the tortoise, and other animal anomalies are to the Lele as the camel, the hare, and the rock-badger to the ancient Hebrews.

THE PANGOLIN

The pangolin is described by the Lele in terms in which there is no mistaking its anomalous character. They say: 'In our forest there is an animal with the body and tail of a fish, covered in scales. It has four little legs and it climbs in the trees.' If I had not by chance identified it at once as the scaly ant-eater, but had thought of it always as a scaly fish-like monster that ought to abide in the waters, but creeps on the land, its symbolic role would not have eluded me for so long.

Anomalous characteristics, like the scaly tail, would set the pangolin apart but would not explain its association with fertility. The fertility of humans is thought to be controlled by the spirits inhabiting the deepest, dampest parts of the forest. The symbolic connection of water with fertility and with the spirits who control human fertility, is fairly explicit for the Lele. All aquatic things – fishes, water animals, and water plants, as well as amphibians – are associated with the spirits and with fertility. Creatures which have the same outward characteristics as aquatics, but live on the land (the pangolin), or which are essentially land animals but frequent the water (the water chevrotain), are also

Figure 3.1 Tree pangolins

associated with the spirits. In this context the pangolin's association with fertility becomes clear.

According to the Lele, the pangolin is anomalous in other ways. Unlike other animals it does not shun men but offers itself patiently to the hunter. If you see a pangolin in the forest, you come up quietly behind it and smack it sharply on the back. It falls off the branch and, instead of scuttling away as other animals would do, it curls into a tightly armoured ball. You wait quietly until it eventually uncurls and pokes its head out, then you strike it dead. Furthermore, the pangolin reproduces itself after the human rather than the fish or lizard pattern, as one might expect from its appearance. Lele say that, like humans, it gives birth to one child at a time. This in itself is sufficiently unusual to mark the pangolin out from the rest of the animal creation and cause it to be treated as a special kind of link between humans and animals.

In this respect the pangolin would seem to stand towards humans as parents of twins stand towards animals. Parents of twins and triplets are, of course, regarded as anomalous humans who produce their young in the manner of animals.

For a human to be classed with animals in any other connection – because, for instance, of unmannerly behaviour – is reprehensible. But to vie with animals in fertility is good. Men do not beget by their own efforts alone, but because the spirits in the forest consent. The parents of twins are considered to have been specially honoured by the spirits. They are treated as diviners and are exempt from the initiation which ordinary men must undergo if they wish to acquire magic powers. Twin children are spoken of as spirits and their parents as Twin Diviners (*Bangang bamayeh*). They pay an entrance fee into their own cult group, and learn 'twin magic' for fertility and good hunting.

The most striking proof of the high ritual status enjoyed by parents of twins is that the usual ritual disabilities of women are disregarded in the case of a woman who has borne twins. She attends the conferences on twin magic on exactly the same footing as the men, performs the rites with them, and at her death is supposed to be buried with all the other diviners. This is quite out of character with the normally subordinate position of women in Lele ritual. Parents of twins are regarded as having been selected by the spirits for a special role, mediating between humans and animals and spirits. Pangolins perform a corresponding role in the animal sphere.

HUMANS, ANIMALS, AND SPIRITS

Lele religion is based on certain assumptions about the interrelation of humans, animals, and spirits. Each has a defined sphere, but there is interaction between them. The whole is regarded as a single system. A major disorder in the human sphere is presumed to disturb the relations which ought to exist between all the parts. Major disorders in the other spheres are not expected to occur.

Animals live their lives, each behaving according to its kind. Their sphere does not impinge on the human sphere. No animal will molest a human, enter a human habitation, or steal chickens and goats, unless made to do so by sorcery. Nor will an animal become a victim to a hunter unless the spirits are willing. For their part, humans cannot expect to intervene in animal affairs, even to sight or pursue, still less to kill an animal, unless their relations with the spirits are harmonious. The approval of the spirits is assured if human relations with each other are peaceful and if ritual is correctly performed. The goodwill of the spirits notwithstanding, the hunter's success may be spoilt by sorcery.

The hunt is the point at which the three spheres touch. Its significance far surpasses its primary object – the supply of meat. The whole range of human aspirations – for food, fertility, health, and longevity – is controlled by the spirits and may be thwarted by sorcery. If the hunt fails, the Lele fear that their other enterprises also are in danger. Not only do they feel angry at a wasted day and meatless fare, but they feel anxious for the recovery of the sick, for the efficacy of their medicines, for their whole future prosperity.

In the delicate balance between humans, animals, and spirits, certain humans and certain animals occupy key positions of influence. Among humans, the Begetters' Group honours those who have been blessed with a child. At their initiation rites ribald songs mock the sterile. The Pangolin cult honours those who have been blessed with children of both sexes; the Twin cult honours those who have been blessed with multiple births. The qualification for membership of any of these cults is not something which a man can achieve by his own efforts. He must have been chosen by the spirits for his role as mediator between the human and the supernatural. In theory, the candidates for the Diviners' Group are also believed to have been made aware of their vocation in a dream or by spirit-possession, though in practice men are known to fake this qualification. Once initiated these men have access to magical powers which can be used on behalf of their fellows.

In the animal world certain creatures mediate between animals and humans. Among these the pangolin is pre-eminent. It has the character of a denatured fish: a fish-like creature which lives on dry land, which bears its young after the manner of humans, and which does not run away from humans. In order to see the full significance of its fish-like scales, one should know more of the symbolic role of fish for the Lele.

Fishes belong so completely to the watery element that they cannot survive out of it. Bringing fish out of the water and the forest into the village is an act surrounded with precautionary ritual. Women abstain from sexual intercourse before going fishing. Fish and fishing gear, and certain water plants, cannot be brought into the village on the day they are taken from the water unless ritual is performed. The woman who is carrying the fish sends a child ahead to fetch a live firebrand with which she touches the fish. The other things are left for one night in the grassland before being taken into the village (see Figure 3.2).

I might interpret this behaviour by saying that they wish to avoid any

Figure 3.2

confusion of the dry and the watery elements, but this would not be a translation of any Lele explanation. If asked why they do it, they reply: 'To prevent an
outbreak of coughing and illness', or 'Otherwise the furry animals (*hutapok*) will
get in and steal our chickens, and coughing will break out among our children.'
But these are merely elliptical references to the communion between spirit,
animal, and human spheres. The furry animals which steal chickens and cause
illness are not ordinary carnivorous animals, but sorcerers' familiars, whose
access to the sphere of living humans is made more difficult if the proper

distinctions between human and animal, day and night, water and land,[10] are correctly observed.

In accordance with the symbolism relating fishes with fertility and with spirits, pregnant women and novices for initiation must totally avoid eating fish. Certain fishes are more specially associated with spirits than others, and Diviners are supposed to avoid eating them. Fishes do nothing to bridge the gap between human society and the creatures of the forest. Unprepared contact with them is potentially dangerous and is hedged with ritual. People in a marginal ritual condition avoid them altogether. But pangolins, part fish, part animal, friendly to humans, are apt for a mediatory role. This, I suggest, is the context of the underlying assumptions by means of which the Lele cult of pangolins, is intelligible to themselves. This is why killing and eating pangolins with proper ritual observances, are believed to bring animals in droves to the hunters' arrows and babies to women.

PANGOLIN RITUAL

In a village of forty men and fifty women, all the adult male pagans save one were Begetters, sixteen were initiated Diviners, three men and their wives were Twin Parents, four men were Pangolin initiates. I was present and able to record the results of a number of hunts in the dry season of 1953.

All the villages to the north, and many to the south of my village had adopted a new anti-sorcery cult, Kabengabenga, which was sweeping across the whole Kasai district. It promised hunting success, health, and long life to its initiates by threatening automatic death to anyone who attempted sorcery after initiation. Men and women in Kabengabenga villages brought pressure to bear on their kinsmen in other villages to follow their example and rid themselves of sorcery, and those who hesitated were accused by the initiates of culpable neglect if any of their kinsmen fell ill or died. Deaths in Kabengabenga villages were attributed to the boomerang action of the cult magic, so that anyone who died was held to be convicted of attempted sorcery. The mission and the Administration had taken strong action to stop the spread of the Kabangabenga cult, and in our own village the young Christians threatened to run away if the village were initiated.

Tension was running high in the village. Hunting failures, personal or communal, were attributed to sorcery; so also was sickness. Scarcely a night passed without someone shouting warnings to unnamed sorcerers to desist, to leave the sick to recover, to leave the hunter in peace to kill his quarry. They were begged to consider the reputation of the village in the eyes of other villages. One old man declared: 'The villages to the north and the villages to the south have taken Kabengabenga. They are all watching us. They used to say: "The men of Lubello kill quantities of game, without taking Kabengabenga." Now we go out hunting, and we come back empty-handed. That is a disgrace. They watch us and say we have sorcerers in our midst.'

Alternative explanations for misfortunes were offered. The senior Pangolin man said that after a strange woman had entered the village recently, it was discovered that she had borne twins; no twin rites had been performed to prevent her entry from spoiling the village; the Twin Parents should now perform rites and send the village on a hunt that would make good the breach of the twin ritual.

On 6 August the Twin Parents duly consulted together. A Twin Parent is supposed to be an 'owner' of the village (*muna bola*) in the sense that his or her anger would render hunting fruitless unless a rite of blessing were performed. One of them, therefore, drew attention to her ulcerated leg, and protested that, in spite of the callous disregard of others in the village, she held no grudge against them for their neglect. If she had been heard to complain, it was in pain, not in anger. She performed the ritual of blessing. Instructions were given for a hunt for the next day.

7 August. The hunt was moderately successful; although four duikers escaped, two small 'blue duikers', one water chevrotain, and one young bay duiker were killed. The success was attributed to the performance of the twin ritual.

There was no more communal hunting until 12 August. Individual hunters complained of their lack of success, and considered the village to be 'bad'. The senior official diviner of the village, the *ilumbi*, was informally approached and asked to take up his magic for the next hunt. It required some courage and tact to ask him to do this, as he was widely thought to be the sorcerer responsible for the bad condition of the village. On the eve of the hunt, he ordered those who had quarrelled to pay fines, and announced that he would do magic. Before the hunt one of the Pangolin men spoke a blessing, in case his grief at the obstinate and rude behaviour of the young Christians should spoil the hunt. They drew three covers, saw little game, killed only one adult and one young 'blue duiker' – a quite negligible bag. The *ilumbi* felt discredited. He announced that the animals which he had seen by divination had been escaping behind the hunters; next time he would do different magic.

13 August. In the dawn an old man got up and harangued the sorcerers, asking what they ate if they didn't like animal meat? Dogs? People? What? He warned them that he did not consent to the illness of children in the village.

During the day it transpired that the twin ritual was still outstanding. The village had been tricked into believing that the successful hunt on 7 August had been the result of twin rituals whereas, in fact, the junior *ilumbi*, himself a Twin Parent, had persuaded the others to let him try a 'spirit magic' which had been highly successful a month earlier. Everyone was angry at the deception. The senior Pangolin man, who had originally diagnosed that a breach of twin ritual had 'spoilt the village', declared that if only the Twin Parents had been frank, the Diviners themselves would have stepped in to perform the necessary twin rites. Twins (*mayehe*) and spirits (*mingehe*) are all the same, he said, and initiated Diviners do not need to beget twins in order to do twin rites. Angriest of all was the senior *ilumbi*, hurt in his pride of magic, who now saw the reason for the failure of the hunt he had arranged on 12 August. More serious than being made to look a fool, he had looked like a sorcerer chasing away the game. In the next village the *ilumbi* had been hounded out for failure to produce game, and in the old days he would have been made to take the poison ordeal. He was obliged to dissemble his anger, as the village could be 'spoilt' by the ill will of any of its ritual officers.

In the next week men refused to go on a communal hunt as the village seemed obviously 'bad', i.e. infected with sorcery. Individual hunters had some success: a duiker was caught in a trap; a man chanced on a wild sow just after she had farrowed and easily shot her and killed her young; and a large harnessed bush-buck was shot. In spite of these successes, there was an atmosphere of frustration and acrimony in the village.

On 24 and 27 August the women went on two long fishing expeditions. While they were away there was little food, and work in the village just ticked over till their return. On 28th two pangolins were killed. When the women came back the atmosphere in the village had changed overnight to one of general rejoicing. The village evidently was felt to be vindicated in the eyes of its Kabengabenga critics. A neighbouring village asked to be allowed to send a candidate for initiation into the Pangolin cult. Among the ritual specialists, annoyance about the overdue twin rite still rankled, but the Pangolin rites had to take precedence now.

The junior Pangolin man announced on behalf of the initiates that the village was 'tied' (*kanda*), that is, that sexual intercourse was banned until after the eating of the pangolin and the shedding of animal blood in the hunt that should follow the feast. Etiquette appropriate to the presence of a chief in the village was to be observed. He used the words: '*Kum ma wa*: The master is dead. Let no one fight.' *Kum* can be translated as master or chief. Unfortunately a quarrel between children dancing broke out, adults took sides, and blows were struck. A fine had to be paid to the Pangolin group for this breach of ritual peace.

29 August. A meeting was called. The village was in a ferment because a man had been caught seducing the wife of the senior Pangolin man. The latter refused to carry on with the Pangolin initiation and feast.

30 August. There was a spate of early morning speeches. The senior Pangolin man was reproached for turning household affairs into village affairs, and for making the village suffer for his private wrong. Someone pointed out that if the pangolins were left to rot, the people of the next village, who wanted their candidate vested with Pangolin power, would think we had refused to eat the pangolin to spite them. All those who had quarrelled were roundly taken to task in public speeches. All were convinced that to go hunting while the senior Pangolin man was feeling angry would be useless.

31 August. Village opinion, originally sympathetic to the senior Pangolin man, now turned against him. He was insisting that full adultery damages should be paid before he proceeded with the Pangolin rites. There was anxiety lest the pangolins should go bad; they had already been dead five days. If they were to go bad without being eaten with proper ritual, the whole village would go 'hard' and suffer for a long time, until Pangolin magic had been done again. Repeated injunctions were made to keep the peace until the pangolin hunt. Two more cases of fighting occurred.

2 September. Fines for fighting were all paid up, and the major part of the adultery damages had been given. Ritual was performed to make the way clear for hunting the next day. The two *ilumbi*, the four Pangolin men, and the Twin Parents met and agreed to do two rites: Twin ritual and Pangolin ritual, for the hunt.

3 September. Before the hunt, two Twin Parents aired their grievances; one on account of her ulcerated leg, which she felt no one took trouble to diagnose and cure; the other complained that her husband had abandoned her for a new young wife. Her husband's colleagues replied for him that it was nonsense to suppose that a man would leave a woman through whom he had attained three of God's callings or vocations (*mapok manjambi*). He was, through her, an initiate of the Begetters, of Twins and of the Pangolin. She was reminded of the danger to the village if a woman who was in these three senses one of its 'owners' were allowed to nurse her anger.

The hunt that followed this concerted ritual effort was a failure. Seven animals in all were seen, but only two small duikers were killed. There was great anger and agreement that the village was bad. However, blood had been shed and the Pangolin feast could proceed. After the Pangolin rites had been performed, people assured each other, we should all see great quantities of game being brought back. The pangolin would draw animals to the village. The next day was fixed for the feast.

That very afternoon a third pangolin was killed. There was great satisfaction. 'Just as we were saying "Tomorrow we shall eat pangolin, and invest new members" . . . behold, another pangolin comes into the village!' They spoke as if the pangolin had died voluntarily, as if it had elected to be the object of Pangolin ritual and to offer itself for the feast of initiates; as if it had honoured this village by choosing it.

At night the junior Pangolin man announced that no one was to fight, above all no one was to fight secretly. 'If you must fight, do it openly and pay up. He who fights tonight, let him be rich. The fine will be twenty raffia cloths.'

5 September. The Pangolin feast and initiation rite were eventually held. I was unfortunately unable to see the rites. I was told that emphasis was laid on the chiefship of the pangolin. We call him *kum*, they said, because he makes women conceive. They expressed shame and embarrassment at having eaten a *kum*. No one is allowed to see the pangolins being roasted over the fire. The tongues, necks, ribs, and stomachs were not eaten, but buried under a palm tree whose wine thenceforth becomes the sole prerogative of the Begetters. Apparently the new initiate was made to eat some of the flesh of the first two pangolins which were in process of decay; the more rotten parts, together with the scales and bones, were given to the dogs. The senior initiates ate the flesh of the more recently killed animal. All were confident that the hunt on the following day would be successful.

6 September. The hunt went off in good heart, twenty men and eight dogs. It was an abject failure. Powerful sorcery was evidently at work, since all ritual had been duly performed. People discussed the possible significance of a leopard that had been heard to bark in the precincts of the village that night, and of leopard tracks that had been seen on the way to the hunt. The leopard is one of the forms which the *ilumbi* is supposed to be able to take, and the *ilumbi* was suspected of having gone ahead of the hunters in leopard's guise, and scared off the game. The *ilumbi* himself, realising that suspicions of sorcery were again directed at him, suggested that he would glady go with the rest of the village to take Kabengabenga magic, if only the Christians did not hold such strong objections. He evidently saw it as a means of clearing his own name. In his youth he had twice taken the poison ordeal and confounded his accusers. He also suggested to me privately that he might leave the village and live elsewhere, as his enemies had never forgiven him for the disputes over women in which he had been embroiled.

In the meanwhile, the village was still 'tied': the ban on sexual intercourse had not been lifted since 28 August, and could not be until blood had been shed in a hunt following the feast of Pangolin initiates.

9 September. A hunt took place in which one small duiker was killed. The ritual requirement was fulfilled, and the ban on sexual intercourse was lifted, but from every other point of view it was felt to have been a failure.

ACCURACY OF LELE OBSERVATION OF ANIMALS

Writing strictly from the point of view of religious symbolism it is not relevant to ask how accurate is Lele observation of animal behaviour. A symbol based on mistaken information can be fully effective as a symbol, so long as the fable in question is well known. The dove, it would seem, can be one of the most relentlessly savage of birds.[11] The pelican does not nourish its young from its own living flesh. Yet the one bird has provided a symbol of peace, and the other of maternal devotion, for centuries.

However, it would be interesting to know whether the symbolism described above is based on fables or not. I must confess that I was able only with great difficulty to identify most of the animals. Many of the rarer ones I never saw alive or dead and in any case should not have been able to recognise them at sight. I was fortunate in securing the kind collaboration of Monsieur A.J. Jobaert, Warden of the Muene Ditu Game Reserve, who knew the Kasai and several of the local languages well. By sending him the native names in two local languages, together with a description, I obtained translation into French, Latin, and English, and these names were checked again by Mr R.B. Freeman, the Reader in Taxonomy at University College, London. My remarks are based on identification obtained in this roundabout and unreliable way. The point I thought it most important to check was whether the Lele are right in considering the breeding habits of pangolins anomalous: first, do pangolins give birth to their young one at a time? Second, how unusual is this among the smaller mammals? In pursuing this inquiry I was interested to find how little scientifically tested knowledge there is concerning the manner of reproduction of mammals, common and uncommon. Such information as is available serves to justify the Lele in both these views.[12]

One interesting point that I am still unable to elucidate is the principle on which the Lele discriminate between the small pangolin (*Manis tricuspis*) which they call *luwawa*, and the giant pangolin (*Manis gigantea*) which they call *yolabọndu*, making a major cult of the first but not of the second. Zoologists may be able to give information about the distribution and habits of the two species which may throw light on the question. It may require an historical solution, since pangolin cults are found in other parts of the Congo.[13]

NOTES

1 The pangolin is a scaly ant-eater.
2 The Begetters are an exception, their initiation being mainly a *rite de passage*. They give indirect support to the other fertility cults by honouring virility and penalising impotence.
3 See Chapter 2, in which I give in detail the various situations of cooking, eating, washing, quarrelling, etc., in which these categories become evident.
4 Domestic animals and vermin are major exceptions. Before the recent introduction of goats, pigs, and ducks, the only domestic animals which the Lele kept were dogs and chickens. There is a fable which describes how the first ancestors of these, a jackal and a partridge, came to throw in their lot with man, and how both dogs and poultry are continually begged by their forest kin to leave the villages of humans. Conventional attitudes to both of these in a number of situations are consistent with the notion that a domestic animal is essentially an anomaly. For rats, which infest the huts of humans, Lele feel nothing but disgust. In conformity with their attitude to other anomalous animals, they never eat dog, domestic rats, or mice, and women extend the avoidance to a number of other rats and to all poultry.
5 For brevity's sake I use here some terms of our own categorisation. Lele use no one word to render 'carnivorous' exactly, but they indicate carnivorous animals by the term *hutapok* – animals with skins, or 'furry animals'. I do not know any Lele term for 'oviparous' or 'mammalian', but it is clear that the manner of reproduction provides criteria for classification as surely for the Lele as for our zoologists, for their descriptions never fail to mention an animal's breeding habits.
6 Significantly, its zoological name is *Anomalurus beecroftii*.
7 Chapter 2.
8 *Le Soulier de Satin*, Troisième Journée, Scène II.
9 Deuteronomy 14: 7; Leviticus II: 4–5.

10 I have given an outline of the most important of these distinctions as they appear in ritual, in Chapter 1.

11 K. Lorenz, *King Solomon's Ring*, London, Methuen, 1952.

12 S.A. Asdell, *Patterns of Mammalian Reproduction*, Ithaca, New York, Comstock 1946, p. 184.

13 D. Biebuyck, 'Répartitions et droits du Pangolin chez les Balega', *Zaïre*, 9 November 1953, vii. Subsequently Professor Vansina pointed out to me that the answer to this question is contained in the text. The small pangolin is the only beast that is a fish-like, bird-like quadruped mammal. This paragraph has been discussed by I.M. Lewis in the journal *Man*, *26*, 3, 1991, with further letters from myself, Roy Ellen and Luc de Heusch.

Chapter 4

Techniques of sorcery control in Central Africa

First published in John Middleton and E. Winter (eds) (1963), *Witchcraft and Sorcery in East Africa*, London, Routledge & Kegan Paul.

Ten years ago Professor Marwick published a comparison of witch-finding movements in Central Africa.[1] Summarising what Dr Richards had earlier reported of the Mcape movement[2] he showed that later witch-finding movements were adapted to avoid the European opposition provoked by Mcape. The latter too obviously resembled the poison ordeals which had been the customary method of dealing with witches throughout the region: medicines had been taken orally, and witches had been exposed, as in the poison ordeal. Furthermore, charms had been sold, rendering the vendors liable to prosecution for fraudulent dealings. But in the Bwanali-Mpulumutsi movement of 1947, medicines were given by incision in the skin, no payment was taken, and witches confessed voluntarily.

This approach somewhat undervalues the resemblance which the Bwanali-Mpulumutsi movement still bore to the poison ordeals. In form there was similarity, in that the treated persons (on one account at least) responded by vomiting if they were innocent, and by not vomiting if they were guilty. In function the similarity was even stronger. If the treated persons were witches, next time they tried to commit witchcraft they would themselves die; if innocent, they would be immune to the witchcraft of others. 'If a man has been treated with Mpulumutsi's medicine, he cannot die from witch-sent diseases, but from God-sent diseases only'.[3] The witches were thought to be automatically revealed by the treament; they were impelled to confess their witchcraft voluntarily, and were then cleansed from it. Submission to Mpulumutsi was very like undergoing an ordeal: those who underwent it were cleared of the charge of witchcraft, so long as they continued to live. Of the stream of pilgrims who ostensibly went to gain immunity from witchcraft, Mpulumutsi's own remarks show that many went to gain proof of their own innocence with which to silence their accusers at home.

Interpretations of witchcraft have not hitherto paid enough attention to the poison ordeal. It is worth re-examining the now classic analyses of Professor Marwick[4] and of Professor Mitchell[5] with the poison ordeal in mind. Both have stressed the normative function of witchcraft beliefs, and this none would wish to qualify. I doubt if anyone would disagree with their second hypothesis, that witchcraft beliefs and accusations provide a means of rupturing relations which have become intolerably strained. But this point is developed in terms which import a great deal more. Cewa witchcraft beliefs help to 'dissolve relations which have become redundant'; they have a 'socially cathartic nature'; they 'blast down the dilapidated parts of the social structure, and clear the rubble in preparation for new ones'; they 'maintain the virility of the indigenous social structure by allowing periodic redistribution of structural forces'.[6]

In Professor Mitchell's account of Yao society, witchcraft accusations appear as something like the switch in a control mechanism, which reacts to an increase of population in excess of what the social unit can bear. They are harnessed to a man's ambition to become a headman himself. He accuses the existing headman, and the case ends when he triumphantly splits the village and founds his own new one.[7]

On this view witchcraft is tidily tucked into the analysis of social structure as a necessary inconvenience, comparable to a temporary rise in unemployment following changes in the structure of industry. However, certain inconsistencies and omissions tempt us to question this sanguine view.

The poison ordeal, which disappeared so recently, had at least two functions: oracular and punitive. The oracular function in the detection of witches has been separately preserved among the Azande.[8] The speciality of the poison ordeal as an oracle was to give a final verdict, from which there could be no appeal. Among the Azande this aspect is saved in the theory of the infallibility of the prince's oracle, essential for the system of belief, as well as for the political system. Without some such device, divination cannot give a final verdict. One is struck with the inconclusiveness of the cases recounted by Professor Marwick, except for the few accused who took the poison ordeal, and survived to confound their accusers.

Getting an oracular verdict against one's rival is a game that two can play, and from Professor Marwick's own account it seems that either party to a Cewa dispute is capable of doing it. The younger men, whose success in ousting their senior rivals would no doubt make for the virility of the society, are often the ones accused of witchcraft. 'Men are tempted to kill their elder brothers or mother's brothers with witchcraft if the latter have property they are likely to inherit'.[9] Evidently it would have been the sister's sons who would have been put to the ordeal, rather than the mother's brothers. With or without the poison ordeal, it seems likely that witchcraft beliefs only dissolve impediments to lineage segmentation in so far as they provide an idiom for phrasing the necessary repudiations.

But the idiom is equally suited to attempts to resist threatening change. Without some specially adapted controls, witchcraft accusations are only a neutral weapon, which either party to a dispute can use. The Azande beliefs are weighted with supplementary beliefs which control the direction of accusations, so that a man and his son do not accuse one another, and no one accuses the ruling dynasty. In the Congo, Lele beliefs in sorcery are weighted so that an accusation against a young man is less plausible than one against an old man. But nothing of this kind is recorded for the Cewa or Yao. If anything, the bias is against the younger men. Out of eight cases of witchcraft related to lineage segmentation among the Cewa, all except one, and that an ambiguous one, are cases in which the accused person is the one desiring office or possessions of the victim. If Cewa witchcraft beliefs were operating in a system with normal checks on frivolous accusations and with serious accusations leading to the ordeal, it would evidently be these ambitious upstarts who would be put to the ordeal. So the case histories show that the action of their witchcraft beliefs would tend to be conservative, upholding men in office, delaying and not encouraging any 'periodic redistribution of structural forces'.

We conclude that in the old days witchcraft accusations were a clumsy and double-edged weapon in the struggle for office; they might be used to consolidate an existing office-holder's position by ruining his junior rivals, as much as by the latter, pressing for fission of the group under the old man's control. The poison ordeal, in which prolonged quarrels were likely to culminate, might blast away the rubble and dilapidated parts of the social structure, or it might serve the forces of reaction, by removing the junior contenders. The very threat of it might inculcate in them a livelier sense of respect for seniority, and thus tend to check lineage segmentation. In any case, it is very likely that the poison ordeal was the king-pin of the system of witchcraft beliefs and that without it their effect on the social structure is considerably modified.

Modern movements of witchfinders may have had counterparts in the pre-colonial period. In the Belgian Congo, where poison ordeals were not suppressed by law until 1924, and where the local application of the law was sometimes even later, similar movements[10] have been recorded since the turn of the century.[11] The history of those witchfinding cults among the Lele suggests that they were an accepted alternative technique of sorcery control, less drastic than the poison ordeal, but promising to be more effective in eradicating sorcery.

Among the Lele the effective suppression of the poison ordeal dates from the 1930s, about fifteen years before fieldwork.[12] Poison ordeals were then no longer practised in the main part of their territory, but it was said that they were administered in secret in the border areas. Men who had witnessed the ordeals were still alive.

One, whose innocence had twice been vindicated by it, in about 1924 and 1927, described the scene to me. An enclosure was built at the edge of the village, into which the accused of several villages would be gathered. For three days they ate nothing but bananas, a diet thought to give them the fairest chance of survival. Their kin and friends wailed and mourned for them. Devoted kinsmen of the various accused would step out of the crowd and enter the enclosure, saying: 'If you drink *ipome*, I shall drink it with you. If you die, we will die together.' Lele always speak of dying together when they mean living together, as they speak of starving together when they mean sharing the last crumb. So this was a gesture of confidence in the happy outcome of the ordeal, not the reverse. In this way the number of candidates was increased.

When finally the concoction was ready, the officials in charge, *bahaki*, would first drink it themselves to show their fitness to perform the rite. They would then ladle it out, a dose to each of the accused. The latter would be made to keep moving, to walk, dance, run, for movement was thought to help the stomach to reject the poison. Some would start to vomit. My narrator graphically described his own experience. He vomited to left, vomited to right, to the applause of his friends he danced and vomited, and finally danced all the way home in triumph, shouting songs of defiance against his accusers.

Others did not react in this way. They felt pain. They wanted to be left alone. But the *bahaki* chivvied them around, beat them until they ran up a hill. Finally they collapsed and died, convicted, punished, and eliminated in a single act.

It was impossible to discover how often the ordeal was used, or how many people died in it. Lele said, frequently, and that many were killed. The verdicts of *ipome* feature quite often in histories of blood-compensation for killing by sorcery. By 1950 the institution seemed to have disappeared, almost without a trace. I could not study it at first hand. But I learnt much about a cult movement which was spreading through the region at the same time, which threw some light on the function of ordeals in Lele society. First, we need to fill in some details about the Lele.

They are a small tribe, an offshoot of the Kuba empire, formerly as much isolated by their dislike of foreigners as by the river system which bounds three sides of their territory, and the rocky Angolan plateau on the south. Even in 1950 Luba tribesmen would be afraid to walk unprotected near Lele villages after dark. These villages are thinly scattered in forest parkland bordering tropical forest. Each has its allies and enemies, and each used to be in permanent hostility with certain of its neighbours. It is relevant to this study to recognise the shut-off, enclosed nature of life in these villages, and their atmosphere of aggressive suspicion against outsiders.

Anything which arouses a Lele man's distrust, or makes him doubt the goodwill of another, any clash of interests or quarrel, may cause him to anticipate sorcery. When illness or death strikes his home, these suspicions are renewed, and he starts to consult oracles.

In practice all deaths and most illnesses are attributed to sorcery. Lele believe that natural death is possible: when a man has reached the end of his allotted span he will inevitably die. But only rarely does it happen that a very old person's death is attributed to the advanced senility which strikes the outside observer as the most likely cause. Deaths of women in childbirth and deaths of infants are an exception, since these lives are held to be liable to special risks from adultery. In such cases the adulterer should pay blood compensation. In other cases compensation is demanded from the convicted sorcerer. Lele have developed elaborate institutions,[13] peculiar to themselves, for arranging blood-compensation. So much advantage is to be gained from a successful claim for compensation that at every death there is an attempt to pin responsibility on someone who can be sued for damages. Thus it is that there is a practical material interest in convicting a man of killing by sorcery, and pressure to seek an authoritative, final verdict.

The Lele idea of a sorcerer changes from one context to another. At some times he is a joke, or a bogy to frighten children; or an intimate enemy, on the doorstep, in the house, sharing drinks and food. Sometimes he is thought of as the beloved uncle or grandfather, who suffers an occasional lapse from righteousness. Sometimes his image evokes horror and disgust, as an unnatural perversion of humanity. Anyone can become a sorcerer, by obtaining the means of sorcery from another, paying the price, and using it against his enemy. A sorcerer acts from *bupih*, which is spite, malice, envy. Most people feel *bupih* at some time, but the real sorcerer is consumed with *bupih* all the time. He is old, so he resents the young. He is poor, so he resents the rich. He is hungry and neglected, so he begrudges the meat and wine his kin do not share with him. He is ugly, so resents beauty and strength. He buys his way into deeper and deeper knowledge of sorcery techniques, the price being always a human life. He gives his own clansman and children, the only people over whose lives he has any right, and with their deaths he buys power to hurt his enemies.

Some of his techniques are thought to depend on control of the spirits of his victims. The spirits of dead babies can see before and behind the present moment, and can be used by him for divinations. Others among his victims are turned into a pack of carnivorous animals, hyena, mongoose, leopard, civet, jackal, which do his bidding, but which demand human flesh for food. If he does not satisfy them, they may turn and kill him too. Thus he is pressed on, by the requirements of the trade he has entered, to kill more and more extensively.

It is this idea of the fully committed sorcerer, completely given over to necromancy, that fills the Lele with horror. Whatever the accusations against him, they will rarely believe that a father or mother's brother with whom they are on good terms has become such a sorcerer, though they admit it is conceivable that he should have committed one or two isolated acts of sorcery. Their interest in not paying blood-compensation ensures that they will defend his innocence in any particular case. This means that no sorcerer is ever accused unanimously, there are always two views about his guilt, two parties pressing for a settlement for or against him.

Note that the image of the committed sorcerer is always an old man, and one who kills his own clansmen as a means of reaching his enemies. Case histories show that others are often accused, old women, or middle-aged men. But whenever Lele discuss sorcery, they talk about jealous, angry old men.

There are at least two reasons for this. One follows from the nature of their beliefs about counter-sorcery ritual. Much of Lele ritual is directed to countering sorcery attacks. Sorcerers and diviners use the same forces, draw on the same knowledge for their opposed intentions. It follows that the higher the repute of a great diviner, the more capable he is thought of committing sorcery.

He is even expected to use sorcery for some of his divinatory techniques, to keep the skulls of his own mother and children in his hut for control over their spirits, to be able to transform himself into a leopard, to meet other sorcerers at night and outwit them on their own ground. The belief in the unity of know-ledge inexorably indicates leading cult officiants as possible suspects when sorcery is feared. Add to this that leading cult officials are usually old men, and you have one half of the explanation of the image of the old man as a sorcerer.

The other half lies in the precarious privileges of age in Lele society. In one perspective it appears that old men enjoy all the advantages. They are polygynists, while, correspondingly, the younger men have a long period of bachelorhood. They control wealth, and the young men come to them asking for help in paying cult dues and payments. Yet the idea of the sorcerer depicts a disappointed, neglected old man. Indeed, in another perspective one sees how vulnerable is their position of privilege. If the young man's maturity is retarded for the sake of polygyny for their elders, young men have their own correspond-ing privileges, notably, freedom from control. It seems likely that the theory of old men as sorcerers reflects their real weaknesses in the authority structure, weaknesses which result in disappointment for many. It is indeed hard not to feel *bupih*, envy and malice, when, having always been trained to show defer-ence to seniors, now that they have reached the peak of the scale of seniority, they realise that deference does not mean obedience or support from their junior clansmen, any more than it did when they themselves were young. Some old men are more fortunate than others. Those who have had no daughters, or whose children have not survived, or whose wives have run away, taking their children with them, or who for any reason are unable to command the goods and services of sons-in-law, these old men find that the deference of junior clansmen is a somewhat empty formality.

Individual old men have to be careful not to abuse their powers or to attract antagonism against their persons, for a few well-aimed accusations of sorcery could easily destroy them. Just as the Azande conform to a high standard of good manners for fear of being accused of witchcraft, so with the Lele, the danger of being accused of sorcery encourages a modest, placatory demeanour in older men.

The fact that it is their own clansmen that sorcerers are thought to sacrifice in the first instance reflects a conflict of interests between young and old within the local clan sections, the frustration of the senior men's claims on their juniors, and also the guilt which the juniors may feel when, steering between the conflicting demands of kinship, they play off one mother's brother against another, and attend seriously to none.

In any society there are likely to be conflicting roles, strained relations, and disappointed hopes. Lele society is no exception, and its institutions certainly lead people to entertain unrealistic expectations. Some roles are very weakly defined and incompatible ideals are held. Furthermore, when relations become intolerably strained, people cannot easily break them off.

Unlike the Cewa-Yao-Nyasa people, Lele society is not based on segmented matrilineages. True, the village is composed of a number of matrilineal descent groups, but these are widely recruited, regardless of genealogical ties. They increase or dwindle according to their success in recruiting young men from other villages, but they are not internally organised into competing lineage segments, and there is no overt competition for the role of leader. The headship of the local descent group is unequivocally defined as the oldest resident male member. Since this has no ambiguity, it gives no scope for rival claims, and in any case the office is hardly a prize worth competing for. The local descent group does not segment on genealogical lines, thought it may eject an un-assimilable member.

Second, the village itself is not primarily a structure of matrilineal descent groups. It has an age-organisation, and cult societies, which cut right across descent groupings and take some of the strains of rivalry between them.

Third, each Lele village is a corporate enduring entity, with a heritage of rights in wealth and women. True, each has originally been formed by a process of splitting, but the rate of fission is slowed up by the political disadvantages which would hamper a new village. The parent village would retain the whole heritage of wealth; the new village would need to muster a minimum defence force if it were to play any political part, and protect its women from abduction. At least twenty men are necessary to form a team for the Lele style of hunt. These combine to put real brakes on the tendency to form new villages. And, as we have seen, the villages are internally constructed so that they do not easily split apart.

Finally, Lele do not compete for the office of village headman. Their village head is chosen on the principle of seniority as the oldest member of one of the founding clans. A man becomes head of a village, not by showing signs of vigorous personality, generosity, and skill in reconciling rivals, but by discreetly ageing in a village where his clan is dominant. The more obscurely he has lived, the more likely he is to attain the post, and indeed it is one which calls for little in the way of personal qualities. Certainly here is one area in which the Lele have eliminated what is evidently a potent cause of conflict in other central African societies.

Although they do not institute a hierarchy of responsibility or channel authority through well-defined offices, yet the Lele expect the village to be a united group. Quarrels, especially violence, are fined, in the interests of good hunting, since it is thought that forest spirits will punish discord by hiding away the game.[14] In short, they make use of external, automatic sanctions to uphold the peace which they desire, but which they do not seek to achieve through overt leadership. They dread (and rightly, according to other central African experience) the disruptive effects of jealousy. They try to achieve harmony by persuading, admonishing, and keeping up a constant pervasive moral pressure.

Their anxiety about peace and their removal of certain roles from the sphere of competition are consistent with the brakes on village fission which I have indicated.

The Lele idea of the good life is a very fine one. When they describe the ideal behaviour of junior clansmen, co-husbands, brother, etc., they evidently expect a high standard of selflessness and spontaneous self-discipline, with a minimum of organisation. Yet, by the time he is past his middle years, a Lele man is quite likely to be embroiled with a number of people in his village. His own infirmities prove to him that he is the victim of sorcery. The ill-health of his enemies suggests to them that he is a sorcerer. The sure way to avoid sorcery is to move out of its geographical range. Young men can do this, for they are sure of a welcome wherever they go. But an old man's arrival is less welcome, for he adds little to the labour force, and disturbs the pattern of seniority among his hosts.

Since voluntary removal does not appeal to him as a solution of his personal problems, his village becomes something like a closed unit for him. A few accusations of sorcery against him may serve as a pretext for not honouring kinship obligations. But if his quarrels build up cumulatively, a man can find himself surrounded by a wall of hostility. He can easily acquire the reputation of a fully committed sorcerer, responsible for every death in the village. No ordinary oracle could convince his accusers of his innocence. If he cannot clear his name, he faces social extinction, and his clansmen face loss in the system of blood-compensation. One can see how he would be pushed towards welcoming the poison ordeal as a deliverance from his troubles.

In the absence of the poison ordeal, enforced exile was often the only prospect for certain irascible characters. In each of the three villages I knew best, there were such persons. Some had been driven away, others had been temporarily given refuge from other villages whence they had been chased. In all cases they had been famous diviners. Each had his own supporters in his clan and family, who thought him unjustly accused. The gap he had left remained a festering point of conflict in the village which had exiled him.

For example, an old diviner, Makut, had many times been accused of sorcery in the village of Ngoie. He fell into the hands of his accusers by bad luck when one of his patients died during the visit of a young medical officer fresh from Europe. The doctor, called in to see the corpse, certified that death had occurred. Told that the dead man had been poisoned (the euphemism for sorcery), he asked to see the poison. Makut, as one doctor to another, readily showed him the old lemonade bottle containing the potion he had used. The doctor considered it to be indeed noxious; Makut was arrested, tried for manslaughter, and sentenced to prison in Luebo. The village was delirious with delight, since, for the first time in their experience of Europeans, it seemed that sorcery was being treated as a legally punishable offence. They saw the beginning of a happy rapprochement of Lele and European views on the subject.

It was a triumph to have sent their sorcerer to prison for life, as they thought. But Makut's wife, his full brother, and his next senior clansman all insisted he was innocent. They collected a fine to be paid for his offence, and after a short term in prison, his sentence was shortened, and he was released at the time of my stay in the village. His brother and fellow clansman went to fetch him from Port Francqui and carried him home on their shoulders, as the old man's feet were crippled with rheumatism.

Great was the anger and alarm in the village awaiting his return. Visitors left precipitately, wives suddenly decided to take their children to see their mothers. People asked me to intervene to stop his return, asking how I proposed to pursue my studies in a deserted village. A few days after he arrived, Makut's wife was ordered by her brother to leave her husband, since it was hoped that without a woman to cook for him he could not stay on. But he stayed. A meeting was held, and then his hut was attacked, the roof torn down, and he was forcibly driven out of the village. No other village would receive him. I heard that he lived on in the forest, where he had been voluntarily joined by his brother. Two old men could not survive there alone, and I understood that friends were secretly bringing food to them.

Other persons in that village, women as well as men, were thought to be sorcerers; some were residents, others were new arrivals from other villages, but each similarly had his body of devoted supporters. The same held good in other villages. Each time that a supposed sorcerer was chased away, his removal left a legacy of enmity between his supporters and accusers that was not automatically cancelled by the eviction. It was impossible not to recognise the gap in their institutions which the poison ordeal filled.

The verdict of the poison ordeal was above challenge. If a man survived it, he confounded his accusers. The whole knot of antagonisms and accusations, which probably carried many separate charges of sorcery, was cut. Of the many who took the ordeal at one time, some did not survive, and the whole onus of the refuted charges was passed on to the dead. The acquitted man could demand compensation, and start again, richer and more powerful than before. If he died, convicted, his physical existence was cut off at the point where social life had become impossible. His kin and supporters had no longer any ground for taking his part in the village. They had no choice but to pay compensation for the deaths he had caused, and this done, they could start again, in a new alignment of social forces.

An old man whose mother had died in a poison ordeal told me that he could not refuse to pay compensation for the deaths she was convicted of, since she had died by the hand of God; *ipome* was God's thing, and if God said she was guilty, she was.

If this is a sound view of the function of the poison ordeal in Lele society, we can judge the quandary into which they were thrown by its abolition. The one sure means of eliminating sorcerers was prohibited, but sorcerers were still at large. However, another means appeared intermittently in their history. We can suppose that even to Lele the poison ordeal, with its trail of victims, appeared sometimes as a too drastic remedy for a scourge which was as usual as the common cold. Some accounts of the old days would say that no sooner did they come home from killing off their sorcerers in the ordeal, than they would find that sorcery had struck again.

'Is it a coincidence,' asked De Jonghe, 'that so many secret societies took their origin in Bashilele country?'[15] Between 1900 and my second visit to the field, in 1953, no less than seven cult movements had been introduced, of which five were directed against sorcery. De Jonghe's researches pointed to the Lele as the origin of several movements which had a much wider distribution in the Congo. But, when they recall the history of their cult movements Lele claim a foreign origin for many of them.

The following is the list of cults, the names by which they were known to the Lele, their objectives, and a rough approximation to the dates at which they were introduced.

1910 *Mambwi*, an anti-sorcery cult.

1929 *Ngendu*, an anti-sorcery cult, adopted specially to cure sickness. Among its cult objects was a wooden image, dressed in a hat and monkey skin skirt, used for divination. It only lasted a year.

1930 *Lukwoh* or *Lukwosh*, a cult to end sorcery, which came to the Lele from the east, was also short-lived.

1932 *Imbwanga*, a cult introduced from the north, which promised the return of the ancestors. Recognised almost at once as a hoax.

1933 *Ngwata*, a cult introduced from the west, with the object of chasing away the whites. Lele were told that if they performed the rites and honoured the prohibitions of the cult, the Europeans would pass them by without seeing them, and therefore would turn back to their own country. Its promises were also discovered immediately to be worthless. This was about the time that Lele laid their last armed ambush for colonial officials. In 1935 a motor-road running north and south was completed, and all villages were moved to easy distance of it. From this date Belgian authority over them became highly effective.

1943 *Melu*, an anti-sorcery cult, whose prohibitions were still being observed in a somewhat disillusioned way at the time of my first visit in 1949–50.

1952 *Kabengabenga*, introduced from the east, where it was called *Mikomi Yool*, to a few of the northern villages of the Lele. At the time of my visit in 1953 it was in the process of spreading southwards from village to village.

Such a history of credulity seems to accord poorly with the intelligence and wit of individual Lele. The impression is increased when one knows that each of these impositions on their credulity cost them considerable material wealth, but here lies part of the explanation. The process by which new cult movements are spread in the Congo has an important economic aspect, comparable to that of the Mcape movement described by Dr Richards. Whoever starts the movement, or introduces it to his own tribe, expects the same accumulation of financial profit as the European who starts a chain-letter series, writing to five acquaintances, inviting each to send him £1, and to write five similar letters to their friends.

A couple of Lele men, with the support of their village, crossed the Kasai in 1952 to acquire the Kabengabenga cult from the Bushong.[16] In return for a substantial down payment, they were taught the secrets of the cult, its rites, mythology, and songs. They acquired material emblems in the form of armbands, which, when fully paid for, endowed them with power to administer the cult, to use its divining techniques, and to initiate others on the same terms. Lele said that this was the way in which all cults spread. The initial fee was regarded as an investment on which one would recoup one's outlay when other villages came asking for initiation. There was therefore an interest in spreading the cult.

Kabengabenga diviners could be consulted by individuals from other villages. Their oracles carried great prestige. A stream of visitors from the south went up to the Kabengabenga villages, to pay a consultation fee and have their names cleared of sorcery charges. They all seemed to go home vindicated, and ready to sow in their own villages the seeds of enthusiasm for the new cult.

It spread in other ways too. When anyone was seriously ill in an uninitiated village, there were never wanting kinsmen in a Kabengabenga village to bewail the sorcery that was evidently rife there, and who marvelled at the irresponsibility of those who did not immediately favour initiation to the cult. Anyone who opposed acceptance of the cult was presumed to be himself a sorcerer, afraid of the curtailment of his activities. Inevitably, while discussing the pros and cons of initiation, individuals foresaw that it would be difficult to stand aside, and began to wonder whether it would not be wiser to make a contribution to the cost, and become themselves one of the cult officials for their own village.

Kabengabenga had some other features in common with earlier anti-sorcery cults. Each cult had its own set of prohibitions, which if not observed, would make it ineffective, and often would bring misfortune, even death. For each, the village was the unit of initiation. No one could reside in an initiated village without adhering to the cult. Nor, once initiated, could inmates of a village go to live in one which had not adopted the cult. The rule was based on fear of the danger of contact between treated and untreated persons.[17] This contributed to the pressure to enter the movement. For example, according to the rules of Kabengabenga, no initiate could set eyes on a non-initiate before going to the forest to hunt or cultivate, or his work would be in vain. And vice versa, the same danger applied to non-initiates setting eyes on initiates. A woman from an initiated village, determined against the rules to visit her sick daughter living in an uninitiated village, had to spend the first part of every morning hiding in the hut, until everyone had safely gone to work without seeing her. Her dietary restrictions made common meals almost impossible.

When a village has adopted an anti-sorcery cult such as Kabengabenga, all its diviners are required to renounce their former profession. Their tools of divination are handed in to the officials of the cult – horns, rubbing oracles, whistles – another point of similarity with Bwanali-Mpulumutsi and Mcape. The new cult officials use their own techniques, proper to the cult, and their rites supersede all previous rites. All the former diviners who do not find a role in the new cult are put out of business. Fortunately there are many new roles to be filled, some through co-option, others by private inspiration.

All the cults had another feature in common with those of Mcape and Bwanali-Mpulumutsi, that is the belief in a kind of boomerang action which destroys any initiate who tries to commit sorcery. This supposed power in the cult further explains why no one who is not an initiate is tolerated in a village which has adopted it, for he may be the only sorcerer whose fangs have not been drawn.

The assurances which the cult makes give it something of the air of a millennial cult. For it promises that the community which embraces it will not suffer again from sorcery. Since all misfortune, illness, and death is attributed to sorcery, an initiated community therefore hopes to enter a new era of peace and prosperity, in which no one will die until their hair is white with age. The only early deaths will be those of sorcerers, killed by their own art turned against themselves.

Among the Lele the effect of their belief in the boomerang action of Kabengabenga was very similar to a happy outcome of a poison ordeal. For the men who had been driven out of their villages were able to return, not reinstated in their old roles, but allowed to live on peaceably in the community. So long as all believe in the efficacy of the cult to kill any sorcerer before he can reach a victim, then it is safe to re-admit sorcerers who have been driven out of the village in the days before the cult was adopted. If they dare to be initiated into the cult, to abjure former practices, knowing that they will die as soon as they attempt sorcery again, then their friends are at liberty to welcome them back. This is an example of the remarkable spirit of pragmatism which stands out in so many accounts of African witchcraft and sorcery.

Old Makut, who was chased out of Ngoie in 1949, was living there peacefully again, thanks to Kabengabenga, when I returned in 1953. In another village an old diviner was driven out for sorcery between 1950 and 1952, but in 1953, after the village had adopted Kabengabenga, he asked to be received back and I heard that he would be re-admitted. In a village which had not adopted Kabengabenga, and where the argument to-adopt or not-to-adopt was being waged between Christians and pagans, the man who was involved in more quarrels than anyone else and was most generally thought to be a sorcerer, often spoke of the need to introduce Kabengabenga. He was then the official diviner of the village and I do not doubt that he would have been the first to volunteer for office in the new cult.

De Jonghe, though he also mentioned economic crisis as a cause of these cult movements, was probably nearer the mark when he regarded them as attempts to control sorcery. But to say this, and no more, implies the crassest gullibility on the part of a community which keeps paying out its wealth for one implausible panacea after another. In the light of what we have said, the behaviour of the Lele becomes more intelligible. Their picture of a sorcerer indicates an old man, greatly disappointed in his life-expectations. A glance at their institutions shows that older men may well be surrounded by enemies, as well as disappointed. In the old days the thought of the poison ordeal not only modified the behaviour of such persons, but limited the freedom with which accusations of sorcery were made. Acquittal by the poison ordeal used to entitle a man to demand heavy compensation from his false accusers. Nowadays each accusation builds up tension to an unbearable point, since those most commonly accused are unable to go to live elsewhere, and their accusers do not intend to move. In the absence of the ordeal the situation is not satisfactorily resolved by the expulsion of the accused, since there is still no final verdict on him.

A new anti-sorcery cult offers another kind of solution. It gives everyone in the village a chance to start again, without the multiplier effect that sorcery fears have on strained relations. It is like a resolution not to believe in sorcery any more, to ignore its influence. If a village pays one hundred raffia cloths, and four bars of camwood, for a cult which enables exiles to return, and old enemies to cooperate amicably again, the new start seems cheap at the price, if only it would work.

We are reminded of the charmingly described Welsh village[18] which constantly undertook new ventures, sports clubs, or charity bazaars, a new committee being formed as soon as an old venture petered out, in valiant attempts to create a unity out of disparate elements. So we should think of the anti-sorcery cults, and the other cults to promote hunting, or to avoid the whites, which sweep in turn through Lele society.

Unfortunately, the Welsh football club or flower show is a better adapted instrument, since it makes no improbable promises. Kabengabenga promised that no one should die prematurely, except sorcerers self-convicted by their own deaths. If a small baby died, the diviners might explain the death as resulting from breach of the Kabengabenga prohibitions. If an adult died, as a proven sorcerer he was to be denied an honourable burial, his corpse to be thrown into the grassland like a dog's. However, these two possibilities do not cover all the contingencies. If a young woman with small children died, her kin could not be convinced that she had committed sorcery. That anyone happily fulfilled in normal motherhood could be ruled by *bupih* and commit sorcery was incompatible with their preconceptions concerning sorcery. Unbelievers, in villages not yet committed to Kabengabenga, scoffingly noted such discrepancies. Sooner or later the cult would be exposed by its failure to fit reality as the Lele persisted in seeing it. On these lines each of the preceding cults had been discredited in their turn: '*Ba mak chu dimb*' (They deceived us). An expression of amused indignation, curiously detached, ends the story of each of the previous cults, even while the narrators are on the brink of a new one.

By 1959 it is understandable that the Lele and other Kuba peoples had exhausted the possibilities of anti-sorcery cults, and that they should have seized the opportunity of waning Belgian control to try poison ordeals again. In 1959–60, before the formal independence of the Congo, but after Belgian administration had collapsed, an outbreak of poison ordeals was reported among the Kuba. Large numbers are said to have submitted to the ordeals, and hundreds to have died.

This description of Lele attempts to control sorcery suggests that we should reconsider what might be called the obstetric view of witchcraft and sorcery. If the believers themselves regard it as an unmitigated scourge, this too is a datum to be fitted into the analysis. Witchcraft is not merely a brutal midwife delivering new forms to society, though it may be this; it is also an aggravator of all hostilities and fears, an obstacle to peaceful cooperation. I suggest that both Mcape and Bwanali-Mpulumutsi had much in common with Kabengabenga and Mikomi Yool. They expressed revulsion against indiscriminate witchcraft accusations, and the havoc which the latter make of orderly social relations.

NOTES

1 M.G. Marwick, 'Another modern anti-witchcraft movement in East Central Africa', *Africa*, XX, 2, 1950. This study was written before I learnt of Professor Marwick's new research on this subject.
2 A.I. Richards, 'A modern movement of witch-finders', *Africa*, VIII, 1935, 448–61.
3 Marwick, 1950, p. 107.
4 M.G. Marwick, 'The social context of Cewa witch beliefs', *Africa*, XXII, 1952.
5 J.C. Mitchell, *The Yao Village*, 1956.
6 Marwick, 1952, p. 232.
7 Mitchell, 1956, p. 155.
8 E.E. Evans-Pritchard, *Witchcraft, Oracles and Magic among the Azande*, 1936.
9 Marwick, 1952, p. 217. The failure of ordinary divination to convince people against their will among the Yao is well illustrated by the account in Mitchell, 1956, pp. 173–4.
10 Assuming that we can treat anti-sorcery movements as similar to anti-witchcraft movements.
11 E. de Jonghe, 'Formations Récentes de Sociétés Secrètes au Congo Belge', *Africa*, IX, 1936, 56–63.
12 'Ordalies, Épreuves superstitieuses' art. 57. C.P., Dâcret du 24.12.1923.
13 M. Douglas, 'Blood debts and clientship among the Lele', *Journal of The Royal Anthropological Institute*, 90, i, 1960, 1–28.
14 See Chapter 1.
15 E. de Jonghe, 1936.
16 J. Vansina, 'Mikomi Yool', *Aequatoria*, XXII, 2, 1959.
17 Compare Bwanali-Mpulumutsi: 'Your wife must be done, otherwise there will be no marriage, only death', Marwick, 1950.
18 R. Frankenberg, *Village on the Border*, 1957.

Chapter 5

Sorcery accusations unleashed
The Lele revisited, 1987

1999 version

The story I am about to relate is painful, as the events themselves were for those who were tortured and died, and also for the others who had to live through them. I am still not sure that it should be exposed to the light. Reputations will be at risk, so I have held it back for ten years. Perhaps I will not be forgiven for recounting it now. The first version seemed such a tall story to European readers that I was rebuked for scandal-mongering. As I persisted I was advised to give more circumstantial detail, such as names and dates. Then I found that published in that form it would endanger the persons named. Now I know that it is too common a story to need the extra signs of authenticity, so I have removed the names in this shortened version. After many conversations with African and other scholars I realise that the topic has far-reaching significance. The story may still be worth reading, so that we can reflect on our own deep conflicts of loyalty and morals.

My title seeks to place in a large context a small, local case of rage against sorcery. Some nations support institutions whose express purpose is to detect, disable, and punish sorcerers. Under the term 'sorcerers' I would include any witches, demon-possessed persons, or wizards supposed to have secret power to wreak harm, not like a robber might work secretly at night, but by occult, super-natural means. Sorcerers are evildoers, and the context here is how believers try to combat them. Belief in sorcery is nothing unusual. It is common in traditional African religions, in Islamic as well as in Christianised countries, and common throughout the Third World. It has been seriously said among anthropologists that to reject something so central as sorcery is surreptitiously to impose the beliefs that uphold my own culture on the people I am purporting to study; even disbelief in sorcery's power to harm would reveal a basic contempt, a failure of objectivity. The question forces me to explain and justify my disbelief. I am not bringing into doubt the possible existence of magicians and sorcerers, any more than of angels, or immortal souls, or demons. What I doubt is that such beings have autonomous supernatural power to hurt or kill and I person-ally do not think it right to prosecute anyone for evildoings of which no proof is possible. My sympathies are liberal, roused on behalf of those who are (often maliciously) accused of doing impossible things. They are usually without means of proving their innocence. Sometimes it is no good arguing on their behalf that what they are charged with is physically impossible. The sheer impossibility is taken for another proof of their occult power.

THE LELE OF THE KASAI

The case I will describe occurred among the Lele of the Kasai in the late 1970s and early 1980s. I first met the Lele in 1949, that is fifty years ago. I went to the Kasai region of what was then called the Belgian Congo as a graduate student to do fieldwork among them as part of my training as an anthropologist. The next visit to the Congo was in 1953, after which I wrote a monograph, *The Lele of the Kasai* (1963). Thanks to my friend Ngokwey Ndolamb, who took six weeks' leave from his office in Benin to be my companion and guide, I was able in 1987 to make what he described as *un voyage de nostalgie* to the same region. By that time it was called Zaïre, and now after the fall of President Mobutu is called La République Démocratique du Congo. Inevitably over that long period, which included political independence, transfer of power, civil war, dictatorship, and economic ruin, there were many changes.

Some were to be expected, some minor, like the change of the name of Leopoldville to Kinshasa, and others major. Though I had not anticipated it, the way the Lele had seized the opportunity of education offered by the missions should have been predictable. The Lele are intellectually gifted and a determined people, so it was a deep satisfaction to find so many of the children of my old friends gracing professional circles in Kinshasa in 1987. General Christianisation of the young was also predictable. I observed that the appeal of Christianity had a lot to do with the tension between generations, between the interests of the old men as polygamists and the young ones as bachelors.[1] What I did not expect, but should have expected, was the anxiety of the new generation of Catholics about the dangers of sorcery.

Belief in sorcery was part of their ancient tradition, but before they were Christianised they had established ways of controlling their fear and of limiting accusations. Father Hubert, the founder and head of the OMI (Ordre de Marie Immaculée) mission at Mapangu, taught the converted Christians not to believe in sorcery. Instead he told them to trust in divine grace and the power of the Church's sacraments, not to resort to the old-time divination and healing, and above all not to join the anti-sorcery cults which from time to time swept the region. Now it was a different scene. Fear of sorcery had been assimilated into Christian thought and practice and had ballooned right out of control.

FROM MONOTHEISM TO DUALISM

On my first visit, in 1949, Father Hubert was always fulminating against Christian converts who let themselves be deceived by false pagan beliefs.

With that training you might have expected that by 1987, when most of the younger generation had been baptised, the young Catholics would deride their father's beliefs as a bunch of absurd superstitions. This had not happened. The god of the Lele had become the Satan of Christian traditions. The old religion was completely monotheist, but the one, unique divine creator worshipped by the Lele ancestors, and their grandfathers and fathers, was now set up in opposition to the Christian God. The Christians associated the deity of their pagan parents with the devil and his minions, and took it from Genesis that there was implacable enmity between him and the human race. Whereas before they had believed in one God, the universe now was governed by two deities, one good, one bad. And the bad one often seemed to be the most powerful. So by a perverse paradox they remained as strongly as ever convinced of the power of the old religion. The new Christian teaching was not saying, as it had in Father Hubert's day, that the pagan religion was a foolish delusion. It now trashed the old religion as sorcery, its priests as sorcerers, sorcery as Satan's weapon, a grim menace. Sorcerers were Satan's servants and the people lived under continual fear of attack. And at the same time, everyone, old and young, lived under fear of being accused of sorcery.

At the times of my first visits, in 1949 and 1953, the religious rites of the Lele had been benign. Cult had been paid to the pangolin spirit, twin spirits and forest spirits, in the belief that the rites would bring prosperity, with abundant fertility and food. Curses of dead ancestors had pursued the wicked with misfortune. Breaches in friendship and solidarity had been swiftly punished by divine sanctions. Diviners were honoured for their knowledge of healing rites. Forty years later, memory of the past culture had gone out of balance, everything that was part of it was reduced to sorcery and judged to be bad, nothing of the old beliefs was good. Even the ancient lore of herbs and symbols was condemned.

What that meant for the tension between the generations can be guessed. It meant contempt for the old, liberation for the young, mutual hatred and mistrust for young and old. Newly ordained Catholic priests were persecuting the practitioners of the old religion. Most paradoxical of all, the mission was running its own anti-sorcery cult. Although its last episode had been finished eight years before, the memory was so fresh and so scandalous still that in 1987 I seemed to have arrived in its immediate aftermath. The last thing I had wanted to study on this visit was sorcery. I had written enough about it before.[2] But in these few weeks there was no way of escaping the topic. Sorcery themes were on everyone's lips. To explain what had happened I need to backtrack a little.

MISSIONARY TACTICS

The missionaries loved their Lele congregation, their school was a great success, their charges did very well educationally, and went on to thrive in the competititive professional world beyond their district. For their part, the Lele were devoted to the mission, and to Catholicism. I never met one who spoke disloyally or was even critical. Strong ties of affection and loyalty united the proselytisers and their flock. After independence, during the civil war troubles of the 1960s, it was said that bands of revolutionary soldiers roamed the former colony, looting, raping nuns, killing priests, wreaking death and destruction on Africans who resisted them. The missionaries at Mapangu might certainly have been in danger. But the Lele round the mission station sponta- neously formed an armed guard, two black men to watch over each white man, night and day, bow and arrows at the ready. All the missionaries came unscathed through the civil war.

If the economy had flourished after independence, if the politics had stabilised at Kinshasa and throughout the provinces, it is possible that the priests would have been satisfied that their mission was making headway against the paganism of the villages. This is just speculation. What is sure is that they were confronted with miserable economic decline, arbitrary political dictatorship at the top, and corrupt officialdom all the way down. Their best students left the Kasai to find rewarding work in Kinshasa, and many succeeded. The parents of these *evolués* as they called themselves, had not spoken any European language, but here were the offspring, equipped with elegant French and adequate English, occupying esteemed positions in the modern world of the capital as lawyers, politicians, business men and business women, and also as ministers in new religions. But back in the villages, 500 kilometres inland, reached by jeep over dangerous dirt tracks because they lay beyond the tarmac route to the diamond mines of Kikwit, the market economy had left them behind. They needed cash to operate in it, but could not get their agricultural products to market.

The villagers were already poor, but by the 1970s their economic position was much worse, and in the 1980s they were well on the path to destitution. The missionaries were in a position of tremendous pressure and anxiety. They made some very excusable mistakes. One major failure was to suppose that an entrenched belief can be uprooted by preaching, or that teaching contempt for the elders was compatible with teaching respect for family values. The main mistake was not to see anything that was good in the old Lele religion that could be salvaged. But this is an endemic problem for missions, to which I shall return below.

GOD IN THE TRADITIONAL RELIGION

To align the Lele religion with sorcery is a complete travesty, since its rites have always been dedicated to counter sorcery and to healing its effects. I will write about it in the present tense as it is by no means certain that the religion is dead and gone. It is an uncompromisingly monotheistic religion in which Njambi, the creator God, is lord of everything. He is the justifier of the good and punisher of evildoers. All the Lele are, as they often would say, his children: 'Are we not all children of Njambi?' would be the slogan in a peacemaking negotiation or in a protest against injustice. His name enters into conversation easily and frequently. He is cited as backing rightful curses and solemn oaths, he sees into people's hearts, he helps and gives. So prominent is his benign aspect that his name, *njambi*, is used familiarly in phrases like 'God willing' or even like we use the word for 'luck'. If a person does not want to boast of his success he attributes it easily to *njambi*.

Under God are the nature spirits, also his creatures, obediently doing his bidding. Their role is somewhat like that of angels in Christian theology, or perhaps more like friendly djinns in Arabia. They are disembodied intelligences who befriend humans if they respect certain rules. The rules were set up by God in the first place. The spirits also punish on God's behalf. They are in charge of specific places, streams, hills, caves. They teach humans cures for illnesses and the uses of healing plants. Their remedies involve consecration of herbs with set words and gestures. If humans only had to deal with God and the spirits, their misfortunes would be small and ill-health easily remedied. God wants humans to live their lives healthily until old age. This is how the world was before sorcery entered it. The religion has no way of explaining chronic illness and early deaths apart from the theory of sorcery.

It was God who made sorcery. The myth is that a Lele chief asked for it and God gave it to him. The chief was not supposed to tell anyone, but he revealed the secret to his friend, and so knowledge of sorcery spread. As God is one, the world is one, knowledge is one, so it follows that the sorcerer taps into the same channels as the priest and diviner. You might say he is a spoiled priest, but very spoiled. The more profoundly he is trained in religious techniques for ensuring fertility, curing sickness and sterility, the more he has at his fingertips the techniques for dealing death or striking barren. The knowledge is the same, the difference is entirely moral, and the result depends on opportunity. This point is very important for understanding the balance of power between the generations.

The definitions of sacred knowledge have laid the trail for accusing the diviners of sorcery. If an old man tries to defend himself by counter-accusations against a young man, the case is just not prima facie plausible. How can a young man, who has not been initiated through the series of cults, and has never practised healing in consultation with his confreres, how can he possibly know any sorcery? The same argument protects women from accusation, since women are excluded from most cults, but not all. These are two of several ways in which Lele religion restricts the scope of sorcery accusations. I mention two more. Interminable lawsuits dragging on for years destroyed the peace of the villages. Every so often the unresolved sorcery cases would all be grouped together in a big ceremony in which the poison ordeal was administered. Those who died in the ordeal were proven guilty. Thus many outstanding cases could be settled in one day, compensations paid over, good names cleared, and peace restored. But it was a drastic procedure and only applied to accusations which had somehow been made to stick. Lastly, accusations were held in check by the rule that anyone who forced his enemy to submit to the poison ordeal would have to take the same ordeal himself. If he was innocent he had nothing to fear. In short, suspicions were strongly steered towards the guilt of the old diviners.

Under Belgian colonial rule the poison ordeal was made illegal, so that resource for deterring frivolous or self-interested accusations was lost. This meant that unless the Lele were successfully persuaded by the Christian missionaries to give up their belief in sorcery, they were stranded in a sorcery-ridden environment in which they could do nothing to protect themselves. The next step for us is to see why it was so difficult to disbelieve in sorcery. Like any other well entrenched belief, this one was deeply embedded in the central institutions. The institutions of sorcery effectively evened up the distribution of power in a village. Accusations of sorcery provided the laity with a weapon against the schools of diviners, and also a weapon for the young to use against the overweening demands of the old.[3] Without being able to accuse old men of sorcery, the weak and the young would feel more vulnerable than ever.

This is how it worked. The senior men controlled entry into the cults, and cult members enjoyed a large pecuniary benefit from fees of new entrants and fees for ritual services. This accumulation of wealth in their hands compensated for their actual dependence on the young for work and for war. On the other hand, the young achieved some balance by making life difficult for any old man who was tempted to abuse his power. If he shouted, looked angry, or made exorbitant demands, he risked being accused of sorcery. Even on my first visit I observed that the old men had a furtive, almost cringing demeanour. They managed to get their way as a group, because they were rich, but as individuals they were very careful never to be seen asserting themselves. If a man was convicted by divination of killing by sorcery, his clansmen would have to pay heavy damages for the lives of his victims. The wealth that came to the victim's kin in this way would usually have to be redistributed quite quickly as damages for similar sorcery crimes. Indeed, sorcery beliefs drove the means of payments, raffia cloths and Congo francs, through the economy. That was one of a whole slew of reasons why sorcery beliefs had such a strong hold. Everybody had an interest in the system. Every death was an opportunity for claims on allegedly responsible sorcerers, and a single claim would blossom into multiple reciprocal claims for deaths several generations back.

The fact that the young men received very little of the redistribution is a part of the story. A series of exactions impoverished the young men: fines for misbehaviour, marriage dues, and fees for entry to cults, meant that they were always going, cap-in-hand as it were, to their uncles for financial help. They could not expect to be granted the wherewithal to marry a wife until they were into their thirties. Here lies the beginning of the skein that tied them into suppressed hostility against their elders, and that led them to believe readily that their sicknesses and fevers were caused by the jealousy of their rich old sorcerer uncles. The balance was not a happy one, but there was a balance. When the missionaries encouraged them to despise the religion of their ancestors, the young men were not unwilling to see the old men delegitimated. When the missionaries told the Lele that everyone's right to make a Christian mono-gamous marriage would be protected by law, the involuntarily celibate young men enthusiastically lined up for baptism, and so did the women.

The missionaries pushed one wedge after another into a deepening fissure between the generations. One can fully understand that they felt that this was the way to make progress in missionising the region. And perhaps also that they did not care as much as they might for the unravelling of the social structure that would ensue. They certainly did not realise how sorcery pumped the material wealth through the economy. Sorcery beliefs maintained a kind of precarious gerontocracy, they upheld a venerable system of marriage exchanges, they explained illness and death and justified compensations being paid out to grieving relatives. In the old days girls were transferred in payment of sorcery debts incurred generations before they were born. Christian marriage ended the hegemony of the old men. It meant the collapse of their marriage alliances. I suppose one could have predicted that the old men would lose out as soon as their levies on the young men were stopped. The end of cult initiations did that. It was naïve not to see that sorcery was the most enduring part of their pagan system.

THE THEORY OF SORCERY

In this religion sorcerers are believed to form an evil corporation. Individual members need the help of the others to execute their own evil designs, because no person can become a victim of sorcery without a sorcerer kinsman 'opening the way', that is, withdrawing protection. An individual sorcerer is thought to be under pressure from fellow sorcerers to hand over nephews and nieces by giving permission to kill them. If all the relatives stand firm and refuse per-mission, unrelated sorcerers can do no harm. But sorcerers have a professional incentive to hand over their own kin. Sorcerers are actuated not only by personal spite, but also by greed. Their initiation into the corporation of sorcerers involves shared feasts of human flesh which, eaten once, gives an insatiable lust for more. Anyone who partakes of the feast without contributing to it incurs a 'flesh debt'. The other sorcerers demand that he open the way to their killing and eating a child of his clan. The first act of sorcery, undertaken from spite, sets the new sorcerer on a slippery slope from which repentence will cost him his life. A recusant sorcerer will eventually be killed by his confreres. Notice then that the theory already pointed to the close kinsman of a sick person, father, uncle, brother, as the sorcerer trying to kill him to improve his own necromantic status.

This is the theory of occult evildoing which I heard in 1949 and 1953[4] and which is common throughout Central Africa, with local variations. When the Lele described it to me again in 1987 there was one striking difference. In former times no children, few women, and few young men would ever be suspected. They were exempted because of the emphasis on the esoteric knowledge and formal initiation believed to be necessary. Sorcerers were supposed to need heavy erudition from which young men and women were excluded. Many an old man could expect to die in peace if he had never been initiated since there was no plausibility in the idea that he could be a sorcerer, and some told me that they had shunned initiation into cults for that very reason. Again, Christians could not know sorcery, they had not been initiated. Europeans could not know it, and so would not be accused.

That was in the old days, but now in 1987, returning after so many decades, I found the link between learning and sorcery was snapped. In the old days every accusation was challenged. Every accused sorcerer had his defenders. His kin had every reason to stand by him: if he were to be convicted, they would have to pay up the blood money for his crimes. But the end of the poison ordeal means that no convictions are secure. Personal vendettas can be pursued by accusations of sorcery, and the accusations returned tit for tat, without restraint. Accusers can name children and idiots without exciting ridicule, child evidence is accepted for convicting sorcerers, and senile old men who have never been initiated now stand as obvious targets for suspicion, not because they are rich and powerful but because they are a reproach, or because they are in the way. It is dangerous to defend alleged sorcerers against Christian accusers just as in the 1950s in America it was dangerous to defend Communists against MacCarthyite charges of espionage. The sad thing is that it is risky to speak up for a friend in a neighbourhood terrorised in the name of God.

CATHOLIC ANTI-SORCERY

The story starts innocuously. The mission priests were worried by the lack of trust and by the mutual hate that characterised the lives of their congregation. In 1974 one of the fathers of the OMI (Oblats de Marie Immaculée) mission working in the villages around Idiofa launched a movement to raise the level of Christian awareness and to establish reconciliation and Christian love. This was the first phase of the *Action Mupele* (*Action*, like *Action Francaise*, and *Mupele*, a transliteration of '*Mon pere*'). The movement was known as Kimvuku, the circle, and intended as part of a general *pastorale de conscientisation*, with the motto: *Reconciliez Vous!* The movement was held to be very successful and spread in 1976 to Lele country. The priest who introduced it said he had come to put an end to hatred. He was joyfully welcomed, for to the Lele this could only mean that he was going to put an end to sorcery. The Catholic priests did not believe in sorcery power. They were therefore not issuing threats against sorcerers; their avowed aim was to stop the officiants of the old religion from intimidating the villagers by threats. They rebuked, as they always had done, evildoing, disturbing the peace, and intimidation. But to the Lele this could only mean that they were issuing counter-threats against sorcerers. What else? Diviners got word that a new form of anti-sorcery cult was in the offing and began spontaneously to hand in to the mission their oracles and medicine horns and some very strange-looking ritual objects. This is such common and well-recorded behaviour at the beginning of anti-sorcery cults in Central Africa that it is a wonder that the missionaries did not recognise it as a normal part of the first phase of a new anti-sorcery cult in the region.[5] They felt encouraged and that they were making progress, but actually the movement for Christian love was being assimilated in the people's thought to the pattern of the old anti-sorcery movements, with *Mon Pere* as the cult leader.

In the next phase, called '*l'Action de l'Abbé*', a young and newly ordained priest was put in charge of the mission at Mwembe, in the heart of Lele country. Not a Lele himself, he went to pains to learn as much as he could of the esoteric traditions, the cults and initiation ceremonies, and food taboos, with the object of ridiculing the old religion and loosening its grip on the minds of the young. This was expected to make room for the project of reconciliation. In the third phase another young priest, a Lele himself, ordained in 1976, was put in charge of the mission at Banga in the south, and another Lele priest, ordained in 1978, was established at Mikope. One of these young priests developed tremendous charismatic appeal. He launched a direct attack on sorcerers. He found he had personal power for identifying sorcerers and for healing by laying on of hands. The demand for his services was immense. The Belgian priest who had started the *Mupele* movement among the Lele was completely outclassed. He found it difficult to carry out his normal ministry because all the villages were demanding the young Abbé, and would have no other priest but he.

The Abbé went from one village to another escorted by his 'Choir', a sinister gang of thugs from what I can make out. In God's name they commanded everyone who possessed the paraphernalia of the old religion to bring it out to be publicly destroyed. Those who were suspected of sorcery were beaten and burned until they confessed. Indeed, the most extraordinary confessions were made. The public who were not personally accused, Catholic and pagan alike, rejoiced that Satan was rebuked. God's rule was justified and health and prosperity were assured.

The Abbé's programme was to arrive with his Choir and stay for a few days in a village that had invited him to purge its sorcerers. He would make discreet enquiries. When he was ready, everyone was required to pass before him in file. Each person had to spit the traditional blessing on a piece of white chalk, which he then took into his house to examine. Next morning he was able to say which bits of white chalk had passed his secret test and so were cleared of suspicion. They all filed before him again; those he found guilty he sent in one direction, the innocent in another. The guilty were then rounded up by the

Choir to be confessed and exorcised. Meanwhile, they were fenced off in the middle of the village square. Once they had confessed and had handed over the fetishes and instruments of divination and sorcery, he would proceed to exorcism to undo the harm of their spells. When this was done, he and the Choir would go to another village to repeat the exercise. No one said they were paid for their services, but it would be in the anti-sorcery tradition for them to receive a hefty fee.

Many of the young Christians that I spoke to considered that the Abbé had done right to pursue and condemn the sorcerers, but they agreed that the *Action de l'Abbé* failed because it had been too violent. There were many who were ready to tell me details of the violence.

In the month of July 1979 a French historian in the company of three other Europeans arrived at the village of Kenge, not knowing that the Abbé was officiating there. They saw persons bound and seated round a big fire, and learned that they were accused sorcerers. They saw them being beaten and heard their screams, as well as the music of the singers and drummers. After taking photographs the others went back to Kinshasa and reported what they had witnessed. The historian went on, eventually reaching the village of Malonga Bwanga where the Abbé's progress had also brought him a few days before.

This was the final night of the session. The Choir had collected all the convicted sorcerers, bound them, and seated them in a ring in the centre of the village, around a blazing fire. He observed that suspicion had fallen on the old, the handicapped, the mentally defective, the sick . . . and the sculptors. Why the sculptors? I had to be told what I should have known. Sculptors only hold their talents from God and religion, that is to say from the god and the religion of their ancestors, and so from Satan. As it is they who carve the ritual objects of religion, oracles and medicine horns, and as they have to be initiated, and as they use magic to make these instruments efficacious, they are deeply implicated in sorcery. All this time the village was in a state of high festival. They were dancing and drumming the anti-sorcery hymns. There was a large crowd as other villages had come to see the spectacle. The accused had been under arrest for at least two days. Some confessed, but others went on maintaining their innocence. The Choir was beating the unrepentant or dragging the self-confessed away from the fire for exorcism. This went on all night. Next day it was over. Everything was quiet, the visitors had left, the village was practically deserted.

SYMPATHY FOR THE ACCUSED

When the anti-sorcery priests and their Choir had left a village, the 'Demoiselles' would come to gather up the burnt and wounded, nurse them and take to hospital the ones too mortally afflicted for them to treat. The

'Demoiselles' are not in holy orders. They are Belgian women belonging to a Christian lay society, individually dedicated to a life of working among the poor and the sick. For the last twenty years they have replaced the Sisters of St Vincent de Paul whom I had known and who used to run the hospital and maternity ward in Brabanta. One is a nurse who runs clinics in seven villages from her base at Mwembe; another nurse is based at Mikope, and a third works on agricultural and economic development.

One might expect that the European nurses would be immune to sorcery charges, given the traditional attitude, but as I said, that was all changed in the 1970s. I heard from three independent sources how the Mademioselle at Mikope had been in danger of her life when she had succoured certain accused sorcerers. A number of victims of the *Action de l'Abbé* had been penned up for three days without food or water. She went out at night with a calabash of water and a straw which she pushed through the chinks of their enclosure, to assuage their thirst. The villagers of Mikope, enraged by this interference with justice, besieged the mission house, charging her of being the friend of sorcerers and threatening to kill her. She escaped through the back of the house and hid in the forest for two days. Eventually she got out of the country and returned to Belgium, but three months later, undeterred, she was back at her post. Anger against the Mademoiselle ran so deep in the village that they did not forgive her until seven years later. At the time of my visit a formal reconciliation ceremony was being organised.

The Mademoiselle at Mwembe, who received me hospitably, was discreet on the subject of sorcery. But she was very indignant on behalf of the victims of the purges. She showed me a mentally defective child who had been indicated as responsible for the deaths of her relatives and whose legs had been burned to the shin bone. None of the child's family would have anything to do with her. I also saw an old man whose skin was blotched white from burns on his back, and others whose feet had been whipped and burned and were now incurably lamed.

I was indignant myself on behalf of my friends from thirty-four years ago who had been tortured for confessions. I was also very mystified by the strange confessions they were reputed to have made. The catechist who had welcomed me when I first arrived in the village of Ngoie was now living in retirement near the mission at Mapangu. When the Abbé made a visitation to Ngoie, this man, no longer young, was tied up, burnt and beaten. Finally he confessed to the unlikely deed of having let the measles microbe out of his sorcerer's stew pan so as to kill the children. I met again the widow of another friend, a Christian leper whose fortitude had edified me greatly on my first visit. She told me that he had been bound and burnt to make him confess, but since the advanced stages of leprosy cause anaesthesia he felt nothing. His resistance was taken as a sign of his guilt: only sorcery could enable him to withstand the pain. I tried to follow up the deaths of other friends but found, not surprisingly, great reluctance to speak about them. Whether they had died as victims of sorcery, or as convicted sorcerers, either way the survivors were deeply embarrassed. They did not want to side with sorcerers and did not want to tell me of their own part in the deaths I was mourning.

One man I knew had become a Christian at the time of my first visit. He had told me about the vivid dream that had led him to conversion. Now an old man, he was taunted for having survived: 'Your age-mates are dead, how is it you are still alive? You must be the sorcerer who killed them off.' He asked me bitingly whether I would have ever thought it possible that young Christians would accuse their elders and beat them up.

When the anti-sorcery activities of the clergy came to the attention of the Apostolic Nuncio in Kinshasa, he conferred with the bishop. The result was that both the young priests who had led the Mupele cult were suspended from their work in their diocese. They were sent abroad for two years. Officially this would be the end of the matter. The Nuncio had acted promptly, effectively, and sensitively. But the responses I had received eight years later showed that the affair was not ended in the hearts of the people. It is cruel to reopen old sores. Why am I writing about Christian persecution of sorcerers so long after it has been dealt with? Because I do not think the matter is finished. The problems go very deep. It will recur, and it is not confined to the territory of the Lele.

EXPLANATIONS OF WITCH-HUNTING SCOURGES

A popular sociological explanation points to frustration following social dis-integration and modernisation. In his classic analysis of witchcraft and sorcery in the Yao village Clyde Mitchell (1956) showed how an accusation of witchcraft could be a means of ridding oneself of burdensome obligations of loyalty and support. Alan MacFarlane (1970) applied the argument to the great sixteenth-century outbreak of witch trials in Tudor England. The upheavals of new commerce and industry broke the delicate web of community, so that neither material rewards nor esteem accrued for honouring claims on kinship or good neighbourliness. Accusing the too importunate poor of witchcraft was a way of rejecting responsibility. A more recent version of the relations between sorcery beliefs and power, following these lines, is convincingly proposed for the Cameroon by Rowlands and Warnier (1987).

There was plenty in the Lele situation to warrant the sociological breakdown theory. Incentives for clan cooperation were missing, lines of local solidarity had broken down. The Lele anthropologist, Pierre Ngokwey (1978), has developed a variant of the frustration theory by pointing out how the explosion of population has transformed the demographic structure of the villages. He interprets the cults described above as direct expressions of inter-generational conflict. The pagan anti-sorcery cults were aimed to reconcile factions and smooth tensions between young and old. The Christian anti-sorcery cults had the same intention, but only succeeded in increasing tension on a larger scale.

Recall that in the old pattern of beliefs mistrust was structured, and sorcery beliefs gave the young a weapon againt their elders' abuse of privilege. Very small changes in the belief system intensify the imbalance of age within the village. Economically the old pagans are dependent on the earnings of the young Christians.

Inter-generational conflict is important in this case. The Lele old are not in the towns, they are still at home in their own region, and pauperised. There is not enough to eat, there is no work, no way of earning cash by labour, and yet Zaïre has become a cash economy. They need cash because the old village economy is no longer self-sufficient. A poignant instance illustrates the loss of organising ability and small-scale authority at the level of the domestic economy. In the old days in each hut an ember was always kept burning from which a new fire could be lit. It seemed unnecessary to ask who was responsible for keeping it alight. Probably some arrangement between mother and daughter underpinned the result, but now it does not work and matches are a necessity of existence, but matches have to be bought with cash. The only way to earn cash is by growing manioc and maize corn for sale. In the absence of a regular market they routinely sell their produce for a tenth of what it fetches in Kinshasa. When the chiefs at various levels of authority need cash, they make extortionate levies on the crops. So there is never enough for the villages to sell. When the younger generation of city-dwellers come to visit them, the villagers beg endlessly. But the city folk were in no position to resent their poor country cousins' begging. They were being importunate on their own account.

When I was there, city-dwelling Lele seemed to be doing brilliantly in the new professions and also in the fringes of urban life, as traders in the market and as freelance religious healers. I did not get the impression that they discharge themselves from responding to the claims of their country kinsfolk; they have enough problems of their own and they need every now and again to go home and collect a bag of grain to take back and sell at ten times what they gave for it. In spite of galloping inflation they must pay mortages, educate their children, and salvage their own professional lives from the general ruin. In a world run by bribery and corruption, backed by enormous disparities of wealth, they must fear failure if things turn out badly, and jealousy if they turn out well. According to social change and frustration theories, they ought to be emphasising the dangers of sorcery. But no, they need their kinsfolk's help. They are not disposed to reject their claims. Younger than the rural Lele, the generational imbalance had turned the other way, and they were being blamed for ensorcelling their nephews and nieces at home: a child's failure in the examinations in Mapangu could be laid to the door of an uncle in Kinshasa. So in the same sophisticated tone as they joked about the state of the roads in the city, the pot-holes and rush-hour traffic jams they would mention the sorcery infestation of the villages, trying to make light of it, and implying it was a rural problem.

The weakness of the social disintegration theory is that it lays too much explanatory power upon change. Change is endemic, so is social disintegration. Rejection of the poor and unfortunate goes on all the time. Social disintegration does not explain what needs to be explained, the terrorism of the successive anti-sorcery movements in Zaïre that used to occur roughly every ten years. The explanation of witch-hunting in European history that best fits this case is political, based on rivalry between a dominant religion and the one it has suppressed. In this African case the involvement of the Catholic mission was the central feature.

The Egyptologist and medieval historian, Margaret Murray (1921), argued that witchcraft in Europe should be interpreted as access to supernatural powers claimed by the suppressed pagan religions, and therefore claimed to be heresy by the Christian Church. So the Christians who were charged with witchcraft by ecclesiastical authorities were actually charged with trying to draw on these discredited resources, consulting or behaving as old-time healers, laying on unconsecrated hands, claiming to be visionaries, fortune tellers and exorcists whose lore, Egyptian, zodiacal, or whatever, derived from pre-Christian religions. It was likely, on this argument, that Joan of Arc and Gilles de Raie were rightly accused of witchcraft in that sense. Walter Kaegi (1966) described a close parallel in fifth-century Byzantium.

Other historians remind us that Christianity has always been rough on rival religions. A modern version of Margaret Murray's thesis is offered by Carlos Ginzburg (1983) to account for the burning of witches in sixteenth-century Italy. The Catholic Church, highly centralised, and so more distanced from the lowly concerns of their flock, felt threatened by the practitioners of the old religions who were offering the faithful more immediate help and healing. So the Inquisition prosecuted the religious irregulars for witchcraft and heresy. If the young Lele priests who were suspended by their superiors had wanted to defend their actions historically they could have found plenty of precedent. But as contemporary Catholics they suffered from lack of an accepted demonology.

In modern Zaïre the Catholic Church is no doubt suffering from religious pluralism. Catholic missionaries are disadvantaged in competition with Protestant churches and the neo-apostolic movement, Christian denominations which have clearly defined their doctrines concerning demons in a way that accommodates local sorcery beliefs.[6]

THEOLOGY OF DEMONISM

When another Lele cult promises to end sorcery, the Church authorities will be in a dilemma. They may condemn it, but they will not be able to stop it. The feelings are too deep and too violent. The missions cannot lead the new cult; the priests who led the last one having been reprimanded. Contemporary Western theology is not attuned to answering the questions that plague Africans about the causes of evil in the world, the causes of sickness and death, questions which their pagan traditions answer all too plausibly in terms of sorcery. On this there is a block, or a gap, a pregnant silence. The subject is barely mentionable, which means that the African Christians are unable to contribute their part to the developing moral philosophy of the Christian Church. The old religion of the Lele provided the people with fetishistic protection from their fears, and rituals of solidarity gave them confidence in their community. The Catholic converts in the early days of the mission had the sacraments, confession and absolution, miraculous medals, holy pictures, holy water, special blessings, and the sign of the cross to make them safe. The devil was more ridiculous than dangerous. At the pastoral level some sound substitution was possible. Admittedly, in pagan times the confidence in their religion broke down roughly every decade and witch-hunting would begin again with renewed ferocity. In this arena, confronting and explaining something summed up as evil, post-Vatican II has little to say. It is an undemonstrative, unritualistic and unecstatic, controlled and interior form of religion. It hardly fills the intellectual vacuum. The novitiate training for African clergy cannot give special guidance for dealing with pastoral problems for which the pagan religion had ready answers. There is nothing to say because the theologians and philosophers have not worked out the supporting doctrines.

In Kinshasa University the Faculty of Catholic Theology has a reputation as a lively Centre d'Etudes des Religions Africaines. It has a number of respected journals including *La Revue Africaine de la Théologie* and *Les Cahiers de la Religion*. As I browsed through the special number of the latter on '*Aspects du Catholicisme au Zaire*' I noticed several edifying articles on renewal, and on traditional African notions of God, death and spirits. There was not a word about any needful reappraisal of Christian doctrine to deal with current beliefs in sorcery. One would expect an African theology developed within this tradition to have much to say about guilt, and sorrow. While I was in Congo in 1987 Cardinal Ratzinger made a visit to the theology faculty of the University. He asked them to organise for him a seminar on the subject of Africanisation of the Catholic Church. The two topics he proposed were liturgical: the question of valid orders and the substance of the Eucharist. Both issues responded to the initiatives of the various Protestant churches in Congo. Some of the latter ordain ministers selected by parish assemblies, and consecrate maize meal and palm wine for the Eucharist instead of wheat bread and fruit of the vine. These were the topics he felt were currently most necessary to debate on the occasion of his visit, while the recurrent crises in the interpretation of evil and suffering under the rubric of sorcery were not mentioned.

A Lele philosopher who had been present at this seminar remarked wryly that Africanisation is not just a matter of adding spears and masks to the liturgy. In his view Africanisation must be a two-way exchange about fundamental philosophical issues, and especially those implied in monotheism. Many anthropologists, Europeans and Africans, have reported carefully and even quite fully on particular African religions. There are significant writings on both religious traditions, by Zaïrois and other African thinkers, following the early work of Tempels, for example, but few attempts at any systematic confrontation of crucial doctrines. The African religions are not supposed to have doctrines that need to be reconciled to those of Christianity.

Christianity has held a path between two extremes, not teaching that the world is wholly evil, or denying that evil exists, but always insisting on monotheism. The central issue is not whether to believe or disbelieve in the harm wrought by demons, but whether demons can do anything by their own power, or whether they are always subject to God's control. Aquinas taught that demons could indeed perform miracles by clever deceit and kinds of conjuring tricks. They could change the appearance of things, but not the reality, and their power is always secondary to and dependent on the power of God. For Aquinas evil is real, but negative; it is the real absence of good, rather than a positive principle or agency working in its own right. On the Thomistic view, sorcery, demons and witchcraft can only play a minor part in the order of things. However, as Dr Nogkwey points out to me, belief in Satan is not unchristian, and the various religions of the world have made many subtle and different apportionments of responsibility between humans, God and other spiritual beings. A superb collection of anthropological essays on this subject has recently been assembled by David Parkin (1987). But since the decline of hell in Western thought at the end of the seventeenth century (Walker, 1964) Satan has received little serious attention. He is always a popular figure of dread, but in serious theology Satan has declined with the decline of organised religion.

In suggesting minor clarifications in the lay confusion and official silence, the question of healing and sickness is paramount. The Lele pagan priests are powerful healers. Their knowledge of therapeutic plants and minerals of their region ought to be treated as a rich resource for the world. But while this knowledge is associated with Satan it remains unavailable. Lele understanding of mental tensions and psychological healing is likely to be no less worth serious study than those of other Congolese people. If Christian teaching could divert attention from sorcery by giving due weight to other causes of misfortune and sorrow, and if a positive view of suffering in Christian eschatology could be developed, the dying and the bereaved could be better comforted. Violence might be reduced if the local bishops insisted that the sorcerer is not solely responsible for undoing his own evil. If exorcism were credited with sufficient power in its own right, the need to identify the sorcerer would just evaporate. So he would not have to confess. So he would not have to be tortured. With such adjustments, it would be easier than at present to make it a point of pastoral care that fellow humans be never accused of doing the devil's work.

The Vatican Council promoted ecumenism, not just a new kindness between the branches of the Christian faith, but it surely cannot stop there. The right relation between Christianity and all religions is under the same scrutiny. I hope that it will become impossible to define their deities as devils. Perhaps they will be assimilated to the role of subsidiary deities, somewhat as Japanese Buddhism assimilated the Shinto gods. Perhaps ancestors of converts will be assimilated to the status of Old Testament heroes, who awaited Christ's resurrection before they could enter heaven. Without some such serious respect for African religions the Christian Church will bring to Africa more rage than peace, more hate than love.

NOTES

1 Adrian Hastings (ed.) *The Church and the Nations*, London and New York, Sheed & Ward, 1959.
2 Mary Douglas, *The Lele of the Kasai*, 1963; *Witchcraft Accusations and Confessions*, 1970; 'Techniques of sorcery control in Central Africa', Chapter 4; etc.
3 'Techniques of sorcery control in Central Africa', Chapter 4.
4 *Ibid.*
5 A.I. Richards, 'A modern movement of witch-findings', *Africa*, 8, 1935, pp. 448–61.
6 P.N. Ngokwey, personal communication.

BIBLIOGRAPHY

AQUINAS, THOMAS (1927), *Questiones Disputate*, 2, *De Malo*, Rome, Editio Quinta Taurinens.

AQUINAS, THOMAS (1928), *The Summa Contra Gentiles of Saint Thomas Aquinas*, London, Burns Oates and Washbourne, book 3, pt. 1, ch. 7: 'That Evil is not an Essence', ch.15: 'That there is no Sovereign Evil'.

BUKWASA, G. (1968), 'Notes sure les Kindoki chez les Kongo', in T.K. Mpansu, *Cahiers des Religions Africaines*, 2, 3, 153–68.

BUKWASA, G. (1973), 'L'Impense du discours: "Kindoki" et "nkisi" en pays Kongo du Zaire', Kinshasa, Presses Universitaires du Zaire.

DOUGLAS, MARY (1963), *The Lele of the Kasai*, Oxford, International African Institute.

DOUGLAS, MARY (1970), *Witchcraft Accusations and Confessions*, London, Tavistock.

GINZBURG, CARLOS (1983), *Night Battles, Witchcraft and Agrarian Cults in the 16th and 17th Centuries*, London, Routledge & Kegan Paul.

KAEGI, WALTER E. (1966), 'The fifth century twilight of Byzantine paganism', *Classica et Medievalia*, 27, 250–70.

MACFARLANE, A. (1970), *Witchcraft in Tudor and Stuart England*, London, Routledge & Kegan Paul.

MITCHELL, CLYDE (1956), *The Yao Village*, Manchester University Press.

MURRAY, MARGARET (1921), *The Witch Cult in Western Europe: a Study in Anthropology*, Oxford University Press.

MURRAY, MARGARET (1933), *The God of the Witches*, Oxford University Press.

NGOKWEY, PIERRE NDOLAMB (1987), 'Le désenchantement enchanteur, ou 'D'un mouvement religieux à l'autre', *Cahiers de CEDAF*, 8, Brussels, Centre d'Études et de Documentations Africaines.

PARKIN, DAVID (ed.) (1987), *The Anthropology of Evil*, Cambridge, Cambridge University Press.

ROWLANDS, MICHAEL and WARNIER, JEAN-PIERRE (1987), 'Sorcery, power and the modern state in Cameroon', *Man*, N.S., *3*, 118–32.

WALKER, D.F. (1964), *The Decline of Hell, Seventeenth Century Discussion of Eternal Torment*, London, Routledge & Kegan Paul.

Chapter 6

Looking back on the 1950s essays

The contrast between explicit and implicit does not depend on speech. Gestures can be explicit, very much so, and also images. The implicit does not depend on pre-linguistic bodily, gestural, and iconic experience. It is that which is understood by a speech community to be so much part of their shared assumptions that it does not need to be said in words, shown in gestures or otherwise depicted. In these essays I was trying to show that the implicit derives from shared efforts to organise.

The five essays brought togther here present some details of Lele religion.[1] The first, published in 1954, is about the importance of the communal hunt in the people's lives, as a source of food, and as a spiritual barometer sensitive to the least sign of anger or insult. When an anthropologist says that a people deeply desire social harmony there has to be evidence given. In this case the evidence is the meticulous scrutiny of the fortunes of the hunt. The spirits in the forest are introduced as the main agents of health and well-being, and the sorcerers as the agents of disease and disaster. These ethnographic reportings are included in this volume as the background and the inspiration for the rest. Furthermore, they present a commonsensical, 'bread and butter' aspect of religion that is not usually described outside of anthropologists' reports.

The first essay describes Lele ideas of cleanness and propriety. A mundane organising activity, the everyday distinguishing of dirt and danger, creates an infrastructure of implicit knowledge against which more elaborate and abstract religious ideas are immediately credible. A meticulous reviewer of this volume in 1976 regretted that I had not discarded before going into print the heuristic resources gained from comparing my own toilet and kitchen-based habits and those of the Lele.[2] He also complained that I had said nothing about how the implicit is learnt. But this was what all those cooking and washing details were about. The pragmatic experience of down-to-earth separations and orderings underpin a social order by providing it with a highly classified universe.

The confidence that the universe needs boundaries to function could never be learnt from sermons or be born out of shared custom. It comes from intellectual satisfaction. There is a demand to be satisfied: Why? Why? Why? At each level there is a plausible answer. Why was I ill? Because I ate forbidden foods. Why do I have a chronic illness? Because I keep disregarding the rules. Why did she die? Because a jealous sorcerer got her. What is a sorcerer? One who is inherently immoral, probably my uncle, someone who has brought occult power to transcend the moral rules, to vent his spite. The washings and the separations are not ordained for nothing and the rules are not followed from unthinking habit. The rules are seen to work, their apparent failures can be explained, the coherent social life can be constructed with consistent praising and blaming. The scope it gives for mutual monitoring is the source of the value of the classifications. This idea lies at the origin of *Purity and Danger*.

The essay called 'Social and religious symbolism of the Lele' (Chapter 2) dealt with topics which are still felt to be indelicate in some contexts, such as menstruation, defecation, sexual intercourse. When I presented it in 1954 at the Royal Anthropological Institute the late Godfrey Lienhardt told me it made 'even Lord Raglan blush'. I also remember that it elicited no other comment. In 1970 I gave a paper on 'Couvade and menstruation' (Chapter 12), at a meeting of doctors and psychiatrists on 'Disorders of the Reproductive System'. When a doctor in the audience congratulated me on what he called 'your objectivity' I was momentarily at a loss to know what he meant, but found that he had been surprised to hear me, a woman, speaking in public on such embarassing topics. About the same time, I recall the first London meeting on feminist anthropology. The speaker described how women's lives and women's interests had been suppressed in male-dominated traditions of ethnography, but she herself ignored studies by women anthropologists, Margaret Mead on gender roles and child-rearing, and Audrey Richards and Phyllis Kaberry on women in the domestic economy. In those days the topics of housework and domestic cleaning had not yet entered into academic research. This gives a sense of the period.

How dirt is conceived and dealt with may have been slow to reach the halls of learning because there were so few women there. Hence the unexpectedness of a project that showed the continuity reigning between humble bodily rituals and the grand concepts that divide males and females, humans and animals into their separate spheres. I had hoped others working in Central Africa would delve for comparable material, and that a few fellow workers in the region would compare notes and highlight significant differences. However, a few years later there was Congo independence and civil war, and after that a country dangerously full of strife and suspicion. My four Congo colleagues from Belgium were dispersed, Jan Vansina, young then but soon to be famous for establishing oral history, Daniel Biebeuck, historian of African art, Luc de Heusch, original surrealist and African kinship specialist, and Jacques Maquet, sociologist. All of them very interesting anthropologists, but it was difficult for any of us to send new students out and to develop our research in common. The rest of the work had to be interpretive rather than ethnograpghic.

The essay entitled 'Animals in Lele religious symbolism' (1957; Chapter 3) describes another sequence of hunts and the attempt to use them as oracles to find causes for failure in moral offences. Moral factors make the link between simple classification and complex experience. Classification becomes very interesting in the context of blaming and excusing, in which the regualr workings of the world are invoked to support demands for accountability. Explaining by reference to moral behaviour is intelligible, and satisfactory because actionable. Something can be done, and is usually done at once, and usually the remedies can be shown to have been effective. However, at this time, alas, the forest was very depleted. Day after day, the disappointed hunters came back, assiduously they put their lives in order, hopefully they set forth again, and day after day they still came back empty-handed and baffled. In the days not so long past the forest was thicker and wildlife was abundant. The routine punishment of disturbers of the peace would almost certainly be followed by hunting success next time they set out. Thus the hunt would eventually confirm causal theories. But in the 1950s the old explanations that pointed to transgressions against peace and politeness were no longer self-justifying.

The fourth essay, 'Techniques of sorcery control' (Chapter 4), describes another self-validating chain of reasoning, and emphasises the self-interest which buttresses belief. Taken together these four essays describe a society and its beliefs as two halves of a self-sustaining paradigm. It would be difficult to buy out of part of the belief system without buying out of it all, and this would have meant leaving the community altogether.

I revisited the Lele in 1987 thanks to the friendship and care of the Lele anthropologist, Dr Ngokwey Ndolamba. We found that what had been a structured way of functioning had given way to chaotic mutual accusation, as described in Chapter 5. Their trust and faith had dissolved. Pangolin power was discredited. The breakdown of a complex social system had brought a collapse of their old theories, and doubts about new ones. One certainty remained as vivid as ever, a destructive belief in sorcery's sinister powers. The tidal wave of recrimination, revenge, and punishment that enveloped the Lele in its pall in the 1970s and early 1980s demonstrated tragically the link between confidence in society and confidence in knowledge. This last visit was more that ten years ago. If any one is disposed to think that the Lele crises of law and learning were only a local thing, recall that the Western world currently experiences crises of authority accompanied by fear and anger directed against advanced industrial technology.

NOTES

1 Mary Douglas, *The Lele of the Kasai*, International African Institute, 1963.
2 Dan Sperber, 'Dirt, danger and pangolins', *Times Literacy Supplement*, 30 April 1976, p. 502.

Part II

Critical essays

Introduction
1975

The late Franz Steiner once said that he could never bring himself to use the verb 'to express'. Indeed, it opens the way to at least three fallacies. The first starts with over-extending the contrast (necessary to any exegesis) between the expression and the idea expressed. Let me hasten to separate my range of problems from those in which such a distinction is necessary and right. In any restricted programme of interpretation, the analysis of a medium of discourse such as speaking, riddling, myth, clothing, food, there must be the vocabulary for referring the sign to that which it signifies. This is the straight translation job. In my own essay on 'Deciphering a meal', in the third section of this book (Chapter 18), I am involved in the decoding process as whole-heartedly as anyone. In what follows here I am warning against the fallacy of allowing the language of translation to carry abroad hidden and false assumptions about the relations between media of expression. If we say that speech and writing are media, and also radio and television and gifts of fruit or flowers, we are using the metaphor of a vehicle of conveyance, channel or band or code. Along and through it something else, the message, seems to pass. But if the idea of a medium be extended to all bodily behaviour and all social relations, as it readily can be, the puzzle arises as to what are the messages conveyed.

The fallacy is particularly clear when among all the realisations of a social situation one level is singled out to be privileged above the others. It may be right to say that a handshake expresses 'how do you do', but equally the words express the handshake, or a smile can do for either. If the gesture, the smile and the words express a general willingness for acquaintanceship, then so do the hundred acts of recognition spread over time express the friendship. But it is also true to say that they constitute it. The relationship is non-existent if it never takes any material form. The gestures, verbal and other, are constitutive of social reality. There is no one moment that can be picked out and said to carry the expressive function on its own. The verb 'to express' tempts the sociologist to reify or freeze one part of the action, arbitrarily dub it 'the expression', and so create a puzzle as to what it expresses. We are thus landed with an artificially foregrounded subject matter, symbolism, essential clues thrown into shadow. The solution is to drop the transportation metaphor and to take all the expressions of a situation, at all levels, as equally contributing to it, making it actual.

The other two fallacies arise once expression has been distinguished from what it expresses. For then a choice appears between competing views of reality. On one view, symbol is the reality, the rest is machinery for producing it. This is the front stage bias. The so-called symbolic system, whether a logically intricate set of kinship terms, or names of herbs, animals or totems, is taken to be the enduring image. Such significance as can be attributed to the rest is somehow summed or incorporated in its expression. No one holds exactly this view, but it sustains some protagonists in the long argument about the status of kinship terms. Let David Schneider (1972) speak, who has been giving doughty battle on the subject:

> For Morgan, as for many people even today, words meant things, concrete objects, and they had either one and only one meaning or a primary meaning which could be distinguished from secondary, metaphoric, extended, or connotational meanings. On premises such as these it seemed obvious to Morgan that the mode of classification could be read directly from the kinship terminology; that is, those positions on the genealogical grid which were grouped together under one kinship term could be distinguished from those positions on the geneaological grid grouped under a different kinship term and so on. Hence kinship terminology was *the* key to the mode of classification and in fact, practically the only key, since the kinship terms meant (either only or primarily) specific relationships of blood or marriage. The taxonomy, then, was derived from no other source than the kinship terminology.

He rightly suggests that the same fallacy obscures the interpretation of religion. Ethnoscientists fall into it likewise when they concentrate on verbal behaviour, isolate it, and elevate its power to carry meaning. As Robin Horton (1967) points out, it is a trap into which primitive cultures fall readily. Comparing the magical use of verbal and non-verbal forms, he sets up a scale of attributed concreteness and effectiveness, running from the spoken word to the written word, to the magical object.

> One may still ask, however, why magicians spend so much time choosing objects and actions as surrogate words, when spoken words themselves are believed to have a magical potential. The answer, I suggest, is that speech is an ephemeral form of words, and one which does not lend itself to a great variety of manipulation. Verbal designation of material objects converts them into a more permanent and more readily manipulable form of words . . .

But certainly Robin Horton would never argue that only traditional thought falls into the error of attributing concreteness to verbal formula. It is usual to think of this as a characteristic of primitive religions. The following remarks by Godfrey Lienhardt (1956) make the application to our scientists clear enough:

> Since for Max Muller God was an idea rather than an active power, he was surprised by a characteristic of primitive religion which he nevertheless intelligently noted – its preference for the concrete, its attachment to material symbols. He noted that there were two distinct tendencies to be observed in the growth of ancient religion . . . on the one side, the struggle of the mind against the material character of language, a constant attempt to strip words of their coarse meaning, and fit them, by main force, for the purposes of abstract thought. But . . . on the other side, a predilection for the material sense instead of the spiritual.

The same cap fits the anthropologist as the people he studies. Anyone who cares to follow up David Schneider's description of the modern anthropologist will recognise a predilection for concretising written words and treating them as the only hard and solid objects of study. This anthropologist starts by saying that the only accessible reality lies in the words of classificatory systems. He goes on to write as if this externally visible and audible reality represents another more real but hidden one, the categories inside the heads of the informants. The system of classification is credited with autonomy and fixity, neither of which it plausibly has. According to this presentation the rest of human behaviour is a bloodless affair, without strife or feeling. These anthropologists spiritualise social life, like vegetarians who depreciate their own carnal existence by feeding on only fruit and seeds. On their record, an awful lot of human behaviour is discarded as unworthy of a scholar's time. This view has something of the attraction of plastic flowers. The verb 'to express' allows the transient to be fixed. Life moves too fast for easy analysis. Exclusive focusing upon expression and its logical categories detaches from the flux of living something that will stay still long enough to be contemplated. The echo of scholastic theology is heard. To concentrate research upon the logical categories and their expression has the satisfaction of seeming to confront mind in its pure state. But if this is the goal that draws the scholar, why not plunge straight into the *Principia Mathematica* and, going back and forward from there, become a pure logician? I would not deny that the analysis of logical forms, in kinship terminology or religious categories, in folklore or studies of riddles, is an arduous, technical, and highly important task. But the anthropologists who train to specialise in it must also be interested in how the category systems are generated. The subject needs both kinds of approach, and neither should exclude the other, or remain unaware of how they are related.

The backstage bias takes the reverse view of the same issues. From this angle, the symbolic system is what appears on the surface. It is mere show, an illusion. Only the work is real which produces it. The mumming performed on stage is hardly relevant: the real stuff of sociological concern lies in the dealings that go on backstage. Sidney and Beatrice Webb are reported to have enjoyed an evening at Covent Garden calculating from the average box-office takings what the dancers earned. These anthropologists likewise are content with the truth which can be reached after stripping off the fancy dress and laying bare the transactions between management and artists. A strong movement in anthropology would focus exclusively on transactions, following on the development of exchange theory in political science and psychology.

In sum the terminology which separates symbolic orders from the rest of the action fits either of two rival positions in anthropology and is therefore hard to dislodge. But they both leave important issues unformulated. Many pay lip-service to the unity of experience, claiming that their approach does it no violence. But they underestimate the challenge of attempting to control the sociological vision in both dimensions. The pioneers who attempt the enormously difficult synthesis are easily belittled by those who stay with either logic or transactions. But soon they will develop their own critical canons and common terminology. Surely, as their work converges on a technical plane, they will become, like the Oxford anthropologists under Professor Evans-Pritchard in the 1950s, a self-recognising élite, turning inwards to bound their field of interest and hammer out their validating procedures, and it will greatly advance the subject when they do – but I will not be there.

In the meanwhile, the review essays in this section plead for the symbolic system always to be presented with a scrutiny of the social system in which it is generated. It would be a pity to take them for factious requests for validation in a narrow tradition of English empiricism. It is true that they praise the insight into socio-economic relationships of my contemporaries here, while pointing to the sociological gaps in the work of some overseas anthropologists. But at the time of their writing it seemed necessary to insist that the sociological dimension is not easy to fill in. They say that interpretation which spans many levels of experience is more convincing than one supported with a shallower depth of documentation and that those who shirk the sociological route suffer a grave problem of validation. Re-read, the reviews show the need for a better vocabulary for discussing the generation of meaning. The vocabulary should clearly recognise that society is entirely constituted by exchanges, verbal and material, that are loaded with significance. It should not minister to our bias for splitting behaviour into levels of more or less symbolic value. Splitting is necessary for examining particular segments. But it should not carelessly relegate precious information to the waste-bin. Any one realisation of society is sustained by many others. The present analytic challenge is to identify and isolate for scrutiny areas of experience that are sufficiently coherent and well-bounded for the ethnographer to record all and only the information necessary to convince colleagues by his interpretation.

Frontstage and backstage are opposed preferences held by the social scientists. If they raise ancient questions of philosophy concerning illusion and reality, sign and signified, they are by no means remote or lacking practical effect. According to such predilections teachers guide their students, and thesis subjects are defined. But the matter goes deeper still. The historians of European thought commonly attribute to Descartes the philosophy based on a dichotomy between ideas and the external world. They suggest that but for him the division between mind and matter would never have stayed to bedevil us. But he had merely found that the older one between substance and form needed to be questioned. And before the schoolmen were Aristotle and Plato themselves. The essay reprinted here on the Dogon reminds us that a people who use oracular techniques of divination are likely to be landed with their own dichotomies between different kinds of reality. Instead of rebuking Descartes, it would be constructive to admit that thinking about the process of thinking encourages the tendency to treat thought as something apart. When anthropology can recognise that thought is the central organising activity, that all social activity is symbolic, and that all behaviour contributes to the constituting of reality, it will be ready for a big theoretical revolution. From there, the next conclusion is that all apprehended reality is socially constituted. And then at last there is scope for the questions about different kinds of socially constituted reality, questions which afford escape from negative relativism.

BIBLIOGRAPHY

HORTON, R. (1967), 'African traditional thought and Western science', *Africa*, *37*, 2, 50–187.

LIENHARDT, R.G. (1956), 'Religion', in *Man, Culture and Society*, ed. H.L. Shapiro, New York, Oxford University Press, ch. xiv, pp. 313ff.

SCHNEIDER, D. (1972), 'What is kinship all about?', in *Kinship Studies in the Morgan Centennial Year*, ed. P. Reining, Anthropological Society of Washington, DC, pp. 32–63.

Chapter 7

Pollution

First published (1968) in *International Encyclopedia of the Social Sciences*, New York, Macmillan Co. and the Free Press.

One of the great puzzles in comparative studies of religion has been the reconciliation of the concept of pollution, or defilement, with that of holiness. In the last half of the nineteenth century, Robertson Smith asserted that the religion of primitive peoples developed out of the relation between a community and its gods, who were seen as just and benevolent. Dependent on a sociological approach to religion, Robertson Smith continued always to draw a line between religious behaviour, concerned with ethics and gods, and non-religious, magical behaviour. He used the term *taboo* to describe non-religious rules of conduct, especially those concerned with pollution, in order to distinguish them from the rules of holiness protecting sanctuaries, priests, and everything pertaining to gods. The latter behaviour he held to be intelligible and praiseworthy and the former to be primitive, savage, and irrational – 'magical superstition based on mere terror'.

He clearly felt that magic and superstition were not worth a scholar's attention. But Sir James Frazer, who dedicated *The Golden Bough* to Robertson Smith, tried to classify and understand the nature of magical thinking. He formulated the two principles of sympathetic magic: action by contagion and action by likeness. Frazer followed Robertson Smith in assuming that magic was more primitive than religion, and he worked out an evolutionary scheme in which primitive man's earliest thinking was oriented to mechanical ideas of contagion. Magic gradually gave way to another cosmology, the idea of a universe dominated by supernatural beings similar to man but greatly superior to him. Magic thus came to be accepted as a word for ritual which is not enacted within a cult of divine beings. But obviously there is an overlap between non-religious ideas of contagion and rules of holiness. Robertson Smith accounted for this by making the distinction between holiness and uncleanness a criterion of the advanced religions ([1889] 1927: 153):

> The person under taboo is not regarded as holy, for he is separated from approach to the sanctuary as well as from contact with men, but his act or condition is somehow associated with supernatural dangers, arising, according to the common savage explanation, from the presence of formidable

spirits which are shunned like an infectious disease. In most savage societies no sharp line seems to be drawn between the two kinds of taboo . . . and even in more advanced nations the notions of holiness and uncleanness often touch . . . [to] distinguish between the holy and the unclean, marks a real advance above savagery.

Frazer echoes the notion that confusion between uncleanness and holiness marks primitive thinking. In a long passage in which he considers the Syrian attitude to pigs, he concludes ([1890] 1955, vol. 2, part 5: 23):

Some said this was because the pigs were unclean; others said it was because the pigs were sacred. This . . . points to a hazy state of religious thought in which the ideas of sanctity and uncleanness are not yet sharply distinguished, both being blent in a sort of vaporous solution to which we give the name taboo.

The work of several modern-day students of comparative religion derives not directly from Frazer but from the earlier work of Durkheim, whose debt to Robertson Smith is obvious in many ways. On the one hand, Durkheim was content to ignore aspects of defilement which are not part of a religious cult. He developed the notion that magical injunctions are the consequence of primitive man's attempt to explain the nature of the universe. Durkheim suggested that experimentation with magical injunctions, having thus arisen, has given way to medical science. But on the other hand, Durkheim tried to show that the contagiousness of the sacred is an inherent, necessary, and peculiar part of its character.

His idea of the sacred as the expression of society's awareness of itself draws heavily on Robertson Smith's thesis that man's relation to the gods, his religious behaviour, is an aspect of prescribed social behaviour. It followed, for Durkheim, that religious ideas are different from other ideas. They are not referable to any ultimate material reality, since religious shrines and emblems are only themselves representations of abstract ideas. Religious experience is an experience of a coercive moral force. Consequently, religious ideas are volatile and fluid; they float in the mind, unattached, and are always likely to shift, or to merge into other contexts at the risk of losing their essential character: there is always the danger that the sacred will invade the profane and the profane invade the sacred. The sacred must be continually protected from the profane by interdictions. Thus, relations with the sacred are always expressed through rituals of separation and demarcation, and are reinforced with beliefs in the danger of crossing forbidden boundaries.

If contemporary thinkers were not already well prepared to accept the idea that 'religious' restrictions were utterly different from primitive superstitions about contagion, this circular distinction between two kinds of contagion could hardly have gone unchallenged. How can it be argued that contagiousness is the peculiar characteristic of ideas about the sacred when another kind of contagiousness has been bracketed away by definition as irrelevant?

This criticism of Durkheim's treatment of sacred contagion is implicit in Lévy-Bruhl's massive work on primitive mentality (1922). Lévy-Bruhl documented a special kind of outlook on the universe, one in which the power to act and to be acted upon regardless of restrictions of space and time is widely attributed to symbolical representations of persons and animals. He himself explained the belief in such remote contagion by the dominance of the idea of the supernatural in the primitive view of the world. And since he would expect 'supernatural' to be equated with Durkheim's 'sacred', he seems to have seen no conflict between his and the master's views.

We cannot accept Durkheim's argument that there are two kinds of contagion, one the origin of primitive hygiene and the other intrinsic to ideas about the sacred, because it is circular. If we approach the problem of contagion in Lévy-Bruhl's terms, then the scope of the answer is broadened: there is not simply a residual area of magical behaviour that remains to be explained after primitive religious behaviour has been understood but rather a whole mentality, a view of how the universe is constituted. This view of the universe differs essentially from that of civilised man in that sympathetic magic provides the key to its control. Lévy-Bruhl is open to criticism; his statement of the problem is oversimple. He bluntly contrasts primitive mentality with scientific thought, not fully appreciating what a rare and specialised activity scientific thinking is and in what well-defined and isolated conditions it takes place. His use of the word 'pre-logical' in his first formulation of primitive thinking was unfortunate, and he later discarded it. But although his work seems to be discredited at present, the general problem still stands. There is a whole class of cultures, call them what you will, in which great attention is paid to symbolic demarcation and separation of the sacred and the profane and in which dangerous consequences are expected to follow from neglect of the rituals of separation. In these cultures lustrations, fumigations, and purifications of various kinds are applied to avert the dangerous effect of breach of rules, and symbolic actions based on likeness to real causes are used as instruments for creating positive effects.

THE CULTURAL DEFINITION

If we are not to follow Robertson Smith in treating the rules of uncleanness as irrational and beyond analysis, we need to clear away some of the barriers which divide up this whole field of inquiry. While the initial problem is posed by the difference between 'our' kind of thinking and 'theirs', it is a mistake to treat 'us' the moderns and 'them' the ancients as utterly different. We can only approach primitive mentality through introspection and understanding of our own mentality. The distinction between religious behaviour and secular behaviour also tends to be misleadingly rigid. To solve the puzzle of sacred contagion we can start with more familiar ideas about secular contagion and defilement. In English-speaking cultures, the key word is the ancient, primitive, and still current 'dirt'. Lord Chesterfield defined dirt as matter out of place. This implies only two conditions, a set of ordered relations and a contravention of that order. Thus the idea of dirt implies a structure of ideal. For us dirt is a kind of compendium category for all events which blur, smudge, contradict, or otherwise confuse accepted classifications. The underlying feeling is that a system of values which is habitually expressed in a given arrangement of things has been violated.

This definition of defilement avoids some historical peculiarities of Western civilisation. For example, it says nothing about the relation between dirt and hygiene. We know that the discovery of pathogenic organisms is recent, but the idea of dirt antedates the idea of pathogenicity. It is therefore more likely to have universal application. If we treat all pollution behaviour as the reaction to any event likely to confuse or contradict cherished classifications, we can bring two new approaches to bear on the problem: the work of psychologists on perception and of anthropologists on the structural analysis of culture.

Perception is a process in which the perceiver actively interprets and, in the course of his interpreting, adapts and even supplements his sensory experiences. Hebb has shown that in the process of perception, the perceiver imposes patterns of organisation on the masses of sensory stimuli in the environment (1949; 1958). The imposed pattern organises sequences into units – fills in missing events which would be necessary to justify the recognition of familiar units. The perceiver learns to adjust his response to allow for modification of stimuli according to changes in lighting, angle of regard, distance, and so forth. In this way the learner develops a scheme or structure of assumptions in the light of which new experiences are interpreted. Learning takes place when new experience lends itself to assimilation in the existing structure of assumption or when the scheme of past assumptions is modified in order to accommodate what is unfamiliar. In the normal process of interpretation, the existing scheme of assumptions tends to be protected from challenge, for the learner recognises and absorbs cues which harmonise with past experience and usually ignores cues which are discordant. Thus, those assumptions which have worked well before are reinforced. Because the selection and treatment of new experiences validates the principles which have been learned, the structure of established assumptions can be applied quickly and automatically to current problems of interpretation. In animals this stabilising, selective tendency serves the biological function of survival. In men the same tendency appears to govern learning. If every new experience laid all past interpretations open to doubt, no scheme of established assumptions could be developed and no learning could take place.

This approach may be extended to the learning of cultural phenomena. Language, for example, learned and spoken by individuals, is a social phenomenon produced by continuous interaction between individuals. The regular discriminations which constitute linguistic structure are the spontaneous outcome of continual control, exercised on an individual attempting to communicate with others. Expressions which are ambiguous or which deviate from the norm are less effective in communication, and speakers experience a direct feedback encouraging conformity. Language has more loosely and more strictly patterned domains in which ambiguity has either more or less serious repercussions on effective communication. Thus there are certain domains in which ambiguity can be better tolerated than in others (Osgood and Sebeok, 1954: 129).

Similar pressures affect the discrimination of cultural themes. During the process of enculturation the individual is engaged in ordering newly received experiences and bringing them into conformity with those already absorbed. He is also interacting with other members of his community and striving to reduce dissonance between his structure of assumptions and theirs (Festinger, 1957). Frenkel-Brunswik's research among school-children who had been variously exposed to racial prejudice illustrates the effects of ambiguity on learning at this level. The children listened to stories which they were afterwards asked to recall. In the stories the good and bad roles were not consistently allocated to white and Negro characters. When there was dissonance between their established pattern of assumptions about racial values and the actual stories they heard, an ambiguous effect was received. They were unable to recall the stories accurately. There are implications here for the extent to which a culture (in the sense of a consistent structure of themes, postulates, and evaluations) can tolerate ambiguity. It is now common to approach cultural behaviour as if it were susceptible to structural analysis on lines similar to those used in linguistics (Lévi-Strauss, 1958; Leach, 1961). For a culture to have any recognisable character, a process of discrimination and evaluation must have taken place very similar to the process of language development – with an important difference. For language the conditions requiring clear verbal communication provide the main control on the pattern which emerges, but for the wider culture in which any language is set, communication with others is not the only or principal function. The culture affords a hierarchy of goals and values which the community can apply as a general guide to action in a wide variety of contexts. Cultural interaction, like linguistic interaction, involves the individual in communication with others. But it also helps the individual to reflect upon and order his own experience.

The general processes by which language structure changes and resists change have their analogues at the higher level of cultural structure. The response to ambiguity is generally to encourage clearer discrimination of differences. As in language, there are different degrees of tolerance of ambiguity. Linguistic intolerance is expressed by avoidance of ambiguous utterances and by pressure to use well-discriminated forms where differences are important to interpretation and appropriate responses. Cultural intolerance of ambiguity is expressed by avoidance, by discrimination, and by pressure to conform.

THE FUNCTIONS OF POLLUTION BELIEFS

To return to pollution behaviour, we have already seen that the idea of dirt implies system. Dirt avoidance is a process of tidying up, ensuring that the order in external physical events conforms to the structure of ideas. Pollution rules can thus be seen as an extension of the perceptual process: insofar as they impose order on experience, they support clarification of forms and thus reduce dissonance.

Much attention has been paid to the sanctions by which pollution rules are enforced (see Steiner, 1956: 22). Sometimes the breach is punished by political decree, sometimes by attack on the transgressor, and sometimes by grave or trivial sanctions; the sanction used reflects several aspects of the matter. We can assume that the community, insofar as it shares a common culture, is collectively interested in pressing for conformity to its norms. In some areas of organisation the community is capable of punishing deviants directly, but in others this is not practicable. This may happen, for example, if political organisation is not sufficiently developed or if it is developed in such a way as to make certain offences inaccessible to police action. Homicide is a type of offence which is variously treated according to the relationship between killer and victim. If the offender is himself a member of the victim's group and if this is the group which is normally entrusted with protection of its members' interests, it may be held contradictory and impossible for the group to inflict punishment. Then the sanction is likely to be couched in terms of a misfortune that falls upon the offender without human intervention. This kind of homicide is treated as a pollution.

We would expect to find that the pollution beliefs of a culture are related to its moral values, since these form part of the structure of ideas for which pollution behaviour is a protective device. But we would not expect to find any close correspondence between the gravity with which offences are judged and the danger of pollution connected with them. Some moral failings are likely to be met with prompt and unpleasant social consequences. These self-punishing offences are less likely to be sanctioned by pollution beliefs than by other moral rules. Pollution beliefs not only reinforce the cultural and social structure, but they can actively reduce ambiguity in the moral sphere. For example, if two moral standards are applied to adultery, so that it is condemned in women and tolerated in men, there will inevitably be some ambiguity in the moral judgment since adultery involves a man and a woman. A pollution belief can reduce the ambiguity. If the man is treated as dangerously contagious, his adulterous condition, while not in itself condemned, endangers the outraged husband or the children; moral support can be mustered against him. Alternatively, if attention is focused on the pollution aspect of the case, a rite of purification can mitigate the force of the moral condemnation.

This approach to pollution allows further applications of Durkheimian analysis. If we follow him in assuming that symbolism and ritual, whether strictly religious or not, express society's awareness of its own configuration and necessities, and if we assume that pollution rules indicate the areas of greater systematisation of ideas, then we have an additional instrument of sociological analysis. Durkheim held that the dangerous powers imputed to the gods are, in actual fact, powers vested in the social structure for defending itself, as a structure, against the deviant behaviour of its members. His approach is strengthened by including all pollution rules and not merely those which form part of the religious cult. Indeed, deriving pollution behaviour from processes similar to perception comes close to Durkheim's intention of understanding society by developing a social theory of knowledge.

Pollution rules in essence prohibit physical contact. They tend to be applied to products or functions of human physiology; thus they regulate contact with blood, excreta, vomit, hair clippings, nail clippings, cooked food, and so on. But the anthropologist notes that the incidence of beliefs in physiological pollution varies from place to place. In some communities menstrual pollution is gravely feared and in others not at all; in some, pollution by contact with the dead is feared, in others pollution of food or blood. Since our common human condition does not give rise to a common pattern of pollution observances, the differences become interesting as an index of different cultural patterning. It seems that physiological pollutions become important as symbolic expressions of other undesirable contacts which would have repercussions on the structure of social or cosmological ideas. In some societies the social definition of the sexes is more important than in others. In some societies social units are more rigorously defined than in others. Then we find that physical contact between sexes or between social units is restricted even at second or third remove. Not only may social intercourse be restricted, but sitting on the same chair, sharing the same latrine, or using the same cooking utensils, spoons, or combs may be prohibited and negatively sanctioned by pollution beliefs. By such avoidances social definitions are clarified and maintained. Colour bars and caste barriers are enforced by these means. As to the ordered relation of social units and the total structure of social life, this must depend on the clear definition of roles and allegiances. We would therefore expect to find pollution concepts guarding threatened disturbances of the social order. On this, nearly everything has been said by van Gennep. His metaphor of society as a kind of house divided into rooms and corridors, the compartments carefully isolated and the passages between them protected by ceremonial, shows insight into the social aspects of pollution. So also does his insistence on the relative character of the sacred (Gennep, [1909] 1960: 12–13):

> Sacredness as an attribute is not absolute, it is brought into play by the nature of particular situations. . . . Thus the 'magic circles' pivot, shifting as a person moves from one place in society to another. The categories and concepts which embody them operate in such a way that whoever passes through the various positions of a lifetime one day sees the sacred where

before he has seen the profane, or vice versa. Such changes of condition do not occur without disturbing the life of society and the individual, and it is the function of rites of passage to reduce their harmful effects.

Van Gennep saw that rites of transition treat all marginal or ill-defined social states as dangerous. His treatment of margins is fully compatible with the sociological approach to pollution. But van Gennep's ideas must be vastly expanded. Not only marginal social states, but all margins, the edges of all boundaries which are used in ordering the social experience, are treated as dangerous and polluting.

Rites of passage are not purificatory but are prophylactic. They do not redefine and restore a lost former status or purify from the effect of contamination, but they define entrance to a new status. In this way the permanence and value of the classifications embracing all sections of society are emphasised.

When we come to consider cosmological pollution, we are again faced with the problem unresolved by Lévy-Bruhl. Cosmological pollution is to the Westerner the most elusive, yet the most interesting case. Our own culture has largely given up the attempt to unify, to interpenetrate, and to cross-interpret the various fields of knowledge it encompasses. Or rather, the task has been taken over by natural science. A major part of pollution behaviour therefore lies outside the realm of our own experience: this is the violent reaction of condemnation provoked by anything which seems to defy the apparently implicit categories of the universe. Our culture trains us to believe that anomalies are only due to a temporarily inadequate formulation of general natural laws. We have to approach this kind of pollution behaviour at second hand.

The obvious source of information on the place of cosmic abnormality in the mind of the primitive is again Lévy-Bruhl. Earthquakes, typhoons, eclipses, and monstrous births defy the order of the universe. If something is thought to be frightening because it is abnormal or anomalous, this implies a conception of normality or at least of categories into which the monstrous portent does not fit. The more surprising that anomaly is taken to be, the clearer the evidence that the categories which it contradicts are deeply valued.

At this point we can take up again the question of how the culture of civilisation differs from that which Lévy-Bruhl called primitive. Recalling that dirt implies system and that pollution beliefs indicate the areas of greatest systematisation, we can assume that the answer must be along the same lines. The different elements in the primitive world view are closely integrated; the categories of social structure embrace the universe in a single, symbolic whole. In any primitive culture the urge to unify experience to create order and wholeness has been effectively at work. In 'scientific culture' the apparent movement is the other way. We are led by our scientists to specialisation and compartmentalism of spheres of knowledge. We suffer the continual breakup of established ideas. Lévy-Bruhl, looking to define the distinction between the scientific and the primitive outlook, would have been well served if he had followed Kant's famous passage on his own Copernican revolution. Here Kant describes each great advance in thought as a stage in the process of freeing 'mind' from the shackles of its own subjective tendencies. In scientific work the thinker tries to be aware of the provisional and artificial character of the categories of thought which he uses. He is ready to reform or reject his concepts in the interests of making a more accurate statement.

Any culture which allows its guiding concepts to be continually under review is immune from cosmological pollutions. To the extent that we have no established world view, our ways of thinking are different from those of people living in primitive cultures. For the latter, by long and spontaneous evolution, have adapted their patterns of assumption from one context to another until the whole experience is embraced. But such a comprehensive structure of ideas is precarious to the extent that it is an arbitrary selection from the range of possible structures in the same environment. Other ways of dividing up and evaluating reality are conceivable. Hence, pollution beliefs protect the most vulnerable domains, where ambiguity would most weaken the fragile structure.

EMOTIONAL ASPECTS OF POLLUTION BEHAVIOUR

Pollution beliefs are often discussed in terms of the emotions which they are thought to express. But there is no justification for assuming that terror, or even mild anxiety, inspires them any more than it inspires the housewife's daily tidying up. For pollution beliefs are cultural phenomena. They are institutions that can keep their forms only by bringing pressure to bear on deviant individuals. There is no reason to suppose that the individual in a primitive culture experiences fear, still less unreasoning terror, if his actions threaten to modify the form of the culture he shares. His position is exactly comparable to a speaker whose own linguistic deviations cause him to produce responses which vary with his success in communicating. The dangers and punishments attached to pollution act simply as means of enforcing conformity.

As to the question of the rational or irrational character of rules of uncleanness, Robertson Smith is shown to have been partly right. Pollution beliefs certainly derive from rational activity, from the process of classifying and ordering experience. They are, however, not produced by strictly rational or even conscious processes but rather as a spontaneous by-product of these processes.

BIBLIOGRAPHY

DOUGLAS, MARY (1966), *Purity and Danger: an Analysis of Concepts of Pollution and Taboo*, London, Routledge & Kegan Paul.
DURKHEIM, ÉMILE ([1912] 1954), *The Elementary Forms of the Religious Life*, London,

Allen & Unwin; New York, Macmillan. First published as *Les Formes élémentaires de la vie religieuse, le système totémique en Australie*. A paperback edition was published in 1961 by Collier.

ELIADE, MIRCEA ([1957] 1959), *The Sacred and the Profane: The Nature of Religion*, New York, Harcourt. First published in German. A paperback edition was published in 1961 by Harper.

FESTINGER, LEON (1957), *A Theory of Cognitive Dissonance*, Evanston, Ill., Row.

FRAZER, JAMES ([1890] 1955), *The Golden Bough: a Study in Magic and Religion*, 3rd ed., rev. London, Macmillan. An abridged edition was published in 1922 and reprinted in 1955.

FRENKEL-BRUNSWIK, ELSE (1949), 'Intolerance of ambiguity as an emotional and perceptual personality variable', *Journal of Personality*, 18, 108–43.

GENNEP, ARNOLD VAN ([1909] 1960), *The Rites of Passage*, London, Routledge; University of Chicago Press. First published in French.

HEBB, DONALD O. (1949), *The Organization of Behavior: a Neuropsychological Theory*, New York, Wiley.

HEBB, DONALD O. (1958), *A Textbook of Psychology*, Philadelphia, Saunders.

LEACH, EDMUND R. (1961), *Rethinking Anthropology*, London School of Economics and Political Science Monographs on Social Anthropology, no. 22. London, Athlone.

LÉVI-STRAUSS, CLAUDE ([1958] 1963), *Structural Anthropology*, New York, Basic Books. First published in French.

LÉVY-BRUHL, LUCIEN ([1910] 1926), *How Natives Think*, London, Allen & Unwin. First published as *Les Fonctions Mentales dans les sociétés primitives*.

LÉVY-BRUHL, LUCIEN ([1922] 1923), *Primitive Mentality*, New York, Macmillan. First published in French.

OSGOOD, CHARLES E. and SEBEOK, THOMAS A. (eds) ([1954] 1965), *Psycholinguistics: a Survey of Theory and Research Problems*, Bloomington, Ill., Indiana University Press.

SMITH, WILLIAM ROBERTSON ([1889] 1927), *Lectures on the Religion of the Semites*, 3rd ed., New York, Macmillan.

STEINER, FRANZ (1956), *Taboo*, New York, Philosophical Library.

Chapter 8

If the Dogon . . .

First published in *Cahiers d'Etudes Africaines*, 7, 28 (1967)

There are German scholars who so much admire Shakespeare that they some-times call him 'our Shakespeare'. I have something of this feeling about the Dogon. Yet, would Dogon studies strike this note of sympathy if they had been actually carried out by the English? If the Nuer had been studied by the Missions Griaule how much more would we know about them today. How much poorer our knowledge of Dogon culture, if we ourselves had studied them.

Some of the differences between the two schools of ethnography depend on concentration of time and effort. It is true that Evans-Pritchard was only able to study the Nuer for a very short time. The poverty of their recorded cosmology partly reflects this. Compare his two brief visits with the many years of dedicated teamwork of the Missions Griaule. But it is certain too that very different points of view inspired the two kinds of ethnography. What would we know of the Nuer if they had been in the French Sudan – and of the Dogon if they had been on the banks of the White Nile? It is hard to imagine because the Dogon now seem so unmistakably French, so urbane, so articulate, with such philosophical insight. The very themes central to their philosophy are themes in the main-stream of Greek and Christian thought. For example, their reflections on sexual dualism echo those of Plato in very similar vein. And their use of anthro-pomorphic symbolism for the corpus politic and the mystical body is a pre-occupation of Christian philosophers as well. Nuer myths, by contrast, are as crude as their way of life. Their manners are blunt, not to say rude. Their cosmological ideas are confused. To complete the contrast, the Dogon work out their metaphysics in terms of speech symbolism, the Nuer use more concrete cattle symbolism. The man whose personality and initiative give him a little leadership they call 'the bull of the herd'. The British, too, use a bovine metaphor to designate the man whose confident buying gives a lead to the stock market. 'The market is "bullish",' they say, or: 'Today bulls were active.' The Nuer may one day feel satisfaction that the national sobriquet of their ethno-graphers is John Bull. Thus while the Dogon seem pre-eminently susceptible to the literary and aesthetic investigation at which the French excel, the Nuer seem only apt for the discoveries in primitive politics and kinship which interest the

British. Yet I long to subject each tribe to a fusion of the British and French techniques of research.

Of all the plays of Shakespeare it is said to be *Hamlet, Prince of Denmark* for which the Germans feel such strong affection. Of all the books on the Dogon it is Mme Calame-Griaule's *Ethnologie et langage* which draws me to Dogon studies. This great book is not a linguist's book about a language. Rather it is an account of Dogon reflections on language in general and their own language in particular. Out of their reflections on speech, the Dogon have created a symbolic structure uniformly embracing their entire universe. The grain of millet in its husk – the human foetus in the uterus – the world in its atmospheric envelope, are each analogues of the others. The constituent materials and morphology of speech are seen to correspond to those of cereals, of man, of woven cloth, of the whole cosmos. The same intricate harmony of images is drawn down and across from one level of experience to the next. Reading it is like gazing through a microscope at a flourishing form of life, confusingly alien and familiar. The lens through which the Dogon see themselves is their theory of speech.

Many primitive cultures use one relatively narrow range of experience for developing a symbolic code. Nilotic peoples do this to some extent with cattle symbolism. Lienhardt has shown how such primary experiences as those of colour are mediated for Dinka children by prior reference to cattle colours; a man's image of himself is mediated by his identification with an ox, his experience of society is summed up in a series of animal sacrifices which give material for profound reflections on the nature of life and truth (Lienhardt, 1961). Ndembu develop something comparable by reflecting on the common qualities of juicy elements in men and trees; different coloured saps are classified with blood and milk and bile, and from their likenesses a cosmic harmony is derived (Turner, 1966). The Bushmen, reflecting on the morphology of human and animal bodies, have developed what Lévi-Strauss has called anatomical totemism. And so on. But the originality of the Dogon in this list is that the intellectual unity which they confer on experience is derived from reflecting on the nature, power, and effects of language.

On first view this would presuppose a degree of self-consciousness about the processes of thought which would lift their culture clear out of the class of primitives. It is not fantastic to hope that the fully recorded epistemology of an ancient West African culture should produce a kind of breakthrough for us. It could at least produce a new perspective such as that produced in European art at the turn of the century by the impact of African sculpture. If traditional African art had an effect on the artistic vision of Europe at that time, it was because it was welcomed in French artistic circles. Conversely I predict that if African linguistics are to make a stir in modern Europe, the greatest impact is likely to be through Anglo-Saxon appreciation. For we regard ourselves as the home of several kinds of linguistic studies. Linguistic philosophy, let's face it, was born in Austria but naturalised British. Linguistics have several roots in our country, though the richest flowering has been in the United States. I can bring home to you our special claim on the Dogon by mentioning a few points of controversy to which their reflections made a definite contribution.

First, consider the support they lend to Malinowski. His main contribution to linguistics was to discover the relevance of social context. The stone he thus threw into the pond has made big ripples, but there are a few linguists who are not convinced. In this argument the Dogon come down clearly on the side of Malinowski. They have no doubt that language is a social activity and should be analysed as such. 'Dans la mesure où tout acte social suppose un échange de paroles, où tout acte individuel est lui-même une manière de s'exprimer, la "parole" est parfois synonyme d'action' (Calame-Griaule, 1965: 24).

Second, linguistic philosophy started by analysing statements and considering the relation between statements and facts on which they impart information. Following this track they come to the position at which they have forgotten that some statements do not convey information but are performances of actions. J.L. Austin (1962) drew the attention of his colleagues to the class of performative sentences in which the utterance is the performance of an act.

> For example, some performative statements are contractual:
> 'I do take this woman to be my lawful wedded wife.'
> 'I bet you sixpence it will rain tomorrow.'
> Some are declaratory:
> 'I name this ship *Queen Elizabeth*.'
> 'I declare war.'

The Dogon do not need to be reminded of this faculty of speech. 'Acte et parole sont liés dans la pensée dogon, c'est pourquoi on appellera aussi symboliquement "parole" le résultat de l'acte, l'oeuvre, la création matérielle qui en résulte' (Calame-Griaule, 1965: 24). Dogon would even enlarge the performative class of speech to include insults and blessings (Calame-Griaule, 1965: 422–9), which they consider to have immediate material efficacy.

In these two instances the Dogon are on the side of contemporary thought. The things that our philosophers and linguists are now remarking are things the Dogon know well. But this is because among ourselves the movement to greater and greater specialisation has run itself to a halt in certain directions. We are forced to return to more naïve approaches. It is not so remarkable that a traditional African philosophy should be found to enshrine some old truths we have forgotten.

More impressive is Dogon subtlety in respect of truth. As is well known, the Dogon divide their universe between Nommo and Yourougou. Nommo is the heavenly power who represents right, reason, society, ritual, and order in all its forms. Yourougou or the Pale Fox is his brother, fallen from grace by an initial act of disobedience. He represents enigma, disorder. Dogon classify speech into twenty-four forms belonging to Nommo and twenty-four belonging to the Fox.

The analysis of this classification shows the speech attributed to the Fox is the obverse of the speech attributed to Nommo. And it is fascinating to note that truth is associated with the Fox: that is, truth in all its forms, both unexpressed and truth expressed. Formal judgments are the speech of Nommo. They lay down the law, as it were. But the speech which predicts the future and the speech which sifts the truth from lies belong to the Fox. Here we can hail a really sophisticated approach to the sociology of truth.

Franz Steiner pointed out a similar native wisdom when he analysed Chagga concepts of truth (1954). A true statement, for the Chagga, had to be formally vested with an extra charge of value. For them the true word differs from ordinary speech in much the same way as we would distinguish sworn affidavits from other kinds of statement. Lienhardt, taking up this line of thought (1961), has observed an elaboration of the difference between ritual truth and actual truth among the Dinka. If the Dinka perform a sacrifice to turn aside the ill-effects of quarrelling, the sacrificer is likely, in his oration, to deny the existence of past quarrels. As Lienhardt says, he is not attempting to deceive divinity or hoping to get away with a false representation of what has happened. The ritual and prayer are used to control experience, to put an imprint on men's minds of what their life should be like and to bridge the gap between actual behaviour and moral intentions. So the Chagga give us sworn truth which is more fully guaranteed than ordinary statements, and the Dinka recognise ritual truth which may be very different from remembered experience.

Both these approaches allow less validity for the statements which are not ritualised. To this extent I find them naïve and superficial. The Dogon recognise another kind of reality, that which is not expressed in ritual. For them formal judgments, curses, and blessings are efficacious rites. They belong to Nommo. But truth belongs to the Fox. This is a marvellous insight. They recognise oracular truth and locate it somewhere beyond formal appearances. The truth of the Fox is discovered in oracles and it is held a truer truth than the judgments of priests and elders. This Fox should be a great surrealist figure, for he challenges the validity of realist perspectives. The Pale Fox is an obvious emblem for André Breton since he honours the riches and truth of the imagination. May we claim him also as an emblem for English anthropology? It is flattering, no doubt, to see ourselves in the guise of diviners. But here is the source of the paradoxical affinity which I see between our way of thinking and that of the Dogon.

Any culture which admits the use of oracles and divination is committed to a distinction between appearances and reality. The oracle offers a way of reaching behind appearances to another source of knowledge. We can therefore place Dogon thought in a historical perspective. For this is a perennial problem of philosophy. It is as alive today as it was for Parmenides and Plato.

As I understand Dogon philosophy, they place the world of appearances under the control of Nommo. It is a well-defined, well-illumined field. Their theory of speech and of thought is part of a crudely mechanistic physiology and psychology of hot and cold emotions. Their formal sociology deals only with external behaviour and it treats formal judgments and ritual statements in a formalistic way. An example of their concrete treatment of the world of appearances is the physical efficacy they attribute to speech. At the level of language analysis, I find the Dogon have only used their complex classification to produce another highly structured type of symbolic patterning, a totemism of linguistics, as it were. At the level of socio-linguistics, again, I find their insights less subtle and profound than I had hoped. Socio-linguistics is specially concerned with what is not said, the suppressed idea, the unexpressed choices which control use of verbal forms. The object of all behavioural sciences is to go behind the external forms of behaviour and discover other information than that which is overtly expressed.

At first sight Dogon formal theory of language is extremely simple on these points. Dogon comments on silence, hesitation, and confused speech are not specially profound. They seem to be more concerned to classify their material rather than to solve any problem. The speech of the drunkard has neither oil nor grain, it has more beer than water and goes in gusty zigzags. The deaf-mute is like a child who has never acquired control of speech. The stutterer is not much better. False promises are equivalent to theft. The Dogon seem not to admit that it is possible for one sort of speech to rise up in the mind while another issues involuntarily from the mouth. They could not begin to discuss Benjamin Lee-Whorf's hypotheses about how language may shape our inchoate thoughts, since they do not recognise one except as the manifestation of the other. Their mechanical linguistic theory cannot deal with the case of a thinker deceived by the structures of his own words. Mme Calame-Griaule (1965: 546–7) notes this rigidity: '. . . on peut craindre que trop de codifications n'aboutissent à un formalisme stérile, qui ramènerait la société au péril d'immobilisme qu'elle voulait justement éviter. Nous pouvons nous demander quelle place la société dogon fait à la liberté.'

She indicates that the answer to this lies in the theory of divination. The oracle, by the obscure sign language of the Fox, aims at freedom from the formal conditons of knowledge. The oracle gives access to a form of reality which is free from the restrictive frame of time. The Fox, by his initial incest with his mother, defied the order of the generations and so of time itself: thus he can read the future. Death lies in the domain of the Fox and the Fox knows secret remedies and poisons by which life and death can be controlled. It is clear that the Dogon are not misled by their solidly material theory of speech into seeing no difference between symbols and symbolised. Half of their coding system deals formally with knowledge of the world of appearances and half of it attempts to find shortcuts by another method. The clear words of Nommo are contrasted with those of the Fox, which include false promises, contradictions, stuttering, and dreaming. Nommo is respectable, while the Fox is a shady character.

Thus the Dogon are as convinced as Plato that the world of appearances and sensation is not the whole of truth. They recognise another kind of reality. Plato used the metaphor of the prisoners in the cave who took their shadows to be real. They disbelieved the man who had been in the daylight of logic and philosophy, but he alone understood how the shadows were cast. For Plato the world of appearance is confused and shadowy and the world of ideas is bright. The Dogon reverse the light and shade. They situate real truth (the sifting of lies and contradictions) in the shadowy realm of the Pale Fox. Formal appearances they place in the daylight world of Nommo.

I ask you here to note the extraordinary sympathy between the Dogon and the surrealists, a sympathy of both methods and aims. André Breton was a poet, reflecting on the conditions of poetic inspiration. His problem was to go behind the screen of realist control and release the imagination. Stimulated by Freud's work on dreams, he also reversed Plato's pattern of light and shade. Wakefulness, logic, and necessity for him distort and limit human experience. Revelation comes with dreams in the night, by means of nonsense, disjunction, total relaxation of control. There is not time to quote here his account of how he developed techniques for escaping the dreary perspectives of realism (Breton, 1924: 30–5). But one is struck at once by their close relation to techniques of oracular consultation.

From here we can place the British anthropologists in a new light. Apparently so down to earth, so practical, so interested in realist themes – now we turn out to be allies of the surrealists on the one hand, and of the Pale Fox of the Dogon on the other. For we also are passionately interested in getting behind the screen of appearance. All our professed interest in politics and kinship is an interest in the machinery that casts the shadows on the wall. The field in which our efforts have been most successful is in trying to discover the social determinants of cosmology. We have done regrettably little in the recording of cosmologies, but something more in what can be called pre-cosmology.

There is one field which is characteristically ours. That is the question of how mystical powers are distributed. There are at base only two classes of mystical power. On the one hand there is mystical knowledge, the power to see and reveal. On the other hand there is power to do harm or good to fellow men. The allocation of these powers is undoubtedly the part of cosmology which excites our interest. It is the mechanism which links cosmos to social structure. If we could understand this link, we could explain the intricate peculiarities of a particular cosmology by the channelling of energies in the particular social system. This is not the same as treating the cosmology as a mirror-image of the society. It is not showing the congruence of the infrastructure with superstructure. The programme is more ambitious – an attempt to discover how the two are generated. We start by assuming that society consists of individuals who seek to manipulate any given situation to their private intentions. Thus we have concentrated largely on the drive for power and legitimacy.

Durkheim rivetted our attention on cosmology as a source of legitimation. Evans-Pritchard has been called the Stendhal of anthropology. Certainly he has revealed the secrets of men's hearts. He first showed how Azande used oracles to manipulate social situations. He also saw that accusations of witchcraft are found in limited niches of the social structure. Since then, our best work has followed on these lines. I cite the work of Turner in Ndembu (1961) and Middleton in Lugbara (1960) on how divination serves political ends. And the work of Gellner on the Islamic cosmology of Berbers of Morocco. He found the alleged distribution of *baraka* or divine power is sensitively attuned to the distribution of political strength and has a practical effect in reinforcing the strong. Not only is *baraka* on the side of the big battalions, but they become even bigger as change of allegiance is justified by the appearance of *baraka* on the winning side. The exact mechanism of how *vox populi* becomes *vox dei* is our favourite puzzle. As to witchcraft, we should one day be able to map the areas of social structure in which men are likely to blame their misfortunes on others, and those in which the victim is held responsible for his own misfortunes.

In 'Spirits, witches and sorcerers in the supernatural economy of the Yakö', Daryll Forde has sought to show the human concerns for health and prosperity which energise the cosmological system. Here he was countering a tendency to attribute all cosmological variations too narrowly to variations in the social dimension. But elsewhere he has probably come closest to formulating a testable hypothesis on the relationship between cosmology and social structure. In *The Context of Belief* he suggests that the peculiarly fragmented and un-coordinated character of the Yakö cosmology and the lack of sharp definition given to the principal mystic forces which control their lives may be related to characteristics of their social structure: 'Where the field of interaction of the individual is both wide and heterogeneous as a result of activities and interests in a series of distinct, non-congruent units' (Forde, 1958b: 208–11), we may expect that beliefs in mystical forces are not closely coordinated in a harmonious and complex cosmology.

Now to draw the parallel between our consuming interest in pre-cosmology and those of the Dogon Pale Fox. Denise Paulme, in an important article (1937), tells us that any fine evening a number of Dogon men can be seen stooping over the flat sandy rocks outside the village. They are preparing their divining tables. They represent a man's personal problems by drawing a rectangular box with three sub-sections, one for heaven, one for man and one for the Fox. The box of heaven has an upper half for dealing with all the divine powers and their attitudes to the consulter, and a lower half for dealing with his specific ritual duties. The rectangle for man has an upper section dealing with outsiders and enemies, and a lower section dealing with the consulter's own family. The upper section of the rectangle for the Fox deals with death in general, and the lower part with the grave of the consulter himself. Here is a reduced and entirely abstract model of the universe. In these empty squares a man fills in little pebbles and sticks, to represent his personal problems. He diagrammatises the interplay of his ambition and his conscience. Psychologists use something of the same technique in devising games for child

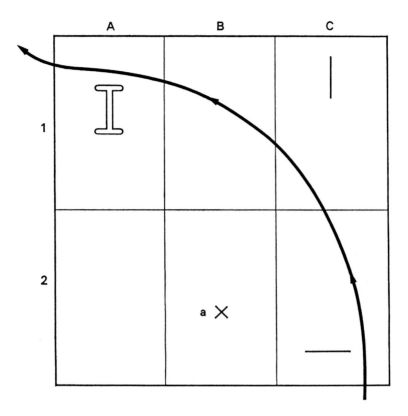

Figure 8.1
Question: Will the pale fox tell the truth?
Answer: Yes, because the tracks lead upwards

analysis. But I am struck with the efficiency and economy of the Fox oracle. Note that the symbols used for posing the problem are lifted out of their general context. They are stripped bare – mere tools for setting a limited question. Then note, and most important of all, that having posed the question the enquirer goes to bed. In the night the Pale Foxes will come and make mute signs with their paws on the sand and thus the truth will be revealed. The consulter abandons conscious control of the oracle. He does not expect that his rational analysis will yield results. He is even ready to admit that the way the problem has been posed is all wrong. If one Fox runs along the divining table from heaven to the grave, and another runs the other way, he is forced to reconsider the whole matter and pose it again the next day. In many ways the process of consultation reminds me of the nightly examination of conscience recommended by St Ignatius. But the Ignatian system put great stress on duty and rational control. The Fox oracle, with its homage to the free imagination,

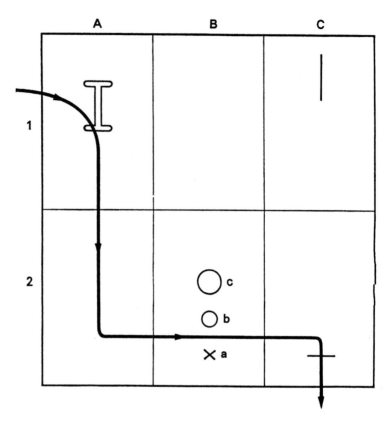

Figure 8.2
A member of the family will die. The tracks bypass B1 into B2, the enquirer's house,
and come out by C2, squashing the object representing the graveyard. In B2 objects are
placed to stand for the enquirer (a), his mouth (b) and his food (c)

could have spiritual advantages. Perhaps the Fox oracle fits closer to the
religious genius of St Francis of Assisi who used little oracles to teach his monks
humble dependence on the will of God.

In reading of the techniques of the Fox oracle I am haunted by the correspondence between this and the techniques of certain surrealists. Artistic
creation bristles with technical and personal problems and the great work of
art is always one in which the artist has succeeded in organising both himself
and his technical apparatus at the same time. I do not understand Raymond
Roussel's poetry. But two of his books in prose, *Locus Solus* and *Impressions
d'Afrique* are wonderfully rich fantasies. They serve as a perfect illustration
for my theme. He has described for us his elaborate technique in *Comment
j'ai écrit certains de mes livres.* He would construct a kind of acrostic or

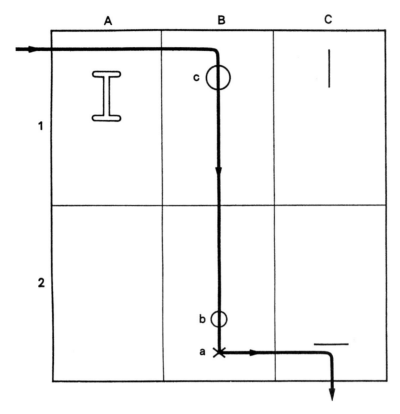

Figure 8.3
The enquirer will die. The tracks have squashed (c), the object representing food in general in B1, gone on to tread on the enquirer's own food (b) in B2, and finally knocked over the stick representing the enquirer himself (a), walking off through the graveyard in C2

métagramme as he called it. 'Je choisissais deux mots presque semblables (faisant penser aux métagrammes). Par exemple *billard* et *pillard*. Puis j'y ajoutais des mots pareils mais pris dans deux sens différents, et j'obtenais ainsi deux phrases presque identiques' (Roussel, 1963: 11). Then he would use these two phrases, so close in sound but different in meaning, as a problem for his imagination. Somehow within these artificial constraints a story had to be worked out. At first, when he was a very young writer, he set himself the task of opening his tale with the phrase in its more obvious meaning, and closing it with the same phrase in the more recondite sense. In between the two phrases the story hardly mattered. He used banal little Breton folk tales. The result was not a literary masterpiece – more a clever parlour trick, rather as Dr Johnson said of women novelists: If we are amazed at a dog standing on its

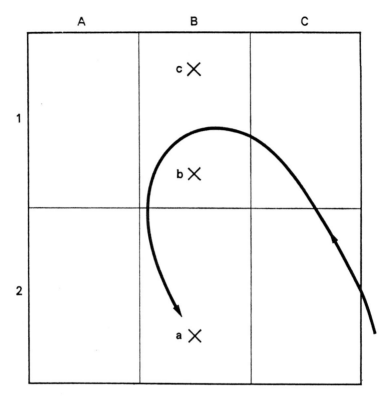

Figure 8.4
Question: Should the enquirer (a) ask the girl (b) to marry him? The answer is favourable: the tracks encircle both (a) and (b). It would have been negative if the tracks had gone between them. The girl's family are represented by the cross at (c) in B1

hind legs it is not because it does it well, but that it does it al all! However, the young Roussel was cast down because his techniques did not bring him instant glory. Observe that one thing was missing from his early experiments. He had discovered a technique of creative writing but he had not learnt to use it to express his own preoccupations. As I see his early work, he was at the same point at which the late Marcel Griaule and Denise Paulme were in 1937 when they recorded the system of divination by the Fox. The technique was well demonstrated, but only by the use of hypothetical examples. They neither knew how the Dogon used it to solve *their* dominant preoccupations, *nor* how to use it to solve their *own* problems as investigators.

The cold neglect of his work drove Raymond Roussel to intensify his efforts. His technique became more elaborate and more supple. He used it to bore a narrow well into his imagination and then watched artesian waters gush up. The two books I admire give passionate expression to the writer's own personal concerns. They consist of loosely strung together episodes. Each describes the creation of a work of art which brings glory and renown to its author. Sometimes the episodes describe a man watching a crowd which is admiring a work of art, which portrays a crowd admiring a work of art, which portrays . . . and so on.

Generally the work of genius consisted in discovering how to make a work of art create itself. The inventor pushes a lever and starts the machinery working of its own accord. Michel Butor in his critical essay on Roussel has made it abundantly clear what personal driving force lies behind these stories. Here we have a writer who found a technique which harnessed the guiding power of his own ambition to his problems as a creative artist. Granted that he was one of the most richly imaginative writers of his generation, we only need to note three things about his technique: one, the violence done to the association between word and meaning, between symbol and thing symbolised; second, his adherence to rigid, artificial constraints; third, the indirect approach to the problem. This last is the true surrealist respect for the unfettered imagination. Somehow the work of art must be made free to produce itself. Note also that many of the fantastic inventions which Roussel described are no more and no less than oracular techniques which produce mysterious writings or hidden truths.

Now, finally, I must try to convince you that British anthropology is not inspired by down to earth concern with problems of colonialism. We must be classed along with other allies of the Fox, both in our aims and our techniques.

To start with the techniques, we reduce the universe to small-scale abstract models, such as genealogies and tables of village composition. These do not serve a love of genealogical lore for its own sake. They are designed to isolate the dynamic conflict of politics and conscience. Take, for example, Marwick's interpretation of Cewa witchcraft in 1952. He suspected that accusations of witchcraft expressed rival claims for political control. To demonstrate this he needed to depict the structure of political units: hence the need for lineage tables. Similarly, John Middleton in 1960 had an insight about how the ancestral cult of the Lugbara interacted dynamically with their witch beliefs. Above all, the insight itself derived from reflecting on the struggle for power and the channelling of private ambition through the lineage structure.

These techniques require a suspension of respect for the symbolic order. Raymond Roussel tore words apart and stripped them of fixed associations, to make them tools for richer uses. Less savagely than James Joyce, he treated words irreverently. He would take a common phrase and chop it up phonetically into different units. From the phrase 'Napoléon Empereur', he got *nappe, ollé, ombre*, and these gave him the image of a Spanish dancer (*ollé*) on a table, so clearly seen that even the shadow (*ombre*) of the crumbs on the cloth (*nappe*) were visible. He thus made a practice of ignoring the stock meanings attached to verbal symbols and finding alternative readings. Surely the Dogon who consults the Fox oracle is also led to analyse his stock allegiances and confront himself with alternative readings of a situation. In a very sensitive perception,

Denise Paulme suggests that the oracle consulter is torn between two desires. He must pose his problem unequivocally so as to get a clear answer for himself. But he must choose ambiguous symbols so as to disguise his problem from inquisitive eyes. Such a procedure would lead these tribal philosophers far into the problem of the relation between appearance and reality. No wonder their treatment of it in their cosmology is so sophisticated. Let me claim as much sophistication for the British anthropologists.

We also show little respect for symbols and try to prize them apart from the reality they represent. For example, David Tait in 1950 published an analysis of Dogon social structure with detailed lineage diagrams. By means of this tool of inquiry he discovered that Dogon social reality is less symmetrical than Dogon official theory claims. He found, for instance, that the arrangement of paired joking clans is not symmetrical. We should not be surprised, of course, that the pressure of living distorts the actual pattern from its ideal form. But the question then becomes more acute: What is the actual experience to which corresponds the Dogon ideal pattern of symmetrical pairs of twins? One final point as to technique: Only the oblique approach will yield the results we seek. The scrupulous setting down of informants' views merely sets up the screen which must then somehow be passed or penetrated. The kind of truths we seek to reveal are hidden from informants themselves. Hence our attempts to develop a foxy cunning in checking statements against action. In the nursery stories about Brer Fox, remember that he always 'laid low and said nuffin'. We try likewise to lie low and to eschew direct questions. We aim to let the informants reveal, by contradiction and inconsistency, the practical social uses to which their cosmological schemes are put.

So much for technique. I hesitate whether to count Professor Lévi-Strauss among the followers of the Fox. Obviously he too is passionately interested in going behind the screen and finding hidden meanings. He is a great diviner. His techniques are as rigid and as oblique as any, and he certainly succeeds in catching the informant unawares. Above all, he seeks to reveal the mechanism which casts the shadows on the wall. His prodigious achievement has dealt precisely with the relation between infrastructure and superstructure. On all these counts he is with us up to the hilt, only one detail is missing. He works at the cognitive level of experience. He is not interested in the self-regarding passions. I feel he is hardly at all concerned with the effect of men's ambition and remorse on society and its cosmos. This is the crucial difference between his work and the kind of English anthropology in Africa that I am talking about. Working on this same problem of Plato's World of Forms, he stays with Plato and we stay, perhaps benightedly, with the Fox.

To conclude. The ethnographers of the Dogon and the Nuer are following different trails and use different techniques to pursue different kinds of quarry. Their combined research would open a new era of advance in these sciences. The French would map the marvellous world of forms, whilst the English would burrow underground. Who are these sorcerers whom the

Dogon fear? Who is accused and why, and what is the result of an accusation? What is the real balance of power which is expressed in the honouring of twins and the rejection of odd numbers? Where is authority most precarious? What is the ladder to advancement? In these subterranean corridors we are more at home.

NOTE

This Chapter is based on a paper given on 9 March 1967 at the École Pratique des Hautes Études (VIth Section, Sorbonne). I wish to record my gratitude to Mme Denise Paulme for her discussion. I am grateful to the Société des Africanistes for permission to reproduce Figures 8.1–4 from Paulme (1937).

BIBLIOGRAPHY

AUSTIN, J.L. (1962), *How to Do Things with Words, The William James Lectures at Harvard, 1955*, Oxford University Press.

BRETON, A. (1924), *Manifeste du surréalisme*, Paris.

BUTOR, M. (1966), *Essais sur les modernes*, Paris.

CALAME-GRIAULE, G. (1965), *Ethnologie et langage. La parole chez les Dogon*, Paris.

EVANS-PRITCHARD, E. (1937), *Witchcraft, Oracles and Magic among the Azande*, Oxford, Clarendon Press.

FORDE, D. (1958a), 'Spirits, witches and sorcerers in the supernatural economy of the Yokö', *Journal of the Royal Anthropological Institute*, 88, 2, 165–78.

FORDE, D. (1958b), *The Context of Belief, a Consideration of Fetishism among the Yakö*, The Frazer Lecture for 1957, Liverpool University Press.

GELLNER, E. (1961), 'Role and organisation of a Berber Zawiya', London, Ph.D. Thesis. (1969), *Saints of the Atlas*, London, Weidenfeld & Nicolson.

GRIAULE, M. (1937), 'Notes sur la divination par le chacal', *Bulletin du Comité d'Études Historiques et Scientifiques et l'Afrique Occidentale Française*, 20, 1–2, 113–41.

LIENHARDT, G. (1961), *Divinity and Experience, the Religion of the Dinka*, London, Oxford University Press.

MARWICK, M.G. (1952), 'The social context of Cewa witch beliefs', *Africa*, 22, 120–35, 215–33.

MIDDLETON, J. (1960), *Lugbara Religion*, London, Oxford University Press.

PAULME, D. (1937), 'La divination par les chacals chez les Dogon de Sanga', *Journal de la Société des Africanistes*, 7, 1–15.

ROUSSEL, R. (n.d.), *Locus Solus* [Paris].

ROUSSEL, R. (n.d.), *Impressions d'Afrique* [Paris].

ROUSSEL, R. (1963), *Comment j'ai écrit certains de mes livres* [Paris].

STEINER, F. (1954), 'Chagga truth', *Africa*, 24, 364–9.

TAIT, D. (1950), 'An analytical commentary on the social structure of the Dogon', *Africa*, 20, 3, 175–99.

TURNER, V.W. (1961), 'Ndembu divination: its symbolism and techniques' (*Rhodes-Livingstone Paper*, 31), Manchester University Press.

TURNER, V.W. (1966), 'Colour classification in Ndembu ritual', *Anthropological Approaches to the Study of Religion*, general editor M. Banton, ASA, 3, London.

WHORF, B.L. (1956), *Language, Thought and Reality, Selected Writings of Benjamin Lee Whorf*, ed. J.B. Carroll, Cambridge, Mass., Harvard University Press.

Chapter 9

The meaning of myth

First published as 'The meaning of myth with special reference to "La Geste d'Asdiwal"', in E. Leach (ed.) (1967), *The Structural Study of Myth and Totemism*, ASA, 5

Social anthropology, as we know it, was born of a professedly empirical approach. And it was first developed in Britain. These two marks, of being British and empirical, are not accidentally linked. This is the home of philosophical scepticism, an attitude of thought which has insulated us more effectively than the North Sea and the Channel from Continental movements of ideas. Our intellectual climate is plodding and anti-metaphysical. Yet, in spite of these traditions, we cannot read much of Lévi-Strauss without feeling some excitement. To social studies he holds out a promise of the sudden lift that new methods of science could give. He has developed his vision so elaborately and documented it so massively for so many fields of our subject that he commands our attention.

He has developed most explicitly in connection with myth his ideas of the place of sociology within a single grand discipline of Communication. This part of his teaching draws very broadly on the structural analysis of linguistics, and on cybernetics and communication theory in general, and to some extent on the related theory of games. Briefly, its starting-point is that it is the nature of the mind to work through form. Any experience is received in a structured form, and these forms or structures, which are a condition of knowing, are generally unconscious (as, for example, unconscious categories of language). Furthermore, they vary little in modern or in ancient times. They always consist in the creation of pairs of opposites, which are balanced against one another and built up in various (algebraically representable) ways. All the different kinds of patterned activity can be analysed according to the different structures they produce. For example, social life is a matter of interaction between persons. There are three different types of social communication. First, there is kinship, the structure underlying the rules for transferring women; second, there is the economy, that is the structure underlying transfer of goods and services; third, there is the underlying structure of language. The promise is that if we can get at these structures, display and compare them, the way is open for a true science of society, so far a will-o'-the-wisp for sociologists.

So far myth has not been mentioned. Lévi-Strauss recognises that its structures belong to a different level of mental activity from those of language, and the technique of analysis must be correspondingly different. The technique is described in his 'Structural study of myth' (1955) and is also made very clear in Edmund Leach's two articles (1961, 1962) in which he applies the technique to the Book of Genesis. It assumes that the analysis of myth should proceed like the analysis of language. In both language and myth the separate units have no meaning by themselves, they acquire it only because of the way in which they are combined. The best comparison is with musical notation: there is no musical meaning in a single isolated note. Describing the new science of mythologics which is to parallel linguistics, Lévi-Strauss unguardedly says that the units of mythological structure are sentences. If he took this statement seriously it would be an absurd limitation on analysis. But in fact, quite rightly, he abandons it at once, making great play with the structure underlying the meaning of a set of names. What are sentences, anyway? Linguists would be at a loss to identify these units of language structure which Lévi-Strauss claims to be able to put on punched cards and into a computing machine as surely and simply as if they were phonemes and morphemes. For me and for most of us, computer talk is a mysterious language very apt for prestidigitation. Does he really mean that he can chop a myth into semantic units, put them through a machine, and get out at the other end an underlying pattern which is not precisely the one he used for selecting his units? The quickness of the hand deceives the eye. Does he further believe that this underlying structure is the real meaning or sense of the myth? He says that it is the deepest kind of sense, more important than the uninitiated reader would suspect. However, I do not think it is fair to such an ebullient writer to take him literally. In other contexts it is plain that Lévi-Strauss realises that any myth has multiple meanings and that no one of them can be labelled the deepest or the truest. More of this later.

From the point of view of anthropology, one of his novel departures is to treat all versions of a myth as equally authentic or relevant. This is right, of course. Linguistic analysis can be applied to any literary unit, and the longer the better, so long as there is real unity underlying the stretches of language that are analysed together. Why stop short at one of Shakespeare's historical plays? Why not include the whole of Shakespeare? Or the whole of Elizabethan drama? Here Lévi-Strauss gives one of his disturbing twists of thought that make the plodding reader uneasily suspect that he is being duped. For by 'version' we find that Lévi-Strauss means both version and interpretation. He insists that Freud's treatment of the Oedipus myth must be put through the machine together with other earlier versions. This challenging idea is not merely for the fun of shocking the bourgeois mythologist out of his search for original versions. Freud used the Oedipus myth to stand for his own discovery that humans are each individually concerned with precisely the problem of 'birth from one' or 'birth from two' parents. On Lévi-Strauss's analysis of its structure, this problem is revealed as underlying the Oedipus cycle. So there is no inconsistency between Freud and Sophocles. But the reference to Freud interestingly vindicates Lévi-Strauss on a separate charge. Some must feel that the themes which his technique reveals are too trivial and childish either to have been worth the excavation, or to have been worth the erecting of an elaborate myth series in the first place. But after Freud no one can be sure that an individual's speculation about his own genesis is a trivial puzzle without emotional force.

I admit that the use of all interpretations of a great myth might not always so triumphantly vindicate this method. Meyer Fortes (1959) treated Oedipus rather differently in *Oedipus and Job in West Africa*. Compare St Augustine, Simone Weil (1950), and Edmund Leach (1962) on the Biblical story of Noah drunk in the vineyard: for one the drunken, naked Noah is Christ humiliated; for the other he is the Dionysian mysteries too austerely rejected by the Jewish priesthood, and for the last the tale is a trite lesson about Hebrew sexual morality. I will say more below of how these 'versions' would look coming out of the mythologic computer. At this stage of the discussion we should treat the computer as a red herring and forget for the moment the quest for the real meaning. We can then begin seriously to evaluate Lévi-Strauss's approach to mythology.

First, we should recognise his debt to the dialectical method of Hegelian–Marxist philosophy. The dialectic was Hegel's speculation about the nature of reality and about the logical technique by which it could be grasped. When Lévi-Strauss says that mythic thought follows a strict logic of its own, he means a Hegelian logic of thesis, antithesis, and synthesis, moving in ever more complex cycles to comprehend all the oppositions and limitations inherent in thought. According to Lévi-Strauss, the structure of myth is a dialectic structure in which opposed logical positions are stated, the oppositions mediated by a restatement, which again, when its internal structure becomes clear, gives rise to another kind of opposition, which in its turn is mediated or resolved, and so on.

On the assumption that it is the nature of myth to mediate contradictions, the method of analysis must proceed by distinguishing the oppositions and the mediating elements. And it follows, too, that the function of myth is to portray the contradictions in the basic premises of the culture. The same goes for the relation of myth to social reality. The myth is a contemplation of the un-satisfactory compromises which, after all, compose social life. In the devious statements of the myth, people can recognise indirectly what it would be difficult to admit openly and yet what is patently clear to all and sundry, that the ideal is not attainable.

Lévi-Strauss does not stick his neck out so far as to say that people are reconciled better or worse to their makeshift arrangements and contradictory formulae – but merely that myth makes explicit their experience of the contra-dictoriness of reality.

A summary of 'La Geste d'Asdiwal' best demonstrates how this is to be understood. It is a cycle of myths told by the Tsimshian tribes. These are a sparse population of migratory hunters and fishers who live on the Pacific coast, south of Alaska. They are culturally in the same group with Haida and Tlingit, northernmost representatives of Northwest Coast culture. Topographically their territory is dominated by the two parallel rivers, Nass and Skeena, which flow southwest to the sea. In the summer they live on vegetable products collected by women, and in winter on marine and land animals and fish killed by the men. The movements of fish and game dictate their seasonal movements between sea and mountains, and the northern and southern rivers. The Tsimshian were organised in dispersed matrilineal clans and lived in typical Northwest Coast composite dwellings which housed several families. They tended to live with their close maternal kin, generally practising avunculocal residence at marriage and the ideal was to marry a mother's brother's daughter.

The myth begins during the winter famine in the Skeena valley. A mother and daughter, separated hitherto by their marriages but now both widowed by the famine, set out from east and west, one from upstream and one from downstream of the frozen Skeena, to meet each other half-way. The daughter becomes the wife of a mysterious bird who feeds them both and when she gives birth to a miraculous child, Asdiwal, its bird father gives him a magic bow and arrow, lance, snow-shoes, cloak, and hat which make him invisible at will, invincible, and able to produce an inexhaustible supply of food. The old mother dies and the bird father disappears. Asdiwal and his mother walk west to her natal village. From there he follows a white bear into the sky where it is revealed as Evening-Star, the daughter of the Sun. When Asdiwal has succeeded, thanks to his magic equipment, in a series of impossible tasks, the Sun allows him to marry Evening-Star, and, because he is homesick, to take his wife back to the earth generously supplied with magic food. On earth, because Asdiwal is unfaithful to her, his sky wife leaves him. He follows her half-way to the sky, where she kills him with a thunderbolt. His father-in-law, the Sun, brings him to life and they live together in the sky until Asdiwal feels homesick again. Once home, Asdiwal finds his mother is dead and, since nothing keeps him in her village, he continues walking to the west. This time he makes a Tsimshian marriage, which starts off well, Asdiwal using his magic hunting-weapons to good effect. In the spring he, his wife, and her four brothers move along the coast northwards, towards the River Nass, but Asdiwal challenges his brothers-in-law to prove that their sea-hunting is better than his land-hunting. Asdiwal wins the contest by bringing home four dead bears from his mountain hunt, one for each of the four brothers, who return empty handed from their sea expedition. Furious at their defeat, they carry off their sister and abandon Asdiwal, who then joins some strangers also going north towards the Nass for the candlefish season. Once again, there are four brothers, and a sister whom Asdiwal marries. After a good fishing season, Asdiwal returns with his in-laws and wife to their village, where his wife bears them a son. One day, however, he boasts that he is better than his brothers-in-law at walrus-hunting. Put to the test, he succeeds brilliantly, again infuriating his wife's brothers, who abandon him without food or fire to die on a rocky reef. His bird father preserves him through a raging storm. Finally, he is taken by a mouse to the underground home of the walruses whom he has wounded. Asdiwal cures them and asks in exchange a safe return. The King of the Walruses lends Asdiwal his stomach as a boat, on which he sails home. There he finds his faithful wife, who helps him to kill her own brothers. But again Asdiwal, assailed by homesickness, leaves his wife and returns to the Skeena valley, where his son joins him. When winter comes, Asdiwal goes hunting in the mountains, but forgetting his snow-shoes, can go neither up nor down and is changed into stone.

This is the end of the story. In the analysis which follows, Lévi-Strauss draws out the remarkably complex symmetry of different levels of structure. Asdiwal's journeys take him from east to west, then north to the Nass, then southwest to the sea fishing of walrus, and finally southeast back to the Skeena River. So the points of the compass and the salient points of order of Tsimshian migration are laid out. This is the geographical sequence. There is another sequence concerned with residence at marriage, as follows.

The two women who open the tale have been separated by the daughter's virilocal residence at marriage. Living together, they set up what Lévi-Strauss calls a 'matrilocal residence of the simplest kind, mother and daughter'. Lévi-Strauss counts the first marriage of the bird father of Asdiwal as matrilocal. Then the sky marriage of Asdiwal himself with Evening-Star is counted as matrilocal, and matrilocal again the two human marriages of Asdiwal, until after has has come back from the walrus kingdom, when his wife betrays her brothers. So, Lévi-Strauss remarks that all the marriages of Asdiwal are matrilocal until the end. Then the regular pattern is inverted and 'patrilocalism triumphs' because Asdiwal abandons his wife and goes home, accompanied by his son. The story starts with the reunion of a mother and daughter, liberated from their spouses (and paternal kin in the case of the daughter), and ends with the reunion of a father and son, liberated from their spouses (and maternal kin in the case of the son). To the English anthropologist some of this symmetry and inversion seems rather far-fetched. The evidence for counting the bird marriage as matrilocal is dubious and the sky marriage is plain groom service. The rejection of the third wife is hardly 'patrilocalism'. But more about inversion below. I want to go into details of another sociological sequence which produces two more pairs of oppositions which are also inverted at the end.

The same symmetry is traced in the cosmological sequence. First, the hero sojourns in the sky where he is wounded and cured by the sky people; then he makes an underground sojourn where he finds underground people whom *he* has wounded, and whom *he* cures. There is a similar elaboration of recurring themes of famine and plenty. They correspond faithfully enough to the economic reality of Tsimshian life. Using his knowledge of another myth of the region, Lévi-Strauss explains their implication. The Northwest Coast

Indians attribute the present condition of the world to the disturbances made by a great Crow, whose voracious appetite initiated all the processes of creation. So hunger is the condition of movement, glut is a static condition. The first phase of the Asdiwal tale opposes Sky and Earth, the Sun and the earthly human. These oppositions the hero overcomes, thanks to his bird father. But Asdiwal breaks the harmony established between these elements: first he feels homesick, then, once at home, he betrays his sky wife for a terrestrial girl, and then, in the sky, he feels homesick again. Thus the whole sky episode ends on a negative position. In the second phase, when Asdiwal makes his first human marriage, a new set of oppositions are released: mountain-hunting and sea-hunting; land and sea.

Asdiwal wins the contest as a land-hunter, and in consequence is abandoned by his wife's brothers. Next time Asdiwal's marriage allies him with island-dwellers, and the same conflict between land and sea takes place, this time on the sea in a boat, which Asdiwal has to leave in the final stage of the hunt in order to climb onto the reef of rock. Taken together, these two phases can be broken down into a series of unsuccessful mediations between opposites arranged on an ever-diminishing scale: above and below, water and earth, maritime hunting and mountain-hunting. In the sea hunt the gap is almost closed between sea- and mountain-hunting, since Asdiwal succeeds where his brothers-in-law fail beacause he clambers onto the rock. The technique by which the oppositions are reduced is by paradox and reversal: the great mountain-hunter nearly dies on a little half-submerged rock: the great killer of bears is rescued by a little mouse; the slayer of animals now cures them; and, most paradoxical of all, the great provider of food himself has provender become – since he goes home in the stomach of a walrus. In the final dénouement, Asdiwal, once more a hunter in the mountains, is immobilised when he is neither up nor down, and is changed to stone, the most extreme possible expression of his earthly nature.

Some have doubted that myths can have an elaborate symmetrical structure. If so, they should be convinced of their error.

Lévi-Strauss's analysis slowly and intricately reveals the internal structure of this myth. Although I have suggested that the symmetry has here and there been pushed too hard, the structure is indisputably there, in the material and not merely in the eye of the beholder. I am not sure who would have argued to the contrary, but myths must henceforth be conceded to have a structure as recognisable as that of a poem or a tune.

But Lévi-Strauss is not content with revealing structure for its own sake. Structural analysis has long been a respectable tool of literary criticism and Lévi-Strauss is not interested in a mere literary exercise.

He wants to use myth to demonstrate that structural analysis has socio-logical value. So instead of going on to analyse and compare formal myth structures, he asks what is the relation of myth to life. His answer in a word is 'dialectical'. Not only is the nature of reality dialectical, and the structure of any myth dialectical, but the relation of the first to the second is dialectical too.

This could mean that there is a feedback between the worlds of mythical and social discourse – a statement in the myth sets off a response which modifies the social universe, which itself then touches off a new response in the realm of myth, and so on. Elsewhere, Lévi-Strauss (1962: 283–4) has shown that this complex interaction is indeed how he sees the relation between symbolic thought and social reality. And he even attempts to demonstrate with a single example how this interaction takes place (1963b; cf. 1962, ch. IV). But in his analysis of myth itself he leaves out this meaning of dialectic. This is a pity, but perhaps inevitable because there is so little historical information about the tribes in question, and still less about the dating of different versions of the myth.

Rather, he develops the idea that myth expresses a social dialectic. It states the salient social contradictions, restates them in more and more modified fashion, until in the final statement the contradictions are resolved, or so modified and masked as to be minimised. According to Lévi-Strauss, the real burden of the whole Asdiwal myth and the one burning issue to which all the antinomies of sky and earth, land and sea, etc., are assimilated, is the contra-diction implicit in patrilocal, matrilateral cross-cousin marriage. This comes as a surprise, since there has never been any mention whatever of matrilateral cross-cousin marriage in the myth of Asdiwal. But the Asdiwal story has a sequel. His son, Waux, grows up with his maternal kin, and his mother arranges for him to marry a cousin. He inherits his father's magic weapons and becomes, like him, a great hunter. One day he goes out hunting, having forgotten his magic spear which enables him to split rocks and open paths through the mountains. There is an earthquake. Waux sees his wife in the valley and shouts to her to make a sacrifice of fat to appease the supernatural powers. But his wife gets it wrong and thinks he is telling her to eat the fat, on which she proceeds to stuff herself until, gorged, she bursts and turns into a rock. Waux, now without either his father's spear or his wife's help, also turns into stone. With this story the Asdiwal cycle is completed. Waux's wife dies of glut, thus reversing the opening gambit in which Asdiwal's mother is started on her journey by a famine. So the movement set going by famine ends in the immobility of fullness. Asdiwal's marriages were all with strangers, Waux makes the approved Tsimshian marriage with his maternal cousin, but she ends by ruining him; the myth makes thus the comment that matrilateral cross-cousin marriage is nothing but a feeble pallia-tive for the social ills it seeks to cure.

Lévi-Strauss points out that the Tsimshian, along with other Northwest Coast cultures, do not benefit from the equilibrium which cross-cousin marriage could produce for them in the form of a fixed hierarchy of wife-givers and wife-receivers. They have chosen instead to be free to revise their whole system of ranking at each marriage and potlatch. So they are committed to deep-seated disequilibrium. Following Rodney Needham (1962), one suspects that this far-fetched reference to Lévi-Strauss's theory of elementary structures of kinship is misplaced. There is no reason to suppose that matrilateral cross-cousin marriage among the Tsimshian is prescribed. However, in reaching these basic antagonisms of social structure, Lévi-Strauss feels he has got to the rock bottom of the myth's meaning (1958a: 27, 28).

> All the paradoxes . . . geographic, economic, sociological, and even cosmo-
> logical, are, when all is said and done, assimilated to that less obvious yet so
> real paradox which marriage with the matrilateral cousin attempts but fails
> to resolve . . .

A great deal of this myth certainly centres on marriage, though very little on the cross-cousin marriage which is preferred. Lévi-Strauss says that the whole myth's burden is a negative comment on social reality. By examining all the possibilities in marriage and showng every extreme position to be untenable, it has as its core message to reconcile the Tsimshian to their usual compromises by showing that any other solution they attempt is equally beset with difficulty. But as I have said, we cannot allow Lévi-Strauss to claim the real meaning of such a complex and rich myth. His analysis is far from exhaustive. Furthermore, there are other themes which are positive, not negative, as regards social reality.

In the first place, this area of Northwest Coast culture combines a very elaborate and strict division of labour between the sexes with a strong expression of male dominance. The myth could well be interpreted as playing on the paradox of male dominance and male dependence on female help. The first hero, Asdiwal, shows his independence of womankind by betraying his first wife. He is betrayed by his second wife, abandons his third wife, but in the sequel his son, Waux, dies because of his wife's stupidity and greed – so the general effect is that women are necessary but inferior beings, and men are superior. Surely this is a positive comment?

In the second place, the potlatch too is built on a paradox that the receiver of gifts is an enemy. One-up-manship, in potlatch terms, brings success, rank, and followers, but two-up-manship inflicts defeat on the opponent and creates hostility. Asdiwal went too far when he brought four huge bears down from the mountain to confront his empty-handed brothers-in-law. Here again, the myth is positive and true to life, so no wonder they abandoned him. The ambivalent attitude in Northwest Coast culture to the successful shaman is a third theme that can plausibly be detected in the myth. Great shamans are always victims of jealousy. Asdiwal, the great shaman, is abandoned. So the myth is plain and simply true to life.

I feel that we are being asked to suspend our critical faculties if we are to believe that this myth mirrors the reverse of reality. I shall return again to give a closer look at the social realities of Tsimshian life.

The ideas of reversal and of inversion figure prominently in Lévi-Strauss's argument. First, he suggests that the myth is the reverse of reality in the country of its origin. Then he has formulated a curious law according to which a myth turns upside down (in relation to its normal position) at a certain distance from its place of origin. These are both developed in the Asdiwal analysis. Third, a myth which appears to have no counterpart in the ritual of the tribe in which it is told is found to be an inversion of the rites of another tribe (cf. Lévi-Strauss, 1956). On this subject the stolid English suspicion of cleverness begins to crystallise.

If ever one could suspect a scholar of trailing his coat with his tongue in his cheek, one would suspect this law of myth-inversion. The metaphor is borrowed from optics, without any explanation of why the same process should be observed in the unrelated science of mythics (Lévi-Strauss, 1956: 42):

> When a mythical schema is transmitted from one population to another, and there exist difference of language, social organization or way of life which makes the myth difficult to communicate, it begins to become impoverished or confused. But one can find a limiting situation in which, instead of being finally obliterated by losing all its outlines, the myth is inverted and regains part of its precision.

So we must expect that exported myths will give a negative or upside-down picture of what the original myth portrayed. Is the scholar being ingenuous, or disingenuous? He must recognise that opposition is a pliable concept in the interpreter's hands. The whole notion of dialectic rests on the assumption that opposition can be unequivocally recognised. But this is an unwarranted assumption, as appears from a critical reading of his treatment of a Pawnee myth (Lévi-Strauss, 1956).

To demonstrate the relation of myth to rite he takes the Pawnee myth of the pregnant boy. An ignorant young boy suddenly finds he has magical powers of healing and the makings of a great shaman. An old-established shaman, always accompanied by his wife, tries to winkle his secret from him. He fails, since there is no secret learning to transmit, and then ensorcells the boy. As a result of the sorcery the boy becomes pregnant, and goes in shame and confusion to die among wild beasts. But the beasts cure him and he returns with even greater power, and kills his enemy. The analysis distinguishes at least three sets of oppositions.

Shamanistic powers through initiation : without initiation
child : old man
confusion of sex : distinction of sex

Lévi-Strauss then invites us to consider what rite this Pawnee myth corresponds to. His problem, which seems very artificial, is that there is at first sight no correlated rite. The myth underlines the opposition of the generations, and yet the Pawnee do not oppose their generations: they do not base their cult associations on age-classes, and entry to their cult societies is not by ordeals or by fee; a teacher trains his pupil to succeed him on his death. But, as he puts it, all the elements of the myth fall into place confronted with the symmetrical and opposite ritual of the neighbouring Plains Indian tribes. Here the shamanistic societies are the inverse of those of the Pawnee, since entry is by payment and organisation is by age. The sponsor and his sponsored candidate for entry are treated as if in a father–son relation, the candidate is accompanied by his wife, whom he offers for ritual intercourse to his sponsor. 'Here we find again all the oppositions which have been analysed on the plane of the myth, with inversion of all the values attributed to each couple.' The initiated and un-initiated are as father to son, instead of as enemies; the uninitiated knows less than the initiated, whereas in the myth he is the better shaman; in the ritual of the Plains Societies it is the youth who is accompanied by his wife, while in the myth it is the old man. 'The semantic values are the same but changed in relation to the symbols which sustain them. The Pawnee myth exposes a ritual system which is the inverse, not of that prevailing in this tribe, but of a system which does not apply here, and which belongs to related tribes whose ritual organisation is the exact opposite.'

Mere difference is made to qualify as opposition. Some of the oppositions which Lévi-Strauss detects in myth are undeniably part of the artistic structure. But opposition can be imposed on any material by the interpreter. Here we have an unguarded example of the latter process. To me it seems highly implausible that we can affirm any opposition worthy of the name between cult organisation with age-grading and entrance fees, and cult organisation by apprenticeship without age-grading. Old male with wife versus young man without wife, and with confusion of sex, these seem equally contrived as oppositions. If the alleged oppositions are not above challenge, the whole demonstration of inversion falls to the ground.

Here we should turn to the relation of myth to literature in general. Lévi-Strauss recognises that a myth is 'a work of art arousing deep aesthetic emotion' (Jakobson and Lévi-Strauss, 1962: 5). But he strenuously rejects the idea that myth is a kind of primitive poetry (Lévi-Strauss, 1963a: 210).

> Myth [he says] should be placed in the gamut of linguistic expressions at the end opposite to that of poetry. . . . Poetry is a kind of speech which cannot be translated except at the cost of serious distortions; whereas the mythical value of the myth is preserved even through the worst translation.

He goes on in terms more emotional than scientific to declare that anyone can recognise the mythic quality of myth. Why does he want so vigorously to detach myth criticism from literary criticism? It is on the literary plane that we have his best contribution to the subject of mythology. He himself wrote a splendid vindication of his own technique of literary analysis by working it out with Jakobson on a sonnet of Baudelaire (Jakobson and Lévi-Strauss, 1962). This essay is an exercise in what T.S. Eliot calls 'the lemon-squeezer school of criticism, in which the critics take a poem to pieces, stanza by stanza, line by line, and extract, squeeze, tease, press every drop of meaning out of it' (Eliot, 1957: 112). After reading the analysis, we perceive the poem's unity, economy, and completeness, and its tremendous range of implication.

When the lemon-squeezer technique is applied to poetry it has a high rate of extraction and the meaning flows out in rich cupfuls. Furthermore, what is extracted is not a surprise – we can see that it was there all the time. Unfortunately, something goes wrong when the technique is applied to myth: the machine seems to spring a leak. Instead of more and richer depths of understanding, we get a surprise, a totally new theme, and often a paltry one at that. All the majestic themes which we had previously thought the Oedipus myth was about – destiny, duty, and self-knowledge – have been strained off, and we are left with a worry about how the species began. When Edmund Leach applies the same technique to the Book of Genesis, the rich metaphysical themes of salvation and cosmic oneness are replaced by practical rules for the regulation of sex. When Lévi-Strauss has finished with the Tsimshian myth it is reduced to anxieties about problems of matrilateral cross-cousin marriage (which anyway only apply to the heirs of chiefs and headmen). It seems that whenever anthropologists apply structural analysis to myth they extract not only a different but a lesser meaning. The reasons for this reductionism are important. First, there is the computer analogy, for the sake of which Lévi-Strauss commits himself to treating the structural units of myth as if they were unambiguous. This takes us back to the basic difference between words and phonemes. The best words are ambiguous, and the more richly ambiguous the more suitable for the poet's or the myth-maker's job. Hence there is no end to the number of meanings which can be read into a good myth. When dealing with poetry, Lévi-Strauss gives full value to the rich ambiguity of the words. When dealing with myth he suggests that their meaning is clear cut, lending itself to being chopped into objectively recognisable, precisely defined units. It is partly in this process of semantic chopping that so much of the meaning of myth gets lost.

But there is another reason, more central to the whole programme. There are two possible objectives in analysing a piece of discourse.[1] One is to analyse the particular discourse itself, to analyse what has been said. The other is to analyse the language, seen as the instrument of what is said. No reason has so far been given to suppose that the structure of discourse is necessarily similar to that of language. But there is reason to point out that if the language analogy is adopted, research will look for a similar structure, a logic of correlations, oppositions, and differences (Ricoeur, 1963). We can say that the first kind of analysis, of what has been said in a discourse, aims at discovering a particular structure. This is what the literary critics do and what Jakobson and Lévi-Strauss did in 'Les Chats', and what Lévi-Strauss in practice does most of the time. This kind of analysis is not intended to yield a compressed statement of the theme. It is not reductionist in any sense. The other kind of analysis discovers a formal or general structure which is not particular to any given stretch of language. For instance, the alexandrine or the sonnet form is not particular to a given poem, and to know that a particular poem has been written in sonnet form tells you nothing about what that poem is about. In the same way, a grammatical structure is formal. A book of grammar gives the conditions under which communication of a certain kind can take place. It does not give a communication.

Lévi-Strauss claims to be revealing the formal structures of myths. But he can never put aside his interest in what the myth discourse is about. He seems to think that if he had the formal structure it would look not so much like a grammar book as like a summary of the themes which analysing the particular structure of a myth cycle has produced. Hence the reductionist tendency is built into his type of myth analysis. He falls into the trap of claiming to discover the real underlying meanings of myths because he never separates the particular artistic structure of a particular set of myths from their general or purely formal structure. Just as knowing that the rhyme structure is a, b, b, a, does not tell us anything about the content of a sonnet, so the formal structure of a myth would not help very much in interpreting it. Lévi-Strauss (1957) comes very near this when he says that the structural analysis of a Pawnee myth consists of a dialectical balancing of the themes of life and death. It might have been better to have said that it was a balanced structure of pluses and minuses, or of positives and negatives. If he had actually used algebra to present the pattern he discerned, then Edmund Leach might have been less tempted to speculate on the similarity of mythic themes all over the world. He himself had found a structure of pluses and minuses in the Garden of Eden myth (1961) and remarked that the recurrence of these themes of death versus life, procreation versus vegetable reproduction, have the greatest psychological and sociological significance. But I think that their significance is that of verb/noun relations in language. Their presence signifies the possibility of finding in them formal structures. But they are not the formal myth structures that we have been promised. These can hardly be knowable in ordinary language. If they are to be discovered special terms will have to be invented for recording them, comparable to the highly specialised terminology of grammar. To say simply that myth structures are built of oppositions and mediations is not to say what the structures are. It is simply to say that there are structures.

I will return later to the question of whether these formal myth structures are likely to be important for sociology. At this stage of publication (though three new volumes are in the press), Lévi-Strauss has not succeeded in revealing them. I should therefore do better to concentrate on the particular artistic structures he has revealed.

The meaning of a myth is partly the sense that the author intended it to convey, and the sense intended by each of its recounters. But every listener can find in it references to his own experience, so the myth can be enlightening, consoling, depressing, irrespective of the intentions of the tellers. Part of the anthropologist's task is to understand enough of the background of the myth to be able to construct its range of reference for its native hearers. To this

Lévi-Strauss applies himself energetically, as for example when he finds that the myth of the creative Great Crow illustrates the themes of hunger and plenty in Tsimshian life.

From a study of any work of art we can infer to some extent the conditions under which it was made. The maidservant who said of St Peter, 'His speech betrays him as a Galilean', was inferring from his dialect; similarly the critic who used computer analysis to show that the same author did not write all the epistles attributed to St Paul. This kind of information is like that to be obtained from analysing the track of an animal or the finger-prints of a thief. The anthropologist studying tribal myths can do a job of criticism very like that of art critics who decide what 'attribution' to give to a painting or to figures in a painting. Lévi-Strauss, after minute analysis of the Asdiwal myth, could come forward and, like a good antiquarian, affirm that it is a real, genuine Tsimshian article. He can guarantee that it is an authentic piece of Northwest Coast mythology. His analysis of the structure of the myth can show that it draws fully on the premises of Tsimshian culture.

Inferences, of course, can also be made within the culture; the native listener can infer a moral, and indeed myths are one of the ways in which cultural values are transmitted. Structural analysis can reveal unsuspected depths of reference and inference meaning for any particular series of myths. In order to squeeze this significance out, the anthropologist must apply his prior knowledge of the culture to his analysis. He uses inference the other way round, from the known culture to the interpretation of the obscure myth. This is how he discerns the elements of structure. All would agree that this is a worthwhile task. But in order to analyse particular structures, he has to know his culture well first.

At this stage we should like to be able to judge how well Lévi-Strauss knows the social reality of the Tsimshian. Alas, very little is known about this tribe. He has to make do with very poor ethnographic materials. There are several minor doubts one can entertain about his interpretation of the facts, but the information here is altogether very thin. A critic of Lévi-Strauss (Ricoeur) has been struck by the fact that all his examples of mythic thought have been taken from the geographical areas of totemism and never from Semitic, pre-Hellenic, or Indo-European areas, whence our own culture arose. Lévi-Strauss would have it that his examples are typical of a certain kind of thought, a type in which the arrangement of items of culture is more important and more stable than the content. Ricoeur asks whether the totemic cultures are not so much typical as selected, extreme types? This is a very central question which every anthropologist has to face. Is *La Pensée sauvage* as revealed by myth and rite analysis typical, or peculiar, or is it an illusion produced by the method? Here we are bound to mention Lévi-Strauss's idea of mythic thinking as *bricolage*. The *bricoleur*, for whom we have no word, is a craftsman who works with material that has not been produced for the task he has in hand. I am tempted to see him as an Emmett engineer whose products always look alike whether they are bridges, stoves, or trains, because they are always composed of odd pieces of drainpipe and string, with the bells and chains and bits of Gothic railing arranged in a similar crazy way. In practice this would be a wrong illustration of *bricolage*. Lévi-Strauss himself is the real Emmett engineer because he changes his rules as he goes along. For mythic thought a card-player could be a better analogy, because Emmett can use his bits how he likes, whereas the *bricolage* type of culture is limited by pattern-restricting rules. Its units are like a pack of cards continually shuffled for the same game. The rules of the game would correspond to the general structure underlying the myths. If all that the myths and rites do is to arrange and rearrange the elements of the culture, then structural analysis would be exhaustive, and for that reason very important.

At the outset of any scientific enterprise, a worker must know the limitations of his method. Linguistics and any analysis modelled on linguistics can only be synchronic sciences. They analyse systems. Insofar as they can be diachronic it is in analysing the before-and-after evolution of systems. Their techniques can be applied to any behaviour that is systematic. But if the behaviour is not very systematic, they will extract whatever amount of regularity there is, and leave a residue. Edmund Leach has shown that the techniques of Lévi-Strauss can be applied to early Greek myths, to Buddhist, and to Israelite myths. But I suppose he would never claim that the analysis is exhaustive. In the case of his analysis of Genesis, I have already mentioned above that the residue is the greater part.

Lévi-Strauss in his publication so far seems blithely unconscious that his instrument can produce only one kind of tune. More aware of the limitations of his analysis, he would have to restrict what he says about the attitude of mythic thought to time, past and future. Structural analysis cannot but reveal myths as timeless, as synchronic structures outside time. From this bias built into the method there are two consequences. First, we cannot deduce anything whatever from it about the attitudes to time prevailing in the cultures in question. Our method reduces all to synchrony. Everything which Lévi-Strauss writes in *La Pensée sauvage* about time in certain cultures or at a certain level of thinking, should be rephrased to apply only to the method he uses. Second, if myths have got an irreversible order and if this is significant, this part of their meaning will escape the analysis. This, as Ricoeur points out, is why the culture of the Old Testament does not fit into the *briocolage* category.

We know a lot about the Israelites and about the Jews and Christians who tell and retell these stories.[2] We know little about the Australian aborigines and about the no longer surviving American Indian tribes. Would this be the anthropologist's frankest answer to Ricoeur? We cannot say whether the *bricolage* level of thought is an extreme type or what it is typical of, for lack of sufficient supporting data about the examples. But we must say that the *bricolage* effect is produced by the method of analysis. For a final judgment, then, we can only wait for a perfect experiment. For this, richly abundant mythical material should be analysed against a known background of equally rich ethnographic records. We can then see how exhaustive the structural analysis can be and also how relevant its formulas are to the understanding of the culture.

NOTES

1 In what follows I am indebted to Professor Cyril Barrett, S.J. for criticism.
2 Edmund Leach makes the following point in an editorial note: Lévi-Strauss's own justification for *not* applying his method to Biblical materials seems to rest on the proposition that we do not know enough about the ancient Israelites! See *Esprit*, November 1963, p. 632 but cf. Leach (1966) *passim*.

BIBLIOGRAPHY

ELIOT, T.S. (1957), *On Poetry and Poets*, London, Faber & Faber.

FORTES, M. (1959), *Oedipus and Job in West African Religion*, Cambridge University Press.

JAKOBSON, R. and LÉVI-STRAUSS, C. (1962), '"Les Chats" de Charles Baudelaire', *L'Homme*, 2, 5–21.

LEACH, E.R. (1961), 'Lévi-Strauss in the Garden of Eden: an examination of some recent developments in the analysis of myth', *Transactions of the New York Academy of Sciences*, series 2, 386–96.

LEACH, E.R. (1962), 'Genesis as myth', *Discovery*, May, 30–5.

LEACH, E.R. (1966), 'The legitimacy of Solomon: some structural aspects of Old Testament history', *European Journal of Sociology*, 7, 58–101.

LÉVI-STRAUSS, C. (1955), 'The structural study of myth', *Journal of American Folklore*, 28, 428–44. Reprinted with modifications in Lévi-Strauss (1963a).

LÉVI-STRAUSS, C. (1956), 'Structure et dialectique', in *For Roman Jakobson on the Occasion of his Sixtieth Birthday*, The Hague, Mouton. Reprinted in Lévi-Strauss (1963a).

LÉVI-STRAUSS, C. (1957), 'Le symbolisme cosmique dans la structure sociale et l'organisation cérémonielle des tribus americaines', *Serie Orientale Roma*, *XIV*, Institut pour l'Étude de l'Orient et de l'Extrême-Orient, Rome, pp. 47–56.

LÉVI-STRAUSS, C. (1958a), 'La Geste d'Asdiwal', *École Pratique des Sciences Religieuses*. Extr. Annuaire 1958–9: 3–43. Reprinted in *Les Temps modernes*, March 1961.

LÉVI-STRAUSS, C. (1958b), *Anthropologie structurale*, Paris, Plon. (English translation, 1963a, *Structural Anthropology*, New York: Basic Books.)

LÉVI-STRAUSS, C. (1962), *La Pensée sauvage*, Paris, Plon.

LÉVI-STRAUSS, C. (1963a), *Structural Anthropology*, New York: Basic Books.

LÉVI-STRAUSS, C. (1963b), 'The bear and the barber', *Journal of the Royal Anthropological Institute*, *93*, part I: 1-11.

NEEDHAM, R. (1962), *Structure and Sentiment*, University of Chicago Press.

RICOEUR, P. (1963), 'Structure et herméneutique', *Esprit*, November, 598–625.

WEIL, S. (1950), *Attente de Dieu*, Paris, La Colombe.

Chapter 10

Jokes

First published as 'The social control of cognition: Some factors in joke perception', *Man*, 5, 2 (1970)

Anthropologists tend to approach ritual joking from scratch, with merely an introspective glance at the cases in which they themselves feel impelled to joke. Consequently they have treated joking rituals as if they arise spontaneously from social situations and as if the anthropologist's sole task is to classify the relations involved. The jokes have not been considered as jokes in themselves, nor has our own cultural tradition been applied to interpreting the joke situation. Certain new trends invite us now to make a more open approach. Anthropology has moved from the simple analysis of social structures current in the 1940s to the structural analysis of thought systems. One of the central problems now is the relation between categories of thought and categories of social experience. Joking as one mode of expression has yet to be interpreted in its total relation to other modes of expression.

Such an approach suggests that the alternatives of joking and of not joking would be susceptible to the kind of structural analysis which Leach (1961: 23) has applied to controlled and uncontrolled modes of mystical power. His original model for this was the linguistic patterning of voiced and unvoiced consonants; his sole concern to show that the contrasts were used in regular patterns. It was not relevant to his argument to ask whether the patterning of contrasted elements in the system of communication was arbitrary or not. But it is possible that the patterning of articulate and less articulate sounds corresponds to a similar patterning in the experiences which they are used to express. This question raises the general problem of the relation between symbolic systems and experience. It is true that in language the process of symbolic differentiation may start with arbitrarily selected elements at the simple phonemic level and combine them into consistent patterns. But at more complex levels each sign carries into the patterning an ever richer load of association. To return to Leach's case of modes of mystical power, I have elsewhere argued (Douglas, 1966: 101–3) that the discrimination of articulate and inarticulate forms of mystical power is not arbitrary. The use of spell and rite is attributed to people occupying articulate areas of the social structure, the use of unconscious psychic powers to others in inarticulate areas. There is a play upon articulateness and its absence, both in the kinds of mystic power being wielded and in the areas of the social structure to which they are allocated. The same appropriateness of symbolic forms to the situations they express can be illustrated with ritual joking. I am confident that where the joke rite is highly elaborated, joking is not used merely diacritically to contrast with seriousness, but that the full human experience of the joke is exploited. If we could be clear about the nature of joking, we could approach the interpretation of the joke rite at a more profound level than hitherto.

Fortunately, a new, more general trend enables this generation to make a fresh approach to joke rites. At the turn of the century when European thought turned an analytic eye upon humour, anthropologists were either antiquarians or specialists, or both. It would not have been in the tradition to look to recent thinkers for illumination. When Radcliffe-Brown wrote on joking relations in the 1940s (Radcliffe-Brown, 1940, 1949) it was still natural that he should not have taken account of Bergson or Freud. Still less would he have turned to the surrealist movement, whose passionate frivolity would estrange one who wished above all to establish the scientific status of his subject. He therefore wrote on the subject of joking in a very desiccated perspective. But there is a great difference in the form in which Freud's ideas are now available to the ordinary public. For us, thanks largely to the surrealists, it is not possible to read new fiction, to go to the theatre, to read the catalogue of any exhibition of painting or sculpture without taking note of an attitude which derives from the thinkers of the beginning of this century. Awareness of the contrast between form and formlessness, and awareness of the subjective character of the categories in which experience is structured have become the cultural premises of our age. They are no longer erudite preoccupations of the learned, but get expressed at an entirely popular level. Continual experimentation with form has given us now an intuitive sympathy for symbolic behaviour which is, after all, a play upon form. What is implicit in some other cultures has become an implicit part of our own. At the same time we can also bring to bear a tradition of explicit analysis. Thus we can have insights at the two levels necessary for understanding joking.

African joking institutions combine the following elements: first, a crude scatology; second, a range of specific relationships; and third, certain ritual occasions (namely funerals and purifications) expressed scatologically. The subject is therefore closely related to ritual pollution in general. I myself am drawn to it because I hope that it will prove possible to distinguish jokes from pollutions by analysing some aspects of humour. This is a task which I shirked in my essay on ritual pollution (1966).

As a key question in this exercise I take Griaule's controversy with Radcliffe-Brown about the whole status of so-called 'joking relationships'. According to Griaule (1948), the Dogon joking partners do not exchange witticisms but rather gross insults. Although Dogon find these exchanges very hilarious, Griaule found it arbitrary to fasten on the laughter-provoking aspect of a complex institution. Now what is the difference between an insult and a joke? When does a joke get beyond a joke? Is the perception of a joke culturally determined so that the anthropologist must take it on trust when a joke has been made? Is no general culture-free analysis of joking possible? When people throw excrement at one another whenever they meet, either verbally or actually, can this be interpreted as a case of wit, or merely written down as a case of throwing excrement? This is the central problem of all interpretation.

First, let me bracket aside the whole subject of laughter. It would be wrong to suppose that the acid test of a joke is whether it provokes laughter or not. It is not necessary to go into the physiology and psychology of laughter, since it is generally recognised that one can appreciate a joke without actually laughing, and one can laugh for other reasons than from having perceived a joke. As the two experiences are not completely congruent, I shall only touch on laughter incidentally. Here I am following Bergson, whose essay on laughter was first published in 1899 in the *Revue de Paris*, and Freud (1916), whose analysis of wit, first published in 1905, says very little about laughter.

Both Bergson and Freud assume that it is possible to identify a structure of ideas characteristic of humour. If this were a valid assumption, all that would be necessary here would be to identify this joke form in the African joke rite. But in practice, it is a very elusive form to nail down. We face the dilemma either of finding that all utterances are capable of being jokes, or that many of those which pass for jokes in Africa do not conform to the laid-down requirements. My argument will be that the joke form rarely lies in the utterance alone, but that it can be identified in the total social situation.

Bergson and Freud are in fact very close: the difference between them lies in the different place of joke analysis in their respective philosophies. Bergson's reflections on laughter are a distillation of his general philosophy on the nature of man. He takes humour as a field in which to demonstrate the superiority of intuition to logic, of life to mechanism. It is part of his general protest against the threatened mechanisation of humanity. According to Bergson the essence of man is spontaneity and freedom: laughter asserts this by erupting whenever a man behaves in a rigid way, like an automaton no longer under intelligent control. 'Humour consists in perceiving something mechanical encrusted on something living' (1950: 29). It is funny when persons behave as if they were inanimate things. So a person caught in a repetitive routine, such as stammering or dancing after the music has stopped, is funny. Frozen posture, too rigid dignity, irrelevant mannerism, the noble pose interrupted by urgent physical needs, all are funny for the same reason. Humour chastises insincerity, pomposity, stupidity.

This analysis is adequate for a vast number of funny situations and jokes. There is no denying that it covers the style of much African joking, the grotesque tricks of Lodagaba funeral partners (Goody, 1962) and the obscene insults of Dogon and Bozo joking partners (Griaule, 1948). But I find it inadequate for two reasons. First, it imports a moral judgment into the analysis. For Bergson the joke is always a chastisement: something 'bad', mechanical, rigid, encrusted is attacked by something 'good', spontaneous, instinctive. I am not convinced either that there is any moral judgment, or that if there is one, it always works in this direction. Second, Bergson includes too much. It is not always humorous to recognise 'something encrusted on something living': it is more usually sinister, as the whole trend of Bergson's philosophy asserts. Bergson's approach to humour does not allow for punning or for the more complex forms of wit in which two forms of life are confronted without judgment being passed on either. For example, Bemba joking partners (Richards, 1937) exchange elaborate references to the relationship between their clan totems; members of the Crocodile clan, for instance, point out to members of the Fish clan that fishes are food for crocodiles, but the latter riposte that crocodiles are therefore dependent on fishes. These are jokes which allegorise the political interdependence of the clans.

If we leave Bergson and turn to Freud, the essence of wit is neatly to span gulfs between different ideas. The pleasure of a joke lies in a kind of economy. At all times we are expending energy in monitoring our subconscious so as to ensure that our conscious perceptions come through a filtering control. The joke, because it breaks down the control, gives the monitoring system a holiday. Or, as Freud puts it, since monitoring costs effort, there is a saving in psychic expenditure. For a moment the unconscious is allowed to bubble up without restraint, hence the sense of enjoyment and freedom.

The late Anton Ehrenzweig (1953) extended the Freudian analysis of wit to aesthetic pleasure. In appreciating a work of art there is a perception of form, and underlying the articulate or dominant form there are other submerged forms half-perceived. These are inarticulate areas, sub-patternings or reversals of the main theme. Ehrenzweig argues that the perception of inarticulate forms is itself a direct source of pleasure. The inarticulate forms are experienced as an image of the subconscious. As they are perceived there is a release of energy, for they allow the subconscious itself to be expressed. Aesthetic pleasure would then have this in common with the joy of a joke; something is saved in psychic effort, something which might have been repressed has been allowed to appear, a new improbable form of life has been glimpsed. For Bergson it is lifeless encrustation which is attacked in the joke, for Freud the joke lies in the release from control. If I may sum up the differences of emphasis between Bergson and Freud I would suggest that for Bergson the man who slips on a banana peel would be funny because he has lost his bodily control and so becomes a helpless automaton: for Freud this man would be funny because his stiff body has for two seconds moved with the swiftness of a gazelle, as if a new form of life had been hidden there. In short, they have a common approach which Freud uses more abstractly and flexibly. For both, the essence of the joke is that something formal is attacked by something informal, something organised and controlled, by something vital, energetic, an upsurge of life for Bergson, of libido for Freud. The common denominator underlying both approaches is the joke seen as an attack on control.

Here we can see why scatology is potentially funny. Take any pun or funny story: it offers alternative patterns, one apparent, one hidden: the latter, by being brought to the surface impugns the validity of the first. Bergson said: 'Est comique tout incident qui appelle notre attention sur le physique d'une personne alors que le moral est en cause' (1950: 391). Reference to the physical pattern of events takes the dignity out of the moral pattern, yes. But this is not all. The symbols are not necessarily loaded the same way. Freud's approach is more complex because it allows that the relation of physical and moral could equally well be the other way round. What is crucial is that one accepted pattern is confronted by something else.

All jokes have this subversive effect on the dominant structure of ideas. Those which bring forward the physiological exigencies to which moral beings are subject, are using one universal, never-failing technique of subversion. But it would be a great mistake to think that humour can be reduced to scatology. Beidelman (1966) seems to do this, I think unintentionally, when he reduces Kaguru joking relations to cosmological ideas about dirt and sex. Structural analysis does not work by reducing all symbols to one or two of their number; rather, it requires an abstract statement of the patterned relations of all the symbols to one another. The same applies to moral bias. It may be incidentally worked into the structure of many jokes, but it is not the essence of joking. Compare the *Comedy of Errors* with *Le Jeu de l'amour et du hazard*. In the latter, Marivaux makes the girl of noble birth pretend to be her own handmaid so as to spy on her suitor; he adopts the same trick to observe her unrecognised. The joke lies in the ridiculous display of valet and handmaid disguised as lord and lady. In Bergson's terms the essence of the joke is that 'something living', natural nobility, triumphs over 'something encrusted', false imitation of breeding. Shakespeare, on the other hand, does not moralise when he successfully entangles the separate worlds of twin brothers and their twin servants and disengages them at the end. His is no less a comedy for all that the social messages are weaker.

By this stage we seem to have a formula for identifying jokes. A joke is a play upon form. It brings into relation disparate elements in such a way that one accepted pattern is challenged by the appearance of another which in some way was hidden in the first. I confess that I find Freud's definition of the joke highly satisfactory. The joke is an image of the relaxation of conscious control in favour of the unconscious. For the rest of this article I shall be assuming that any recognisable joke falls into this joke pattern which needs two elements, the juxtaposition of a control against that which is controlled, this juxtaposition being such that the latter triumphs. Needless to say, a successful subversion of one form by another completes or ends the joke, for it changes the balance of power. It is implicit in the Freudian model that the unconscious does not take over the control system. The wise sayings of lunatics, talking animals, children, and drunkards are funny because they are not in control; otherwise they would not be an image of the unconscious. The joke merely affords opportunity for realising that an accepted pattern has no necessity. Its excitement lies in the suggestion that any particular ordering of experience may be arbitrary and subjective. It is frivolous in that it produces no real alternative, only an exhilarating sense of freedom from form in general.

SOCIAL CONTROL OF PERCEPTION

While hailing this joke pattern as authentic, it is a very different matter to use it for identifying jokes. First we should distinguish standardised jokes, which are set in a conventional context, from spontaneous jokes. Freud's claim to have found the same joke pattern in all joking situations hides an important shift in levels of analysis. The standard joke, starting for instance with 'Have you heard this one?' or 'There were three men, an Irishman, etc.', contains the whole joke pattern within its verbal form. So does the pun. The joke pattern can easily be identified within the verbal form of standard jokes and puns. But the spontaneous joke organises the total situation in its joke pattern. Thus we get into difficulties in trying to recognise the essence of a spontaneous joke if we only have the utterance or the gesture and not the full pattern of relationships. If the Kaguru think it witty to throw excrement at certain cousins or the Lodagaba to dance grotesquely at funerals or the Dogon to refer to the parents' sexual organs when they meet a friend, then to recognise the joke that sends all present into huge enjoyment we need not retreat into cultural relativism and give up a claim to interpret. The problem has merely shifted to the relation between joking and the social structure.

The social dimension enters at all levels into the perception of a joke. Even its typical patterning depends on a social valuation of the elements. A twentieth-century audience finds the Marivaux comedy weak because it one-sidely presents the aristocrats' manners as live and their servants' manners as lifeless imitations. But to an eighteenth-century audience of French aristocrats any dramatist presenting both lords and commoners as equally lively in thier own right would have had, not a comedy, but a theme of social reform to tempt only a Bernard Shaw in his most tendentious vein. In every period there is a pile of submerged jokes, unperceived because they are irrelevant or wrongly balanced for the perspective of the day. Here let me try to save the definition of the joke pattern from the charge that it does not include modern forms of humour, such as the shaggy dog story or the sick joke. The shaggy dog is only told in a society which has been satiated with joke stories. The joke of the tale that goes on in a declining spiral to a nadir of pointlessness lies in the dashed expectations of the listeners: the humour is not in the verbal utterances but in the total situation in which it is a practical joke. The sick joke expresses a parallel sophistication in joke forms. It plays with a reversal of the values of social life; the hearer is left uncertain which is the man and which the machine, who is the good and who the bad, or where is the legitimate pattern of control. There is no need to labour the point that such a joke form relates to a particular kind of social experience and could not be perceived by those who have not been exposed to a thoroughgoing relativising of moral values.

So much for the social control of perception. As to the permitting of a joke, there are jokes which can be perceived clearly enough by all present but which are rejected at once. Here again the social dimension is at work. Social requirements may judge a joke to be in bad taste, risky, too near the bone, improper, or irrelevant. Such controls are exerted either on behalf of hierarchy as such, or on behalf of values which are judged too precious and too precarious to be exposed to challenge. Whatever the joke, however remote its subject, the telling of it is potentially subversive. Since its form consists of a victorious tilting of uncontrol against control, it is an image of the levelling of hierarchy, the triumph of intimacy over formality, of unofficial values over official ones. Our question is now much clearer. We must ask what are the social conditions for a joke to be both perceived and permitted. We could start to answer it by examining the literature of various joking situations. My hpothesis is that a joke is seen and allowed when it offers a symbolic pattern of a social pattern occurring at the same time. As I see it, all jokes are expressive of the social situations in which they occur. The one social condition necessary for a joke to be enjoyed is that the social group in which it is received should develop the formal characteristics of a 'told' joke: that is, a dominant pattern of relations is challenged by another. If there is no joke in the social structure, no other joking can appear.

Take as an example Fredrik Barth's (1966) analysis of the social situation on board a Norwegian fishing boat. Here the skipper is in full charge of the crew until the boats are lowered into the water. Then the net boss takes over. Before that point the net boss is not subject to the skipper as are other crew members. He is there on the boat, nominally under the skipper, but potentially a source of authority which will supplant the skipper for a brief period. There is in this social pattern the perfect joke form. All the time that the skipper and the other members of the crew are busily expressing superordination and subordination within the frame of common commitment to the enterprise, the net boss expresses his detachment and individuality by witty sallies. As soon as he takes over responsibility, however, his joking stops short. The essential point is that the joking by the net boss expresses a pattern of authority which arises out of the technicalities of fishing: it does nothing to create the situation, it merely expresses it.

Take as a second example the rather unexpected story about laughter in the beginning of the *Iliad*. At first sight the social situation seems to be all wrong, if my account of a proper joke form is accepted. Thersites, a common soldier, insults the Greek leaders; Odysseus strikes him brutally with a metal studded rod; Thersites is crushed and the troops have a hearty laugh at his expense. On this showing there seems to be no joke to provoke the laughter, for the Greek leaders represent the dominant elements in the social structure. Odysseus's act merely asserts their authority. But this would be to take the story out of context. The Greek leaders' plan to mount a new attack on Troy is about to be thwarted by their men. The argument between Odysseus and Thersites takes place when the former has been trying single-handed to check a wild dash for the ships by hordes of men who have been nine years away from home. In the context of threatened mob rule, the leaders are not the dominant element in the pattern, but the weak, endangered element. One could say that everyone laughs with relief that their scramble for home is not allowed to overwhelm the delicate balance of power between a handful of leaders and a mass of followers. Thersites, the rude and ugly cripple, usually takes Odysseus and Achilles for his butts; this time the pattern is reversed. The men laugh to find themselves on the side of the leaders, in reverse of their behaviour a short time before.

As a final example, I would like to turn to the parables in the New Testament to suggest that when the social structure is not depicted, it is unlikely that we can perceive 'told' jokes even when the joke form is clearly present in the verbal utterance. Many of the parables have an obvious joke pattern: the kindom of heaven likened to a mustard seed (Luke 13: 19; Mark 4: 31–2), the prayers of the complacent Pharisee placed second after the humble prayer of the publican (Luke 18: 10–14), the guest who takes the lowest place and is brought up to the top, to cite a few. Many incidents in the Gospel narrative itself also have a joke form, the wedding at Cana to take only one. But whereas the Gospel incidents present little difficulty in the light of the messages that 'the things that are impossible with men are possible with God' (Luke 18: 27), some of the parables do. Why was the poor fellow with no wedding garment bound and cast into the place of darkness with weeping and gnashing of teeth (Matthew 22: 11–14)? Why was the unjust steward commended for making friends with Mammon (Luke 16: 1–9)? How does this accord with the message of love and truth? I suggest that the difficulties arise because we are lacking signals from the social situation. Suppose that the Galilee audience, as soon as it heard 'Let me tell you a parable' settled into the same expectant joking mood that we do on hearing 'Do you know the riddle about . . .?' Then we could interpret the parables frankly as jokes, told at a rattling pace, with dramatic pauses for effect, each reaching higher and higher climaxes of absurdity and ridicule. The punishment of the man with no wedding garment then appears as a necessary correction to the obviously funny story of the rich man whose social equals, having refused his invitation to a feast, found their places were filled by beggars from the street (Matthew 22: 2–10). Could the kingdom of heaven be filled with any kind of riff-raff then? No – that would be to miss the point of the story. True, the socially uppermost are not necessarily the best qualified for the kingdom of heaven. But to correct the wrong impression about riff-raff, a new joke has to be introduced against the gate-crasher. There will be more to say later about the joke form as a vehicle of religious thought.

I hope that I have established that a joke cannot be perceived unless it corresponds to the form of the social experience: but I would go a step further and even suggest that the experience of a joke form in the social structure calls imperatively for an explicit joke to express it. Hence the disproportionate joy which a feeble joke often releases. In the case of a bishop being stuck in the lift, a group of people are related together in a newly relevant pattern which over-throws the normal one: when one of them makes the smallest jest, something pertinent has been said about the social structure. Hence the enthusiasm with which a joke at the right time is always hailed. Whatever happens next will be seen to be funny: whether the lowliest in the no longer relevant hierarchy discovers the right switch and becomes saviour of the mighty, or whether the bishop himself turns out to be the best mechanic, the atmosphere will become heady with joy, unless the bishop has made the mistake of imposing the external hierarchy.

To the pleasure of the joke itself, whatever that may be, is added enjoyment of a hidden wit, the congruence of the joke structure with the social structure. With laughter there is a third level of appositeness: for disturbed bodily control mirrors both the joke structure and the social structure. Here there is the germ of an answer to the puzzle of why tickling should provoke laughter, discussed by Koestler (1964).

Tickling, says Koestler, using the same Bergson–Freud analysis of wit, is funny because it is interpreted as a mock attack. The baby laughs more when it is tickled by its own mother than by a stranger; with strangers one can never be sure (Koestler, 1964: 80–2). But to the uncertainty about whether a stranger is really making a serious or a mock attack add the fact that there is no social relation with strangers. Hence the wit is not in play in the social dimension to anything like the same extent. From the content of the joke, to the analogy of the joke structure with the social structure, on to the analogy of these two with the physical experience, the transfer of formal patterns goes on even to a fourth level, that revealed by Freud. A joke unleashes the energy of the unconscious against the control of the conscious. This, I argue, is the essential joke experience, a fourfold perception of the congruence of a formal pattern.

JOKES AS RITES

In classing the joke as a symbol of social, physical and mental experience, we are already treating it as a rite. How then should we treat the joke which is set aside for specified ritual occasions?

Once again, as with standardised and spontaneous jokes, it is necessary to distinguish spontaneous rites from routinised or standard rites. The joke, in its social context as we have discussed it so far, is a spontaneous symbol. It expresses something that is happening, but that is all. The social niche in which it belongs is quite distinct from that of ritual which is enacted to express what ought to happen. Similarly, the spontaneous rite is morally neutral, while the standard rite is not. Indeed, there is a paradox in talking about joke rites at all, for the peculiar expressive character of the joke is in contrast with ritual as such.

Here I need to return to the general idea of joke structure derived from Freud, and to contrast the way a joke relates disparate ideas with the way a standard ritual does the same.

A standard rite is a symbolic act which draws its meaning from a cluster of standard symbols. When I use the word 'rite' in what follows, I combine the action and the cluster of symbols associated with it. A joke has it in common with a rite that both connect widely differing concepts. But the kind of connection of pattern A with pattern B in a joke is such that B disparages or supplants A, while the connection made in a rite is such that A and B support each other in a unified system. The rite imposes order and harmony, while the joke disorganises. From the physical to the personal, to the social, to the cosmic, great rituals create unity in experience. They assert hierarchy and order. In doing so, they affirm the value of the symbolic patterning of the universe. Each level of patterning is validated and enriched by association with the rest. But jokes have the opposite effect. They connect widely differing fields, but the connection destroys hierarchy and order. They do not affirm the dominant values, but denigrate and devalue. Essentially a joke is an anti-rite.

I have analysed elsewhere (Douglas, 1966: 114–28) rituals which use bodily symbolism to express ideas about the body politic. The caste system in India is a case in point. The symbolism underlying the ideas about pollution and purification has something in common with wit; it transfers patterns of value on a declining slope of prestige from one context to another with elegant economy. The lowest social ranks in the caste systems are those required to reform social functions equivalent to the excretory functions of the body. There is the basis for a joke in the congruence of bodily and social symbolism, but the joke is absent since two patterns are related without either being challenged. The hierarchy is not undermined by the comparison, but rather reinforced.

Totemic systems make play with formal analogues. The same patterns are transposed from context to context with exquisite economy and grace. But they are not funny. One of the essential requirements of a joke is absent, the element of challenge. I give an example from Madame Calame-Griaule's recent book (1966) on Dogon language. She has analysed something that might be called a kind of linguistic totemism. The Dogon use a limited number of classes of speech as a basis for classifying wide ranges of other experience. With speech of the market place, for instance, are classified commerce and weaving. There is an obvious analogy from two kinds of constructive interaction. Here we have economy in connecting up disparate activities, but no humour. Take the class of speech that Dogon call 'trivial speech', the speech of women. This includes certain forms of insect, animal, and human life. The controlling idea for the class associated with 'trivial speech' is dissipation. The work of this class is the sower's broadcasting of seed; the red monkey who comes to eat the crops after the farmer has planted is the appropriate animal in the class; the despised Fulani herder who pastures his cattle on the stubble after harvesting it is the human associated with it. The insect is the grasshopper, alleged to defecate as fast as it eats, an obvious type of fruitless effort. The references to despised forms of activity and to uncontrolled bowel movements have a derogatory implication for the idle chatter of women. The range of behaviour on which the pattern of 'trivial speech' is imposed degenerates from human Dogon to human Fulani, from human to animal pest, then to insect pest, and finally to the excretory functions of the body. As the classification moves down from one context to the next, it slights and devalues. There is the possibility of a joke here. If it were challenging the known pretensions of women to utter important speech, it would have the making of a joke. But, given the low place of women in Dogon esteem, it is more likely to be the deadly earnest affirmation of male superiority, in which case this classification supports the established social order. The message of a standard rite is that the ordained patterns of social life are inescapable. The message of a joke is that they are escapable. A joke is by nature an anti-rite.

When joking is used in a ritual, it should be approached nonetheless as a rite. Like any other rite the joke rite is first and foremost a set of symbols. Its symbolism draws on the full experience of joking, just as communion rites draw on the full experience of eating, right down to the digestive process, and sexual rites and sacrifice draw on the experience of sex and death. So we should expect the joke rite to exploit all the elements of the joke in its essential nature. This will give the full explanation of ritual joking. Jokes, being themselves a play upon forms, can well serve to express something about social forms. Recall that the joke connects and disorganises. It attacks sense and hierarchy. The joke rite then must express a comparable situation. If it devalues social structure, perhaps it celebrates something else instead. It could be saying something about the value of individuals as against the value of the social relations in which they are organised. Or it could be saying something about different levels of social structure; the irrelevance of one obvious level and the relevance of a submerged and unappreciated one.

John Barnes (1954: 43) used the term 'network' to indicate an undifferentiated field of friendship and acquaintance. In his Morgan Lectures, Victor Turner has suggested that the word 'community' could be applied to this part of social life. In 'community' the personal relations of men and women appear in a special light. They form part of the ongoing process which is only partly organised in the wider social 'structure'. Whereas 'structure' is differentiated and channels authority through the system, in the context of 'community', roles are ambiguous, lacking hierarchy, disorganised. 'Community' in this sense has positive values associated with it: good fellowship, spontaneity, warm contact. Turner sees some Dionysian ritual as expressing the value of 'community' as against 'structure'. This analysis gives a better name to, and clarifies, what I have elsewhere crudely called the experience of the non-structure in contrast to the structure (Douglas, 1966: 102). Laughter and jokes, since they attack classification and hierarchy, are obviously apt symbols for expressing community in this sense of unhierarchised, undifferentiated social relations.

Peter Rigby (1968) has developed this approach in his survey of all types of relationship in which joking is required in Gogo culture. He starts with interclan joking, then goes on to affinal joking, grandparent/grandchild joking, and finally joking between mother's brother and sister's sons and between cross-cousins. Each kind of joking has its own rules and quality of joke required. He concludes from his survey that he needs the concept of 'community' as distinct from 'structure' in order to interpret this pattern of behaviour: 'In Gogo society it is relationships with and through women which establish the "community"; that is affinal, matrilateral and uterine kin' (Rigby, 1968: 152).

Interclan links and links with aliens and enemies are included in a general class along with links through women. Starting from an ego-centred universe of kin, the Gogo have developed a cosmic model: joking categories are contrasted with control categories; joking categories are links or mediators between different organised domains. Gogo use the idea of joking categories to express the fading out of social control at all points and in all directions. It is a boundary image, but the boundaries are fuzzy and face two ways; one is structured, the other is unstructured. Boundaries connect as well as separate. Women are the boundaries of the patrilineal lineage. Affines stand out of reach of clan and lineage control but they are links. Clans are bounded as clans, but are linked by exogamy. 'Grandfathers are links or mediators with the un-structured world of the spirits of the dead who are not distinguished on the basis of lineal descent' (Rigby, 1968: 152).

Here we have an analysis which brings out cosmological implications hidden in the nature of joking. A joke confronts one relevant structure by another less clearly relevant, one well differentiated view by a less coherent one, a system of control by another independent one to which it does not apply. By using jokes at social boundary points the Gogo are being witty at several levels: they comment on the nature of society, and on the nature of life and death. Their joke rites play upon one central abstraction, the contrast of articulation, and they develop the applica-tion of this symbol with the energy of inveterate punners. At the division of meat at a funeral, the heirs are told by the elders to speak clearly: if they mumble the sister's son will take everything (Rigby, 1968: 149). Here is an explicit reference to articulateness in speech as the symbol of structured relationships and inarticu-lateness as the symbol of the personal, undifferentiated network.

The interpretation of the Gogo joke rites as an abstract statement of two kinds of social interaction is highly satisfactory. The interpretation of Kaguru joke rites as an expression of an association made between sex, filth, and liminality I find dubious. According to Beidelman, the Kaguru use joking to express 'liminal' relations, that is ambiguous ones. The range of relationships in which Kaguru require joking is much the same as the range of Gogo joking relations. It would seem plausible that the ego-oriented view of social life (as either differentiated by a pattern of control or undifferentiated), is enough to warrant joking between these categories, and that dirt is an apt enough expres-sion of undifferentiated, unorganised, uncontrolled relations.

It still remains to distinguish jokes in general from obscenity as such. They are obviously very close. A joke confronts one accepted pattern with another. So does an obscene image. The first amuses, the second shocks. Both consist of the intrusion of one meaning on another, but whereas the joke discloses a meaning hidden under the appearance of the first, the obscenity is a gratuitous intrusion. We are unable to identify joke patterns without considering the total social situation. Similarly for obscenity, abominations depend upon social context to be perceived as such. Language which is normal in male company is regarded as obscene in mixed society; the language of intimacy is offensive where social distance reigns and, similarly, the language of the dissecting room where intimacy belongs. Inevitably, the best way of stating the difference between joking and obscenity is by reference to the social context. The joke works only when it mirrors social forms; it exists by virtue of its congruence with the social structure. But the obscenity is identified by its opposition to the social structure, hence its offence.

In the modern industrial world the categories of social life do not embrace the physical universe in a single moral order. If there is a social offence, there are moral implications such as cruelty, impiety, corruption of the innocent, and so on. But the social offence is not thought to release floods, famines or epidemics. Obscenity for us is a mild offence, since it can now be accounted for entirely in terms of offence against social categories. This leaves us unqualified to comprehend the much greater offence of obscenity in a primitive culture. For there the categories of social life coordinate the whole of experience: a direct attack on social forms is as disturbing as an attack on any of the symbolic categories in which the social forms are expressed – and vice versa. The idea of obscenity then has a much greater range and power, and the response it triggers is stronger. It is better to use a quite different word, such as abomination or ritual pollution, for the primitive cultures' equivalent to obscenity and to look for a much more whole-hearted and systematic wiping out of the offence than we can muster for dealing with obscenity.

Abomination is an act or event which contradicts the basic categories of experience and in doing so threatens both the order of reason and the order of society. A joke does nothing of the sort. It represents a temporary suspension of the social structure, or rather it makes a little disturbance in which the particular structuring of society becomes less relevant than another. But the strength of its attack is entirely restricted by the consensus on which it depends for recognition.

THE JOKER

Now we should turn to the role of the joker. He appears to be a privileged person who can say certain things in a certain way which confers immunity. He is by no means anything like a taboo breaker whose polluting act is a real offence to society. He *is* worth contrasting with persons undergoing rituals of transition, mourners, and initiands. Symbolically, they are in marginal states, passing from one clearly defined status to another. They are held to be dangerous to themselves and to others until they have gone through the whole ritual of redefinition. In the symbolisation of the social structure, they have let go their moorings and are temporarily displaced. But the joker is not exposed to danger. He has a firm hold on his own position in the structure and the disruptive comments which he makes upon it are in a sense the comments of the social group upon itself. He merely expresses consensus. Safe within the permitted range of attack, he lightens for everyone the oppressiveness of social reality, demonstrates its arbitrariness by making light of formality in general, and expresses the creative possibilities of the situation.

From this we can see the appropriateness of the joker as ritual purifier. Among the Kaguru, certain common sexual offences such as sexual intercourse between affines are thought to bring illness, sterility or death on the kin of the two offenders. There are other graver sexual offences, but these relatively minor ones can be ritually cleansed by the joking partners of the transgressors (Beidelman, 1966: 361–2). A similar responsibility falling on joking partners among the Dogon led Griaule to describe their partnership as cathartic (1948). Rites of purification are a very widespread responsibility of joking partners in central and east Africa, as Stefaniszyn (1950) has pointed out. I myself commented (Tew, 1951) that the joking aspects of the relationships could not be understood without an analysis of the relation between joking and purification. Now I suggest that the relevance of joking to purification emerges as another elaborate ritual pun. These rites make a double play on the joke experience: laughter itself is cathartic at the level of emotions; the joke consists in challenging a dominant structure and belittling it; the joker who provokes the laughter is chosen to challenge the relevance of the dominant structure and to perform with immunity the act which wipes out the venial offence.

The joker's own immunity can be derived philosophically from his apparent access to other reality than that mediated by the relevant structure. Such access is implied in the contrast of forms in which he deals. His jokes expose the inadequacy of realist structurings of experience and so release the pent-up power of the imagination.

Perhaps the joker should be classed as a kind of minor mystic. Though only a mundane and borderline type, he is one of those people who pass beyond the bounds of reason and society and give glimpses of a truth which escapes though the mesh of structured concepts. Naturally he is only a humble, poor brother of the true mystic, for his insights are given by accident. They do not combine to form a whole new vision of life, but remain disorganised as a result of the technique which produces them. He is distinctly gimmicky. One would expect him to be the object of a hilarious mythology, as among the Winnebago, but hardly the focus of a religious cult. And yet there he is, enshrined – Proteus in ancient Greece; the elephant god who gives luck and surprises in Hinduism; and the unpredictable, disruptive, creative force called Legba in Yoruba religion (Wescott, 1962). Needless to say, he is always a subordinate deity in a complex pantheon. The joker as god promises a wealth of new, unforeseeable kinds of interpretation. He exploits the symbol of creativity which is contained in a joke, for a joke implies that anything is possible.

It is much easier now to see the role of the joker at a funeral. By restraining excessive grief he asserts the demands of the living. I would expect joking at funerals to be more possible and more required the more the community is confident that it will turn the mourner's desolation into a temporary phase. Then the question is: who must joke and what should be his precise degree of relationship with the bereaved and the dead? The central African joking partner is a friend cultivated by gifts and hospitality, and is by definition not a close kinsman: his role at a funeral is to cheer the bereaved and to relieve them of the polluting duties of burial. There are here the elements of another ritual pun; for it is the kin who are ritually endangered by contact with the dead, the kin who are involved in the social structure of inheritance and succession, and it is the personal friend, the joking partner, who is uninvolved in the social structure and is the person who is immune from pollution of death.

There are many ways in which it can be appropriate to joke at a funeral. When a man dies his friends fall to reviewing his life. They try to see in it some artistic pattern, some fulfilment which can comfort him and them. At this moment obvious inconsistencies and disharmonies are distressing. If he is a great man, a national figure, of course his achievements are cited, but it seems important to be able to say that in his private life he also had fulfilled his family roles. If he is an ordinary citizen then the assessment of his success goes on entirely at the level of family and community. He is judged as a man, not as an item of social structure.

The role of the joker at the funeral could call attention to his individual personality. Indeed, in the Jewish *shib'ah*, a week of mourning after burial, the friends who come in to comfort the bereaved and praise the departed, invariably find themselves joking at his expense. Thus they affirm that he was an individual, not only a father or brother in a series of descending generations, but a man. So much for the social symbolism.

On the subject of funeral joking it is tempting to consider some metaphysical implications. A joke symbolises levelling, dissolution, and recreation. As a symbol of social relations it is destructive (somewhat like fire?) and regenerative (somewhat like water?). The joke, working on its own materials, mimics a kind of death. Its form in itself suggests the theme of rebirth. It is no coincidence that practical jokes are common in initiation rites, along with more concrete expressions of dying and being reborn. When Jan Vansina underwent the Bushong boys' initiation (1955) he was continually involved in practical joking, either at the expense of non-initiates or at the expense of the group of novices to which he belonged. One after another the much dreaded ordeals were revealed to be only tricks.

METAPHYSICAL JOKES

If the joke form can symbolise so much, it could be capable of saying something about death itself in the context of religion.

We have traced the pun from its social to its psychological form, from these to its physical expression in laughter, and from the spontaneous symbol of social relationships to the standardised joke rite, expressing the value of less articulate sectors of social relationships compared with formalised structures. At funerals it expresses the value of the man himself, or the value of disinterested friendship or the value of the level of community in which most of a man's life is effective. It seems, after all this, not too bold to suggest that by the path of ritual joking these African cultures too have reached a philosophy of the absurd. By revealing the arbitrary, provisional nature of the very categories of thought, by lifting their pressure for a moment and suggesting other ways of structuring reality, the joke rite in the middle of the sacred moments of religion hints at unfathomable mysteries. This is the message which Turner attributes to the practical joke at the centre of the cult of Chihamba performed by the Ndembu tribe in Zambia.

First the initiates pay homage to the great white spirit, Kavula, as the source of all power; then as they approach his tabernacle, they are told to strike his effigy under a white cloth with their rattles, and then that they have killed him. Soon after they are told that they are innocent, and that he is not dead, and the paraphernalia under the white cloth is revealed to be no more than some everyday implements. Everyone then laughs joyfully. Following an elaborate exegesis, Turner (1962: 87) says:

> we have in Chihamba the local expression of a universal-human problem, that of expressing what cannot be *thought of*, in view of thought's subjugation to essences. It is a problem which has engaged the passionate attention of ritual man in all places and ages. It is a problem, furthermore, which has confronted artists, musicians and poets whenever these have gone beyond the consideration of aesthetic form and social manners.

It is unfortunate that Turner presented his novel interpretation of a primitive cult in neo-scholastic terms. The only serious consideration which his study has received attacks this presentation. Horton (1964) argues that the whole complex of ontological problems with which Turner has saddled Ndembu theologians, the distinction between the act-of-being itself (an act) and the concept of being (an essence) only makes sense in the terms of Thomist–Aristotelian philosophy. He deftly applies the logical positivist criticism to this approach. Further, Horton rejects the idea that 'a dominant concern to "say the unsayable" about the ultimate ground of all particular forms of existence' can be found in all African religions (1964: 96–7), still less, as Turner says, universally in all religions whatever.

These criticisms bypass the main challenge of Turner's thesis. Merely to dare to interpret a ritual mock-killing of a god in one particular African religion as an attempt to express unfathomable mysteries about the inadequacy of the categories of thought for expressing the nature of existence is bold enough. Leave out Turner's claim that this is a universal human preoccupation; it may be or it may not be. Forget his presentation in scholastic terms; it could as well have been presented through Kant or Kierkegaarde or modern phenomenologists as through Aquinas. It is still a daring claim that he makes for the profound meaning of an African joke rite. For all the subtlety and complexity with which he spins out the symbolism, my own first response was one of doubt. It was the first serious suggestion by a contemporary anthropologist that rituals which have no formal philosophical exegesis in their native culture could be concerned with problems about the relation of thought to experience which are, undeniably, a universal preoccupation of philosophy. After reflecting on the use of the joke rite in Africa, I am now much more convinced that Turner may be right. African cultures have clearly reached an apotheosis of wit by playing upon the joke at various levels of meaning. It is not a great leap from attributing to the joke rite a subtle image of society to attributing also to it an image of the conditions of human knowledge.

But this is not the point at which I would wish to end this article. There is another implication which should be underlined: the social control of experience. It is here argued that the patterning of social forms limits and conditions the apprehension of symbolic forms. This may be extended from the perception of the joke form to the perception of other patterns, hierarchy, part–whole relations, unity, schism, incorporation, exclusion. The control exerted by experience in the social dimension over the perception of conceptual patterns is already taken into account in learning theory and in religious sociology. This study of the joke rite suggests that the achievement of consonance between different realms of experience is a source of profound satisfaction. It suggests that the drive to reduce dissonance may work at a more abstract level than has been recognised hitherto. The exercise of tracing the analogies drawn in joke rites gives additional meaning to Kandinsky's famous saying that the impact of an acute triangle on a circle produces an effect no less powerful than the finger of God touching the finger of Adam in Michelangelo's famous fresco.

NOTES TO THIS EDITION [1975]

Early versions of this article received valuable criticism from the Makerere Conference on Joking Relationships, in December 1966, and from the Muirhead Society, Birmingham.

Professor John Beattie has pointed out that the difference I make between Freud and Bergson is almost indiscernible and with this criticism I agree.

Dr Audrey Richards makes a more serious criticism that my use of her writings on the Bemba distorts the information. Either I should leave them out or say a great deal more about them, giving a survey of all the occasions in which formalised joking occurs in Bemba society. It is quite incorrect to say that 'the jokes categorise the political interdependence of the clans' since the clans are neither corporate nor interdependent, nor do they have any function except the regulation of exogamy and the right to appoint to one or two court offices. She has agreed to publishing the following useful note for which I am extremely grateful:

> I realise that you have not really concentrated on the reciprocal clan relationships. You say that the use of these jokes 'categorises the interdependence of the clans' using the Bemba, but I do not think that they are interdependent now except at the court when the clan membership of the bakabilo has a good deal of significance, and of course they remain exogamous for some extraordinary reason considering that they have really *no* other corporate functions as regards commoners.
>
> Of course the reciprocal clan relationships cannot fit in with your view that 'whatever the joke, however remote its subject, the telling of it is potentially subversive' and further that it 'destroys harmony and order'. But you could expand your idea to say that in the case of the royal Crocodile clan, this would be true, although it would be untrue of the other clans. When the head of the Fish clan dances in front of the Chitimukulu, threatening him with a broad-bladed fishing spear and insulting him, there is just this element of the subversive in everyone's behaviour. Everyone present enjoys the situation and comes round to watch the affair and to laugh. The chief does not enjoy it although he smiles in a sickly way. He takes special routes across the river in order to avoid having his goods plundered by members of the Fish clan. He told me it was very tiresome and that he thought that now the Europeans were there, they ought to put an end to such 'things of the past'. I suppose it depends on whether your theory needs for its support an account of the emotions of the people actually expressed at the time as well as the descriptions of Banungwe relations.
>
> As regards commoners, the parallels between the behaviour of marriageable classes, for example, cross-cousins, is rather striking and in some cases was made explicit to me but only by old men. One man said to me that *Bunungwe* were enemies whom we married when we first came into the country. (I think I mention this in my article but do not seem to have any copy at all.) Cross-cousins joke in this way together and can snatch each others goods. *Banungwe* joke and take each others' things once a month when the new moon comes – but bury each other which of course cross-cousins do not do. The joking is stereotyped for clan opposites but not for cross-cousins.

BIBLIOGRAPHY

BARNES, J.A. (1954), 'Class and committees in a Norwegian island parish', *Human Relationships*, 7, 39–58.

BARTH, F. (1966), *Models of Social Organisation* (Occasional Papers Royal Anthropological Institute, 23), London, Royal Anthropological Institute.

BEIDELMAN, T.O. (1966), '*Utani*: some Kagura notions of death, sexuality and affinity', *South West Journal of Anthropology*, 22–4, 354–80.

BERGSON, H. (1950), *Le Rire: essai sur la signification du comique*, first published Paris, Presses Universitaires de France.

CALAME-GRIAULE, G. (1966), *Ethnologie et langage: la parole chez les Dogon*, Paris, Gallimard.

DOUGLAS, M. (1966), *Purity and Danger: an Analysis of Concepts of Pollution and Taboo*, London, Routledge & Kegan Paul.

EHRENZWEIG, A. (1953), *The Psychoanalysis of Artistic Vision and Hearing: a Theory of Unconscious Perception*, London, Routledge & Kegan Paul.

FREUD, S. (1916), *Wit and its Relation to the Unconscious* (trans. A. A. Brill), London, Fisher & Unwin.

GOODY, J. R. (1962), *Death, Property and the Ancestors*, London, Tavistock Publications.

GRIAULE, M. (1948), 'L'Alliance cathartique', *Africa*, *16*, 242–58.

HORTON, R. (1964), 'Ritual man in Africa', *Africa*, *34*, 85–104.

KOESTLER, A. (1964), *The Act of Creation*, London, Hutchinson.

LEACH, E.R. (1961), *Re-thinking Anthropology* (London School of Economics Monographs in Social Anthropology, 22), London, Athlone Press.

RADCLIFFE-BROWN, A.R. (1940), 'On joking relationships', *Africa*, *13*, 195–210.

RADCLIFFE-BROWN, A.R. (1949), 'A further note on joking relationships', *Africa*, *19*, 133–40.

RICHARDS, A.I. (1937), 'Reciprocal clan relationships among the Bemba', *Man*, *37*, 188–93.

RIGBY, P. (1968), 'Joking relationships, kin categories and clanship among the Gogo', *Africa*, *38*, 133–55.

STEFANISZYN, B. (1950), 'Funeral friendship in central Africa', *Africa*, *20*, 290–306.

TEW, M. (1951), 'A further note on funeral friendship', *Africa*, *21*, 122–4.

TURNER, V.W. (1962), *Chihamba, the White Spirit (Rhodes-Livingstone Papers, 33)*, Manchester University Press.

VANSINA, J. (1955), 'Initiation rituals of the Bushong', *Africa*, *25*, 138–52.

WESCOTT, J. (1962), 'The sculpture and myths of Eshu-Elegba the Yoruba trickster: definition and interpretation in Yoruba iconography', *Africa*, *32*, 336–65.

Chapter 11

Do dogs laugh?

A cross-cultural approach to body symbolism

First published in *Journal of Psychosomatic Research*, 15 (1971)

The body, as a vehicle of communication, is misunderstood if it is treated as a signal box, a static framework emitting and receiving strictly coded messages. The body communicates information for and from the social system in which it is a part. It should be seen as mediating the social situation in at least three ways. It is itself the field in which a feedback interaction takes place. It is itself available to be given as the proper tender for some of the exchanges which constitute the social situation. And further, it mediates the social structure by itself becoming its image. Some of this I discussed in the *Journal of Psychosomatic Research* (Douglas, 1968a) and in *Purity and Danger* (Douglas, 1966). To adapt the signal box metaphor to show the full involvement of the body in communication we should have to imagine a signal box which folds down and straightens up, shakes, dances, goes into a frenzy or stiffens to the tune of the more precise messages its lights and signal arms are transmitting. This paper is offered as a background to those others in this conference which treat of specialised signalling systems such as the voice and the face. It is above all offered as a preface to Professor Jenner's discussion of *endogenous* factors. I will suggest a parallel set of social factors *exogenous* to the biological organism, feedback pathways which control the rhythm of social interaction.

A young zoologist who asked my advice about a study he was making of laughter in human and non-human species, complained that sociologists had given him very little help. Indeed it is very difficult for us to produce a theory or even a vague hypothesis on the subject. My own idea on the body's role in joke symbolism is not easily adapted to an experimental approach to laughter (Douglas, 1968b). We know that some tribes are said to be dour and unlaughing. Others laugh easily. Pygmies lie on the ground and kick their legs in the air, panting and shaking in paroxysms of laughter (Turnbull, 1961). Francis Huxley noted the same bodily abandonment to convulsions of gaiety in Haiti (Huxley, 1966). But we have nothing to say about these differences that could help the zoologist. It is just as difficult for us to suppose that laughter in different tribes means the same thing, as to be sure that animals are laughing when they grin and splutter.

Bergson (1900) declared that laughter is the unique prerogative of humans.

However, we have it from a biologist that dogs laugh as they play. Lorenz in *Man Meets Dog* (1954) describes the case:

> an invitation to play always follows; here the slightly opened jaws which reveal the tongue, and the tilted angle of the mouth which stretches almost from ear to ear give a still stronger impression of laughing. This 'laughing' is most often seen in dogs playing with an adored master and which become so excited that they soon start panting.

He suggests that the same facial expression marks the beginning of erotic excitement.

Here is a description of the beloved master playing with his dog. Thomas Mann (1961) describes ways of rousing and stimulating his dog.

> Or we amuse ourselves, I by tapping him on the nose, and he, by snapping at my hand as though it were a fly. It makes us both laugh. Yes. Bashan has to laugh too; and as I laugh I marvel at the sight, to me the oddest and most touching thing in the world. It is moving to see how under my teasing his thin animal cheeks and the corners of his mouth will twitch, and over his dark animal mask will pass an expression like a human smile.

The play produces in the dog 'a state of ecstasy, a sort of intoxication with his own identity so that he begins to whirl around on himself and send up loud exultant barks'. Both accounts take the laugh to be essentially a facial expression, but both, being good observers, note the panting, the more generally visible excitement or ecstasy. I shall return to these two useful clues to the nature of laughter. First, it is a process which begins in a small way, observable on the face, and is capable of ending in involving the whole body. Second, it is normally a social response; private laughing is a special case. Here I should set out my assumptions about a systematic approach to the body as a channel of communication. The upshot will be to throw doubt on the attempt to isolate a complex such as laughter, or indeed facial expression, for comparative study.

I see the relation of the spoken word to non-verbal communication as analogous to the relation between written word and the physical materials and visible manner of its presentation. Californian sociologists are paying attention now to the unspoken part of any discourse, its reliance on shared, implicit assumptions (Garfinkel, 1967). In the same way, a written document communicates through a physical, metaphysical, and social dimension. The typography, arrangement of footnotes, layout of margins and headings, acknowledgments, all witness to a set of implicit meanings about the realm of discourse it belongs in. Its physical embodiment indicates a social sphere to which it is directed. In the same way, the body comes into play to support the meanings of a spoken communication. Posture, voice, speed, articulation, tonality, all contribute to the meaning. The words alone mean very little. Verbal symbols depend on the speaker manipulating his whole environment to get the meaning across. We have to make a special effort if we wish to consider the meanings conveyed by the typography of a literary text in isolation from the verbal message. The whole trend of our education has been the other way. We now realise that we have unduly privileged the verbal channel and tended to suppose it could be effective in disembodied form. In the same way we should now make an effort to think of the body as a medium in its own right, distinct from the words issuing from the mouth. Speech has been over-emphasised as the privileged means of human communication, and the body neglected. It is time to rectify this neglect and to become aware of the body as the physical channel of meaning.

My first assumption is that normally the physical channel supports and agrees with the spoken one. The case in which the channels contradict one another is a special one, for conveying the special meanings of banter, irony, mistrust, etc. I have discussed this general concordance between channels of communication in *Natural Symbols* (1970). My second assumption follows: that conscious and unconscious bodily expressions need not be distinguished, since both exhibit the same tendency to reinforce speech. The degree of consciousness can be ignored. My third assumption is based on observation. The body is not always under perfect control. A screening process divests uncontrolled noises of meaning. The small hiccups, sneezes, heavy breathing, and throat clearings can and must be screened out as irrelevant noise, not to be treated as part of the bodily channel's message. There are limits of tolerance. Once the limit is passed, the discourse has to be stopped. A prolonged sneezing fit or other uncontrolled bodily movement forces the owner of the interrupting machine to withdraw if the noises cannot be framed with an apology. I would like to ask the zoologist whether animals screen off bodily interruptions or whether Bergson should have selected this capacity to ignore them, rather than laughter, as the distinctively human accomplishment.

The fourth assumption is that there is a cross-cultural, universal language of bodily interruptions. Instead of being ignored, they can be deliberately brought back artificially into the discourse to convey well understood messages based on a hierarchy of bodily orifices. Back and lower orifices rank below frontal and upper. A development of Freudian symbolism to the social dimension fits the meanings in a quite straightforward way (Hallpike, 1969). Fifth, here we come to the crux of the matter. Laughter, though not controlled any more than any other upper/front eruptions such as coughing or breaking wind, is not screened off and ignored. Laughter is a unique bodily eruption which is always taken to be a communication. I suggest that this is because a laugh is a culmination of a series of bodily communications which have had to be interpreted in the usual way as part of the discourse. The finally erupting laugh cannot be screened off because all the changes in bodily posture preceding it have been taken as part of the dialogue.

If this approach can be developed it will give a sociological perspective to those working on the study of facial signals. At this stage my provisional answer to the young zoologist asking for guidance in the sociology of laughter is this. Laughter is too complex a process; at the same time it is too narrowly defined for identification. It would be better to start by considering the exogenous social factors which govern the thresholds of tolerance of bodily relaxation and control. These thresholds are set socially. In some social situations it is proper to take cognisance fully of bodily eruptions as part of the symbolising of familiarity and relaxation, in others the thresholds are lowered in response to the need to express formality and social distance.

If we ask of any form of communication the simple question, What is being communicated?, the answer is: information from the social system. The exchanges which are being communicated constitute the social system. Let us assume a sensitive feedback between all the parties to the social exchange. The body is expressing both the social situation at a given moment, and also a particular contribution to that situation. Inevitably, then, since the body is mediating the relevant social structure, it does the work of communicating by becoming an image of the total social situation as perceived, and the acceptable tender in the exchanges which constitute it. The possibilities of change and development arise in the first instance in the spontaneous bodily responses, precisely because they are treated as modifying messages by those who receive them. The uncontrolled frown or giggle can effectively rechannel all subsequent exchanges into a different set of pathways.

In its role as an image of society, the body's main scope is to express the relation of the individual to the group. This it does along the dimension from strong to weak control, according to whether the social demands are strong, weak, acceptable or not. From total relaxation to total self-control the body has a wide gamut for expressing this social variable.

What does it mean when one tribe laughs a lot and another tribe rarely? I would argue that it means that the level of social tensions has set low or high thresholds for bodily control. In the first case, the full range of the body's power of expression is more readily available to respond fully to a small stimulus. If the general social control settings are slack, the thresholds of tolerance of bodily interruption will be set higher. Comparisons of laughter should take account of the load of social meaning which the body has to carry. Where we seek to compare laughter, we should compare also the pressure on the individual from the social structure. The two cases of the Pygmies and the Haitians cited above are instructive. The first, living in the equatorial Congo forest, sparse and freely mobile, are free from obvious social pressure. The second were admittedly part of a modern police state which was at a low level of economic development. The people whom Francis Huxley studied in Haiti were haphazard in their means of livelihood and their obligations to one another were tenuous and short-lived. Both peoples seemed to use the full bodily range of expression for grief and joy. In *Natural Symbols* I have said more about the significance of such variations in the strength and permanence of social relations for bodily expression.

Another aspect of social organisation which is likely to be expressed in bodily symbolism is the length and complexity of messages. Social systems which vary on this point will have corresponding variations in the amount of pause that can be tolerated in the process of verbal communication. An important experiment on hesitation phenomena was reported by Professor Bernstein (1962). The speech of middle-class and working-class boys was timed. It was found that cutting across measured differences of intelligence, the middle-class boys were more tolerant of long pauses in the discourse. Bernstein argued that the hesitation phenomenon reflected an expectation on their part that speech was subject to a complex and therefore slow process of programming. I would like to see this experiment repeated and developed as a valuable clue to understanding non-verbal symbolic behaviour. I would also like to see something comparable devised for primates of like intelligence and different social organisation. For example, when full studies are made of savannah chimpanzees, the comparison with forest chimpanzees along the lines indicated here would be interesting. Since their social organisation would be likely to be more rigidly hierarchised in the savannah, we would predict more strictly defined and less variable responses, more control, longer pauses – less 'laughing'.

NOTE

I acknowledge here my thanks to Dr Robert Martin for his discussion of this chapter and his suggestion of how the question could be treated experimentally with chimpanzees.

BIBLIOGRAPHY

BERGSON, H. (1900), *Le Rire: essai sur la signification du comique*, Paris, Presses Universitaires de France.

BERNSTEIN, B. (1962), 'Linguistic codes, hesitation phenomena and intelligence', *Language and Speech*, 5, 1, 31–46.

DOUGLAS, M. (1966), *Purity and Danger: an Analysis of Concepts of Pollution and Taboo*, London, Routledge & Kegan Paul.

DOUGLAS, M. (1968a), 'The relevance of tribal studies', *Journal of Psychosomatic Research*, 1, 12.

DOUGLAS, M. (1968b), 'The social control of cognition: some factors in joke perception', *Manchester Journal of the Royal Anthropological Institute*, 3, 3, 361–76.

DOUGLAS, M. (1970), *Natural Symbols, Explorations in Cosmology*, London, Barrie & Rockliff.

GARFINKEL, H. (1967), *Studies in Ethnomethodology*, New Jersey, Prentice-Hall.

HALLPIKE, C.R. (1969), 'Social hair', *Manchester Journal of the Royal Anthropological Institute*, 2, 256–64.

HUXLEY, F. (1966), *The Invisibles*, London, Hart-Davies.

LORENZ, K. (1954), *Man Meets Dog*, London, Methuen.

MANN, T. (1961), 'A man and his dog' in *Stories of a Lifetime*, London, Secker & Warburg.

TURNBULL, C.M. (1961), *The Forest People*, London, Chatto & Windus.

Chapter 12

Couvade and menstruation

The relevance of tribal studies

First published in *Journal of Psychosomatic Research*, *12*, 1 (1968)

We all have the same human body, with the same number of orifices, using the same energies and seeking the same biological satisfactions. Yet tribal rituals are highly selective in their treatment of these themes. I cannot think of any physical condition of which the ritual treatment is constant across the globe. Even fear of the dead, even corpse pollution which Malinowski thought to be a universal human experience, has not been taken up universally in ritual. There are cultures, such as the Mae Enga of the New Guinea Highlands, where contact with corpses does not have to be ritually cleansed though they cleanse themselves from sex pollution (Meggitt, 1964). While in other parts, say the Nyakyusa of Tanzania, elaborate washings, seclusions, and fumigations are necessary to make the mourners and burial party fit for normal society again (Wilson, 1957). The same holds good for menstruation: in tribal society it is not universally hedged with ritual taboos. Each primitive culture makes its own selection of bodily functions which it emphasises as dangerous or good. The problem then is to understand the principles of selection.

Another point to consider is that rituals are not fixed from time immemorial. They are not unchanging hard cores of some mystic cosmology. It is a mistake to think of people as being set somewhere below and apart from their cosmological ideas. To some extent they themselves (or we, ourselves) get this feeling of being controlled by an external, fixed environment of ideas. But the feeling is an illusion. People are living in the middle of their cosmology, down in amongst it; they are energetically manipulating it, evading its implications in their own lives if they can, but using it for hitting each other and forcing one another to conform to something they have in mind. If we can realise how much a language changes in a lifetime, without the speakers recognising their own contribution, we can realise how rituals and beliefs change. They are extremely plastic. These two points should be taken together: first, that rituals select some bodily conditions and ignore others; second, that they are being manipulated by people trying to live together. Jointly they provide a clue to the interpretation of ritual, for we should look for circumstances that are not universal, not common to all mankind, to discover the principles of selection. These we are likely to find in the social environment, the dimension in which people are using everything they can, particularly mystic ideas, to influence one another.

The next stage is to distinguish various levels of meaning. Take a common bodily condition and consider the range of rites which seek to control it: there will be several psychological meanings, some potent for the person undergoing that condition and others for persons responding as an audience. Rites dealing with menstruation will use a cluster of culturally standardised meanings concerning blood, womanhood, fertility, barrenness. Then there will be sociological meanings: at one level there is scope for using the situation to manipulate other people, that is at the level of interpersonal relations; at a more inclusive social level the ritual may be made to say something public about social groupings and their relation to one another.

I propose to discuss some rituals concerning menstruation to demonstrate these two distinct sociological dimensions of meaning.

First, beliefs which claim that women are dangerous while menstruating give scope for playing out interpersonal conflicts. These beliefs give rise to rituals which seclude women or require them to be purified before return to mixed society. In order to understand any such belief you have to place yourself in the shoes of a man whose career is in reality liable to be frustrated by female wiles and infidelity. For such a man the danger beliefs can be seized upon as a clear symbolic statement of several things he believes to be true and important in the social sphere. Belief in the dangers of menstruation may be useful:

1   *To assert male superiority.* This is expressed in ideas about cleanness and impurity. To express female uncleanness is to express female inferiority, a point which it may be vitally important to get across to a particular wife in a given home at any time.

2   *To assert separate male and female social spheres.* Men may wish to set clear limits to female intrusion in male affairs or the beliefs may reflect the *de facto* existence of separate male and female spheres of interest. To require a menstruating woman to keep to female quarters can make this point quite effectively. To blame her carelessness in this respect for *his* failure in fishing or hunting or farming is a way of using the cosmos to constrain other people: the man does not directly blame the bad weather for driving the fish deeper into the stream or the game deep into the forest or for drowning or drying the crops. He argues that the weather was bad, but would not have been if menstruating women had kept to the bounds laid down for them. I have heard this being furiously argued by Lele in the Kasai.

3   *To attack a rival.* Women can fasten on these beliefs and use them against one another. Lele believe that food cooked by a menstruating woman is dangerous, and women are not above using these beliefs to fasten blame for family disasters on rival co-wives.

All this is straightforward and obvious. The case of menstruation rites is only one example of a whole range of danger beliefs which are used to underline roles and obligations and to maintain statuses. They not only express people's interest in these social distinctions and duties – they give a handle for coercing everyone into conforming to the pattern. For example, beliefs in dangers following adultery clearly have an expressive function and a coercive potential. Similarly for beliefs in pollution of homicide, pollution of strangers, pollution of royalty by commoners, and so on. Menstrual impurity is a consistent part of a wide general category of pollution beliefs.

In a recent publication (Douglas, 1966) I have seemed to subscribe to the view that danger beliefs have a positive role in enforcing morality. I gave the impression that the beliefs are able to hold down deviance and to enforce conformity to a common code, setting an independent sanction on behaviour. Such a view is certainly wrong. The beliefs are the product of common assent to a set of norms: they express it publicly and visibly, but their power to hold people to a code of behaviour is not more than the power of those people's respect for that code. This, of course, sets limits to the scope for manipulating a social situation by citing danger beliefs. Other people who are not committed to that code will not take the danger beliefs seriously.

There is another quite different way in which danger beliefs can be used to manipulate a social situation:

4   *To lay claim to a special relation.* Among the Hadza, a small, poor tribe of hunters in Tanzania, all social groupings are very fluid. A band loses members, gains others, disbands, reconstitutes itself with a largely different membership in a matter of weeks. At the group level people come and go very freely and set little store on belonging to this or that social unit. But at the interpersonal level there are certain strong pressures. Men want to have sexual access to women, this is a dominant preoccupation. But women are able to live independently of men, for the division of labour is very weak, and they can look after their own needs and those of their children except for getting meat and trade goods. On this unsymmetrical basis of sexual and economic dependence of one sex upon the other, the marriage tie is fragile and easily broken. Here a belief in the dangers of menstruation serves to define the married couple. Dr James Woodburn, from whose unpublished Ph.D. thesis this material is drawn (Woodburn, 1964), describes certain risks which the whole band is thought to run, if the husband of a menstruating woman pursues his usual occupations. While his wife is menstruating the husband is restricted in two important respects: he may not touch poisoned arrows and he may not put his arm into a bees' nest. If he fails to observe these restrictions, the poison on the arrows he touches will lose its efficacy and all the honey in the bees' nests in the area will be eaten by the bees. Other people have an interest in making sure that a man does acknowledge and continues to acknowledge cohabitation by

observing these restrictions: men do not want the poison of their arrows to be spoiled by being handled during gambling by such a man and both men and women would be alarmed at the prospect of all the honey in the district disappearing. The effect is that husband and wife are thus at these times both partially segregated from their sexual groups. While she menstruates, he abstains from certain manly activities. Dr Woodburn writes charmingly of this observance which withdraws both husband and wife from the wider community as a monthly reaffirmation of their union. But as I see it, the husband, whose claim to the woman is always open to challenge and who never knows from month to month how long she will accept him, this precarious husband is using danger beliefs to proclaim publicly his relationship. In ostentatiously *not* joining his comrades and not doing the usual day's round, sitting around while his wife also abstains from certain female occupations, he is being conspicuously public-spirited in trying to avert hardship from the community. But his primary interest is in drawing attention to some alleged physical aspects of the social link between spouses. He is calling on the physical universe to prove his claim to her. Given the lack of other definition of the marital role in this society, one can even imagine two rivals abstaining from work during a woman's menstruation, of competing to apologise for hunting and honey failures due to their carelessness on this point – just as rival lineage elders among the Lugbara put in claims for being responsible for illnesses among their followers in a ritual duel for the succession (Middleton, 1960).

This example of a social use for menstrual taboos suggests a parallel inter-pretation for couvade, the custom whereby a man takes to his bed while his wife is in labour of child-birth, and often simulates her pains. On this approach, I suggest it would be worth looking for a correlation between practice of the couvade, weak definition of marriage, and a strong interest on the husband's part in asserting his claim to the wife and her child. In England we might expect the couvade to be found in sectors of society where the husband is forced to be absent for long periods from home; in tribal society where the marriage tie is weak. The couvading husband is saying, 'Look at me, having cramps and contractions even more than she! Doesn't this prove I am the father of her child?' It is a primitive proof of paternity. It is apparent that I am here seeking to restore to sociological investigation the hypotheses entertained by Tylor and Bachofen and discussed by Crawley (1902). For these anthropologists the practice of the couvade was a missing link in the evolutionary sequence from matriarchal to patriarchal society. I am suggesting that it is a danger belief in the same class as those others by which individuals seek to manipulate their social environment.

I am now ready to turn to the next sociological level of interpretation. Here I am talking about grand public rituals which involve everyone, initiations, funerals, marriages, rituals of peace and war. These are the occasions for arousing emotion and fastening it on focal values: the propositions they make are general, consensus-producing statements about the essential nature of society. These are not the occasions which individual X can use for coercing his enemy, or rival, Y. I contend that if the universal human experience of sex is taken up at this level of ritual it is used to say something publicly, not about sex, but about society. I am going to take for my example the very difficult case of initiation rites in which the genital organs of boys are cut so that they bleed with the explicit intention of making a parallel to female menstruation. Bettelheim (1955: 260) has discussed two examples of this rite among the Murngin and Arunta Australian aborigines. He interpreted them as expressions of male envy of the female procreative role. Indeed, he has ample justification for this interpretation in the texts which he quotes and which give native statements consistent with his view. 'We make the boys bleed so that they become like women,' they say, over and over again in different forms. He concludes (p. 204):

> Anthropological observations lend themselves better to the interpretation that initiation rites were designed to compensate for what might have been considered male physical deficiency in procreation, perhaps reinforced by women because of penis envy or resentment of menstruation, than to the more familiar anthropological and psychoanalytic interpretation.

And again:

> These practices suggest that human beings' envy of the genital apparatus of the other sex leads to the desire to acquire similar organs and to gain power and control over the genitals of the other sex. The former desire is repre- sented in men by subincision and possibly also circumcision; in women it is shown in manipulation to enlarge the clitoris and labia.

His argument, which is well known, derived from insights gained in his clinic for schizophrenic children approaching adolescence. These children had never heard of Murngin aborigines, or of Arunta, or Arapesh or Wogeo. They invented actions which were startlingly close to the practice of induced genital bleeding in boys which figures prominently in the initiation rites of these tribes. They even gave the same reasons for doing so, reasons which Bettelheim sums up as male envy of the womb. There is no need in this paper to take Bettelheim's argument to pieces and show why his generalisations about primi- tive personality development are unacceptable as stated. The point is to be grateful to him for drawing attention so graphically to the central problem of interpretation of ritual, that is, the relation between individual psychological needs and public social needs, both expressed by symbolic acts. Take the case of the couvade: some tribes practise a ritual which requires a man to lie-in while his wife is in child-labour and which is supported by beliefs that the outcome will be unfortunate if he does not lie-in. Here is a publicly recognised standard ritual. Then take the cases reported by contemporary doctors in Europe of men who claim to feel labour pains while their wives are in labour. This is not a public ritual, but a private situation, a pain felt by an individual. What the two cases have in common, whether it is public and private couvade or public and private womb envy, is the subject of this paper. The first step is to understand what the public enactment is about. Is it intended to bring relief to those whose private mental condition is disturbed or would be disturbed and who may gain balance and reassurance by the enactment? In my opinion, no. This is not what public rituals are about, though incidentally they may achieve this effect. A public ritual, with all its attendant beliefs in danger if it is not performed, is the summation of a whole community's experience. It expresses a common, public concern, and uses whatever symbolic language is to hand for bringing the point home. No one is going to be able to foist his private anxieties on the community unless they correspond to everyone's private anxieties, arising out of a common situation. In the case of the couvade in modern Europe, it is easy to see why some men might resort to it spontaneously in their anxiety to lay claim to their wives, and easy to see why it has not become a common practice. It is not likely to appeal to men who have a marriage settlement deposited with the solicitor; or men in tribes where dowry and marriage payments give the husband security. It could become much commoner at the spontaneous level in an England of the future in which the marriage bond were much looser, and then we could predict the pundits dreaming up physical dangers to the unborn child likely to be averted by the father lying-in. Already one notices a new emphasis on the father's role in the lying-in of the mother, and a new responsibility for the mental health of his children, an emphasis which I would expect to be increasing with the greater ease of divorce.

Rituals expressing envy of the womb are not susceptible of a parallel interpretation. In the case of the couvade, I am taking the sociological dimension at the interpersonal level and suggesting that couvade is like menstrual and adultery pollution, a belief used directly for manipulating social realtions. But there is the other dimension, the graphic expression of social forms. To place Murngin and Arunta boys' initiation in this dimension we need to consider other kinds of bodily symbolism.

When the Dinka, a tribe of cattle-herders in the Sudan, sacrifice an ox, they prescribe a variety of different ways of killing it (Lienhardt, 1961). Each method is symbolically appropriate to what the sacrifice is intended to bring about. If it is a truce between two groups of kin separated by a blood feud, they cut the beast in half across the middle and divide the whole animal between both parties; the quarrel is no more to be a division between them. For some occasions they trample it to death, for others they suffocate it. If the sacrifice is to cancel the effects of incest, the animal is cut in half longways, through the genital organs. What is being carved upon the body of the animal is a division to be recognised in future between two lineages: formerly they begot children in one line, now they are divided as to begetting: hence the cut through the genital organs.

There is no difficulty in seeing the body of a sacrificial ox as an image of the body politic. The way it is carved up is clearly the diagram of a social situation. It is clear that what is enacted states something of common concern. We must be prepared to make the same interpretation when the symbolic statement is being carved upon human flesh. This is a central clue to the incision rites which use womb envy to express something about the constitution of society.

When I read Bettelheim's *Symbolic Wounds,* I asked myself why these aboriginal tribes should be so anxious to emphasise symmetry even where symmetry most manifestly is absent, and why in their initiation rites they should try to make the boys acquire procreative powers like women's. It struck me that the artificial creation of symmetry between the sexes might correspond to a dual division within the tribes. True enough, the Murngin are divided into moieties, that is into exogamous, woman-exchanging halves, and the Arunta have a section system, which basically means that moieties have themselves been divided into half again. It seemed plausible then to suggest that the symmetry of the sexes created by initiation expresses the duality of society. If everyone in the system has a strong stake in maintaining the exchanges between the two parts of society, and if this exchange requires that the two parts be symmetrical and equal, then the incision of boys would express a common social concern. I have not had a chance to develop this interpretation. It requires detailed re-examination of the social situation and of the texts about the initiation ceremonies in the tribes cited by Bettleheim. But to make it sound less far-fetched, I will mention two other cases in which male-genital bleeding is ritually required, explicitly as a parallel with female menstruation; two other cases in which the same ritual emphasis on the symmetry of the sexes is found in societies with division into moieties. I take Margaret Mead's account (1938, 1940) of the Mountain Arapesh of New Guinea and Ian Hogbin's first account (1934-5) of the neighbouring Wogeo.

The cosmology of the Arapesh associates all power and energy with sex; it emphasises the equality of male and female sexual power and their equal dangers. Each sex is concerned to control its own sexual power in the interests of fertility and growth. Excessive sexual energy, if uncontrolled, is dangerous to all in contact with it. Not only is a woman dangerous in her sexuality and especially in menstruation to men and children, but a man too is dangerous to women. The sexual power is manifested in blood: the female nourishes the young in her womb with good blood, her menstrual blood is dangerous; the male has equivalent blood in the penis which is good, life-giving and which he draws to feed to his child, once born, in exact parallel to the feeding of the foetus in the womb. Female menstruation strengthens the woman, because it is a means of discharging from her body the dangerous fluids of the opposite sex received in intercourse. This natural purifying discharge men achieve artificially by letting blood from the penis. The centre of the initiation rite of boys is the incision of the penis. Here we have duality and symmetry clearly expressed in rite and cosmology. What of the social structure? We read that this reaches only a very low level of organisation.

> The typical picture is a cluster of hamlets, bound together by ties of inter-marriage, ceremonial co-operation – but within which there is little genuine integration, no centralized system for punishing offenders, no institution-alized leadership, and no mechanism for preventing any one of the associated hamlets from forming stronger ties with hamlets outside the temporary aggregation. The entire region depends on kinship ties as the major social mechanism and the tendency, so conspicuous in Polynesia and in Africa, of elaborating kinship ties into effective political superstructures is lacking.

The Arapesh have two patterns which combine this low-level organisation of kinship into a larger unit: one concerns initiation and one concerns feasting. Mead says, 'Arapesh have two sorts of dual organisation, both are virtually functionless, except for their value in oratory; one is vaguely connected with feasting and the other as vaguely associated with the initiatory cult.' This was in 1938, and nowadays an anthropologist would have to go to some trouble to demonstrate that a reported lack of function and vagueness in institutions is not subjectively imparted by the observer. The Arapesh evidently felt strongly about their dual system for she goes on to report that when a local schism resulted in one locality being entirely represented in one half of the dual division associated with initiation, they split themselves into two again, 'taking as their totems two varieties of the emblem bird, the hawk'.

Hogbin tells us that the cosmology of the Wogeo is also energised by sexual powers.

> The chief source of peril is sexual intercourse, when contact is at a maximum. . . . The juices of the male then enter the female, and vice versa. Women are automatically cleansed by the process of menstruation, but men, in order to guard against disease, have periodically to incise the penis and allow a quantity of blood to flow. This operation is often referred to as men's menstruation. . . . Men also incise the penis after they have performed certain tasks which for magical reasons are held to be very dangerous.

These include building a new men's house, burying a corpse, going on a murder expedition, initiating a boy. They also let blood before risky work, to eliminate the danger. As to social organisation, they are organised in small patrilineal clans. Cutting right across them are two exogamous matrilineal divisions.

Here is evidently very rich material for testing my hypothesis. I would not argue that all rites of incision express the symmetry of dual social divisions. But if it is explicitly stated that the incision of the male genital organ is performed to achieve symmetry with the female reproductive system then I would look for important interdependent dual social divisions whose symmetry I would suppose to be expressed in the ritual creating a symmetry of the sexes.

To conclude: if psychologists turn to tribal studies to gain insights into the behaviour of their patients, they will find it difficult to isolate any strictly psychological levels of meaning which derive from the common human experience of sex and reproduction. For in a tribal culture even these intimate experiences can be mediated to the individual through cosmological and ritual categories. Even the physiological differences between male and female can be masked by a categorisation whose primary purpose is to reflect and sustain a particular social order. Therefore I maintain that there is very little validity in the argument which would interpret tribal rituals by the light of psychiatric clinical experience. Tribal rituals are either being used by one individual to coerce another in a particular social situation, or by all members to express a common vision of society. We cannot argue from the rituals of our mentally disturbed patients to those of functioning tribal systems. But there may be some validity in arguing the other way. When I suggested that the couvade may relate to the husband's insecure claim to the wife, I offered a social context in which the couvade might be found, either in established ritual or arising spontaneously from psychosomatic interactions. Could it be that the schizophrenic boy in Bettelheim's clinic, who wanted to menstruate like the adolescent girl, felt his *social* world threatened by a division based on sexual disparity? Then it would be the symmetry of his *social* world that he wished to restore by creating symmetry of the sexes within it? Not womb envy, but reversing the behaviour of the Arapesh community which, when it found itself lopsidely representing only one totem, divided itself into two, the schizophrenic boy could equally well be trying to prevent a splitting of his society.

In sum, my argument is that we can hope for insight into tribal rituals by studying their social dimensions and into psychosomatic phenomena which resemble tribal rituals by studying the social context, both at the level of social manipulation and at the level of expressing social forms.

BIBLIOGRAPHY

BETTELHEIM, B. (1955), *Symbolic Wounds*, Chicago, Free Press.

CRAWLEY, E. (1902), *The Mystic Rose: a Study of Primitive Marriage*, London, Macmillan.

DOUGLAS, M. (1966), *Purity and Danger: an Analysis of Concepts of Pollution and Taboo*, London, Routledge & Kegan Paul.

HOGBIN, H.I. (1934–5), 'Native culture of Wogeo', *Oceania*, 5, 330, 315.

HOGBIN, H.I. (1970), *The Island of Menstruating Men: Religion in Wogeo, New Guinea*, Chandler Publishing Co.

LIENHARDT, R.G. (1961), *Divinity and Experience: the Religion of the Dinka*, London, Oxford University Press.

MEAD, M. (1938), 'The Mountain Arapesh. I: An importing culture', *Anthropology Papers of the American Museum of Natural History*, *36*, (3), 160, 168.

MEAD, M. (1940), 'The Mountain Arapesh. II: Supernaturalism', *Anthropology Papers of the American Museum of Natural History*, *37*, (3), 344.

MEGGITT, M. (1964), 'Male–female relationships in the highlands of Australian New Guinea', *American Anthropologist*, *66*.

MIDDLETON, J. (1960), *Lugbara Religion*, London, International African Institute.

WILSON, M. (1957), *Rituals of Kinship Among the Nyakyusa*, London, Oxford University Press for International African Institute.

WOODBURN, J. (1964), 'Social organisation of the Hadza of North Tanganyika', Ph.D. thesis, University of Cambridge.

Chapter 13

The healing rite

Review of V.W. Turner's *The Forest of Symbols* and *The Drums of Affliction*, first published in *Man*, 5, 2 (June 1970)

The healing power of symbols is central to the whole subject of symbolic meaning. Now that Turner's four volumes on Ndembu are published (1957, 1962, 1967, 1968), we should see where we stand, as anthropologists, on ritual healing. In the long run nearly everything he has written is concerned with the efficacy of symbols. This is partly because Ndembu rituals claim to have power to heal the body as well as to enlighten the mind; consequently every piece of the jigsaw puzzle of how to interpret their symbolic acts contributes to understanding the great moments when sickness is brought under priestly control. So the climax of the sequence of Ndembu studies is the performance of *ihamba*, the rite which cures one Kamahasanyi of his lassitude and backache by extracting from his body the tooth of an angry dead hunter's ghost. His body purged thus of a symbol of jealous backbiting is itself the symbol of the village which is purged, by the same ritual, of intrusive elements in its system. It is also a symbol of the matrilineal principle reaffirmed in its purity and solidarity – to the confusion of intrusive patrilateral segments and unbrotherly brethren. The rite is not only symbolic in the expressive sense. It even brings about the required changes at the physical and social levels.

To show how a rite can achieve all this the anthropologist requires a detailed analysis of the social structure as well as an analysis of the symbolic system. To provide such detailed analyses of life crises, afflictions, and of how the Ndembu ritualise them, creates thorny problems of interpretation. Only when the descriptions are on record and the interpretations justified is Turner ready for a summing up and demonstration. His *Drums of Affliction* is the climax to which the previous studies lead.

The two books under review relate to one another and to previously published Ndembu studies as follows. First in 1957 came *Schism and Continuity*. This was an analysis of the Ndembu social system. It described how the pulls of matrilineal descent and village membership create personal dilemmas. Here was elaborated the concept of social drama, a ritual resolution of conflict, and an affirming of community values. This is the base line, as it were, for subsequent studies of ritual. Then came *Chihamba, the White Spirit* (1962) a short book describing a particular cult. Now we have in *The Forest of Symbols* (1967) a set of papers which originally appeared in various books and journals. Four deal with the interpretation of ritual symbols; two with rituals of healing, one with hunting ritual, one with witchcraft and sorcery, and two with initiation. One of the latter, on boys' circumcision, is entirely new and has not been published elsewhere. Then in 1968, published by the International African Institute, another volume, *The Drums of Affliction*, deals specifically with ritual healing. There is some overlap between the two last books. The first contains two chapters on healing while the second has a long section on girls' puberty ritual which might well have gone into the first. Turner (1968: 198) explains the principle by which he includes life crisis rituals in the book on rites of affliction by a valuable essay on ritual legitimation. While affliction rituals, as distinct from life crisis rituals,

> are *ad hoc* and unpredictable in their origin and represent responses to unprecedented events, the latter accompany the passage of an individual, or a set of similarly circumstanced individuals, from one social status to another. It is on such occasions of life crises, when fairly elaborate *rites de passage* are performed, that the legitimacy of certain crucial principles of Ndembu society is most fully and publicly endorsed. In the rituals of affliction we see these principles under challenge; in the life crisis rituals we see them being renewed and replenished.

Thus there is a true sense in which the study of healing symbols would not be complete without examining the whole context in which symbols are generated and applied. For the same reason, the book dealing specifically with healing condenses a great deal of the previous material on social structure and on interpretation.

It is extremely valuable to have in the 1967 volume articles which have been scattered and relatively inaccessible. It is also of first importance to have within one set of covers a self-sufficient account of the healing rites of one culture. Without further introduction *The Drums of Affliction* can be put into the hands of anthropologists, psychologists, medical sociologists or anyone interested in the subject. The achievement is so extensive that I cannot take up points of detail without losing proportion. Let me say something general about the scope and originality of the project which is now complete. No one else has done quite this: to push as far as possible the relation of the symbolic to the social order, showing how each gives form to the other in a dynamic intermingling of meanings. In this example we have the answer to the ticklish problem of validation. Anthropologists are rightly always worried by the danger of subjectively imposing their categories on the material to be analysed. How can we control this subjective factor? Turner's answer is to require a convincing demonstration of how the cultural categories sustain a given social structure. It should never again be permissible to provide an analysis of an interlocking system of categories of thought which has no demonstrable relation to the social life of the people who think in these terms. For example, my own discussion of animal categories in the Old Testament, an analysis of Leviticus II in *Purity and Danger* (1966), cannot be acceptable on the standards laid down.

Of course Turner is also original in the quality of his fieldwork. In systematic coverage he is unrivalled. The reading may be repetitive, but this is inevitable for one alive to the need to prove that he has not imposed his own patterns on his material. There is pawky humour, tender observation of personality, and many switches of style: expository, narrative, and even lyrical. But these books do not make easy reading. Turner always requires us to be projected into the Ndembu social world. He expects us to understand the micro-history and current micro-social structure of Ndembu villages. Then from a strictly local point of departure he proceeds to analyse their treatment of the common themes of birth, sex, authority, and death. I pride myself on being specially interested in central African ethnography, so it is from a critical vantage point that I confess that his interpretations seem to be as objectively valid as they can be (given the elementary stage of theoretical understanding of the subject). Indeed, my own professional concerns about Turner's reporting are quite the other way. His villages are located, mapped, their history recorded. The in-habitants are placed on genealogical charts. Their ambitions and conflicts with one another are the essential background to learning the meaning of the rituals. Their names are no doubt scrambled, but to little purpose since each individual seems to be entirely and unmistakably identifiable. What will they feel like when they read these pages in years to come? (Turner, 1968: 197, 192).

> Kamahasanyi, sterile as he was, weak, effeminate, formerly suspected of sorcery, slightly paranoid . . .

> For Kamahasanyi appeared to have passive homosexual tendencies, which suggested there might be a conflict between masculine and feminine striv-ings in his unconscious psyche. It is not perhaps too surprising that he had undergone several performances of Ihamba, a ritual which might be con-sidered to provide masochistic gratifications and to imitate, in its emissions of blood, agonised writhings and final expulsion of an object from within the body, certain of the features of parturition.

It may be as well for Turner that Kamahasanyi has no descendants to come to Chicago to avenge their father's dignity.

The study of colour symbolism has been justly celebrated ever since a paper on it was read to the Association of Social Anthropologists in 1963 (Turner, 1965). Curiously enough, Turner himself has been in a poor position to exploit fully the tight little complex of meanings he discovered in the ritual combina-tion of black, red, and white. He was primarily engaged on the exercise I have just described, that of raising the whole standard of fieldwork, of validation of ethnographers' interpretations, of analytically relating the social and cultural processes. This task, once achieved, makes possible more condensed presentations for future fieldworkers whose range of relevance has been established once and for all. However, it is quite certain that the colour meanings are only one important set. If Turner had been the old style cultural anthropologist he would have delved until he revealed other equally tightly organised sets and demonstrated their structural interrelationships. His special originality is to have come close enough to the field of action to show how meanings arise spontaneously in the minds of people, then are polished up and brought out to express great public occasions. Layer after layer of meaning accrues to each symbol as its application is extended. At each context a social consensus isolates a particular sense. Obviously the working out of the lexical consistency and the syntactic flexibility of the whole ritual language would be a very complex task. Turner could hardly have had time to achieve this as well as what he has done. We seem to have come a long way since Leach (1958: 151–2) was able to write that it is

> surely useless to enquire just why one set of symbolisations is employed in preference to another? Europeans wear black for mourning, Chinese white. In each case the special status of the mourner is indicated by the wearing of a special dress. But the question of *why* one culture selects black for this purpose and another white is surely both irrelevant and unanswerable.

Leach of course is assuming that the answer that is not irrelevant is in terms of the total patterning of symbols in the culture. But by demonstrating how these arise Turner is able legitimately to raise interesting questions about the experiences that generate both thought and society – the enterprise which Lévi-Strauss says only a fool or a genius could attempt (Lévi-Strauss, 1962: 173).

It is very revealing to compare Turner's work on the efficacy of symbols with that of Lévi-Strauss on the same theme. Admittedly, for Turner it is the main interest and for Lévi-Strauss a subsidiary one. But each has written about the calling of the diviner in strikingly different vein. Both would agree that his stock-in-trade is a set of symbolic structures which tend towards creating harmony between different layers of experience. Both would agree that the diviner cures by locating discrepancies and by realigning the patient's subjective attitudes to an acceptable pattern of symbols. Lévi-Strauss's model is the wonder-working shaman of the American shamanist tradition. He dazzles by the skill of his conjuring and the force of his personality. He achieves his cures by producing a social consensus in favour of himself and at the expense of rivals. It is very much a question of outwitting and out-shining (Lévi-Strauss, 1958: 198). 'Quesalid did not become a great shaman because he cured his patients; he cured his patients because he had become a great shaman.' The passage quoted goes on to say that the diviner's own neurotic imagination provides a symbolic mode in which normal thought can fathom the problem of illness. The symbolic systems which the shaman employs draw their emotional force from their correspondence with the psychological and physical experiences of the patient. In another essay on the effectiveness of symbols Lévi-Strauss shows how the shaman works directly on the psyche of his patients (1958: ch. 10). The intervening social structure plays no role in investing the symbols with their emotional power: doctor and patient might be alone (for all explanatory purposes) in an imagined universe constructed by the shaman specially for the séance.

Victor Turner's shaman is also a conjuror; he produces by sleight of hand objects from the sufferer's body. But his style so eschews the flamboyantly magical that he rather suggests a psychiatric social worker. His task is to size up a social problem in terms of an accepted and usual pattern of symbols, and then to encourage his clients to conform to the moral norms of their culture. To this end he gets them to dramatise their situation in an established ritual idiom. At the same time he skilfully manipulates their relationships. Any personal charisma is masked. According to Turner's account, knowing how the social structure works and is symbolised is much more important for the Ndembu shaman than to make a brilliant dazzle.

Place the Anglo-Saxon and the Gaul side by side and we have two anthropologists speaking to us in just such contrasted styles about the way to understand symbols. But any *ad hominem* conclusion is very out of place. They are talking about two different cultures, oceans apart. Each anthropologist forms his bias in association with his informants. The culture interacts with the researcher and to disallow this factor is to lose the rightful impact of his teaching. No doubt at all, ritual healing and social structures are very different, between America and Africa. If Lévi-Strauss had been instructed at an impressionable age by Ndembu teachers hé would have written differently. He would surely have been as apt a pupil as Turner for the scholarly Windson, Muchona, Ihembi, and the others. Take the portrait of Muchona, contrasted with his rival (Turner, 1967: 132, 134):

> Kasonda was worldly and a shade spiteful, *au fait* with the seamier side of Ndembu (and indeed human) nature. He took a rancorous zest in the struggle for headmanship, prestige and money that were the bane of village life. Muchona, for all his battling against witchcraft and the moody, punitive dead, had a curious innocence of character and objectivity of outlook. I was to find that in the balance mankind came off well for Muchona. Between these men lay the gap that has at all times divided the true philosopher from the politician. . . . Living as he had done on the margins of many structured groups and not being a member of any particular group, his loyalties could not be narrowly partisan, and his sympathies were broader than those of the majority of his fellow tribesmen. His experience had been richer and more varied than that of most Ndembu, though all Ndembu, being hunters and semi-nomadic cassava cultivators travel considerable distances during their lives.

This was one of the men who held seminars for the anthropologist on the intricate meanings of colours and rituals. Writing of him as a practitioner, Turner is concerned to point out his courage and gentleness (1967: 137, 138):

> Muchona was treating a woman who was suffering from delusions as a result of puerperal fever. My friend was impressed by what he considered the 'compassionateness' of Muchona's demeanour. Gone was the rather uneasy pertness and comicality of his usual manner; in its stead was an almost maternal air – kind, capable hands washing with medicine, a face full of grave concern. My friend commented on the 'heroism' with which Muchona, at one phase of the ritual, ventured out alone into the ghost-ridden graveyard, far from the firelight, to exorcise the agencies of evil that were making the poor victim writhe and babble nonsense. He subdued his fear to his curative vocation.

> In our 'seminars', Muchona seldom betrayed the emotional bases of his calling. A new and exhilarating intellectual dimension had opened up to him as well as to myself in our discussions of symbolism. At such times he had the bright hard eye of some raptor, hawk or kite, as he poised over a definitive explanation. Watching him, I sometimes used to fancy that he would have been truly at home scoring debating points on a don's dais, gowned or perhaps in a habit. He delighted in making explicit what he had known subliminally about his own religion. A curious quirk of fate had brought him an audience and fellow enthisiasts of a kind he could never have encountered in the villages.

Returning to the comparison with Lévi-Strauss and American shamanism, we should recall the difficulties that Lowie voiced about Durkheim's theory of totemism (Lowie, 1925). To Durkheim's thesis that religious beliefs expressed and sustained society, Lowie riposted that Crow religion was emphatically individualistic. But there is no doubt that Crow social organisation, at least at the level of kinship, was nowhere near as highly systematised as that of the Australian aborigines. It thus seems fair to suppose that Durkheim would never have developed the full theme of *The Elementary Forms of the Religious Life* if he had only had access to Crow and other Plains Indian material. So it is interesting to suppose that Turner's approach to rites of affliction, so strongly Durkheimian in feeling, would never have been developed if he had worked under the instruction of American Indian shamans. It may well be possible that a therapeutic tradition in which the patient and doctor construct their own world of fantasy for comprehending the illness may work in a particular kind of social structure and not in others. In two accounts of ritual efficacy (1958: chs 9 and 10) Lévi-Strauss can proceed as if no restrictions from the social structure need to intervene between the individual patient and the pattern of efficacious symbols spun for him by the diviner. There seem to be no limits to what an imaginative and histrionic performer can induce his community to believe. A Zuni boy accused of sorcery cures his alleged victim by spinning fantastic tales. He is quite explicitly said to be inventing his tall stories and the problem to be explained is how he himself comes to believe in his own fiction (1958: 189–92). The Cuna shaman's song (1958: 205–26) describes the dangers faced by the unborn baby in its mother's womb. Lévi-Strauss does not say that any song which endows the labouring woman's body with cosmic significance would equally well affect her emotional power to respond. Indeed, he stresses (pp. 217–8) that the cure requires that she and her community should believe in the mythology. The social processes by which belief is engendered and sustained are not described. Yet it must be quite misleading for an anthropologist to give the impression that efficacious symbols can always be woven out of private fantasy without reference to the social system. The relevance of this for Ronald Laing's psychiatric work is obvious.

No one has done more than Lévi-Strauss to display the interlocking categories of culture. These constitute a public symbolic system which is available for everyone to draw upon who is a member of the culture. He shows how they are based upon basic social categories and how they schematise all the material aspects of life into patterns of meaning. Lévi-Strauss does not take culture to be a static thing. Everything he has written shows his interest in how changes in the social structure such as the erosion of the moiety system or of clans or variations in the division of labour go with corresponding alterations in the cosmological scheme. Therefore he postulates an interaction between individual and society and some kind of mediation of the social system on the kinds of symbolic patterns which the public culture can generate.

When it comes to ritual healing and the efficacy of magic, however, he takes this narrower and less sociological view. It would almost seem as if the healer were free to be a *bricoleur*, fitting together the bits of the local stock of symbols into the patterns that will most impress his audience and his patient. Yet the rest of his writing implies that the *bricolage* is controlled by the exigencies of a particular social structure in which the patient is involved. The symbols the diviner chooses to apply must be those which allow everyone concerned to perceive a desirable social configuration and, having recognised it, to achieve it. Therefore the healer is not working simply on the psyche of the patient, in terms of their widest social concerns. His business is with how they internalise the values of their society. Useless for him to propose heroic sacrifice if it is not already validated; useless to open new perspectives of hitherto unimagined love and harmony which leave his audience unconvinced. If his therapy works it is because the symbols are creative instruments of a particular social structure. It is precisely here that Turner makes his special contribution.

Lévi-Strauss first aroused intense excitement by announcing what he was going to do by applying structural analysis to mythology (1955). He then preceeded to apply it, in volume after volume (1964, 1966, 1968). The anticipatory demand was already created. Clearly Turner's intellectual odyssey has been rather the other way. He approached his material with openness, ready to find what it contained. The surprises in it probably surprised himself. The very integrity with which he has developed his insights has limited their impact. Here we have a Ndembu-style philosopher, relatively home-spun, making a tremendous contribution to discussions going on in the glare and noise of a more spectacular forum. To make sure that it is fully used is the challenge for us.

BIBLIOGRAPHY

DOUGLAS, M. (1966), *Purity and Danger: an Analysis of Concepts of Pollution and Taboo*, London, Routledge & Kegan Paul.

DURKHEIM, É. (1915), *The Elementary Forms of the Religious Life*, London, Allen & Unwin.

LEACH, E.R. (1958), 'Magical hair', *Journal of the Royal Anthropological Institute*, 88, 147–63.

LÉVI-STRAUSS, C. (1955), The Structural study of myth in 'Myth: a symposium', *Journal of American Folklore*, 78, 428–44.

LÉVI-STRAUSS, C. (1958), *Anthropologie structurale*, Paris, Plon.

LÉVI-STRAUSS, C. (1962), *La Pensée sauvage*, Paris, Plon.

LÉVI-STRAUSS, C. (1964), *Le Cru et le cuit (Mythologiques I)*, Paris, Plon.

LÉVI-STRAUSS, C. (1966), *Du Miel aux cendres (Mythologiques 2)*, Paris, Plon.

LÉVI-STRAUSS, C. (1968), *L'Origine des manières de table (Mythologiques 3)*, Paris, Plon.

LOWIE, R.H. (1925), *Primitive Religion*, London, Routledge & Kegan Paul.

TURNER, V.W. (1957), *Schism and Continuity in an African Society: a Study of Ndembu Religious Life*, Manchester University Press.

TURNER, V.W. (1962), 'Chihamba, the White Spirit' (*Rhodes-Livingstone Papers, 33*), Manchester University Press.

TURNER, V.W. (1965), 'Colour classification in Ndembu ritual: a problem in primitive classification' in M. Banton (ed.), *Anthropological Approaches to the Study of Religion* (Assoc. Social Anthrop. Monogr., 3), London, Tavistock.

TURNER, V.W. (1967), *The Forest of Symbols: Aspects of Ndembu Ritual*, New York, Cornell University Press.

TURNER, V.W. (1968), *The Drums of Affliction: a Study of Religious Process among the Ndembu of Zambia*, Oxford, Clarendon Press.

Chapter 14

Obituary of Godfrey Lienhardt

First published in *Anthropology Today*, *10*, 1 (1994), courtesy of the Royal Anthropological Institute

Tributes to Godfrey Lienhardt, who died in Oxford on 9 November [1993] at the age of 72, and particularly to his study of Dinka religion, have gone on to emphasise his personal qualities, especially his remarkable gift for friendship and his dedication to the peoples of the Sudan. My task is to review the scholarly achievement.

I agree fully with Douglas Johnson's judgment that *Divinity and Experience: the Religion of the Dinka* (1961) 'has never been surpassed' (*Independent*, 17 November), but feel more reserve about André Singer's judgment that it was 'one of the most influential works on our understanding of African religion and belief systems in general' (*Guardian*, 19 November) because I do not see that it had as much influence at the time as it might have been expected to have.

In the early years after the war, after Malinowski and Radcliffe-Brown had introduced their different brands of English functionalism, a new form of writing about religion began. It conveyed the personal immediacy of fieldwork, and located the roots of religion firmly in social life, with a scholarly focus on problems of translation and interpretation. At least four very distinguished ethnographic studies of religion of the 1960s should be set alongside Lienhardt's. After Evans-Prichard's *Nuer Religion* (1956), there followed in quick succession two Oxford books, John Middleton's *Lugbara Religion* (1960) and Kenelm Burridge's *Mambu, a study of Melanesian Cargo Movements and their Social and Ideological Background* (1960). A few years later came Victor Turner's *The Ritual Process* (1969) and Ernest Gellner's *Saints of the Atlas* (1969). Lienhardt's book came in the middle of the chronological series.

Since I have been teaching in Religious Studies departments in American and English universities I have come to doubt that any of these works (with the exception of Victor Turner's) has had much influence outside the narrow professional circle of anthropologists, and now within anthropology they are liable to be derided as the legacy of colonialism: to some they are labelled an impious imposition of Western thought styles upon the sacred things of other cultures. The context of these books rebuts the accusation. Composed before the concept of 'Orientalism', they are better seen as deployed, as it were, in a battle against unsympathetic, even contemptuous, accounts of other people and their religions. But the battle was never engaged. A simple time-warp may explain their relative lack of influence in religious studies. One can assume that the agenda of theologians and missionaries in general would have changed over forty years. The anthropologists of the 1960s would have been getting their idea of theological issues from the 1920s. They were reading Rudolph Otto, Wilhelm Grönbech, or Schleiermacher, writing much earlier. It is not the fault of scholars in religion that their battlefields had shifted before the religious ethnographies were ever published, or that the latter were left attacking popular misconceptions about religion.

The anthropologists' famous antecedents had a fine tradition of writing on African and Melanesian religion influenced by Durkheim, Mauss, Hocart, and Van Gennep. Missionaries, such as Van Wing, Maurice Leenhardt and J. Dennet, had respectfully examined the concept of the person and of the body, the doctrines and practice of sacrifice, and ritual. One of the common underlying themes for the new generation of anthropologists was that the religions in question should not be rated as irrational superstitions. Paralleling Malinowski's approach to law and marriage and Raymond Firth's approach to economic activity, the new studies of religion showed how belief embodies necessary cognitive processes for mapping the world, coding the forces of the universe, and protecting cherished public concerns.

Each of these 1960s books was brilliantly executed. Each took up a particular question about the relation of belief to society, they were each very original, but none could have achieved their project without describing very clearly how a part of the social system worked. Godfrey Lienhardt's *Divinity and Experience* (1961) was out of line in that it offered an encompassing thesis in the philosophy of knowledge, how knowing is rooted in action, and developed it without needing to present an account of Dinka social organisation (which he had done elsewhere in special articles).

The surprise that emerges from rereading *Divinity and Experience* in the light of the author's completed life is the close complementarity of the work and the man. How could that extraordinary book have been conceived except by an intellectually fastidious, fiercely independent person? And how necessary to the sustained argument was love of friends and the sensitivity to delicate distinctions cherished by them? He hated hubris, ambition, attempts to domineer and control. The wonder is that he ever could have found the energy to consummate the work if it had not also been the vehicle of expressing his own life's project. There is a connection to be made between the passionate integrity which made him reject office and eschew power in his professional life and the particular type of scholarly exposition that he chose, his methods and his central thesis.

Godfrey Lienhardt had read English in Cambridge. Hyper-sophisticated, fiercely rejecting cant and snobbery, witty and cogent in debate, one could recognise in him one of a formidable generation influenced by F.R. Leavis. At the time certain topics were circulating among anthropologists interested in religion, and Godfrey Lienhardt delighted in causing discomfiture by revealing their origins, whether they arose from heated denominational controversies among Christians, or from smug positions adopted by nineteenth-century rationalists. Above all he was committed to truth in ethnography, that is against falsifying, against stretching, strait-jacketing, magnifying, ennobling or belittling or otherwise misrepresenting the beliefs of the Dinka.

This integrity shows in his punctilious discussion of translations of theological terms. The Aristotelian distinction between natural and supernatural was already discarded by anthropologists as an unwarranted importation of Western ideas. Evans-Pritchard had introduced scruple into the use of the word 'sin' to translate the Nuer words for transgression against God's law. But it had not occured to anyone that in writing about another religion the word 'God' was equally suspect. Lienhardt described the first division in the Dinka cosmology as distinguishing humans from ultra-human beings, spirits, which he decided to call 'Powers' with a capital P. Among Powers one term meaning 'the sky' or 'the above' comes close to 'God', but he said:

> the attributes of our 'God' and their *nhialic* are not identical, and I have thought that the advantages of using the obvious translations are eventually outweighed by disadvantages . . . would raise metaphysical and semantic problems of our own for which there is no parallel among the Dinka and in their language (p. 29).

His solution was to write of Divinity with a capital D without definite article when translating *nhialic*, and 'divinity' with a small d when writing about Powers. Thus he developed a neutral, non-denominational but still intelligible vocabulary for talking about God's dealings with people.

The exercise in authentic translation surely has vast implications for students of the Bible who are interested in the two Hebrew words for God, and who have assumed the *El* and *Yaweh* come from different times or different regions of early Israel, or who have not been prepared to attribute such theological subtlety to the sons of Abraham. Lienhardt's discussion of existences and relationships involved in the concepts of Powers would surely also be an aid in interpreting the presence in the Bible of angels and archangels who speak as if they shared identity with the one omnipotent God. It certainly ought to have put paid to simplistic historical theories that we still read about the surprising presence of monotheism in early Judaism, because under this strict analysis, it is much more difficult to tell monotheism from polytheism.

It may help to mention a few of the current ideas about religion that he explicitly repudiated. One was the idea of a specifically religious emotion that Rudolph Otto the Lutheran theologian called 'Awe' or the sense of numinous, or *mysterium tremendum*. It was taken up by Marett as the basis of animist religion and much used in teaching comparative religion. The Dinka recognised a 'creator goat' which they treated like an itinerant holy man, respectfully feeding and shading it and putting it on its way to the next district when it seemed ready to go, but he insisted that they definitely did not hold the sacred goat in awe (pp. 49–50).

Another topic was magic or symbolic action, to which he brought a well-worked-out cognitive theory about the relation between action and thought mediated by schemes or images (p. 283 ff.). Another of the current ideas was that religious belief is fixed and static; this he corrected with his insistence on religious syncretism and continuous change (p. 83).

Another famous theme in popular accounts of archaic religions was human sacrifice, a term applied to the Dinka custom of burying certain 'spear masters' alive (p. 196). He made it plausible that these famous holy men would be content to accept the honour of spending their last moments in their own graves. They being the embodiment of the spirit of their people, their last breath was not allowed to expire naturally from their bodies, but Lienhardt considered that this applied literally only to the last breath. His account would have given to the theory of human sacrifice of Africa and in the Bible the sceptical sophistication that is applied by anthropologists to unattested reports of cannibalism. The book should also be mined by any scholars interested in spirit possession, and in animal transformations, among other topics which interested anthropologists then and later. However, it would be difficult to mine it for a particular topic, since the integration of the work was very close.

One might wish that Dinka religious ideas had been more systematised. But that would have contradicted the thesis that the systematisation comes from the action. To take systematisation beyond the knowledge of the ethnographer would have been a grave failure in his eyes. He distinguished clan divinities from the free divinities of the sky, the former being aspects of the principle of descent groupings, the latter having powers that affected the whole Dinka people. Presumably if he had offered a further classification of the free divinities, or tried to work out more fully what gender relations held between them, he would have come against something which their thought and practice kept unsystematised, and he would have wanted to do the same. He refused to attempt a classification of the shrines of the Dinka because he said it would falsify the variety of their practice (p. 265).

A very interesting discussion of *Divinity and Experience* is given in the concluding pages of Valerio Valeri's *Kingship and Sacrifice, Rituals and Society in Ancient Hawaii* (1985), where the author refers to 'the relatively explicit theory of Lienhardt' (p. 346). At one point Lienhardt writes of the anchorage of Dinka religious ideas in social practice as something which 'no theory of sacrifice' can neglect (p. 272). But he would most probably repudiate having a theory of his own. For him, much of contemporary writing about religious ideas was over-systematised. 'Theory', 'system' and 'structure' were suspect terms, smacking of intellectual conceit.

However, his book was tightly structured. It makes a consistent progress through his themes, but so carefully concealed are the mechanics of the composition that the argument becomes elusive. The Dinka universe is split between humans and Powers; humans themselves can be split at times between a passive personhood and active Powers, and Divinity itself has its reflections in various Powers. Sacrifice is not only the culminating point of the religion, but the sacrificial animal embodying Dinka aspirations and understanding is at the peak of the book's presentation. To achieve this literary coherence he has in fact systematised a great deal.

The biggest tribute he made to the complexity of Dinka thought was that, by keeping close to Dinka terms such as those for shadow, image, reflection, he formulated their whole experience in an account of symbolic action as depiction. By casting his thesis in the vocabulary of imaging he presented Dinka to us in their own terms. However, I cannot help feeling that with this *tour de force* he had painted himself into a corner. He had meant to write a book about experience, but what he wrote was about experience as pictures, experience mediated by signs. Dinka saw their experience steeped in picture theories of knowing, and he found in our own language a similar resource biased towards representational epistemology. The current efforts among philosophers to clear depiction from our epistemological discourse suggests there could be possible, more distanced, alternative ways of conveying the meanings of the Dinka religion. In other words, the Dinka won over their ethnographer to their outlook – a victory he could not grudge. His ability to bend his own enquiry to the terms of the people he was studying was part of his preference for gentle, personal influence among his friends.

When he went in 1983 to Northwestern University to receive an Honorary Degree for his distinguished services to African Studies, Godfrey Lienhardt was also warmly welcomed by the anthropologists at the University of Chicago. There he found he had become a legendary figure: thirty years earlier he had achieved something that all young anthropologists were now aspiring to do. As one of them told me, his ethnography took account of the whole gamut of experience, the whole person, the whole encounter, the whole scene, in a polished form that seemed to have leaped from the early 1960s to a place ahead of the present day.

Chapter 15

Looking back on the 1960s essays

The 'Critical essays' shift the problem of belief from the subjects studied to the scholars reporting on their studies. Some of the essays still seem to have been on the right track. Some of them are substantially right but fail to give due praise, some are actually wrong. I have added my obituary notice of Godfrey Lienhardt at the end to give a fair idea of what 1960s anthropology could achieve.

Chapter 7 on pollution is a general reflection on the idea of dirt, and following closely the argument of *Purity and Danger* which had been published only two years earlier, it relates the idea of dirt to an underlying system of values and to a habitual arrangement which organises them. I am glad to include it in this edition because it sketches the main concerns of my own later publications. For example, it explains clearly the connection between dirt and a violated classification. It seems as if I was already anticipating the volume of *Essays in the Sociology of Perception* which was not achieved until 1982.[1]

I notice that I made a wildly wrong prediction on the future of pollution ideas in Western industrial societies. Explaining why taboo and pollution were more prominent features of so-called 'primitive societies' than of modern, I put the burden of explanation upon the greater success and the consequently greater stability of the modern systems of knowledge. I wrote that,

> In 'scientific culture . . . we are led by our scientists to specialisation and compartmentalisation of spheres of knowledge. We suffer the continual break-up of established ideas. . . . In scientific work the thinker tries to be aware of the provisional and artificial character of the categories of thought which he uses. He is ready to make a reform or reject his concepts in the interests of making a more accurate statement. Any culture which allows its guiding concepts to be continually under review is immune from cosmological pollutions.

How wrong could I get? The mistake was to overemphasise the intellectual and underemphasise the sociological pressures, the very trap that I was constantly warning my critics against. This was written just before the awareness of environmental pollution had burst upon the Western world. A Harvard political scientist, the late Ithiel de Sola Poole, becoming curious about the threatened pollution of rivers and the fate of the about-to-be-extinct snail-darter, told me that he consulted the heading 'Pollution' in the International Encyclopedia of Social Sciences, and was surprised to read my essay on *The Golden Bough* and religion and taboo.

The first edition had two essays on French anthropology in the 1960s, one on the Dogon studied by the team of Marcel Griaule, and one on the work of Claude Lévi-Strauss on the structural study of myth. In these I explained why it was frustrating to the English anthropologist to read a powerful and elegant anthropological literature that did not link up convincingly with real life. To read accounts of myth unsupported by empirical observation or case histories was discomfitting. I was writing to clarify the difference between two traditions of reporting. The essays speak for themselves. What I now see as a woeful omission from this section was lack of any tribute to the transformation effected by structuralist theory.

Before Lévi-Strauss we, the British social anthropologists descended from Malinowski and Radcliffe-Brown, having disposed of nineteenth-century evolutionary theories, were left with no theory of myth whatever. In mythology we were paupers, grubbing for a material grip. All we could do was to bracket it away as literature, or echo Malinowski's dictum that myth is a sociological charter. We might have felt uncomfortable at having nothing to say about the momentous topic, but we were at a complete loss. That is still to some degree a difficulty. Anyone can do structural analysis, more or less richly and convincingly, but it is difficult to be able to say whether the meanings elicited from the exercise are true. If my comments on Lévi-Strauss in Chapter 8 were grudging it was perhaps because I sensed that this new methodology which allied anthropology with literature would be a threat to the development of social anthropology as I knew it.

Chapter 10 on jokes was written for a conference in Uganda on Joking organised by Victor Turner. It tries to solve a conundrum about what makes a funny joke funny. Unfortunately it has some mistakes. For one, I blush for having orginally attributed to Beaumarchais *Les Jeux de l'Amour* of Marivaux, as kindly pointed out by the dilligent reviewer cited earlier.[2] (I would dispute his further claim that I had misrepresented Freud's theory.) For another, I misinterpreted the interclan joking of the Bemba, and have now included Audrey Richards' comment in the text. By the main argument I take my stand: a joke is not funny unless the context permits it to be recognised, and the funniest jokes project the situation of the laughers. The funniness consists in the licence to comment irreverently on the current situation. Chapter 11 on bodily behaviour (Do dogs laugh?) continues the theme. It makes appeal to the idea that I had first developed in *Natural Symbols* (1970), that communication puts pressure on the communicators to bring all the media of expression into conformity.

This has in it the seed of a postmodernist explanation for the public exuberance of our contemporary sportsmen. The body, I claimed, mediates the relevant social structure, it communicates by presenting itself as an image of the total social situation, and it is the acceptable tender in the exchanges which make the social situation. So while the footballers or cricketers are in the game, the body is wholly absorbed in the game's exchanges; once a goal is scored or a wicket lost, there is respite. Formerly, the players walking staidly across the pitch would hide their triumph or shame, they had to exhibit sportsmanship and emotional control. Now they ecstatically embrace and indulge in widly unconstrained demonstrations of joy. Doing so, they are, I suggest, responding to the change in late capitalist society. Formerly pressures to conform to dignified behaviour were evoked by commitment, lifetime responsibility, and hopes for job security. Now, in postmodernism, there is no security, no commitment, no mutal responsibility, so there is no reason to conceal exultation, nothing to restrain the leaping and frolicking before the cameras.

My initial conception of African healing was pedestrian. I really thought it was all a matter of knowing the right herbs. The Lele regarded themselves as great specialists on healing, and I supposed that this meant that their herbal remedies were effective. I even collected a small herbarium, at the instance of Franz Steiner, and had the plants identified by the kindness of the Natural History Museum. When I first heard Victor Turner describing Ndembu healing I had a sudden illumination about how much I had been missing of the way that symbolism works, and of how powerful African medicine could be to restore tranquillity and confidence to a disturbed mind. This my review in Chapter 13 tries to explain. While I am sure that their healers do have powerful herbal remedies that we know nothing about, African healing is not Western medicine in a more primitive state. It is a highly developed skill, with very different aims and means, as different as psychiatry from physical medicine.

NOTES

1 Mary Douglas (ed.), *Essays in the Sociology of Perception* Routledge, 1982. Contributors were: David Ostrander, Michael Thompson, James Hampton, Celia Bloor, David Bloor, George Gaskell, George Kelly, Katrina McLeod, Don Handelman, Martin Rudwick, Steve Rayner and Denis Owen.
2 Dan Sperber, 'Dirt, danger and Pangolins', *Times Literary Supplement*, 30 April 1976, p. 502.

Part III

Essays on the a priori

Introduction
1975

It is a privilege for a researcher's work to be taken up by another. The neophyte who has spotted a technique or a useful piece of information is lucky if someone more experienced absorbs the initial research and solves the main questions as a footnote to his own work. My experience was the other way round. In Congolese fieldwork among the Lele I observed some material relevant to then current anthropological concerns, and published it summarily in 1955 and 1957 (Chapters 2 and 3 of this book). The material explained some of the assumptions about animals and humans that operated as hidden categories through which the Lele organised their experience. The categories came to the surface as explicit rules of diet, hygiene, and etiquette. Though fragmentary they were remarkably consistent. Clearly, further research into the rules for everyday dealing with animate and inanimate things would reveal a more coherent ordering of the universe and reveal more and more clearly the social imprint it received through their system of classification. In its broad outline this was not specially new to British social anthropology or to any anthropologists trained in the traditions of *L'Année sociologique*. Durkheim and Mauss had dealt in Australian, Eskimo, Chinese and American ethnography, and had gained access to the category system through the grand principles actualised in moiety, phratry or marriage class organisation. My material was African and access to it was gained through staying with the women as they cooked, divided food, talked about illness, babies and proper care of the body. I had added a geographical region to the existing literature on the subject of implicit categories, and also a different social dimension, more intimate than those already studied. In this sense, the reporting was normal science: it extended the application of principles already understood. But the fact that the Lele cults could better be interpreted through knowing their principles of personal hygiene and diet, and that these turned out to be consistent with the principles for classifying animal kinds, could be of more than regional interest. It suggested an even stronger channelling of experience through socially significant categories than was already assumed. This in turn would suggest that a much closer fit between religious and other forms of organisation could be revealed through studying higher level classification systems.

At the time of research I had had the good fortune to attend lectures in Oxford on Nuer sacrifice and on Tallensi ancestral cults. It was impressive to learn how the specialised religious institutions gathered up the varied strands of social and psychological experience and affirmed the normative values in dramatic rituals. The tribal religions were saying something, expressing something, if you must, that was happening independently at a secular level, in clan and lineage organisation. In spite of assertions to the contrary (Evans-Pritchard, 1956: 313) the approach was strongly Durkheimian: religion crystallised the great moments, the deepest emotions, it focused for the individual his relation to society. Lele had no lineages, did not perform sacrifice or venerate ancestors. Most of their cultic energies were devoted to warding off sorcery. Since for them specialised religious institutions were not so apparent as for those other tribal societies, they promised a fertile ground for interpreting ritual more broadly. The Lele case should have been able to show the link between the great moments and the minor ones, the structuring of thought and response in every aspect of lived experience. The principles of classification, when their burden of social concern had all been revealed, would show how culture is created. Obviously, if such a programme lay ahead, it would not do to leave the analysis of animal classification where I put it down in 1957. That article concludes tamely that once the implicit framework of Lele metaphysical ideas had been uncovered, the 'different cult groups no longer seemed to be disconnected and overlapping, but rather appeared as complementary developments of the same basic theme'. Left out of this conclusion was practically everything that really preoccupied the Lele. One gets the impression of a lot of squeamish, hypochondriac old maids, worried about absurdly elaborate etiquette and superstitious hygiene. No sign of their truculence, their raiding and abductions of women, their harping on violent revenge and sexual virility. These values come to the fore in the book on their social organisation (1963). But their principles of classification merely relate their cult groups to their assertion of male dominance over females, human dominance over animals, both given in terms of finer discrimination of food and table manners. And on that platitude the matter rested.

At that time it was likely that each year would see a new batch of anthropologists in Central Africa. Inevitably some of them would be confronted by similar problems. It was reasonable to hope that my analysis would be superseded by more complete recordings of animal taxonomy in other tribes and the rules of behaviour by which they were known. As a result of concerted research on principles of belief in that region, it could be expected that one day the implications for the theory of knowledge, which I could vaguely indicate, would be expounded for wider understanding. At that time, moreover, it did not seem necessary to highlight as a discovery the advantages this kind of data holds over mythology for revealing the basis of culture. The difficulty of controlling a given interpretation of mythology is that there are no criteria of relative importance for the different elements identified. By contrast, beliefs

which are pegged by rules of behaviour and underwritten by beliefs in automatic sanctions have some guarantee of the weight that is attached to them.
The anthropologist's subjective bias is brought under control. But the development of anthropology has gone in other directions.

Not only did anthropology eventually change its focus, with the happy result
that my original assumptions are in favour again, but, less happily, the region I
worked in suffered great change. Congo Independence in 1961 was followed by
civil war. The dispersal of my Belgian colleagues led to some drying up of
research in that region. That is why I can enjoy the rare privilege of cashing my
own cheques, postdated as they seem to have been. Twenty years later I can
chide myself for negligence, and get to work afresh by contemplating the
relation of my own with colleagues' subsequent work.

The earliest paper (1955; Chapter 2 of this book) records some Lele ideas about
cleanliness and propriety. It shows that they reach forth from water-gourd and
cooking-pot to the sphere of religion. Filth here is clearly associated with sexual
shame and improper sex. Rules of avoidance of all kinds, whether for showing
respect between sons and fathers, seniors and juniors or in-laws, is always referred
explicitly to the dominant idea of in-law avoidance. Therefore, if I found that
animals were said to be lacking shame and without respect, the connotations of
sex and marriage could not be ignored – surely not. However, in the 1957 paper
(Chapter 3 of this book), dealing directly with animal catgories and cults, this
connection is completely overlooked. The pangolin is on record there as an animal
which, unlike all other beasts, shows shame and practises respect avoidance. If it
ever occurred to me that the dominant metaphor of sex was dominant here too, I
simply do not know how to interpret the connection. I merely concluded from the
superficial meaning of Lele remarks about the pangolin's human-like characteristics that its politeness made it a fit mediator between the species whose defining
boundaries its physical existence transcended. I was uncomfortably aware that this
was a pretty thin explanation of its awesome power. But it was a private dis-
comfort. No one else I ever consulted disagreed with that particular analysis. I was
sometimes asked when I would write a book on Lele religion, but confessed that I
had recorded all I knew.

When I came back from the first stint of fieldwork, my supervisor, Professor
Evans-Pritchard, looking sympathetically through my sketchy reports, told me
that I had plenty of information – what was wanting was understanding: this
would come with empathy and work, one's own and other people's. I now see
that the problem of understanding foreign beliefs is distorted by the concentration on great moments dramatically enacted. The very category of religion,
focusing, as Victor Turner puts it so well, on rites of life crisis and of affliction
(see Chapter 13 of this book) would be a distraction to the task I should have
had in hand. It implies that a scanning of the grand affirmatory points in social
experience will always turn up the corresponding catalogue of rituals of affirmation, separation and healing, and thus map in advance that part of the culture
which corresponds to religion the world over. But the problem of relating Lele

classification of animals to their ongoing male competition for women did not open to that approach. It could not be solved until posed in a different comparative framework. It involved a conversion to a form of alliance theory, as the penultimate paper here, 'Self-evidence', shows. It involved clarifying the untidy language of magic and religion, the work which was begun in *Purity and Danger* and continued in these essays. To have shown some of the ways in which each tribal universe is constructed out of the mutual coercion of social life did not bring me anywhere near solving the problem of the pangolin's extraordinary power as a sign to the Lele. I was stuck. Stimulus had to come from other research. It was given in handsome endowments from Ralph Bulmer and S. Tambiah.

In *Purity and Danger* I paralleled the Lele classification of animals with that in Leviticus 11. Ralph Bulmer was the only person to protest that in writing on Hebrew cosmology I had done the very thing that the rest of the book was written to stop. It was an analysis of a system of ideas with no demonstration of its connection with the dominant concerns of the people who used it for thinking with. Both Bulmer's and Tambiah's animal classifications brilliantly avoided this defect. In each case a concern about wrong sexual partners came through to the animal classification in the form of concern about uncontrolled boundary-crossing animals. The systems of marriage rules made themselves felt in the systems of rules about touching and eating animals. Full of admiration, my first thought was that it would be impossible to push the Hebrew and Lele analyses to parallel conclusions, for lack of good ethnography. Then I re-read E.R. Leach's *Legitimacy of Solomon*, which brought home to the anthropologist with a resounding thud something which Old Testament scholarship has been agreed upon for a very long time. This was that the Pentateuch was full of concern for the evils that flowed from marriages with foreigners. Israelite marriage laws were not based upon a rule of lineage or tribal exogamy, rather the contrary. Therefore it was reasonable that the Israelites would not manifest the same concerns about wrong sexual partners as tribes whose whole social organisation was based on a rule of exogamic exchange. And if the Israelites were significantly different in their marriage laws, what about the Lele? Here again a more reflective study might show up important differences in their attitude to the son-in-law and his provenance.

Chapters 18 and 19 supplement one another closely. The new approach to animal classification could not proceed without extending the analysis of Hebrew rules of purity. I chose the rules governing the Jewish meal (Chapter 18 of this book) so as to reach beyond the classification of animal kinds to the social and political preoccupations of the Jewish people themselves. This exercise seemed to illustrate well the thesis that a social preoccupation with boundaries will be reflected in the treatment of boundaries in general and therefore that classification systems may be compared according to the way their boundaries are arranged. Having demonstrated the connection between Leviticus 11 on the Mosaic dietary laws and the dominant concerns of the ancient Hebrews,

I was ready to compare the four classification systems, Thai, Karam, Lele and Hebrew, from this very abstract point of view. Their different patterns of insulation and overlap finally provided the context in which I solved the puzzle about the pangolin's power (Chapter 19). A more sophisticated logical exposition is very desirable. The essence of the argument is that the logical patterning in which social relations are ordered affords a bias in the classification of nature, and that in this bias is to be bound the confident intuition of self-evident truth. And here, in this intuition, is the most hidden and inaccessible implicit assumption on which all other knowledge is grounded. It is the ultimate instrument of domination, protected from inspection by every warm emotion that commits the knower to the social system in which his knowledge is guaranteed. Only one who feels coolly towards that society can question its self-evident propositions.

BIBLIOGRAPHY

EVANS-PRITCHARD, E.E. (1956), *Nuer Religion*, Oxford, Clarendon Press.
DOUGLAS, M.M. (1963), *The Lele of the Kasai*, London, Oxford University Press for the International African Institute.
GOODENOUGH, W.H. (1970), *Description and Comparison in Cultural Anthropology*, Chicago, Aldine.

Chapter 16

Environments at risk

Lecture given at ICA, October 1970, first published in (1972) *Ecology in Theory and Practice*, Viking Press.

When the scientist has a very serious message to convey he faces a problem of disbelief. How to be credible? This perennial problem of religious creed is now a worry for ecology. Roughly the same conditions that affect belief in a denominational god affect belief in any particular environment. Therefore, in a series of lectures on ecology, it is right for the social anthropologist to address this particular question. We should be concerned to know how beliefs arise and how they gain support. Tribal views of the environment hold up a mirror to ourselves. Putting ourselves in line with tribal societies, we can try to imagine the figure we would cut in the eyes of an anthropologist from Mars. From our own point of view he would take an agnostic stand. But today, to do justice to this lecture's subject, we should ourselves attempt the difficult trick of letting go of what we know about our environment – not forgetting it, but treating it as so much science fiction. Like the alien anthropologist, let us suspend belief for a little while, so as to confront a fundamental question about credibility.

We are far from being the first civilisation to realise that our environment is at risk. Most tribal environments are held to be in danger in much the same way as ours. The dangers are naturally not identical. Here and now we are concerned with overpopulation. Often they are worried by underpopulation. But we pin the responsibility in quite the same way as they do. Always and everywhere it is human folly, hate, and greed which puts the human environment at risk. Unlike tribal society, we have the chance of self-awareness. Because we can set our own view in a general phenomenological perspective, just because we can compare our beliefs with theirs, we have an extra dimension of responsibility. Self-knowledge is a great burden. I shall be arguing that part of our current anxiety flows from loss of those very blinkering or filtering mechanisms which restrict perception of the sources of knowledge.

First, let us compare the ecology movement with others of historical times. An example that springs to mind is the movement for the abolition of slavery of a century ago. The abolitionists succeeded in revolutionising the image of man. In the same way, the ecology movement will succeed in changing the idea of nature. It will succeed in raising a tide of opinion that will put abuses of the environment under close surveillance. Strong sanctions against particular pollutions will come into force. It will succeed in these necessary changes for the same reason as the slavery abolition movement, partly because of its dedication and mostly because the time is ripe. In many countries in the nineteenth century slavery was becoming more costly than wage labour.[1] If this had not been the case, I doubt if that campaign would ever have got off the ground. Where locally it was not the case, all the arguments about brotherly love, Christianity, and common humanity were of no avail. The Clapham Sect, I believe, abstained from sugar as a protest against plantation slavery. In the same spirit some of my friends have abstained from South African sherry. This is a less impressive sacrifice since there are other better sherries. But those of us who do not own a car will not end exhaust fume pollution any more than the Clapham Sect diminished by one whit the place of sugar in the native diet. The tide of opinion against slavery was not against industrial development. And the tide of opinion which will reduce the worst pollution effects will not stem industrialisation. Here is the crunch of the environmental problem that leads it far beyond the nuisance of water and air pollution and increasing noise. The ecologists have had to raise their sights to the global level. Their gloomy forecasts for the imminent end of our planet put us, the laymen, in the role of the helpless hero of a thriller. Several nasty deaths are in store for us. Time will reveal whether the earth will be burnt up by the unbalancing of its radiation budget, or whether a film of dust will blank out the sun's rays, or whether it will explode in an atomic war. Over-population and over-industrialisation are the twin causes. But herein lies the dilemma. The obviously overpopulated and starving masses are in the non-industrial regions. Their hope of food lies in new technological developments. But these come from the already industrial countries. Must we stop the growth of science which may one day feed the existing hungry? How do we control population anyway? And which ones should we start with? On a giant hoarding over the Chicago Expressway is a notice which says: 'Think before you litter.' A rather coarse expression, I thought, when I first assumed it to be family planning advice. But if I understand Dr Paul Ehrlich aright the anti-litter campaign could do well to take on the double objective, especially in Chicago. The starving millions of Asia are not the ones who own two cars, whose factories discharge effluent into lakes, or whose aeroplanes give off loud bangs. Ehrlich says: 'The birth of every American child is fifty times more of a disaster for the world than the birth of each Indian child. If you take consumption of steel as a measure of overall consumption, you find that the birth of each American child is 300 times more of a disaster for the world than the birth of each Indonesian child.'[2]

At the top global level the scientists speak with different voices, and none has a clear solution. This is the level at which we are free to believe or disbelieve. The scientists would not wish to be treated as so many old sandwich-men bearing placards which say: 'The end is near.' Our disbelief is just as much a problem for them as our gullibility. Therefore, whether their message is true or false, we are forced to study the basis of plausibility.

Another movement of ideas which this current ecology question recalls is the growth of classical economics. A realisation which transfixed thoughtful minds in the eighteenth century and onwards was that the market is a system with its own immutable laws. How can we appreciate the boldness of the illumination with which Ricardo discerned that system and its homeostatic tendencies? In our day and for this audience I can only hope to give an idea of the thrill of analysing its complexity, and the power and even sheer beauty of the system as it revealed itself, by reminding you of the excitement engendered in linguistics by Chomsky's revelation of the structural properties of language. But that is a very pale analogy. Consider how few political decisions are affected by linguistics compared with the implications of economic science. For the sake of that system and its unalterable laws, many good men have had to harden their hearts to the plight of paupers and unemployed. They were deeply convinced that much greater misery would befall if the system was not allowed to work out its due processes. In the same way, the ecologists have perceived system. In fact, their whole science consists in assuming system, reckoning inputs and outputs, and assessing the factors making for equilibrium. The pitch of excitement in the ecological movement rises when the analysis is lifted to the level of whole continents and even to the level of this planet as a whole. In exactly the same way as the old economists, the ecologists find themselves demanding a certain toll of human suffering in the name of the system which, if disturbed, will loose unimaginable misery on the human race. Sometimes there is a question of bringing water a thousand miles to irrigate a desert. The ecologists know how to do it. They can easily make a desert blossom and so bring food and life to starving people. They hesitate to answer for the consequences in the area from which the water has been diverted. Their professional conscience bids them consider the system as a whole. In the same spirit as Ricardo deploring the effects of the Poor Laws, ecologists find themselves unwillingly drawn into negative, even reactionary positions.

These digressions into economics and slavery suggest a way of restricting somewhat the problem of credibility which is altogether too wide. It will be rewarding to watch how belief is committed along the bias towards or away from restriction. For ultimately this is it – restriction or controlled expansion? Which of us tends to believe the experts who warn that our system of resources is limited? And which of us optimistically follow those who teach that they cannot possibly tell yet what resources may lie unknown beneath the soil or in the sea or even in the air? And the same question about our own bias may be raised for the bias of the experts themselves.

Phenomenology, as I understand it, is concerned with what it is we believe we know about reality and with how we come to believe it. An anthropologist's survey of tribal environments is different from the ecologist's survey. Ecology imports objective measures from a scientific standpoint and describes in those terms the effect of the system of cultivation on the soil and of the soil on the crop yield, etc. It is concerned with interacting systems of physical realities. The anthropologist, if he is not lucky enough to have access to an ecological survey in his research area, has to make a rough dab at this kind of assessment and then use it to check with the tribe's own view of their environment. In this sense an anthropologist's survey of tribal environments is an exercise in phenomenology. Each tribe is found to inhabit a universe of its own, with its own laws and its own distinctive set of dangers which can be triggered off by incautious humans. It is almost as if there were no limit on the amount of variation two tribes can incorporate into their view of the same environment. Some objective limits must apply. Nevertheless, if we were to rely entirely on tribal assessments, we would get wildly incongruous views of what physical possibilities and constraints are in force.

For example, I worked in the Congo on the left bank of the Kasai river, among the Lele. On the other bank of the same river lived the Bushong, where my friend Jan Vansina worked a little later on. Here were two tribes, next-door neighbours, who celebrated their cold and hot seasons at opposite points in the calendar. When I first arrived, green to Africa, the Belgians said how wise I had been to arrive in the cold season: a newcomer, they said, would find the hot rainy season unbearable. In fact it was not a good time to arrive, because all the Lele were working flat out to clear the forest and fire the dead wood, and then to plant maize in the ash. No one but the very aged and the sick had time to talk to me and teach me the language, until the rains arrived and ended their period of heavy work. When I knew the language better, I learnt of a total discrepancy between the European and native assessment of the weather. The Lele regarded the short dry season as unbearably hot. They had their sayings and rules about how to endure its heat. 'Never strike a woman in the dry season', for example, 'or she will crumple up and die, because of the heat.' They longed for the first rains as relief from the heat. On the other bank of the Kasai, the Bushong agreed with the Belgians that the dry season was pleasantly cool and they dreaded the onset of the first rains. Fortunately the Belgians had made excellent meteorological records, and I found that in terms of solar radiation, diurnal and nocturnal temperatures, cloud cover, etc., there was very little objective difference that could entitle one season to be called strictly hotter than the other.[3] What the Europeans objected to, apparently, was the humidity of the wet season and the absence of cloud which exposed them directly to the rays of the sun. What the Lele suffered from in the dry season was the increased radiant heat which resulted from the heavy screen of clouds. They recognised and hated the famous glass-house effect that we are told will result from an excessive carbon dioxide screen for ourselves. But above all, the Lele timetable required them to do all their agricultural work in one short, sharp burst, in the dry season. The Bushong, across the river, with a more complex agricultural system, worked away steadily the whole year round. They also distinguished wet and dry seasons, but they concurred with the Europeans about the relative coolness of the dry period. How did the Europeans arrive at their assessment, since objectively there was so little to choose? No doubt because the seasons

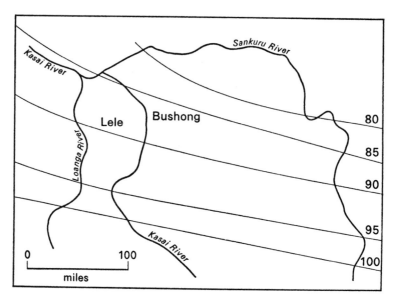

Figure 16.1 Average length of dry season expressed in days (F. Buletot, *Saisons et Périodes Sèches et Pluvieuses au Congo Belge*, Brussels, 1954)

were named and their attributes set at Leopoldville, the capital, where temperature readings showed a difference between the seasons that did not obtain in the interior. In this example, credibility derives from social usage. If the Lele could have changed their timetable, their perception of their climate could have been altered. But so would a great deal else in their life. They were relatively backward technologically, compared with the Bushong. A different timetable, spreading their work through the calendar and through the whole population, would have greatly bettered their exploitation of their environment. But for such a fundamental revolution they would have had to create a different society.

Timetables are near the heart of our problem in the phenomenology of environments. Andrew Baring, in studying a Sudanese people, tells one that their mythology is full of dynastic crises, plots, unrest, and revolution. Whenever discontent reaches boiling-point in the myth cycle, a new king takes over the palace. The upstart always shows his administrative flair by changing the times of meals. Then the discontent simmers down and all is well until something goes wrong again with the order of day in the royal household. Then the stage is set for a new dynastic upheaval and a new king to settle the timetable problem afresh. Largely, the doom ecologists are trying to convince us about a kind of time-bomb. Time is running out they say. Whenever I suggested to the Lele small capital-intensive projects that would improve their hunting or the comfort of their houses, they would answer 'No time'. The allocation of time is a vital determinant of how a given environment is managed. It is also true that time perspective held by an expert determines what answer he will give to a technical problem. Therefore, we should start our discussion of how credibility is engendered by considering the time-dimension.

Among verbal weapons of control, time is one of the four final arbiters. Time, money, God, and nature, usually in that order, are universal trump cards plunked down to win an argument. I have no doubt that our earliest cave ancestress heard the same, when she wanted a new skirt or breakfast in bed. First 'There wouldn't be time', and then, 'We couldn't afford it anyway'. If she still seemed to hanker: 'God doesn't like that sort of thing'. Finally, if she were even prepared to snap her fingers at God, the ace card: 'It's against nature and what is more, your children will suffer'. It is a strong hand when the same player, by holding all these cards, can represent God and nature, as well as control the timetable and the bank account. Then the time-scale, as presented by that player in control, is entirely credible.

It is only just beginning to be appreciated how much the perception of time-scale is the result of bargaining about goals and procedures. For a touching insight, read Julius A. Roth's little book *Timetables, Structuring the Passage of Time in Hospital Treatment and Other Careers.*[4] Here he describes the attempts of long-term patients in a TB hospital to get some satisfactory response out of their doctors. Spontaneously and inevitably the clash of interests expressed itself in a battle about the timetabling of diagnosis and treatment. For the patient, his whole life is held in suspense, no plans can be made, no sense of progress enjoyed until he knows when he can go home. His anxiety concentrates in a passionate study of the time-scaling of the disease and its treatment. With no means of extracting from them any clue to his central preoccupations, and no sanctions to employ to enforce their collaboration, the patient would try to impose on the medical staff a kind of natural timetable. 'I've been here six months now, doctor, by this time you ought to have decided whether I need surgery.' 'Massey got a pass after only three months here – why can't I?' 'Hayton got discharged three months after surgery – why should I have to wait four months?' The doctors' strategy is evasive. They consistently reject the very idea of a rigid timetable, and struggle to refute the culture of the ward where patients go on working out a clear set of phases by which they judge the competence of the doctors and the course of their illness. Sometimes if the doctor does not seem to accept these spontaneously emerging laws of disease and treatment, the patient discharges himself, feeling that the basis of mutual understanding has failed.

The Lele afford another example of how timetabling is used as a weapon of control. They think that they can do something to bring on the rains. This technique of weather control was not a rain-dance, or a magic spell. It was something which any individual might do, with the effect of hastening the onset of the rainy season. The belief in its effectiveness became an instrument for mutual coercion. Laggard farmers would beg others to wait until they had had time to clear their fields and burn the wood. The punctual ones would warn them to hurry up, lest the rain be provoked by action in the north. It seemed to me, sceptical as I was of the value of their technique, exactly like the departmental head who creates artificial deadlines to hasten decisions or otherwise keep his staff on their toes. 'I can only vouch for the students' reaction if we get our policy settled by the next meeting.' Much later I learnt that the Lele techniques of seeding the clouds by the smoke of their burning forests might indeed be effective. Air pollution can increase condensation and precipitation of moisture. It seems that a district in Indiana, thirty miles downwind of South Chicago's smoky steelworks, tends to have 31 per cent more rain than other communities where the air is clearer.[5] The joke was on me that the Lele weather control turned out to be scientifically respectable. For the purpose of my present argument, its efficacy is irrelevant. All that matters is that time is a set of manipulable boundaries. Time is like all the other doom points in the universe. One and all are social weapons of control. Reference to their power sustains a view of the social system. Their influence is thoroughly conservative. For no one can wield the doom points credibly in an argument who is not backed by the majority view of how the society should be run. Credibility depends so much on the consensus of a moral community that it is hardly an exaggeration to say that a given community lays on for itself the sum of the physical conditions which it experiences. I give two well known examples.

In many tribal societies it is widely agreed that wives should be faithful to their husbands. Women probably concur in that ideal, and they would perhaps like to add to it that husbands should be equally faithful to their wives. However, the latter view does not obtain whole-hearted male support. Therefore, since the men are the dominant sex, to sustain their view of sexual morality they need to find in nature a sanction which will enforce the chastity of wives without involving male infidelity. The solution has been to fasten on a natural danger to which only female physiology is exposed. Hence we find very commonly the idea that miscarriage is due to adultery. What a weapon that provides: the woman tempted to adultery knows that her unborn baby is at risk, and her own life too. Sometimes she is taught that the health of her older children will also suffer.[6] What a paraphernalia of confession and cleansing and compensation attends the guilty mother in her labour. What she has done is against nature and nature will retaliate.

For a different example – a warlike tribe of Plains Indians, the Cheyenne, believes that murder of a fellow tribesman is the ultimate wickedness. The tribe used to depend on wandering herds of bison for its food. The bison, it was thought, did not react to the murder of men of other tribes. The bison were not affected by ordinary homicide as such. But a fratricide emitted a putrid stink which frightened off the herd and so put the vital resources of the tribe at risk. This danger from the environment justified special sanctions to outlaw the murderer.[7]

When homicide and adultery are seen to be triggering agents for danger points in a physical environment, the tribal view of nature begins to emerge as a coherent principle of social control. Red in tooth and claw, perhaps, but nature responds in a highly moral and avenging form of aggression. It is on the side of the constitution, motherhood, brotherly love, and it is against human wickedness.

When I first wrote *Purity and Danger* about this moral power in the tribal environment, I thought our own knowledge of the physical environment was different.[8] I now believe this to have been mistaken. If only because they disagree, we are free to select which of our scientists we will harken too, and our selection is subject to the same sociological analysis as that of any tribe.

We find that in tribal society certain classes of people are liable to be classed as polluters. These classes are not the same for all tribes. In some social structures the polluters will be one type, in others another. Imagine a tribal insurance company which set out to cover people against the risk of being accused of causing pollution. Their market researchers and surveyors should be able to work out where they should charge the highest premiums in any particular social system. In some societies the élite possessors of esoteric know-ledge are certain to be charged with owning too much science and misapplying it to selfish ends. Sorcery charges against big operators in New Guinea or against cunning old polygamists among the Lele can be paralleled by our own charges against big business polluting lakes and rivers and poisoning the children's food and air for their commercial profit. The Lele shared with other Congolese tribes an acute anxiety about their population. They believed them-selves to be dying out because of malicious attacks by sorcerers against the fertility of women and on their lack of babies. They continually said that their numbers had declined because of jealousy. 'Look around you', a man said to me on this theme, 'do you see any people? Do you see children?' I looked about. A handful of children played at our feet and a few people sat around. 'Yes', I said, 'I see people and children.' 'Look again', he said, disgusted with my missing the cue. 'There are no people here, no children.' His question had been couched in the rhetorical style expecting the answer 'No'. It took me a long time to learn the tonal pattern which should have led our dialogue to run in this way.[9]

'Look around you! Do you see any people? Tell me – do you?'

Emphatic answer: 'No!'

'Do you see any children? Tell me, do you?'

Emphatic answer: 'No!' Then his answer would come: 'See how we have been finished off. No one is left now, we are destroyed utterly. It's jealousy that destroys us.' For him, the sorcerer's sinful lore was as destructive as for us the science that serves military and business interests with chemical weapons and pesticides.

In another type of society the probability of being accused of pollution will fall on paupers and second-class citizens of various types. Paupers I define as those who, by falling below a required level of achievement, are not able to enter into exchanges of gifts, services, and hospitality. They find themselves not only excluded from the main responsibilities and pleasures of citizenship but a charge upon the community. They are a source of embarrassment to their more prosperous fellows and a living contradiction to any current theories about the equality of man. In tribal societies, wherever such a possibility exists, these unfortunates are likely to be credited with warped emotions. By and large they may be called witches, and risk being accused of causing the natural disasters which other people suffer. Somehow they must be eliminated, controlled, and stopped from multiplying. If you want to intuit from our own culture how such accusations of witchcraft gain plausibility I recommend you to attend a conference of professional social workers. Over and over again you will hear the objects of the social workers' concern being described as 'non-coping'. The explanation given for their non-coping is widely attrributed to their having 'inadequate personalities'. In something of this way, landless clients in the Mandari tribe are said by their patrons to have a hereditary witchcraft streak which makes them vicious and jealous.[10] The fact that they are emotionally warped justifies their fellow-men in withholding the liberties and protections of citizenship.

As for females, in all these societies and anywhere that male dominance is an important value, women are likely to be accused of causing dangerous pollution by their very presence when they invade the men's sphere. I have written enough about female pollution in *Purity and Danger*.

It should be clear now that credibility for any view of how the environment will react is secured by the moral commitment of a community to a particular set of institutions. Nothing will overthrow their beliefs if the institutions which the beliefs support command their loyalty. Nothing is easier than to change the beliefs (overnight!) if the institutions have lost support. If we could finish classifying the kinds of people and kinds of behaviour which pollute the tribal universes we would have performed an ecological exercise. For it would become clear that the view of the universe and a particular kind of society holding this view are closely interdependent. They are a single system. Neither can exist without the other. Tribal peoples who worship their dead ancestors often explicitly recognise that each ancestor only exists insofar as cult is paid to him. When the cult stops, the ancestor has no more credibility. He fades away, unable to intervene, either to punish angrily, or to reward kindly. We should entertain the same insight about any given environment we know. It exists as a structure of meaningful distinctions. Insofar as it is only knowable by the powers attributed to it and the practical action taken in its regard, and insofar as its powers are evoked as techniques of mutual control, a known environment is as fragile as any ancestor. While a limited social reality and a local physical environment are meshed together in a single experience, there is perfect credibility for both. But if the society falls apart, and separate voices claim to know about different environmental constraints, then do credibility problems arise.

At this point I should correct some possible false impressions. I have tried to avoid examples which lend themselves to a skullduggery, conspiracy theory of how the environment is constructed in people's minds. There is no possibility of one group conning another about what nature will stand for, and what is against nature. I certainly would not imply that fears of world overpopulation are spread by frustrated car-owners in the commuter belt who would like a clear run from Surrey to the City. I would not imply that residents on the south coast press for legislation to control population because they know there is no hope of legislating specifically to ban summer crowds from the seaside. But personal experience could make them lend a friendlier ear to those demographers who are most gloomy about population increase, and ignore the optimistic ones. It obviously suits Lele men and Cheyenne men to teach that the physiology of childbirth and the physiology of the wild bison respond to moral situations. But no one can impose a moral view of physical nature on another person who does not share the same moral assumptions. If Lele wives did not believe in married fidelity as a part of the social order they might be more sceptical about an idea which suits husbands extremely well. Because all Cheyenne endorse the idea that murder in the tribe is disastrous they can believe that bison are sensitive to its smell. The common commitment to a set of social meanings makes inferences about the response of nature plausible.

Another misunderstanding concerns the distinction between true and false ideas about the environment. I repeat the invitation to approach this subject in a spirit of science fiction. The scientists find out true, objective things about physical nature. The human society invests these findings about social meaning and constructs a systematic timetabled view of the way that human behaviour and physical nature interact. But I fear that it is an illusion if scientists hope one day to set out a true, systematic, objective view of that interaction. And so it is also illusory to hope for a society whose fears of pollution rest entirely on the scientists' teaching and carry no load of social and moral persuasion. We cannot hope to develop an idea of our environment which has pollution ideas only in the scientists' sense, and none which, in that strict sense, are false. Pollution ideas, however they arise, are the necessary support for a social system. How else can people induce each other to cooperate and behave if they cannot threaten with time, money, God, and nature? These moral imperatives arise from social intercourse. They draw on a view of the environment to support a social order. As normative principles they have an adaptive function. Each society adapts itself to its habitat by precisely these means. Telling each other that there is no time, that we can't afford it, that God wouldn't like it, and that it is against nature and our children will suffer, these are the means by which we adapt our society to our environment, and it to ourselves. In the process our physical possibilities are limited and extended in this way and that, so that there is a real ecological interaction. The concepts of time, money, God, and nature do for human society the adaptive work which is done non-verbally (but otherwise probably by very similar means) in animal society.

I have spoken of pollution ideas which are used by people as controls on themselves and on each other. In this light they seem to be weapons or instruments. However, there is another fundamental aspect of the subject. Pollution ideas draw their power from our own intellectual constitution. Impossible here to describe the learning process by which each individual works out a set of expectations, and derives rules which guide him in his behaviour. The beliefs that there are rules and that future experience is expected to conform to them underlies social intercourse. There is some fascinating experimental work on this aspect of behaviour by American sociologists. However faulty our probings and conclusions may be, we assume a rule-obeying, stable environment. We expect, as we learn a fairly satisfactory set of rules, that the *et cetera* principle can be left to look after the known. The *et cetera* principle is like the automatic pilot which, once the controls are fixed, will keep the plane on course. *Et cetera, et cetera.* Finding rules that work is satisfying as it allows us to suppose that more of the machine can be turned over to the automatic pilot to look after. Discovering a whole system that works is exciting because it suggests an even greater saving of *ad hoc* painful blundering. Hence the emotional response to discovering that market prices work as a system, or that language or mythology has a systematic element.

The deepest emotional investment of all is in the assumption that there is a rule-obeying universe, and that its rules are objective, independent of social validation. Hence the most odious pollutions are those which threaten to attack a system at its intellectual base. The system itself rests on a number of un-challengeable classifications. One of the well known examples in anthropology is that of the Eskimo girl in Labrador who would persistently eat caribou meat after winter had begun.[11] A trivial breach of an abstinence rule, it seems to us. But by a unanimous verdict, she was banished in midwinter for committing what was judged to be a capital offence. These Eskimo have constructed a society whose fundamental category is the distinction of the two seasons. People born in winter are distinguished from those born in summer. Each of the two seasons has a special kind of domestic arrangement, a special seasonal economy, a separate legal practice, almost a distinct religion. The regularity of Eskimo life depends upon the observances connected with each season. Winter hunting equipment is kept apart from summer equipment, summer tents are hidden in winter. No one should touch the skins of animals classed as summer game in winter. As Marcel Mauss put it, 'even in the stomachs of the faithful' salmon, a summer fish, should have no contact with the sea animals of the winter.[12] By disregarding these distinctive categories the girl was committing a wrong against the social system in its fundamental form. A lack of seriousness about the categories of thought was not the reason given for why she was condemned to die by freezing. She had to die because she had committed a dangerous pollution which set everyone's livelihood at risk. Contrast this sharp categorisation and this cruel punishment for contempt with the Eskimo experience of the last millennium. Here is a civilisation which has seen precisely what may well be in store for us, a slow but steady worsening of the environment. Are we going to react, as doom draws near, with rigid applications of the principles out of which our intellectual system has been spun? It is horribly likely that, along with the Eskimo, we will concentrate on eliminating and controlling the polluters. It might be a more worthwhile recourse to think afresh about our environment in a way which was not possible for the Eskimo level of scientific advance. Nor is it only scientific advance which lies in our grasp. We have the chance of understanding our own behaviour.

If the study of pollution ideas teaches us anything it is that, taken too much at face value, such fears tend to mask other wrongs and dangers. For example, take the population problem. A straight response to pollution fears suggests we should urgently try to control population. The question is treated in an unimaginative and mechanical way. It is made a matter of spreading information and making available contraceptive devices. At first, people's eagerness to use them is taken for granted, but soon the clinics report apathy, carelessness, lack of determination, lack of agreement between husbands and wives. Then the question moves from voluntary to automatic methods such as sterilisation or compulsion by law. We are almost back to 'Think before you litter' and forcible control of animal populations. But if we were to learn from biologists, Wynne-Edwards' work on animal populations has many a moral for the demographer.[13] In some human societies social factors encourage the voluntary control of the family size. Not all tribes tolerate unlimited expansion of their numbers. It cannot be ignored that the world demographic problem is an Us/Them situation. Even in Ricardo's day it was They, the labourers, whose improvident fecundity created the pressure on resources, while We, the rich, could be relied on to procreate more cautiously. And today it is We, the rich nations, who wag our fingers at Them, the poor ones, with their astronomical annual increase. Somewhere a social problem about the distribution of prestige and power underlies the stark demographic facts. Let us not miss the lessons of this confrontation with biology and anthropology.

In essence, pollution ideas are adaptive and protective. They protect a social system from unpalatable knowledge. They protect a system of ideas from challenge. The ideas rest on classification. Ultimately any forms of knowledge depend on principles of classification. But these principles arise out of social experience, sustain a given social pattern, and themselves are sustained by it. If this base is grossly disturbed, knowledge itself is at risk.

In a sense the obvious risk to the environment is a distraction. The ecologists are indeed looking into an abyss. But on the other side another abyss yawns as frighteningly. This is the terror of intellectual chaos and blind panic. Pollution is the black side of Plato's good lie[14] on which society must rest: it is the other half of the necessary confidence trick. We should be able to see that we can never ask for a future society in which we can only believe in real, scientifically proved pollution dangers. We *must* talk threateningly about time, money, God, and nature if we hope to get anything done. We must believe in the limitations and boundaries of nature which our community projects.

Here we return to the comparison with the classical economists and the slavery abolitionists. It would be good to know which of our experts is likely to take a restrictive view of the environment, certain that time, money, God, and nature are against change, and which of them is likely to favour expansionary policies. It is easy to see why the laymen can't lift their noses above the immediate horizon. The layman tends to assimilate the total planetary environmental problems to his own immediate ones. His horizon is his back yard. For the scientists, as well as this same tendency, there is another source of bias. To understand a system – any system – is a joy in itself. The more that is known about it the more the specialist is aware of its intricacies, and the more wary he is of the complex disturbances which can result from ignorance. The specialist has thus an emotional investment in his own system. As Professor Kuhn has said, in his *The Structure of Scientific Revolutions*,[15] scientists rarely change their views, they merely retire or die away. If there are to be solutions to a grave problem, they will come from the fringes of the profession, from the amateur even, or from those areas of knowledge in which two or three specialisms meet. This is comforting. In the long run, if there is a long run, unless the man in the street specially wants to choose the pessimistic, restrictionist, view on any ecological problem, he can wait and see. The scientific establishment has its own structure of stability and challenge. Our responsibility as laymen and as social scientists is to probe deeper into the sources of our own bias. Suppose we are really set for the worst terrors that the ecologists can predict. How shall we comport ourselves?

Our worst problem is the lack of moral consensus which gives credibility to warnings of danger. This partly explains why we fail so often to give proper heed to the ecologists. At the same time, for lack of a discriminating principle, we easily become overwhelmed by our pollution fears. Community endows its environment with credibility. Without community, unclassified rubbish mounts up, poisons fill the air and water, food is contaminated, eyesores block the skyline. Flooding in through all our senses, pollution destroys our well-being. Witches and devils ensnare us. Any tribal culture selects this and that danger to fear and sets up demarcation lines to control it. It allows people to live contentedly with a hundred other dangers which ought to terrify them out of their wits. The discriminating principles come from social structure. An unstructured society leaves us prey to every dread. As all the veils are successively ripped away, there is no right or wrong. Relativism is the order of the day. I myself have tried to join the work of taking down some of the veils. We have adopted first this standpoint, then that, seen tribal society from within and from without, seen ourselves as the scientists see us or from the stance of the anthropologist from Mars. This is the invitation to full self-consciousness that is offered in our time. We must accept it. But we should do so knowing that the price is William Burroughs' *Naked Lunch*.[16] The day when everyone can see exactly what it is on the end of everyone's fork, on that day there is no pollution and no purity and nothing edible or inedible, credible or incredible, because the classifications of social life are gone. There is no more meaning. Neither melancholic madness nor mystic ecstasy, the two modes in which boundaries are dispensed, can accept the other invitation of our time. The other task is to recognise each environment as a mask and support for a certain kind of society. It is the value of this social form which demands our scrutiny just as clearly as the purity of milk and air and water.

NOTES

1 John Hicks, *A Theory of Economic History*, London, 1969, pp. 122–40.
2 Paul Ehrlich, *Listener*, 30 August 1970, 215.
3 Mary Douglas, 'The Lele, resistance to change', in *Markets in Africa*, ed. Bohannan and Dalton, Evanston, Ill., 1962. The author is grateful to Northwestern University Press for permission to reproduce Fig. 16.1 from *Markets in Africa*.
4 Julius A. Roth, *Timetables, Structuring the Passage of Time in Hospital Treatment and other Careers*, New York, 1963.
5 Eric Aynsley, 'How air pollution alters weather', *New Scientist*, 9 October 1969, 66–7.
6 Mary Douglas, *The Lele of the Kasai*, International African Institute, Oxford, 1963, p. 51.
7 E.A. Hoebel, *The Cheyénnes, Indians of the Great Plains*, New York, 1960, p. 51.
8 Mary Douglas, *Purity and Danger: an Analysis of Concepts of Pollution and Taboo*, London, 1966.
9 Mary Douglas, 'Elicited responses in Lele language', *Kongo-Over-zee*, xvi, 4, 1950, 224–7.
10 Jean Buxton, 'Mandari witchcraft', in *Witchcraft and Sorcery in East Africa*, ed. John Middleton and Edward Winter, London, 1963.
11 E.A. Hoebel, *The Law of Primitive Man: A Study in Comparative Legal Dynamics*, Harvard, 1954.
12 Marcel Mauss and M.H. Beuchat, 'Essai sur les variations saisonnières des sociétés Eskimos', *L'Année Sociologique*, 9, 1904–5, 39–132.
13 V.C. Wynne-Edwards, *Animal Dispersion in Relation to Social Behaviour*, Edinburgh and New York, 1962.
14 Plato, *The Republic*, paras 376–92, Lindsay translation, Everyman.
15 T.S. Kuhn, *The Structure of Scientific Revolutions*, Chicago, 1962.
16 William Burroughs, *The Naked Lunch*, New York, 1962; London, 1965.

Chapter 17

The depoliticisation of risk

First published in R. Ellis and M. Thompson (eds) (1997), *Culture Matters*, Westview Press

Politics is foremost in the international and national debates about risks, whether they concern risk to the environment, regulation to control risk, or implementation of the laws. But in the accompanying academic discussion politics and justice have very little formal place. This is a complaint against the academics about how political issues are sometimes ignored or muffled in academic work, sometimes espoused unwittingly, and sometimes treated with no concern for objectivity. There are two cleavages within the academic field of risk analysis. First, there is a conflict about nothing less than the nature of reality. Second, at the next level, the conflict is about how the first should be studied. My purpose in writing about these conflicts in academia is to try to reconcile contrary positions.

In 1992 the Royal Society issued a report titled *Risk: Analysis, Perception, and Management*. It was an updating of a Royal Society report of a decade earlier, *Risk Analysis* (1983), which had drawn criticism for saying practically nothing about risk perception and management. The 1992 report, unlike its predecessor, was not issued as a report *of* the Society but rather as a report of the work of the study group chaired by Sir Frederick Warner in the form of six independent chapters each attributed to its subchairman. The preface indicated that this saved editing and delay in publication. The preface also suggested delicately that this dissociating device was not merely intended to serve greater speed and punctuality. Controversial issues were raised, especially in Chapters 5 and 6, which dealt with risk perception and risk management. Evidently the scientists reporting on engineering risk, toxicology, and epidemiology had been able to reach general agreement. But difficulties arose in dealing with the ambiguities of the so-called social sciences.

Sir Frederick, in a later article in *Science and Public Affairs* (Warner, 1992), said quite frankly that the trouble had been caused by the social scientists. It was partly a disagreement between them and the natural scientists on what is real about risk, and partly a disagreement among the social scientists themselves

I wish to thank the Political Economy Research Centre at the University of Sheffield for the opportunity to present an early version of this paper in their seminar series, 17 February 1994.

on method. Joining a dispute between psychologists and anthropologists, and taking sides unabashedly, Sir Frederick praised the solid work of psychologists; he particularly commended the careful sampling and psychometric analysis that had identified factors in risk perception, such as the 'dread factor', and had developed a theory about the 'social amplification of risk'. But these honest souls 'had reckoned', he said, 'without the anthropologists who dismiss their contributions'. He evidently counted the psychometric crowd among the true scientists when at the end of his article he deplored the political isolation of scientists and complained that in Parliament scientists have little influence when pitted against fifty Members from the London School of Economics.

To explain what the dispute was about, let me quote Professor Brian Wynne on the intrinsic difficulties of being understood at all. Citing Kierkegaard, he said, 'We construct the meanings offered to us by others into forms that correspond with our fundamental identities; in the process, the original meanings are transformed, or perhaps we should say violated. Kierkegaard wrote with great power about the tragedy, not just that we are confined to distorting each others' meanings, but more that we are confined to pretending that it is otherwise' (Wynne, 1922: 275–6). Wynne went on to describe his own experience as participant observer of the 1977 Windscale Public Enquiry into a planned oxide fuels reprocessing facility at the Sellafield nuclear complex (Wynne, 1982). In his 1982 book he had 'examined the way that the dominant rationality silently and systematically deleted my questions about institutional commitment, behaviour and trustworthiness, as if they had nothing to do with the risk. This same rationality constructed the decision issue as one of objective discovery rather than social commitment, and hence also constructed the opponents and their concerns as factually wrong or irrational' (1992: 278).

This is how the issue of reality comes up. Wynne also quoted Harry Otway and Philip Pahner (1976) who suggested that risk definitions as framed by experts were taken by the experts to be more real than the definitions of lay people. Beyond the issues of measurement and quantification of risks and risk perceptions were more basic questions about which dimensions of experience should be recognised and which should be denied validity. The feeling that reality is how the experts define it, and that alternative definitions are irrational and possibly subversive, and even based on bad faith, is the issue that disturbed the meetings of the Royal Society study groups. Sir Frederick's constituency wanted to stay with a reality defined by the experts. Why they felt this to be safer has probably to do with politics, as I shall try to show later. That is the first cleavage.

In October 1992 the Foundation for Science and Technology and the Royal Society held a joint meeting to launch the report. Complete decorum reigned until near the end when a psychologist got up from the floor and reproached the Royal Society report for giving undue space to radical views. When he asked that the term 'social construction of risk' be eliminated from the discussion, shouting, clapping, and hissing broke out and the meeting was adjourned.

First let me agree quickly that the term 'social construction of risk' has been a source of confusion. Somehow the engineers and some others understand it as a denial of the reality of the risks. But the emphasis is on the word 'social' as distinct from 'individual construction of risk'. Once we get past the expert's perception and try to assess the wider perception of the non-expert public, we can choose to focus attention on individuals confronting and defining risk on their own, or we can take a collective view. This is where the cleavage on method appears.

All knowledge and everything we talk about is collectively constructed. Language is no private invention. Words are a collective product, and so are meanings. There could not be risks, illnesses, dangers, or any reality, knowledge of which is not constructed. It might be better if the word 'social construal' were used instead of 'construction', because all evidence has to be construed. Construal, being an act of interpretation, does not imply impugning of reality. But I myself protest on behalf of the anthropologists that the Royal Society report granted much too much space to the psychometric approach to risk perception. I welcome this opportunity to tell serious social scientists what is wrong with the psychometric approach, with its biased sampling and alleged 'discovery' of psychological factors attached to particular risks, scientistic pretensions, and claims to objectivity.

THEORIES OF RISK PERCEPTION

In what follows, without trying to make an exhaustive survey, I will introduce four approaches to risk perception. The first (psychometric) and the second (social amplification) try to avoid analysing a political dimension, with varied success. The objectives of the third are connected with achieving justice, and it does not pretend to be apolitical. The fourth grasps the political nettle and aims to incorporate political opposition as part of the analysis as well as part of what is being studied.

Psychometric and rational actor models

This is the approach that completely bypasses political factors and pays no attention to them whatever. Paul Slovic (1992) narrates how in 1970 he and another graduate student in the psychology department of Stanford University were asked by Gilbert White about their research into risk taking and probabilistic judgments for simple gambles. White wondered whether they could throw light on human response to natural hazards such as floods or earthquakes. They realised that their field had been defined too narrowly to tell much about risk taking outside the laboratory, and they forthwith redirected their methods to studying what they came to call 'cognitive processes and societal risk taking'.

At that time the dominant paradigm had been launched by an engineer, Chauncy Starr (1969), who argued that acceptable risks are accepted risks; if the public accepts a risk, it is acceptable. From that assumption his programme was to remind the lay public who were agitating against the risk of exposure to nuclear radiation that they accepted greater risks every day for far less benefit: an hour's sunbathing, a daily glass of cola, crossing the road. Against this approach, the psychologists developed questionnaires to ask the public directly about their perceptions of risk–benefit trade-offs and continued work on the technical and statistical problems entailed.

The underlying objectives of this psychometric programme are those of cognitive science: to identify universal principles of the human mind. This high level of abstraction effectively removes the inquiry from the dust and turmoil of politics. The team of Amos Tversky and Daniel Kahneman (1981) writes with wit and elegance unusual in the social sciences; they uncover quizzical paradoxes and curious anomalies in human behaviour that challenge the rational actor model of economics and political philosophy. This paradigm has given rise to so much experimentation as to deserve the title of 'normal science' in the field of risk research, which means a large investment has been made in its assumptions and procedures.

The excellent summary of this approach given in Chapter 5 of the Royal Society's 1992 report is no doubt oversimplified. But even from the original essays the layperson is no wiser as to why people take risks about living in floodplains or on earthquake faults or near nuclear power stations. The outcomes of the research say little about big decisions. There is a rude question that it is embarrassing to put to such a civilised set of people about their urbane procedures. Why have these seemingly trite discoveries been made the basis of worldwide research programmes on the perception of risk?

It is true that they help to explain various divergences between official statistics and public beliefs. For example, a type of event will tend to be judged more probable to the extent that instances of it are readily available in the memory; questionnaires showed that deaths from the most vivid causes are thought to be the most frequent (Lichtenstein et al., 1978). 'Vivid' catches and holds attention while 'dull' passes into background. Other examples helped to develop what became known as the 'availability heuristic'. This is not denying that laypeople are rational; not at all: just that they have other things on their mind when they listen to the experts. But what does vividness consist in? How does one thing become more available than another?

The overall objective of the psychometric project is to build up gradually a model of individual cognitive response to risk. However, several features of the research design could be improved. Certain criticisms are commonly made: one against the small size of the samples, one against the reliance on subjective responses, and another against the whole procedure of deriving axioms from laboratory questionnaires. I will add a few more. The respondents are chosen and the questions designed as if nothing in their previous lives or personal experience would make a difference to their response to risks and probabilities; this is a rejection of the reciprocal influence between culture and personal beliefs.

Again – and this is another aspect of the neglect of the cultural dimension – individual answers are correlated to individual risks. Both the respondents and the risks are decontextualised for the sake of a universalisable theory of mind. Again, and perhaps the most serious criticism, the respondents are faced with a limited list of risks that the researchers have defined. But life is full of risks; at every step we are dogged by risky decisions, and life without risk is not worth living (Fried, 1970). What guarantees that the spectrum of selected risks gives a fair view of the life choices an individual has to weigh?

If we were being offered a theory of cognition that explained how some events become salient and others backgrounded, it would be very interesting indeed. But a lot of backgrounding and foregrounding has been done in advance, so that implicitly the respondents' answers are being measured against a common idea of what is a salient risk. The common idea is local to our own culture and so does not say anything about the 'human' cognitive process. What has developed is a local theory of psychological meanings attached to separate items called risks or hazards.

Certain risks have associated with them 'dread', uncontrollability, involuntariness of exposure, and inequitable distribution of risk bearing. Within this paradigm there is no research, as far as I know, on how the dread factor arises, and it sounds much like saying that certain events are feared because the dread factor is associated with them. The focus is on the free-floating events and apparently free-floating psychological meanings. All over the world where this paradigm holds sway, field researchers are practising normal science, looking for the dread factor, joyously finding it as predicted, and paying no systematic attention to the processes by which the meanings become attached.

Everyone in the risk perception business agrees that the mind's perceiving involves active organising of the experience by the subject. But in spite of accepting a post-Kantian view of the perceptual process, the research design of the psychometric approach ignores the subject's development of perceptual lenses. The emphasis is on the impact of 'risks' on the mind, like the impact of sense impressions on the retina in seventeenth-century optics. Though they follow with fascination the laboratory subject actively distorting a situation that has supposedly only one right answer, the explanations of what the respondent has done to turn a question around are intended to illustrate universal cognitive tendencies implicitly founded in the human biological heritage. To be frank about my own bias, I cannot take seriously a theory of risk perception that has eliminated cultural factors. When people knowingly take risks, they are not alone; the bigger the risk, the more likely they are to consult among their family and friends and go to experts. Deciding to take a risk is generally a cooperative matter, and this makes the results of questionnaires on the psychometric model implausible as clues to how people think about risks.

Social amplification

Ten years ago when I tried to do a literature review of how the social sciences approached the question of risk acceptability I found practically nothing. I felt that reviewing the literature on a silence was like walking round a hole in the ground. Since then, several new approaches have developed. The social amplification approach tries to supplement some of the deficiencies in the psychometric paradigm. It very properly starts by studying the funnel of social experiences through which the prospect of hazards is filtered to individuals; it is primarily concerned with how social and cultural processes intensify or attenuate perceptions of risk. The key words are 'signals', transmitted through a variety of 'social amplification stations'. Examples of such 'stations' cited in groups of scientists, government agencies, activist groups, and so on. The social amplification approach aims to account for the differential interpretations placed on hazardous events.

This sounds like a promising programme, but for three drawbacks. The first is that it enters the arena of politics unconsciously, with a political bias apparently hidden from its practitioners. Though it claims to be explaining how some hazards come to be played down and others played up by the social filtering mechanisms, the title gives a true idea of the central concern, which is how hazards come to be *amplified*. In other words, without apology or recognition, the research is directed to explaining how things seem to be more dangerous than they really are. In the context of technological risk this is a barely disguised political bias. Though the research does turn its attention to risks that are taken voluntarily and to risks that are apparent to others but not to the chief actors, this seems to be done with the intention of meeting the criticism of lack of balance. A systematic approach would absolutely need to develop a theory of selection. To account for how some risks are selected for attention would mean keeping in mind the concomitant neglect (or 'attenuation') of other dangers.

Second, the whole concept of amplification suggests a focus on what the real hazard truly is (that is, unamplified), and how the public tends to get a false (amplified) view of it. This is an unconscious and naïve realism. It would be safer to admit some indeterminancy about the expert reading of evidence as well as indeterminancy in what the public observes. Brian Wynne (1989) has made famous a case of sheep farmers being more knowledgeable about the effects of nuclear radiation than the scientists.

Third, the idea of signals and signal stations needs to be thoroughly worked out. At present it is at the stage of arm-waving. Signals and signal stations come close to a sociological version of salience. But again, the trouble is that salience is supposed to be the same for everyone. The terms suggest that in any culture some objects, places, persons, or words attract attention, acting as points of reference and producing conspicuous solutions to questions that might otherwise be flooded with ambiguity. Thomas Schelling's (1960) idea about salience is in the air again and being reintroduced in epistemology, economics, and organisation theory. It certainly deserves a good run in studying risk perception under the guise of 'signal stations'. The question about risk perception then would be how salience is bestowed, which is parallel to the previous question about the 'availability heuristic'. This is where the possibility of reconciling the rifts between the social scientists on risk perception should be possible.

Frankly political arguments

It is impossible for readers not to know about the host of political writings warning of risks foisted on the people by unscrupulous industrialists and politicians, about risks being minimised, denied, concealed. A lot of it is intended for journalism. This is where the whole new field of risk analysis started. First there was the public protest, then government and industry called for advice about why the public was so outraged, and then the academic study of risk perception developed somewhat along the lines I have indicated, producing what is now a vast bibliography and including many different types of inquiry.

For our purposes here it will be enought to cite one book that directly addresses questions of justice. Kristin Shrader-Frechette's *Risk and Rationality* (1991) aims to provide a philosophically respectable position on risk. I use it here because the author specifically attacks *Risk and Culture* (Douglas and Wildavsky, 1982). Shrader-Frechette pits her own frankly populist standpoint against two allegedly antipopulist theories of risk. In her vocabulary 'populist' means taking public complaints seriously and giving credit to the people's fears about rising morbidity and death rates due to technology. It means democratic principles and legislation designed to respond to bottom-up claims. 'Antipopulist' in this vocabulary indicates the enemy of the people. In the context of risk the enemy dismisses popular fears of technology as baseless and gives esoteric and suspect reasons for supporting a coalition of government and industry against pollution control and workplace dangers. Shrader-Frechette indicts two approaches to risk: One is the naïve positivism of engineers and scientists for whom a fact is a fact and has nothing to do with values (echoes of the Royal Society's engineers); the other is the grid-group cultural theory espoused by myself and a handful of colleagues. Shrader-Frechette writes passionately in defence of the people's risk aversion, too lightly dismissed by politically biased antipopulists. Risk theory does indeed tend to be muddied by political debating strategies; risk is inevitably politicised, since major values are at stake; employment, poverty, lives, and regions laid waste; budgets emptied; and timetables overturned. I sympathise with the scorn Shrader-Frechette pours on the attempts of professional risk analysts to evade the political aspects of their science, and I offer qualified support for her proposals for improving current methods of risk assessment.

The main positive idea is that risk–cost–benefit analysis could be improved by ethical weighting techniques; alternative analyses should be done to take account of different ethical assumptions; and 'expert opinions' should be weighted according to their past performance. As a defender of the people Shrader-Frechette wishes to end arbitrariness in risk decisions and hopes that improved analysis will curb back-scratching, payoffs, bribes, and ignorance. She wants to find ways of improving cost–benefit analysis by incorporating ethical and political biases. Starting from a political standpoint, she wants to depoliticise the issues, so as to provide an opening for populist views. In a review of this book I said:

> It is probably true that risk-cost-benefit analysis as practiced fails to take account of egalitarian values, social obligations and rights of individuals. And ethical weighting will certainly open the field to a new kind of democratic debate. Passionate interest in carcinogens in parts to the million will be shifted to passionate interest in complex principles of ethical weighting. This would probably restore the prestige of science, for it is widely remarked that science when used to arbitrate in politics loses its authority. If the political strains are transferred to the scrutiny of ethical weighting systems, environmentalists may discover that the populist view is not necessarily in support of what seems to be obviously good and right. Eventually the focus will be directed to cultural differences, and to political disagreement. This is where cultural theory comes in, for it starts by mapping the political and ethical differences engaged beneath the surface of any argument about risks. (Douglas, 1993: 485)

At this point I am ready to introduce grid-group cultural theory as a fourth type of approach that has a method of incorporating the political debate in its analysis.

'Culture' as type of bias or 'culture' as dialogue

Considerable misunderstanding of the methods and objectives of grid-group cultural theory has arisen from its critics' rewriting of the terminology. In the theory a typology of cultures is derived from cultural biases; but overhasty readers take the elements of the typology to be culture 'groups'. It is easy to be scathing about whether communities divide into hierarchical groups, egalitarian groups, individualist groups: They do not, and no one ever said they do. A cultural bias is a point of view, with its own framing assumptions and readily available solutions for standardised problems. Scattered persons not in any group at all may share a similar cultural bias. It is a question of a way of life, and the way of life depends heavily on the way of earning a living and on the social relations that are entailed. A common culture is a source for salient reference points and heuristics and so is complementary to some of the aforementioned approaches to risk. But note also the adversarial element: Each culture in this analysis is thought to be strongly in competition with its alternatives.

Because I need to avoid giving the impression of a culture as a sharply defined group of people, I would like to try presenting culture as a dialogue. This is like joining a powerful movement in the social sciences to turn action into speech and text, and I should say firmly where it is different: I am not taking the Habermasian view of the ideal society as dialogue, because I am not emphasising possible harmony, but the contrary. The aspect of the cultural dialogue that needs to be understood is accountability. Think of culture as essentially a dialogue that allocates praise and blame. Then focus particularly on the blame.

Intercultural dialogue is inherently agonistic; the outcome will at any one point be a victory for one and defeat for another of the contestants; the contest is about the form of the life to be led in common. That is why blaming is so central. Every accident and mishap affords the members of the dialogue an opportunity to call one another to account. Somebody dies, someone is blamed; someone is injured, someone is blamed. Blaming ranges the universe, with all its benefits and hazards, on one side or another. Under this optic it is implausible that risks be perceived except through the accountability that they activate. The blaming process is normal cultural activity, and we have to examine the dangers that are around as made more salient by the handles they provide for blaming. That salience depends on accountability opens the study of cognitive salience to politics.

Each culture is founded on a distinctive institutional base, which gives it interests to protect, and its own conventional way of doing things. Consequently each culture allocates blame to different sectors, and they vary according to the amount of blaming that they tolerate. In this perspective the risk signals for which the social amplification researchers are looking would be features of the systems of accountability in each cultural type.

I can shorten the introduction to the theory of culture that I wrote with the late Aaron Wildavsky (Douglas and Wildavsky, 1982) by summarising four kinds of competing dialogues about risk in any industrial society. The basic discriminator is the attitude to power and authority: There are two ways of exerting power, one bureaucratic and hierarchical, and the other by bargaining and exchanging; there are two ways of resisting the influence from these bases, one by active criticism, and the other by withdrawal. The four cultural types that are thus distinguished (you can call them hierarchy, market, critical activist, and isolate) are always in flux, always open to conversion to one of the other positions. The competition is generally overt and highly political. This comes closer to the dynamic model presented by Steve Rayner (1992) and to Michael Thompson's (1992) insistence that cultures are always counterpoised against one another, than the more static versions I have usually offered. Here is a thumbnail sketch of the three types engaged in political debate:

1   One is based on government and administration, anchored in an established hierarchy, reductionist in reasoning style, and professionally concerned for measurability. It requires objective bases for comparison that can be used to

justify the decisions it makes. It takes a longer view than the others, and this may give it a coolness about accepting disaster. The hierarchists, in their struggle to create analytic operational formulae, tend to prefer a risk research vocabulary that can be formalised without being politicised. Control of information is so important for maintaining their hegemony that they may well be accused of attenuating risks, making them sound less serious than the other quarters of the public believe.

2   Another type is based on the market, individualist in ethics, pragmatic in style of reasoning; it casts suspicion on grand theories; it tends to be incrementalist in politics, positivist in sociology, and behaviourist in psychological theory. It takes such a short view of the future that again it tends to be less tender about the misfortunes of others. Market representatives who want market forces left free to make the world safer by advanced technology would like the language of risk to be contained within technical meanings. For example, the Royal Society risk report of 1983 discussed toxicity, engineering, and epidemiology as technical problems. These people will be much more interested in showing how normally acceptable risks are amplified by social processes, and they may be accused of minimising risks.

3   The third, in opposition to the established hierarchy and to the market, is essentially a radical political discourse; it is the conscience of the community, reformist in objectives and holistic in modes of reasoning; it is the source of the scorn routinely poured on the bureaucratic concerns of the first type and on the materialist goals of the second type. The radical critics, with liberation and radical political change as their programme, find the context of risk a convenient arena for their part of the dialogue. They are much more interested in showing that risks have been concealed and the public misled. They are accused by the others of amplifying dangers, and perhaps with reason.

Thus we have three sources of risk signals, and we would expect at any one time a three-sided policy struggle and from one of the corners a hegemonic discourse dominating the rest.

When we have identified three kinds of cultural signal stations, we should be attending carefully to the favourite words that come to the fore in each culture and how the choice of themes is calculated to draw together the defenders of a cultural type against its opponents. As the debate unfolds, temporary coalitions emerge between members of the three opposing discourses. Common points of reference and some common vocabulary are necessary, however deep the divergence between objectives. Just as transgression became the salient point of reference for blaming for disaster in the Bible, and sin in the history of Christianity, in our secular, scientific world, risk has become the convenient, conspicuous blame term that all parties connive to promote. Steve Rayner (1992) has argued that recently a hegemonic discourse has emerged: International concern about the environment is led by the radical critics, and the language and assumptions of the debate are dominated by those from the radical corner. The keystone of the conversational edifice is 'risk'.

It is difficult to recommend this cultural theory to someone who would really like a social science pure of politics. Its central idea is that any community is engaged in a heavy debate about its own governance. Whatever the scale, whether an African village of a few hundred people, a major bureaucracy, industrial units, or the organised professions, politics always lurks. Insofar as a group of people is worthy of the name of community, blaming goes on as part of the normal political process. By identifying three institutional bases and one neutral position for the isolates, and recognising four dialogues about nature, danger, risk, and responsibility, we can go a long way towards incorporating arguments about politics in the analysis. Ideally this will provide a stronger kind of objectivity than one sought by avoiding politics altogether. And it will be much more revealing about the debate on risk than any questionnaire that homogenises the cultural element.

OBJECTIVITY AND THE EXCLUSION OF POLITICS

By shunning politics the risk analysis profession has won prestige, but in the long-term it puts itself in danger of nullity. If the political dimension is there, it is not safe to evade it; the only thing to do is to confront it and include the political dialogue in your theory.

It has been observed that the psychometric research was originally funded by industry and government at a time of heated national controversy about nuclear power. I have heard it whispered that the researchers receiving grants would be expected to justify the experts and that a result that showed the public's fears of risk to be irrational would have been very acceptable. One member of the team has thought it necessary to deny that anything of this kind was either intended or demonstrated. But more plausibly, in such conditions it would have been dangerous to say anything that could be politically construed, and in practice there is practically nothing that is safe from that attack, as I know from the reviews of *Risk and Culture*. The safe course is to go all out for purity. My personal explanation of the success of this peculiar moment in the history of ideas is precisely that by the rigorous search for universal cognitive laws the profession achieved this pure status, above-and-beyond politics. Research along psychometric lines gave to a newly emergent profession the halo of objectivity.

In a secular society claims to this sort of objectivity are like claims to speak for God in an earlier time. If ever there was such a thing as pure research, this is it. To be able to exhibit purity on the subject of risk is a remarkable achievement, for the risks are prominent and the funds for studying risk perception forthcoming just because the debate is highly political. However elegant its formulae may be, and however useful for charting the basic conditions of the human cognition, the pure scholasticism of the psychometric approach as at present pursued disables it from relevance to risk perception.

If we were invited to make a coalition between grid-group cultural theory and psychometrics, it would be like going to heaven. Given such an invitation we would try to be practical and ask the high priests of the cult to apply its laboratory questionnaires to subjects drawn from well identified opposed cultural types. Not only would this afford a real test of their theorising, but also it would have the advantage of relating it to risk perception. If we were to collaborate with social amplification research, we would help them to identify the cultural equivalent of 'risk stations', and so they would learn to hear the different messages about risks that emanate respectively from each. If we had an option to collaborate in Shrader-Frechette's programme to improve cost–benefit analysis by incorporating ethical weighting, we would ask for different cultural weightings to be included in the exercise.

'Risk' in the present-day international and national political debates is a rhetorical strategy, a convention for allowing conversations to seem to proceed even while attacking. We can conclude this brief survey by noting that the idea of risk bids fair to dominate the scenario for political science and that those universities that leave it out of their curriculum may themselves be left high and dry. Note that this strong risk aversion of academics, which leads them to exclude the main factor from the research that is their very bread and butter, is an Anglo-Saxon bias. In France risk has already started to provide a new vocabulary for questions of justice and justification (Duclos, 1989, 1991; Boltanski and Thévenot, 1991; Laufer, 1993). In Germany Ulrich Beck (1986) has made the first stab at rewriting all of political science in terms of vulnerability to risk. You can expect the French to be more political and philosophical; you can suppose readily that the politicisation of risk has gone further in Germany thanks to the militant Greens; and I suppose you can expect the Anglo-Saxons to be more bureaucratic and hence to seek remoteness from the fracas and to restrict their interests to what can be measured precisely.

Everyone agrees that 'humans do not perceive the world with pristine eyes, but through perceptual lenses such as the family, friends, superordinates and fellow workers' (Renn, 1991). This being so, my claims are that the central problem for risk research is to know more about the lenses, and that this objective places risk assessment squarely in the departments of political culture and political economy.

BIBLIOGRAPHY

BECK, U. (1986), *Die Risikogesellschaft*, Frankfurt, Suhrkamp.

BOLTANSKI, L. and THEVENOT, L. (1991), *De la Justification*, Paris, Gallimard.

DOUGLAS, M. (1993), Review of Schrader-Frechette, *American Political Science Review*, *87*, 485.

DOUGLAS, M. and WILDAVSKY, A. (1982), *Risk and Culture*, University of California Press.

DUCLOS, D. (1989), *La Peur et le Savoir, le Société face à la science, la technique, et leurs dangers*, Paris, Harmattan.

DUCLOS, D. (1991), *Les indistriels et les risques pour l'environnement*, Paris, Harmattan.

FRIED, E. (1970), *An Anatomy of Values*, Cambridge, Mass., Harvard University Press.

LAUFER, R. (1993), *L'entreprise face aux risques majeurs*, Paris, Harmattan.

LICHTENSTEIN, S., SLOVIC, P., FISCHEFF, B. and COMBS, B. (1978), 'Judged frequency of lethal events', *Journal of Experimental Psychology, Human Learning and Memory*, 4, 551–78.

OTWAY, H. and PAHNER, P. (1976), 'Risk assessment', *Futures*, 8, 124–34.

RAYNER, S. (1992), 'Cultural theory and risk analysis', in S. Krimsky and D. Golding (eds), *Social Theories of Risk*, Westport, Conn. and London, Praeger, 1992, pp. 83–116.

RENN, O. (1991), 'Risk communication and the social amplification of risk', in R. Kasperson and P. Stallen (eds), *Communicating Risk to the Public*, Kluwer.

SCHELLING, T. (1960), *Strategy and Conflict*, Cambridge, Mass., Harvard University Press.

SCHRADER-FRECHETTE, K.S. (1991), *Risk and Rationality: Philosophical Foundations for Populist Reform*, University of California Press.

SLOVIC, P. (1992), 'Perceptions of risk: Reflections on the psycho-metric paradigm', in S. Krimsky and D. Golding (eds), *Social Theories of Risk*, Westport, Conn. and London, Praeger, pp. 117–52.

STARR, C. (1969), 'Social benefit versus technological risk', *Science*, 165, 1232–8.

THOMPSON, M. (1992), 'The dynamics of cultural theory and their implications for the enterprise culture', in S.H. Heap and A. Ross (eds), *Understanding the Enterprise Culture*, Edinburgh University Press, pp. 182–202.

WARNER, SIR F. (1992), 'Calculated risks', *Science and Public Affairs*, 44–9.

WYNNE, B. (1982), *Rationality and Ritual: The Windscale Inquiry and Nuclear Decisions in Britain*, British Society for the History of Science.

WYNNE, B. (1989), 'Sheepfarming after Chernobyl', *Environment*, 31, 11–15, 33–9.

WYNNE, B. (1992), 'Risk and social learning', in S. Krimsky and D. Golding (eds), *Social Theories of Risk*, Westport, Conn. and London, Praeger, pp. 275–30.

Chapter 18

Deciphering a meal

First published in *Daedalus*, Winter 1972

If language is a code, where is the precoded message? The question is phrased to expect the answer: nowhere. In these words a linguist is questioning a popular analogy.[1] But try it this way: if food is a code, where is the precoded message? Here, on the anthropologist's home ground, we are able to improve the posing of the question. A code affords a general set of possibilities for sending particular messages. If food is treated as a code, the messages it encodes will be found in the pattern of social relations being expressed. The message is about different degrees of hierarchy, inclusion and exclusion, boundaries and transactions across the boundaries. Like sex, the taking of food has a social component, as well as a biological one.[2] Food categories therefore encode social events. To say this is to echo Roland Barthes[3] on the sartorial encoding of social events. His book, *Système de la mode*, is primarily about methodology, about code-breaking and code-making taken as a subject in itself. The next step for the development of this conceptual tool is to take up a particular series of social events and see how they are coded. This will involve a close understanding of a micro-scale social system. I shall therefore start the exercise by analysing the main food categories used at a particular point in time in a particular social system, our home. The humble and trivial case will open the discussion of more exalted examples.

Sometimes at home, hoping to simplify the cooking, I ask, 'Would you like to have just soup for supper tonight? I mean a good thick soup – instead of supper. It's late and you must be hungry. It won't take a minute to serve'. Then an argument starts: 'Let's have soup now, and supper when you are ready'. 'No no, to serve two meals would be more work. But if you like, why not start with the soup and fill up with pudding?' 'Good heavens! What sort of a meal is that? A beginning and an end and no middle.' 'Oh, all right then, have the soup as it's there, and I'll do a Welsh rarebit as well.' When they have eaten soup, Welsh rarebit, pudding, and cheese: 'What a lot of plates. Why do you make such elaborate suppers?' They proceed to argue that by taking thought I could satisfy the full requirements of a meal with a single, copious dish. Several rounds of this conversation have given me a practical interest in the categories and meaning of food. I needed to know what defines the category of a meal in our home.

The first source for enlightenment will obviously be Claude Lévi-Strauss's *The Raw and the Cooked* and the other volumes of his *Mythologiques*[4] which discuss food categories and table manners. But this is only a beginning. He fails us in two major respects. First, he takes leave of the small-scale social relations which generate the codification and are sustained by it. Here and there his feet touch solid ground, but mostly he is orbiting in rarefied space where he expects to find universal food meanings common to all mankind. He is looking for a precoded, panhuman message in the language of food, and thus exposing himself to the criticism implicit in the quoted linguist's question. Second, he relies entirely on the resources of binary analysis. Therefore he affords no technique for assessing the relative value of the binary pairs that emerge in a local set of expressions. Worse than clumsy, his technical apparatus produces meanings which cannot be validated. Yea, or nay, he and Roman Jakobson may be right on the meanings in a sonnet of Baudelaire's.[5] But even if the poet himself had been able to judge between theirs and Riffaterre's alternative interpretation of the same work[6] and to say that one was closer to his thought than the other, he would be more likely to agree that all these meanings are there. This is fair for literary criticism, but when we are talking of grammar, coding, and the 'science of the concrete',[7] it is not enough.

For analysing the food categories used in a particular family the analysis must start with why those particular categories and not others are employed. We will discover the social boundaries which the food meanings encode by an approach which values the binary pairs according to their position in a series. Between breakfast and the last nightcap, the food of the day comes in an ordered pattern. Between Monday and Sunday, the food of the week is patterned again. Then there is the sequence of holidays and fast days through the year, to say nothing of life cycle feasts, birthdays, and weddings. In other words, the binary or other contrasts must be seen in their syntagmatic relations. The chain which links them together gives each element some of its meaning. Lévi-Strauss discusses the syntagmatic relation in his earlier book, *The Savage Mind*, but uses it only for the static analysis of classification systems (particularly of proper names). It is capable of a much more dynamic application to food categories, as Michael Halliday has shown. On the two axes of syntagm and paradigm, chain and choice, sequence and set, call it what you will, he has shown how food elements can be ranged until they are all accounted for either in grammatical terms, or down to the last lexical item.[8]

> Eating, like talking, is patterned activity, and the daily menu may be made to yield an analogy with linguistic form. Being an analogy, it is limited in relevance; its purpose is to throw light on, and suggest problems of, the categories of grammar by relating these to an activity which is familiar and for much of which a terminology is ready to hand.
>
> The presentation of a framework of categories for the description of eating might proceed as follows:

Units: Daily menu
       Meal
       Course
       Helping
       Mouthful

Unit: Daily Menu	$\rightarrow$
Elements of primary structure	E, M, L, S ('early,' 'main,' 'light,' 'snack')
Primary structures	EML EMLS (conflated as EML(S))
Exponents of these elements	E: 1 (breakfast)
(primary classes of unit 'meal')	M: 2 (dinner)
	L: 3 ⎱ (no names available; see
	S: 4 ⎰ classes)
Secondary structures	EL_aS_aM EL_aM EML_bS_b EMS_aL_c
Exponents of secondary elements	L_a: 3.1 (lunch)
(systems of secondary classes of	L_b: 3.2 (high tea)
unit 'meal')	L_c: 3.3 (supper)
	S_a: 4.1 (afternoon tea)
	S_b: 4.2 (nightcap)
System of sub-classes of unit	E: 1.1 (English breakfast)
'meal'	1.2 (continental breakfast)

Passing to the rank of the 'meal,' we will follow through the class 'dinner:'

Unit: Meal, Class: dinner	$\rightarrow$
Elements of primary structure	F, S, M, W, Z ('first,' 'second,' 'main,' 'sweet,' 'savoury')
Primary structures	MW MWZ MZW FMW FMWZ FMZW FSMW FSMWZ FSMZW (conflated as (F(S)MW(Z)))
Exponents of these elements	F: 1 (antipasta)
(primary classes of unit 'course')	S: 2 (fish)
	M: 3 (entrée)
	W: 4 (dessert)
	Z: 5 (cheese*)
Secondary structures	(various, involving secondary elements $F_{a..d}$, $M_{a.b}$, $W_{a.c}$)
Exponents of secondary elements	F_a: 1.1 (soup)
(systems of secondary classes of	F_b: 1.2 (hors d'oeuvres)
unit 'course')	F_c: 1.3 (fruit)
	F_d: 1.4 (fruit juice)
	M_a: 3.1 (meat dish)
	M_b: 3.2 (poultry dish)
	W_a: 4.1 (fruit*)

	Wb:	4.2 (pudding)
	Wc:	4.3 (ice cream*)
Systems of sub-classes of unit 'course'	Fa:	1.11 (clear soup*) 1.12 (thick soup*)
	S:	2.01 (grilled fish*) 2.02 (fried fish*) 2.03 (poached fish*)
	Wb:	4.21 (steamed pudding*) 4.22 (milk pudding*)
Exponential systems operating in meal structure	Fc:	grapefruit/melon
	Fd:	grapefruit juice/pineapple juice/ tomato juice
	Ma:	beef/mutton/pork
	Mb:	chicken/turkey/duck/goose

At the rank of the 'course,' the primary class 'entrée' has secondary classes 'meat dish' and 'poultry dish.' Each of these two secondary classes carries a grammatical system whose terms are formal items. But this system accounts only for simple structures of the class 'entrée' those made up of only one member of the unit 'helping.' The class 'entrée,' also displays compound structures, whose additional elements have as exponents the (various secondary classes of the) classes 'cereal' and 'vegetable.' We will glance briefly at these:

Unit: Course, Class: entrée

Elements of primary structure	J, T, A ('joint,' 'staple,' 'adjunct')
Primary structures	J JT JA JTA (conflated as J((T)(A)))
Exponents of these elements (primary classes of unit 'helping')	J: 1 (flesh) T: 2 (cereal) A: 3 (vegetable)
Secondary structures	(various, involving – among others – secondary elements Ja,b, Ta,b, Aa,b)
Exponents of secondary elements (systems of secondary classes of unit 'helping')	Ja: 1.1 (meat) } systems as at M Jb: 1.2 (poultry) } in meal structure
	Ta: 2.1 (potato) Tb: 2.2 (rice) Aa: 3.1 (green vegetable*) Ab: 3.2 (root vegetable*)

And so on, until everything is accounted for either in grammatical systems or in classes made up of lexical items (marked *). The presentation has proceeded down the rank scale, but shunting is presupposed throughout:

there is mutual determination among all units, down to the gastronomic morpheme, the 'mouthful.'

This advances considerably the analysis of our family eating patterns. First, it shows how long and tedious the exhaustive analysis would be, even to read. It would be more taxing to observe and record. Our model of ethnographic thoroughness for a microscopic example should not be less exact than that practised by anthropologists working in exotic lands. In India social distinctions are invariably accompanied by distinctions in commensality and categories of edible and inedible foods. Louis Dumont's important work on Indian culture, *Homo Hierarchicus*, discusses the purity of food as an index of hierarchy. He gives praise to Adrian Mayer's detailed study of the relation between food categories and social categories in a village in Central India.[9] Here twenty-three castes group themselves according to the use of the same pipe, the provision of ordinary food for common meals, and the provision of food for feasts. Higher castes share the pipe with almost all castes except four. Between twelve and sixteen castes smoke together, though in some cases a different cloth must be placed between the pipe and the lips of the smoker. When it comes to their food, a subtler analysis is required. Castes which enjoy power in the village are not fussy about what they eat or from whom they receive it. Middle-range castes are extraordinarily restrictive, both as to whom they will accept food from and what they will eat. Invited to family ceremonies by the more powerful and more ritually relaxed castes they puritanically insist on being given their share of the food raw and retire to cook it themselves in their own homes.[10] If I were to follow this example and to include all transmission of food from our home my task would be greater. For certainly we too know situations in which drink is given to be consumed in the homes of the recipient. There are some kinds of service for which it seems that the only possible recognition is half or even a whole bottle of whiskey. With the high standards of the Indian research in mind, I try now to identify the relevant categories of food in our home.

The two major contrasted food categories are meals versus drinks. Both are social events. Outside these categories, of course, food can be taken for private nourishment. Then we speak only of the lexical item itself: 'Have an apple. Get a glass of milk. Are there any sweets?' If likely to interfere with the next meal, such eating is disapproved. But no negative attitude condemns eating before drinks. This and other indices suggest that meals rank higher.

Meals contrast with drinks in the relation between solids and liquids. Meals are a mixture of solid foods accompanied by liquids. With drinks the reverse holds. A complex series of syntagmatic associations governs the elements in a meal, and connects the meals through the day. One can say: 'It can't be lunchtime. I haven't had breakfast yet', and at breakfast itself cereals come before bacon and eggs. Meals in their sequence tend to be named. Drinks sometimes have named categories: 'Come for cocktails, come for coffee, come for tea', but many are not named events: 'What about a drink? What shall we have?' There is no structuring of drinks into early, main, light. They are not invested with any necessity in their ordering. Nor is the event called drinks internally structured into first, second, main, sweet. On the contrary, it is approved to stick with the same kind of drink, and to count drinks at all is impolite. The judgment 'It is too early for alcohol' would be both rare and likely to be contested. The same lack of structure is found in the solid foods accompanying drinks. They are usually cold, served in discrete units which can be eaten tidily with fingers. No order governs the choice of solids. When the children were small and tea was a meal, bread and butter preceded scones, scones preceded cake and biscuits. But now that the adult–child contrast no longer dominates in this family, tea has been demoted from a necessary place in the daily sequence of meals to an irregular appearance among weekend drinks, and no rules govern the accompanying solids.

Meals properly require the use of at least one mouth-entering utensil per head, whereas drinks are limited to mouth-touching ones. A spoon on a saucer is for stirring, not sucking. Meals require a table, a seating order, restriction on movement and on alternative occupations. There is no question of knitting during a meal. Even at Sunday breakfast, reaching for the newspapers is a signal that the meal is over. The meal puts its frame on the gathering. The rules which hedge off and order one kind of social interaction are reflected in the rules which control the internal ordering of the meal itself. Drinks and their solids may all be sweet. But a meal is not a meal if it is all in the bland-sweet-sour dimensions. A meal incorporates a number of contrasts, hot and cold, bland and spiced, liquid and semi-liquid, and various textures. It also incorporates cereals, vegetables, and animal proteins. Criticism easily fastens on the ordering of these elements in a given case.

Obviously the meanings in our food system should be elucidated by much closer observation. I cut it short by drawing conclusions intuitively from the social categories which emerge. Drinks are for strangers, acquaintances, work-men, and family. Meals are for family, close friends, honoured guests. The grand operator of the system is the line between intimacy and distance. Those we know at meals we also know at drinks. The meal expresses close friendship. Those we only know at drinks we know less intimately. So long as this boundary matters to us (and there is no reason to suppose it will always matter) the boundary between drinks and meals has meaning. There are smaller thresholds and half-way points. The entirely cold meal (since it omits a major contrast within a meal) would seem to be such a modifier. So those friends who have never had a hot meal in our home have presumably another threshold of intimacy to cross. The recent popularity of the barbecue and of more elabor-ately structured cocktail events which act as bridges between intimacy and distance suggests that our model of feeding categories is a common one. It can be drawn as in Figure 18.1. Thus far we can go on the basis of binary oppositions and the number of classes and subclasses. But we are left with the general question which must be raised whenever a correspondence is found between a given social structure and the structure of symbols by which it is expressed, that is, the question of consciousness. Those who vehemently reject the possibility of a meal's being constituted by soup and pudding, or cake and fruit, are certainly not conscious that they are thereby sustaining a boundary between share-drinks and share-meals-too. They would be shocked at the very idea. It would be simplistic to trace the food categories direct to the social categories they embrace and leave it at Figure 18.1. Evidently the external boundaries are only a small part of the meaning of the meal. Somewhere else in the family system some other cognitive activity is generating the internal structuring.

We can go much further toward discovering the intensity of meanings and their anchorage in social life by attending to the sequence of meals. For the week's menu has its climax at Sunday lunch. By contrasting the structure of Sunday lunch with weekday lunches a new principle emerges. Weekday lunches tend to have a tripartite structure, one element stressed accompanied by two or more unstressed elements, for example a main course and cold supporting dishes. But Sunday lunch has two main courses, each of which is patterned

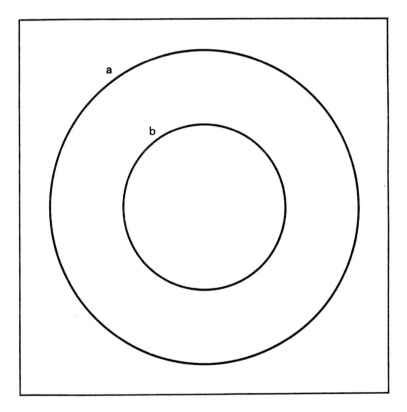

Figure 18.1 Social universe (a) share-drinks; (b) share-meals-too

like the weekday lunch – say, first course, fish or meat (stressed) and two vegetables (unstressed), second course, pudding (stressed), cream and biscuits (unstressed). Christmas lunch has three courses, each on the same tripartite model. Here we stop and realise that the analogy may be read in the reverse sense. Meals are ordered in scale of importance and grandeur through the week and the year. The smallest, meanest meal metonymically figures the structure of the grandest, and each unit of the grand meal figures again the whole meal – or the meanest meal. The perspective created by these repetitive analogies invests the individual meal with additional meaning. Here we have the principle we were seeking, the intensifier of meaning, the selection principle. A meal stays in the category of meal only insofar as it carries this structure which allows the part to recall the whole. Hence the outcry against allowing the sequence of soup and pudding to be called a meal.

As to the social dimension, admission to even the simplest meal incorporates our guest unwittingly into the pattern of solid Sunday dinners, Christmases, and the gamut of life cycle celebrations. Whereas the sharing of drinks (note the fluidity of the central item, the lack of structuring, the small, unsticky accompanying solids) expresses by contrast only too clearly the detachment and impermanence of simpler and less intimate social bonds.

Summing up, syntagmatic relations between meals reveal a restrictive patterning by which the meal is identified as such, graded as a minor or major event of its class, and then judged as a good or bad specimen of its kind. A system of repeated analogies upholds the process of recognition and grading. Thus we can broach the question of interpretation which binary analysis by itself leaves untouched. The features which a single copious dish would need to display before qualifying as a meal in our home would be something like those of the famous chicken Marengo of Napoleon after his defeat of the Austrians.[11]

> Bonaparte, who, on the day of a battle, ate nothing until after it was over, had gone forward with his general staff and was a long way from his supply wagon. Seeing his enemies put to flight, he asked Dunand to prepare dinner for him. The master-chef at once sent men of the quartermaster's staff and ordnance in search of provisions. All they could find were three eggs, four tomatoes, six crayfish, a small hen, a little garlic, some oil and a saucepan . . . the dish was served on a tin plate, the chicken surrounded by the fried eggs and crayfish, with the sauce poured over it.

There must have been many more excellent meals following similar scavenging after the many victories of those campaigns. But only this one has become famous. In my opinion the reason is that it combines the traditional soup, fish, egg, and meat courses of a French celebratory feast all in a *plat unique*.

If I wish to serve anything worthy of the name of supper in one dish it must preserve the minimum structure of a meal. Vegetable soup so long as it had noodles and grated cheese would do, or poached eggs on toast with parsley.

Now I know the formula. A proper meal is A (when A is the stressed main course) plus 2B (when B is an unstressed course). Both A and B contain each of the same structure, in small, a + 2b, when a is the stressed item and b the unstressed item in a course. A weekday lunch is A; Sunday lunch is 2A; Christmas, Easter, and birthdays are A + 2B. Drinks by contrast are unstructured.

To understand the categories we have placed ourselves at the hub of a small world, a home and its neighbourhood. The pre-coded message of the food categories is the boundary system of a series of social events. Our example made only oblique reference to costs in time and work to indicate the concerns involved. But unless the symbolic structure fits squarely to some demonstrable social consideration, the analysis has only begun. For the fit between the medium's symbolic boundaries and the boundaries between categories of people is its only possible validation. The fit may be at different levels; but without being able to show some such matching, the analysis of symbols remains arbitrary and subjective.

The question that now arises is the degree to which a family uses symbolic structures which are available from the wider social system. Obviously this example reeks of the culture of a certain segment of the middle classes of London. The family's idea of what a meal should be is influenced by the Steak House and by the French *cuisine bourgeoise*. Yet herein is implied a synthesis of different traditions. The French version of the grand meal is dominated by the sequence of wines. The cheese platter is the divide between a mounting crescendo of individual savoury dishes and a descending scale of sweet ones ending with coffee. Individual dishes in the French sequence can stand alone. Compare the melon course in a London restaurant and a Bordeaux restaurant. In the first, the half slice is expected to be dusted with powdered ginger and castor sugar (a + 2b) or decorated with a wedge of orange and a crystallised cherry (a + 2b). In the second, half a melon is served with no embellishment but its own perfume and juices. A + 2B is obviously not a formula that our family invented, but one that is current in our social environment. It governs even the structure of the cocktail canapé. The latter, with its cereal base, its meat or cheese middle section, its sauce or pickle topping, and its mixture of colours, suggests a mock meal, a minute metonym of English middle-class meals in general. Whereas the French pattern is more like: $C^1 + B^1 + A^1/A^2 + B^2 + C^2$, when the cheese course divides A^1 (the main savoury dish) from A^2 (the main sweet). It would be completely against the spirit of this essay to hazard a meaning for either structure in its quasi environmental form. French families reaching out to the meal structure of their cultural environment develop it and interact with it according to their intentions. English families reach out and find another which they adapt to their own social purposes. Americans, Chinese, and others do likewise. Since these cultural environments afford an ambient stream of symbols, capable of differentiating and intensifying, but not anchored to a stable social base, we cannot proceed further to interpret them. At this point the analysis stops. But the problems which cannot be answered here, where the cultural universe is unbounded, can usefully be referred to a more closed environment.

To sum up, the meaning of a meal is found in a system of repeated analogies. Each meal carries something of the meaning of the other meals; each meal is a structured social event which structures others in its own image. The upper limit of its meaning is set by the range incorporated in the most important member of its series. The recognition which allows each member to be classed and graded with the others depends upon the structure common to them all. The cognitive energy which demands that a meal look like a meal and not like a drink is performing in the culinary medium the same exercise that it performs in language. First, it distinguishes order, bounds it, and separates it from disorder. Second, it uses economy in the means of expression by allowing only a limited number of structures. Third, it imposes a rank scale upon the repetition of structures. Fourth, the repeated formal analogies multiply the meanings that are carried down any one of them by the power of the most weighty. By these four methods the meanings are enriched. There is no single point in the rank scale, high or low, which provides the basic meaning or real meaning. Each exemplar has the meaning of its structure realised in the examples at other levels.

From coding we are led to a more appropriate comparison for the interpretation of a meal, that is, versification. To treat the meal as a poem requires a more serious example than I have used hitherto. I turn to the Jewish meal, governed by the Mosaic dietary rules. For Lu Chi, a third-century Chinese poet, poetry traffics in some way between the world and mankind. The poet is one who 'traps Heaven and Earth in a cage of form'.[12] On these terms the common meal of the Israelites was a kind of classical poem. Of the Israelite table, too, it could be said that it enclosed boundless space. To quote Lu Chi again: [13]

> We enclose boundless space in a square-foot of paper;
> We pour out deluge from the inch-space of the heart.

But the analogy slows down at Lu Chi's last line. For at first glance it is not certain that the meal can be a tragic medium. The meal is a kind of poem, but by a very limited analogy. The cook may not be able to express the powerful things a poet can say.

In *Purity and Danger*[14] I suggested a rational pattern for the Mosaic rejection of certain animal kinds. Ralph Bulmer has very justly reproached me for offering an animal taxonomy for the explanation of the Hebrew dietary laws. The principles I claimed to discern must remain, he argued, at a subjective and arbitrary level, unless they could take account of the multiple dimensions of thought and activity of the Hebrews concerned.[15] S.J. Tambiah has made similarly effective criticisms of the same shortcoming in my approach.[16] Both have provided from their own fieldwork distinguished examples of how the task should be conducted. In another publication I hope to pay tribute to the importance of their research. But for the present purpose, I am happy to admit the force of their reproach. It was even against the whole spirit of my book to offer an account of an ordered system of thought which did not show the context of social relations in which the categories had meaning. Ralph Bulmer let me down gently by supposing that the ethnographic evidence concerning the ancient Hebrews was too meagre. However, reflection on this new research and methodology has led me to reject that suggestion out of hand. We know plenty about the ancient Hebrews. The problem is how to recognise and relate what we know.

New Guinea and Thailand are far apart, in geography, in history, and in civilisation. Their local fauna are entirely different. Surprisingly, these two analyses of animal classification have one thing in common. Each society projects onto the animal kingdom categories and values which correspond to their categories of marriageable persons. The social categories of descent and affinity dominate their natural categories. The good Thailand son-in-law knows his place and keeps to it: disordered, displaced sex is reprobated and the odium transferred to the domestic dog, symbol of dirt and promiscuity. From the dog to the otter, the transfer of odium is doubled in strength. This amphibian they class as wild, counterpart-dog. But instead of keeping to the wild domain it is apt to leave its sphere at flood time and to paddle about in their watery fields. The ideas they attach to incest are carried forward from the dog to the otter, the image of the utterly wrong son-in-law. For the Karam the social focus is upon the strained relations between affines and cousins. A wide range of manmade rules sustain the categories of a natural world which mirrors these anxieties. In the Thailand and Karam studies, a strong analogy between bed and board lies unmistakably beneath the system of classifying animals. The patterns of rules which categorise animals correspond in form to the patterns of rules governing human relations. Sexual and gastronomic consummation are made equivalents of one another by reasons of analogous restrictions applied to each. Looking back from these examples to the classification of Leviticus we seek in vain a statement, however oblique, of a similar association between eating and sex. Only a very strong analogy between table and altar stares us in the face. On reflection, why should the Israelites have had a similar concern to associate sex with food? Unlike the other two examples, they had no rule requiring them to exchange their womenfolk. On the contrary, they were allowed to marry their parallel paternal first cousins. E.R. Leach has reminded us how strongly exogamy was disapproved at the top political level,[17] and within each tribe of Israel endogamy was even enjoined (Numbers 36). We must seek elsewhere for their dominant preoccupations. At this point I turn to the rules governing the common meal as prescribed in the Jewish religion. It is particularly interesting that these rules have remained the same over centuries. Therefore, if these categories express a relevance to social concerns we must expect those concerns to have remained in some form alive. The three rules about meat are: (1) the rejection of certain animal kinds as unfit for the table (Leviticus 11; Deuteronomy 14), (2) of those admitted as edible, the separation of the meat from blood before cooking

(Leviticus 17: 10; Deuteronomy 12: 23–7), (3) the total separation of milk from meat, which involves the minute specialisation of utensils (Exodus 23: 19; 34: 26; Deuteronomy 14: 21).

I start with the classification of animals whose rationality I claim to have discerned. Diagrams will help to summarise the argument (first outlined in *Purity and Danger*, 1966). First, animals are classified according to degrees of holiness (see Figure 18.2). At the bottom end of the scale some animals are abominable, not to be touched or eaten. Others are fit for the table, but not for the altar. None that are fit for the altar are not edible and vice versa, none that are not edible are sacrificeable. The criteria for this grading are coordinated for the three spheres of land, air, and water. Starting with the simplest, we find the sets as in Figure 18.3.

Water creatures, to be fit for the table, must have fins and scales (Leviticus 13: 9–12; Deuteronomy 14: 19). Creeping swarming worms and snakes, if they go in the water or on the land, are not fit for the table (Deuteronomy 14: 19; Leviticus 11: 41–3). 'The term swarming creatures (*shéreç*) denotes living things which appear in swarms and is applied both to those which teem in the waters (Genesis 1: 20; Leviticus 11: 10) and to those which swarm on the ground, including the smaller land animals, reptiles and creeping insects.'[18] Nothing from this sphere is fit for the altar. The Hebrews only sanctified domesticated animals and these did not include fish. 'When any one of you brings an offering to Jehovah, it shall be a domestic animal, taken either from the herd or from the flock' (Leviticus 1: 2). But, Assyrians and others sacrificed wild beasts, as S.R. Driver and H.A. White point out.

Air creatures (see Figure 18.4) are divided into more complex sets: set (a), those which fly and hop on the earth (Leviticus 11: 12), having wings and two legs, contains two subsets, one of which contains the named birds, abominable

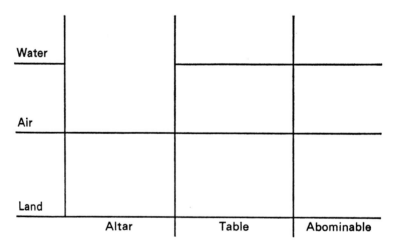

Figure 18.2 Degrees of holiness

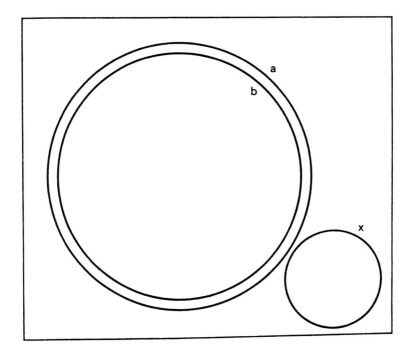

Figure 18.3 Denizens of the water (a) insufficient criteria for (b); (b) fit for table; (x) abominable: swarming

and not fit for the table, and the rest of the birds (b), fit for the table. From this latter subset a sub-subset (c) is drawn, which is suitable for the altar – turtledove and pigeon (Leviticus 14; 5: 7–8) and the sparrow (Leviticus 14: 49–53). Two separate sets of denizens of the air are abominable, untouchable creatures; (f), which have the wrong number of limbs for their habitat, four legs instead of two (Leviticus 9: 20), and (x), the swarming insects we have already noted in the water (Deuteronomy 14: 19).

The largest class of land creatures (a) (see Figure 18.5) walk or hop on the land with four legs. From this set of quadrupeds, those with parted hoofs and which chew the cud (b) are distinguished as fit for the table (Leviticus 11: 3; Dueteronomy 14: 4–6) and of this set subset consists of the domesticated herds and flocks (c). Of these the first born (d) are to be offered to the priests (Deuteronomy 24: 33). Outside the set (b) which part the hoof and chew the cud are three sets of abominable beasts: (g) those which have either the one or the other but not both of the required physical features; (f) those with the wrong number of limbs, two hands instead of four legs (Leviticus 11: 27; 29: 31; and see Proverbs 30: 28); (x) those which crawl upon their bellies (Leviticus 11: 41–4).

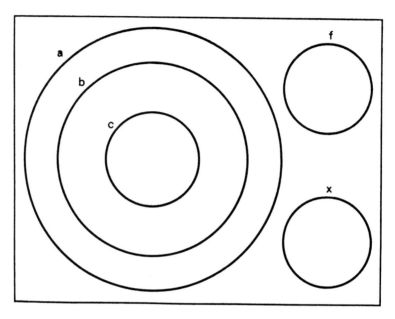

Figure 18.4 Denizens of the air (a) fly and hop: wings and two legs; (b) fit for table; (c) fit for altar; (f) abominable: insufficient criteria for (a); (x) abominable: swarming

The isomorphism which thus appears between the different categories of animal classed as abominable helps us to interpret the meaning of abomination. Those creatures which inhabit a given range, water, air, or land, but do not show all the criteria for (a) or (b) in that range are abominable. The creeping, crawling, teeming creatures do not show criteria for allocation to any class, but cut across them all.

Here we have a very rigid classification. It assigns living creatures to one of three spheres, on a behavioural basis, and selects certain morphological criteria that are found most commonly in the animals inhabiting each sphere. It rejects creatures which are anomalous, whether in living between two spheres, or having defining features of members of another sphere, or lacking defining features. Any living being which falls outside this classification is not to be touched or eaten. To touch it is to be defiled and defilement forbids entry to the temple. Thus it can be summed up fairly by saying that anomalous creatures are unfit for altar and table. This is a peculiarity of the Mosaic code. In other societies anomaly is not always so treated. Indeed, in some, the anomalous creature is treated as the source of blessing and is specially fit for the altar (as the Lele pangolin), or as a noble beast, to be treated as an honourable adversary, as the Karam treat the cassowary. Since in the Mosaic code every degree of holiness in animals has implications one way or the other for edibility,

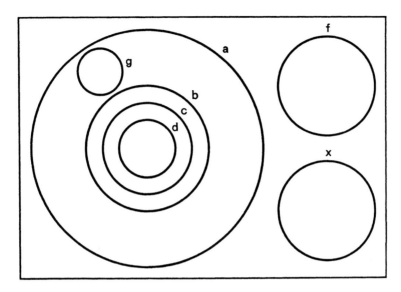

Figure 18.5 Denizens of the land (a) walk or hop with four legs; (b) fit for table; (c) domestic herds and flocks; (d) fit for altar; (f) abominable: insufficient criteria for (a); (g) abominable: insufficient criteria for (b); (x) abominable: swarming

we must follow further the other rules classifying humans and animals. Again I summarise a long argument with diagrams. First, note that a category which divides some humans from others, also divides their animals from others. Israelites descended from Abraham and bound to God by the Covenant between God and Abraham are distinguished from all other peoples and similarly the rules which Israelites obey as part of the Covenant apply to their animals (see Figure 18.6). The rule that the womb opener or first born is consecrated to divine service applies to firstlings of the flocks and herds (Exodus 22: 29–30; Deuteronomy 24: 23) and the rule of Sabbath observance is extended to work animals (Exodus 20: 10). As human and animal firstlings are to God, so a man's own first born is unalterably his heir (Deuteronomy 21: 15–17). The analogy by which Israelites are to other humans as their livestock are to other quadrupeds develops by indefinite stages the analogy between altar and table.

Since Levites who are consecrated to the temple service represent the first born of all Israel (Numbers 3: 12 and 40) there is an analogy between the animal and human firstlings. Among the Israelites, all of whom prosper through the Covenant and observance of the Law, some are necessarily unclean at any given time. No man or woman with issue of seed or blood, or with forbidden contact with an animal classed as unclean, or who has shed blood or been involved in the unsacralised killing of an animal (Leviticus 18), or who has

Under the Covenant

Human	Israelites	others
Nonhuman	their livestock	others

Figure 18.6 Analogy between humans and nonhumans

sinned morally (Leviticus 20), can enter the temple. Nor can one with a blemish (Deuteronomy 23) enter the temple or eat the flesh of sacrifice or peace offerings (Leviticus 8: 20). The Levites are selected by pure descent from all the Israelites. They represent the first born of Israel. They judge the cleanness and purify the uncleanness of Israelites (Leviticus 13, 14, 10: 10; Deuteronomy 21: 5). Only Levites who are without bodily blemish (Leviticus 21: 17–23) and without contact with death can enter the Holy of Holies. Thus we can present these rules as sets in Figures 18.7 and 18.8. The analogy between humans and animals is very clear. So is the analogy created by these rules between the temple and the living body. Further analogies appear between the classification of animals according to holiness (Figure 18.2) and the rules which set up the analogy of the holy temple with its holier and holier inner sanctuaries, and on the other hand between the temple's holiness and the body's purity and the capacity of each to be defiled by the self-same forms of impurity. This analogy is a living part of the Judeo-Christian tradition which has been unfaltering in its interpretation of New Testament allusions. The words of the Last Supper have their meaning from looking backward over the centuries in which the analogy had held good and forward to the future celebrations of that meal. 'This is my body . . . this is my blood' (Luke 22: 19–20; Mark 14: 22-4; Matthew 26: 26–8). Here the meal and the sacrificial victim, the table and the altar are made explicitly to stand for one another.

Lay these rules and their patternings in a straight perspective, each one looking forward and backward to all the others, and we get the same repetition of metonyms that we found to be the key to the full meaning of the categories of food in the home. By itself the body and its rules can carry the whole load of meanings that the temple can carry by itself with its rules. The overlap and repetitions are entirely consistent. What then are these meanings? Between the temple and the body we are in a maze of religious thought. What is its social counterpart? Turning back to my original analysis (in 1966) of the forbidden meats we are now in a much better position to assess intensity and social relevance. For the metonymical patternings are too obvious to ignore. At every moment they are in chorus with a message about the value of purity and the

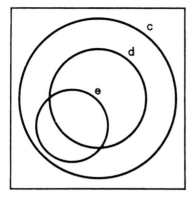
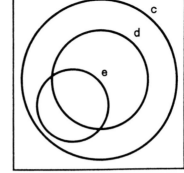

Figure 18.7 The Israelites (c) under the Covenant; (d) fit for temple sacrifice: no blemish; (e) consecrated to temple service, first born

Figure 18.8 Their livestock (c) under the Covenant; (d) fit for temple sacrifice: no blemish; (e) consecrated to temple service, first born

rejection of impurity. At the level of a general taxonomy of living beings the purity in question is the purity of the categories. Creeping, swarming, teeming creatures abominably destroy the taxonomic boundaries. At the level of the individual living being impurity is the imperfect, broken, bleeding specimen. The sanctity of cognitive boundaries is made known by valuing the integrity of the physical forms. The perfect physical specimens point to the perfectly bounded temple, altar, and sanctuary. And these in their turn point to the hard-won and hard-to-defend territorial boundaries of the Promised Land. This is not reductionism. We are not here reducing the dietary rules to any political concern. But we are showing how they are consistently celebrating a theme that has been celebrated in the temple cult and in the whole history of Israel since the first Covenant with Abraham and the first sacrifice of Noah.

Edmund Leach, in his analysis of the genealogy of Solomon, has reminded us of the political problems besetting a people who claim by pure descent and pure religion to own a territory that others held and others continually encroached upon.[19] Israel is the boundary that all the other boundaries celebrate and that gives them their historic load of meaning. Remembering this, the orthodox meal is not difficult to interpret as a poem. The first rule, the rejection of certain animal kinds, we have mostly dealt with. But the identity of the list of named abominable birds is still a question. In the Mishnah it is written: 'The characteristics of birds are not stated, but the Sages have said, every bird that seizes its prey (to tread or attack with claws) is unclean.'[20] The idea that the unclean birds were predators, unclean because they were an image of human predation and homicide, so easily fits the later Hellenicising interpretations that it has been suspect. According to the late Professor S. Hooke (in a personal communication), Professor R.S. Driver once tried out the idea that the Hebrew names were onomatopoeic of the screeches and calls of the birds. He diverted an assembly of learned divines with ingenious vocal exercises combining ornithology and Hebrew scholarship. I have not traced the record of this meeting. But following the method of analysis I have been using, it seems very likely that the traditional predatory idea is sufficient, considering its compatibility with the second rule governing the common meal.

According to the second rule, meat for the table must be drained of its blood. No man eats flesh with blood in it. Blood belongs to God alone, for life is in the blood.[21] This rule relates the meal systematically to all the rules which exclude from the temple on grounds of contact with or responsibility for bloodshed. Since the animal kinds which defy the perfect classification of nature are defiling both as food and for entry to the temple, it is a structural repetition of the general analogy between body and temple to rule that the eating of blood defiles. Thus the birds and beasts which eat carrion (undrained of blood) are likely by the same reasoning to be defiling. In my analysis, the Mishnah's identifying the unclean birds as predators is convincing.

Here we come to a watershed between two kinds of defilement. When the classifications of any metaphysical scheme are imposed on nature, there are several points where it does not fit. So long as the classifications remain in pure metaphysics and are not expected to bite into daily life in the form of rules of behaviour, no problem arises. But if the unity of Godhead is to be related to the unity of Israel and made into a rule of life, the difficulties start. First, there are the creatures whose behaviour defies the rigid classification. It is relatively easy to deal with them by rejection and avoidance. Second, there are the difficulties that arise from our biological condition. It is all very well to worship the holiness of God in the perfection of his creation. But the Israelites must be nourished and must reproduce. It is impossible for a pastoral people to eat their flocks and herds without damaging the bodily completeness they respect. It is impossible to renew Israel without emission of blood and sexual fluids. These problems are met sometimes by avoidance and sometimes by consecration to the temple. The draining of blood from meat is a ritual act which figures the bloody sacrifice at the altar. Meat is thus transformed from a living creature into a food item.

As to the third rule, the separation of meat and milk, it honours the pro-creative functions. The analogy between human and animal parturition is always implied, as the Mishnah shows in its comment on the edibility of the afterbirth found in the slaughtered dam: if the afterbirth had emerged in part, it is forbidden as food; 'it is a token of young in a woman and a token of young in a beast.'[22] Likewise this third rule honours the Hebrew mother and her initial unity with her offspring.

In conclusion I return to the researches of Tambiah and Bulmer. In each case a concern with sexual relations, approved or disapproved, is reflected on to the Thailand and Karam animal classifications. In the case of Israel the dominant concern would seem to be with the integrity of territorial boundaries. But Edmund Leach has pointed out how over and over again they were concerned with the threat to Israel's holy calling from marriages with outsiders. Foreign husbands and foreign wives led to false gods and political defections. So sex is not omitted from the meanings in the common meal. But the question is different. In the other cases the problems arose from rules about exchanging women. In this case the concern is to insist on not exchanging women.

Perhaps I can now suggest an answer to Ralph Bulmer's question about the abhorrence of the pig.

> Dr Douglas tells us that the pig was an unclean beast to the Hebrew quite simply because it was a taxonomic anomaly, literally as the Old Testament says, because like the normal domestic animals it has a cloven hoof, whereas *un*like other cloven-footed beasts, it does not chew the cud. And she pours a certain amount of scorn on the commentators of the last 2,000 years who have taken alternative views and drawn attention to the creature's feeding habits, etc.

Dr Bulmer would be temped to reverse the argument and to say that the other animals are prohibited as part of an elaborate exercise for rationalising[23]

> the prohibition of a beast for which there were probably multiple reasons for avoiding. It would seem equally fair, on the limited evidence available, to argue that the pig was accorded anomalous taxonomic status because it was unclean as to argue that it was unclean because of its anomalous taxonomic status.

On more mature reflection, and with the help of his own research, I can now see that the pig to the Israelites could have had a special taxonomic status equivalent to that of the otter in Thailand. It carries the odium of multiple pollution. First, it pollutes because it defies the classification of ungulates. Second, it pollutes because it eats carrion. Third, it pollutes because it is reared as food (and presumably as prime pork) by non-Israelites. An Israelite who betrothed a foreigner might have been liable to be offered a feast of pork. By these stages it comes plausibly to represent the utterly disapproved form of sexual mating and to carry all the odium that this implies. We now can trace a general analogy between the food rules and the other rules against mixtures: 'Thou shalt not make thy cattle to gender with beasts of any other kind' (Leviticus 19: 19). 'Thou shalt not copulate with any beast' (Leviticus 18: 23). The common meal, decoded, as much as any poem, summarises a stern, tragic religion.

We are left the question of why, when so much else had been forgotten[24] about the rules of purification and their meaning, the three rules governing the Jewish meal have persisted. What meanings do they still encode, unmoored as they partly are from their original social context? It would seem that whenever a people are aware of encroachment and danger, dietary rules controlling what goes into the body would serve as a vivid analogy of the corpus of their cultural categories at risk. But here I am, contrary to my own strictures, suggesting a universal meaning, free of particular social context, one which is likely to make sense whenever the same situation is perceived. We have come full-circle to Figure 18.1, with its two concentric circles. The outside boundary is weak, the inner one strong. Right through the diagrams summarising the Mosaic dietary rules the focus was upon the integrity of the boundary at (b). Abominations of the water are those finless and scaleless creatures which lie outside that boundary. Abominations of the air appear less clearly in this light because the unidentified forbidden birds had to be shown as the widest circle from which the edible selection is drawn. If it be granted that they are predators, then they can be shown as a small subset in the unlisted set, that is as denizens of the air not fit for table because they eat blood. They would then be seen to threaten the boundary at (b) in the same explicit way as among the denizens of the land the circle (g) threatens it. We should therefore not conclude this essay without saying something more positive about what this boundary encloses. In the one case it divides edible from inedible. But it is more than a negative barrier of exclusion. In all the cases we have seen, it bounds the area of structured relations. Within that area rules apply. Outside it, anything goes. Following the argument we have established by which each level of meaning realises the others which share a common structure, we can fairly say that the ordered system which is a meal represents all the ordered systems associated with it. Hence the strong arousal power of a threat to weaken or confuse that category. To take our analysis of the culinary medium further we should study what the poets say about the disciplines that they adopt. A passage from Roy Fuller's lectures helps to explain the flash of recognition and confidence which welcomes an ordered pattern. He is quoting Allen Tate, who said: 'Formal versification is the primary structure of poetic order, the assurance to the reader and to the poet himself that the poet is in control of the disorder both outside him and within his own mind.'[25]

The rules of the menu are not in themselves more or less trivial than the rules of verse to which a poet submits.

NOTES

I am grateful to Professor Basil Bernstein and to Professor M.A.K. Halliday for valuable suggestions and for criticisms, some of which I have not been able to meet. My thanks are due to my son James for working out the Venn diagrams used in this article.

1 Michael A.K. Halliday (1961), 'Categories of the theory of grammar', *World, Journal of the Linguistic Circle of New York, 17,* 241–91.
2 The continuing discussion between anthropologists on the relation between biological and social facts in the understanding of kinship categories is fully relevant to the understanding of food categories.

3 Roland Barthes, *Système de la mode*, Paris, Editions Seuil, 1967.

4 Claude Lévi-Strauss, *The Raw and the Cooked: Introduction to a Science of Mythology*, I, London, Jonathan Cape, 1970. The whole series in French is *Mythologiques*: I. *Le Cru et le cuit*, II. *Du Miel aux cendres*, III. *L'Origine des manières de table*, Paris, Plon, 1964–8.

5 Roman Jakobson and Claude Lévi-Strauss, 'Les Chats de Charles Baudelaire', *L'Homme*, 2, 1962, 5–21.

6 Michael Riffaterre, 'Describing poetic structures: two approaches to Baudelaire's *Les Chats*', *Structuralism*, Yale French Studies 36 and 37, 1967.

7 Claude Lévi-Strauss, *The Savage Mind*, London, Weidenfeld & Nicolson, 1966; University of Chicago Press, 1962, 1966.

8 Halliday, 'Categories of the theory of grammar', pp. 277–9.

9 Adrian C. Mayer, *Caste and Kinship in Central India: a Village and its Region*, London, Routledge, 1960.

10 Louis Dumont, *Homo Hierarchicus: the Caste System and its Implications*, trans. M. Sainsbury, London, Weidenfeld & Nicolson, 1970; French ed., Gallimard, 1966, pp. 86–9.

11 See under 'Marengo', *Larousse Gastronomique*, Hamlyn, 1961.

12 A. MacLeish, *Poetry and Experience*, London, Bodley Head, 1960, p. 4.

13 *Ibid.*

14 Mary Douglas, *Purity and Danger: an Analysis of Concepts of Pollution and Taboo*, London, Routledge, 1966.

15 Ralph Bulmer, 'Why is the cassowary not a bird? A problem of zoological taxonomy among the Karam of the New Guinea Highlands', *Man*, new ser., 2, 1967, 5–25.

16 S.J. Tambiah, 'Animals are good to think and good to prohibit', *Ethnology*, 7, 1969, 423–59.

17 E.R. Leach, 'The legitimacy of Solomon', *Genesis as Myth and Other Essays*, London, Jonathan Cape, 1969.

18 S.R. Driver and H.A. White, *The Polychrome Bible, Leviticus*, v. l. fn. 13.

19 Leach, 'Legitimacy of Solomon'.

20 H. Danby, trans., *The Mishnah*, London, Oxford University Press, 1933, p. 324.

21 See Jacob Milgrom, 'A prolegomena to Leviticus 17: 17', *Journal of Biblical Literature*, 90, II, 1971: 149–56. This contains a textual analysis of the rules forbidding eating flesh with the blood in it which is compatible with the position herein advocated.

22 *Ibid.*, p. 520.

23 Bulmer, 'Why is the cassowary not a bird?', p. 21.

24 Moses Maimonides, *Guide for the Perplexed*, trans. M. Friedlander, London, Routledge, 1904, first ed., 1881.

25 Roy Fuller, *Owls and Artificers: Oxford Lectures on Poetry*, London, Deutsch, 1971, p. 64.

Chapter 19

Self-evidence

The Henry Myers Lecture, given for the Royal Anthropological Institute, 4 May 1972

Over two hundred years ago David Hume declared that there is no necessity in Nature: 'Necessity is something that exists in the mind, not in objects.' In other words, he insisted that knowledge of causality is of the intuitional kind, guts knowledge; causality is no more than a 'construction upon past experience'; it is due to 'force of habit', a part of human nature whose study, he averred, is too much neglected. As anthropologists our work has been precisely to study this habit which constructs for each society its special universe of efficacious principles. This very habit peoples each world with humans, alive and dead, animal bodies and animal spirits, half-humans, half-animals, and divinities mixed with each. From the sheer variety of these constructed worlds, the anthropologist is led to agree, but only guardedly, with Hume. Other people's causal theories are put into two sets: those which accord with our own and need no special explanation, and those which are magical and based on subjective associations as Frazer believed, or on affective rather than cognitive faculties, as Lévy-Bruhl (see Cazeneuve, 1972: 44, 68, 70) when he tried to distinguish the mystical from the scientific mind. But Hume claimed that all causal theories whatever and without exception arise from what he called the sensitive rather than the cognitive part of our nature. Whenever we reserve our own causal theories from sceptical philosophy, our gut response proves him utterly right. But it is almost impossible not to make this reservation. One of the objects of this paper is to propose a more formal mode of discussion in which we can hope to compare causal systems, including our own. Without that shift our only recourse as anthropologists is to translate from other cultures into our own. The better the translation, the more successfully has our provincial logic been imposed on the native thought. So the consequence of good translation is to prevent any confrontation between alien thought systems. We are left as we were at the outset, with our own familiar world divided by its established categories and activated by the principles we know. This world remains our stable point of reference for judging all other worlds as peculiar and other knowledge as faulty. Translation flourishes where experience overlaps. But where there is no overlap, the attempt to translate fails. The challenge of a new meaning by which to test our own ideas is turned into a challenge to find a new expression for our old meanings. The only confrontation takes place when the lack of overlap between our culture and others suggests a few academic puzzles about the peculiarities of native thought. This is the failing I wish to remedy in this essay. Puzzles about native thought are puzzles about thought in general and so puzzles about our own thought. We anthropologists tend to discuss problems of meaning in a too segregated framework. We have to see that the categories and actual principles which we find in our own world present the same problems of rational justification that baffle us in the exotic worlds of foreigners. Just where there is no cultural overlap the effort to interpret should be driven to ascend from the particular puzzling statement to higher and higher levels of generalisation until finally the conflict of opinion is uncovered at its source. Two different sets of hypotheses about the nature of reality and how it is divided up are exposed, each carrying the ring of self-evident truth so clearly that its fundamental assumptions are implicit and considered to need no justification.

By this route we are already in the middle of the question of self-evidence. A self-evident statement is one which carries its evidence within itself. It is true by virtue of the meaning of the words, 'All bachelors are unmarried men'; '2 + 2 = 4'. Quoting Professor Quine, on whose work this discussion draws heavily, a self-evident or analytic statement can be defined 'as any statement which, by putting synonyms for synonyms, is convertible into an instance of a logical form all of whose instances are true' (1943: 120). But what is synonymity? It is 'the relation between expressions that have the same meaning'. And what is the meaning of an expression? It is 'the class of all expressions synonymous with it'. So we are in a circle out of which anthropology can hardly hope to show the way. But our material might explain better how the relation of synonymity is recognised and confirmed. The strategy of this paper is to start with Quine's description of how intuitions of sameness are established, and to improve it by inserting a fuller account of the sociological dimension. As it stands, his account has certain limitations. For one, it leaves the intuition of sameness on the wrong side of rationality: guts are guts and reason is reason, there is still a gap in the account of how the two relate. For another, it leaves us with an empty cultural relativism: each universe is divided up differently, period. From here there is nothing more to say about the comparison of universes, since we are always forced to speak within the categories of our own language. But I dare to hope that I can show a path which will lead out of that particular circle, towards generalisation about kinds of universes. As a by-product of the discussion there is a contribution to comparative religion, because theodicy provides one of the most comprehensive explanatory systems and the argument will therefore be most easily demonstrated by comparing religious doctrines.

Quine is a philosopher who has taken the anthropologist's problems and materials very seriously. His *Word and Object* (1960) is directed straight to the matter in hand and I cannot do justice to the breadth of view and clarity with which it is discussed. His arguments are directed against many of our time-honoured and favourite fallacies, from pre-logical mentality to the idea that meaning is an independent, free-floating entity, which words try to capture more or less completely (1960: 76). Here I only need to summarise the argument that relates to synonymy. The recognition of sameness is firmly anchored in social experience: an individual in the community experiences stimulus-synonymy, which approximates to sameness of confirming experiences and disconfirming experiences. Sameness of meaning is traced to verbal habits which are determined by community-wide collateral information. Thus we are given an outline for the psychological and sociological basis for producing words to which the same meanings are allocated. We are also directed away from worrying about short synonyms towards the longer and more complex ones. This is a relief. The most baffling translations of foreign ideas are the shortest ones, presented out of context, as parts away from their wholes. The Bororo told von den Steinen in 1894 that they were parrots (Lévy-Bruhl, 1910). The Nuer say human twins are birds (Evans-Pritchard, 1956: 128–34). The Karam say that the cassowary is their sister's child (Bulmer, 1967). In certain specifiable contexts the animal or the human member of the class could be substituted, the one for the other, without affecting the meaning. But in the short synonym the translation of the copula 'is' has almost certainly been badly rendered. Edmund Leach has discussed Malinowski's refusal to recognise synonyms where the sameness escaped his own understanding. Each time the word *tabu* appeared as a kinship term Malinowski claimed that it was a homonym modified by context so that differences of meaning were conveyed.

> Malinowski (1935: p. 66ff.) spared his islanders the imputation of pre-logicality by so varying his translations of terms, from occurrence to occurrence, as to side-step contradiction. Leach (p. 130) protested, but no clear criterion emerged. It is understandable that the further alternatives of blaming the translation of conjunctions, copulas or other logical particles is nowhere considered; for any considerable complexity on the part of the English correlates of such words would, of course, present the working translator with forbidding practical difficulties (Quine 1960: 58f.n.).

And so we are absolved. As it happens, Edmund Leach has successfully interpreted the sameness in the kinship relationships of the Trobrianders conveyed by the word *tabu* (1958: 120–45). So anthropology may have reached a stage at which the generous absolution for our neglect of logical particles may be less necessary. I certainly would prefer to discuss longer synonyms which would approximate 'to what it might mean "to speak of two statements as standing in the same germaneness, relating to the same particular experience"' (Quine, 1960, quoting Grice and Strawson 1956: 156). For example, 'in villages in Ceylon the fact that a woman cooks food for a man is a public statement of a conjugal relationship' (Tambiah, 1969). To cook for him is the same as cohabiting with him, 'she is his cook' = 'she is his wife'. This synonym, in any form, is not a puzzling one for us because of the overlap between our customs and theirs. The dividing line between cooks and wives is an unimportant one. The big mysteries arise when an important dividing line of meaning is ignored; when certain human categories, for example, are made synonymous with animal species. Then the short form has to be expanded into its longer form and the logical particles carefully examined. Surely there can be no recognition of sameness without a grasp of the logical relations which hold the class of things with the same meaning to the same particular experiences in the same way. For an account of recognising sameness I turn to Quine (1960: 66–7):

> By an intuitive account I mean one in which terms are used in habitual ways without reflecting how they might be defined or what presuppositions they might conceal [Quine, 1960, note to p. 36]. Intuition figures in the case of analyticity despite the technical sound of the word; sentences like 'No unmarried man is married', 'No bachelor is married', and '2 + 2 = 4' have a feel that everyone appreciates . . . one's reaction to denials of sentences typically felt as analytic has more in it of one's reaction to ungrasped foreign sentences. When the sentence concerned is a law of logic, something of this reaction is discerned . . . dropping a logical law disrupts a pattern on which the communicative use of a logical particle heavily depends . . .
>
> If the mechanism of analyticity intuitions is substantially as I have vaguely suggested, they will in general tend to set in where bewilderment sets in as to what the man who denies the sentence can be talking about. This effect can be gradual and also cumulative.

Avoiding bewilderment and experiencing bewilderment are the two extremes at which it is easy to see how logic bites into the emotional life. In between the extremes, the emotions are channelled down the familiar grooves cut by social relations and their requirements of consistency, clarity and reliability of expectations. I feel we should try to insert between the psychology of the individual and the public use of language, a dimension of social behaviour. In this dimension logical relations also apply. This is the nub of my contribution to how intuitions of self-evidence are formed. Persons are included in or excluded from a given class, classes are ranked, parts are related to wholes. It is argued here that the intuition of the logic of these social experiences is the basis for finding the a priori in nature. The pattern of social relations is fraught with emotional power; great stakes are invested in their permanence by some, in their overthrow by others. This is the level of experience at which the guts reaction of bewilderment at an unintelligible sentence is strengthened by potential fury, shock, and loathing. Apprehending a general pattern of what is right and necessary in social relations is the basis of society: this apprehension generates whatever a priori or set of necessary causes is going to be found in nature. This 'pure, unreconstructed Durkheimianism', as a friend has called it, develops naturally from my earlier work on the idea of pollution (1966). There I tried to show how the world of nature is dragged into the arguments about society, and how it benefits each protagonist in the dialogue to refer to dangers from the allegedly objective system of causes out there. The issue now is to rescue the notion of intuition or guts reaction from any contrast with rationality by anchoring it in the experience the individual has of the logical properties of social forms.

Each universe is to be seen as a whole, generated with a particular kind of social experience. It may be objected that such an infinite number of possible classifications of nature operating for such a variety of social relations can be imagined that there is no sense in talking of universes as wholes. But the wholeness that concerns us lies in the finite range of favoured patternings of reality. I shall develop this argument with special reference to the treatment meted to borderline cases. The idea is that a continuum of social systems could be constructed in which, at one end, outsiders would be excluded completely and irrevocably, and working through various modifications, at the other extreme outsiders would be admitted to full membership of the community. Each point on the continuum would have its corresponding world of nature, with a characteristic way of dealing with hybrids and anomalous beings. Judgments that such and such creatures because they escape through the meshes of the local system of classification are contrary to nature, tend to evoke a further judgment. The monster in question may indeed be ignored. But equally it may be regarded as a vehicle of prosperity or of disaster. The judgment is made evident to the observer by rules about how it is to be treated when encountered. By this route we can rise to a higher level of formal comparison. Instead of talking about particular beliefs, say in unicorns or wombats, and instead of talking about causal systems or synonymy in general, we can identify distinctive predilections for agreeing certain kinds of self-evident propositions, each anchored in its correlated social environment.

By focusing on how anomalous beings may be treated in different systems of classification, we make a frontal attack on the question of how thought, words, and the real world are related. Granted that the known world is socially constructed, no matter how flexible and subtle the principles of classification used, there will be some living beings which fit badly in the local taxonomic scheme. Bulmer and Tambiah give many different examples in their important essays on Karam and Thai classifications of animals, stressing the social nature of the taxonomic system. Creatures that emerge as anomalous on one could be perfectly acceptable on another. For example, Thai villages count domestic land animals as distinct from birds. As if they had no niche for domestic birds, ducks and chickens are counted land animals, their birdlike features notwithstanding. Land animals with wings suggest an anomaly to us, but they do not perceive it. On the other hand, the otter, like voles and seals, has no connotation of monstrosity for us: for the Thai it is a revolting hybrid, a fish as it were, with a head like a dog, a wild beast which invades their domestic fields in flood time.

There are obviously as many kinds of anomaly as there are criteria for classifying. For the purpose in hand, it is enough to speak of creatures which in their morphology show criteria of more than one major class, or not enough criteria to enable them to be assigned to any one class, and of creatures which in themselves belong clearly enough to a recognised class but which have either the habits or which stray into the habitat of another class. An example of the first will be the pangolin or scaly ant-eater, honoured by the Lele as a tree-dwelling mammal with scales like a fish; of the second, the cassowary which Karam reckon has neither the feathers nor the brains of a bird; of the third, nocturnal antelopes distinguished by the Lele on account of this habit from other antelopes; of the fourth, the Thai view of the otter and the Nile monitor and other invasive creatures which stray out of the habitat to which they could be assigned on other criteria.

Any universe is liable to harbour monsters which straddle across its major classes. But such creatures do not necessarily get any attention. If they are noticed, they can be judged very auspicious. Alternatively, they can inspire horror, aversion, disgust. When this is recorded, we have the strong guts reaction. Many are the Old Testament scholars content to explain the abominableness of creeping things in Leviticus 11 by a universal loathing of reptiles and insects, and to accept snakes being lumped together with the uncleanness of leprosy and death as a perfectly self-evident, unnecessary-to-explain collection of same meanings intelligible to all. But some religions pay cult to snakes and others associate them with fertility and the renewal of life. The Christian doctrine of the Incarnation insists that god-man belongs fully to two contrasted sets. For centuries the Israelites were in contact with Egyptian religion which venerated man-gods and god-beasts, and with the Assyrians likewise. But to the Israelites all hybrids and most mixtures were abominable. I have argued and believe that their abomination of creeping things was part of a larger habit of abominating beings which did not tidily conform to their established criteria of air, water, and land creatures. And this was part again of a still larger pattern of social behaviour which used very clear, tight defining lines to distinguish two classes of human beings, the Israelites and the rest.

These remarks summarise too briefly the analysis I made of the Mosaic dietary laws in *Purity and Danger* (1966) and the fuller statement of the meanings enclosed in the Rabbinical interpretation of these laws, given in 'Deciphering a meal' (Chapter 18). It will be easier to understand what follows after reading them, but probably the most important point to clarify if this essay is to stand alone is the status of the pig as a monster in the ancient Israelite classification system. The pig, in Leviticus 11, is put into the class of abominable, unclean creatures, along with the hare, the hyrax, and the camel. The grounds alleged are that these creatures either cleave the hoof or chew the cud, but do not do both. In other words, they don't quite make it into the class of ungulates. By itself, seen from the viewpoint of another pattern of classification, having some but not all the criteria of the class of edible animals would not make them automatically unclean, revolting, abominable. But this classification system, throughout, in all its application, picks on the borderline instance and tags it abominable. The meaning of clean and unclean only gets its full resonance when the classification of the whole universe is complete. When the scheme is drawn in its totality, one of the criteria of cleanness is revealed which before was hidden: the clean species must have all the necessary criteria of its class. To the three major habitats, air, land, water, is assigned a mode of locomotion proper to the clean species inhabiting each one. Conversely, each species must have the necessary physiological characteristics for locomotion in its habitat, fins in the water, wings and two legs in the air, four legs on the land. Creeping things have a mode of locomotion which is not distinctive of any one element: their existence confounds the tidy logical scheme of things: this marks them abominable. The pig, with the right mode of locomotion to get into the same class as sheep, goats and cattle, does not chew the cud. It is the only non-cud-chewing hoof-cleaver in the whole of creation, a monster with no other judgment possible of its improper, law-defying existence than outright abomination.

In *Purity and Danger* I supposed that the Hebrew response of rejecting anomaly was the normal one. I argued that to classify is a necessary human activity and that there is a universal human tendency to pass adverse judgment on that which eludes classification or refuses to fit into the tidy compartments of the mind. A too facile solution. I failed to exploit the full interest of the contrast between my fieldwork in the Congo and my library research in the Bible. For

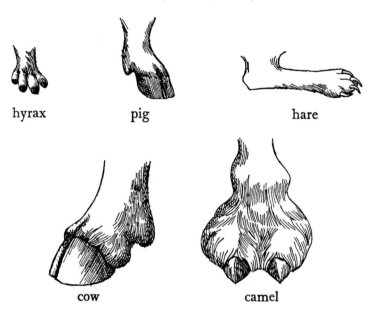

hyrax   pig   hare

cow   camel

Figure 19.1

the Lele, many anomalies are auspicious and they religiously celebrate the most anomalous of all, which carries defining marks of land and water creatures, humans and animals, the pangolin or scaly ant-eater. On the other hand on this showing, every anomaly conceived according to the Biblical classification of nature is a defiling monster (Douglas, 1966). I swept under the carpet, as too difficult for my theorising, the contrast between the abominable pig and the revered pangolin. Bulmer (1967) and Tambiah (1969), who have pointed out these and other shortcomings, have also made such signal advances in their own analyses of animal taxonomy that I am ready, thanks to their work, to have another try. Foul monster or good saviour, the judgment has little to do with the physical attributes of the being in question and much to do with the prevailing social pattern of rules and meanings which creates anomaly. I shall now try to discover the properties of a classification system which will not overlook anomalies, and which, having recognised them, attributes to them efficacy either for evil or for good. Such a response to a mixed category is essentially a gut reaction. It judges the creature at a fundamental level which brooks no question, either to be divinity or to be abominable. The two studies, Tambiah's of north-east Thailand, Bulmer's on the Karam in the New Guinea Highlands, both demonstrate how the classification of animals is imbued with strong social concerns. In each case the taxonomy organises nature so that the categories of animals mirror and reinforce the social rules about marriage and residence. We have known since *Primitive Classification* (Durkheim and Mauss, 1903) and after Lévi-Strauss (1962) we shall never forget that totemic systems of thought stand in this relation to the social system. But it is one thing to know, another to apply. I myself failed to apply this knowledge to my own interpretation of Lele taxonomy. I was able to translate the game-warden's zoological classification into Lele terms and describe the categories which the animals' morphology and behaviour suggested to the Lele. I was able then to relate this native taxonomy to their cult associations. When it came to relating these two levels of realisation (the organising of the world of nature and the organising of cults) to other levels in which meaning is generated, it seemed enough to say there were oppositions and tensions in Lele society which the pangolin cult figuratively transcended as the animal itself transcended the bound- aries of animal kinds (Douglas, 1957). Luc de Heusch developed the theme more richly in a re-analysis of my material.

> On peut se demander pourqoui cette synthèse socio-religieuse se situe sous le signe du pangolin. Le Pangolin est le médiateur par excellence entre le monde humain et le monde animal. A l'intérieur du monde humain l'écart significatif qui oppose le clan matrilinéaire (univers tendu de la 'fraternité') au groupe d'âge (univers agréable du compagnonnage, assiette du village) reproduit à moindre échelle l'écart primordial qui existe, aux yeux, des Lele, entre la nature et la culture. De ce point de vue, les Hommes- pangolins *au village* et les pangolins *en forêt* occupent des positions

homologues. L'une des conditions d'initiation est d'avoir tué un pangolin en forêt; le rituel implique l'absorption de la chair de cet animal. Un rapport de contiguité s'établit donc entre les Hommes-pangolins et les pangolins. Les premiers sont médiaturs entre les deux composantes antag-onistes de la société d'une part, entre l'homme et la femme d'autre part; les seconds sont médiateurs, plus généralement, entre la culture et la nature. L'activité rituelle des Hommes-pangolins intéresse à la fois la chasse (activité masculine) et la fécondité des femmes, alors que les sphères socio-économiques propre aux deux sexes sont rigoureusement séparées . . . la femme et l'homme, le clan et le village, la diachronie et la synchronie réalisent une synthèse harmonieuse, difficile et rare (de Heusch, 1964: 87–109).

At the time we were both satisfied with this result. In their social life the Lele achieved a difficult synthesis: the mediating powers of the pangolin celebrated the synthesis and its cult contributed to it. However, there is a kind of smug incuriosity which is content to analyse a symbolic system until it is phrased in terms of a universal contrast between nature and culture without specifying the particularities of the case in hand. There are different kinds of synthesis, yet not all are expressed by cults of mediators: the problem needs to be posed comparatively.

In north-east Thailand and in New Guinea, Bulmer and Tambiah convin-cingly demonstrate that the interpretation of the natural world is dominated by incest rules and tense relations with in-laws. If the otter in the flooded rice-fields was a foul monster to the Thai villagers it was because it doubly and even trebly imaged disordered sex, the forbidden incestuous partner. The cassowary in the taro plots was tabooed for the Karam, an image of encroaching, untrustworthy affines. The strength of feeling about both animals derived from the strength with which violent passions were contained, passions which flowed in the same pattern which identified these animals with critical phases in human affairs. No need in these two analyses to explain the local attitude to these animals in terms exogenous to the social system under study. By contrast analysis of the pangolin's meaning had little to do with giving and taking in marriage. Yet the Lele were obsessed with the competition for wives; abductions and vengeance were daily preoccupations; they used to fight continually and always for women; their political units were riven by strife. In the light of this other research, the earlier explanations seemed inadequate and some aspects of the later arguments of *Purity and Danger* worse still. There I fell back on the universal human experience of classification and posited a universal human need to recognise its facticity and to transcend it by mediating cults (1966: 159–79). Luc de Heusch (1971) pointed out the difficulties in that argument. On their own showing the Lele categories of spirit animals were not necessarily anomalous or disgusting and their attitude of suspicion towards the anomalous flying squirrel had not made it into a spirit-animal. But even with such detailed criticism, the answer came slowly and was difficult.

The question about the meaning of the Lele pangolin cult had first to be sunk in the wider question about the response to hybrids and anomalous beings. It is rather the question of why Egypt and Mesopotamia should have paid cult to divine animals, man-birds, man-gods, and not Israel. Lévi-Strauss has suggested a natural propensity of mythical thought which postulates mediating existences (1958: 227–55). Following this idea in the analysis of the Garden of Eden story, Edmund Leach (1969: 11) remarks:

> Mediation (in this sense) is always achieved by introducing a third category which is 'abnormal' or 'anomalous' in terms of ordinary 'rational' categories. Thus myths are full of fabulous monsters, incarnate gods, virgin mothers. This middle ground is abnormal, non-natural, holy. It is typically the focus of all taboo and ritual observance.

In the first place it is not the case that all taboo and ritual observance are typically focused on the abnormal; I have already argued that cognitive categories are made external and visible by taboos (1966). As part of an entirely rational process by which categories of thought are stabilised, taboo marks off those experiences which defy classification. Any reflection on any ethnography about taboo shows that these latter are not the only focus of taboo. Many taboos take the form of do-not-touch rules which protect the normal social structure and moral code. Critics of *Purity and Danger* were quick to point out the possible confusion between different kinds of taboo situation (Ardener, 1967: 139; de Heusch, 1971: 10–12). If taboo is to be treated simply and only as a reaction to the abnormal, the non-natural, the holy as opposed to ordinary 'rational' categories, we are no nearer understanding it than were the nineteenth-century anthropologists. In the second place, less plausibly, there is the suggestion that the human mind always and everywhere tends to invent mediating existences to reconcile oppositions. If such a tendency is found in the structure of myth, its presence is often the result of analytic procedures which place it there. Between myth-making and taboo, between recitative and practical situations, we find a puzzle of our own making. If the one bias causes us to accept anomaly and the other to reject it, neither can be taken seriously as an account of how the human mind works. More to the point to recognise the monstrous beings discovered in myth as the product of fully rational analytic and synthesising procedures and the monstrosity-rejecting behaviour of taboo as part of the process of constituting meanings in practical daily life. Both are therefore to be understood by rational procedures of inquiry, according to the approach here advocated, whereas the argument which appeals to a tendency to invent mediators closes inquiry.

Since we are interested centrally in how meanings are constituted, we would do well to avoid mythical material. Apart from being notoriously pliant to the interpreter's whim, it is thought in relatively free play. Myth sits above and athwart the exigencies of social life. It is capable of presenting one picture and then its opposite. We are on more solid ground by concentrating on beliefs which are invoked explicitly to justify behaviour. The more inconvenient the rules of behaviour and the more pervasive their alleged effect, the more weight should be attached to the beliefs invoked to uphold them. With this principle of selection we can turn again to the fact that some cultures accept the possibility of good mediation between man and nature and some do not. For it provides a guarantee that the beliefs under study are taken seriously by the people who act upon them. Thus we avoid the charge of subjective interpretation.

My general argument supposes that in each constructed world of nature, the contrast between man and not-man provides an analogy for the contrast between the member of the human community and the outsider. In the last most inclusive set of categories, nature represents the outsider. If the boundaries defining membership of the social group have regulated crossing points where useful exchanges take place, then the contrast of man and nature takes the imprint of this exchange. The number of different exchanges envisaged, their possible good and bad outcomes and the rules which govern them are all projected onto the natural world. If the institutions allow for some much more generous and rewarding exchange with more than normally distant partners, then we have the conditions for a positive mediator. If all exchanges are suspect and every outsider is a threat, then some parts of nature are due to be singled out to represent the abominable intruder who breaches boundaries that should be kept intact. In sum, the argument here advanced is that when boundary-crossing is forbidden, a theology of mediation is not acceptable, and that every theology of mediation finds its adherents in a society which expects to do well out of regulated exchange.

To demonstrate the imprinting upon nature of the rules and categories which are dominant in social life, I turn again in single detail to Ralph Bulmer's analysis of Karam animal kinds. When he tries to understand why the Karam count the cassowary as a game animal and not a bird he is led to piece together the rules which set the creature apart. Note that the rules are part of a general causal theory. If they are not obeyed, root crops wither and nut crops rot. One of the rules prevents the cassowary from being domesticated. Though other neighbouring peoples do so, Karam believe that the cassowary is a creature whose eggs they cannot hatch and whose young will not thrive if they try to rear them in the village. So it remains by this rule and belief in the class of wild creatures which are hunted for their meat. When the hunt is successful, the hunter who has killed a cassowary has to observe a period of pollution and undergo long rites of purification as if for killing a man. The rites are only slightly modified for the cassowary. When he slays a man, to purify himself he must eat the heart of a pig. When he slays a cassowary he must eat his victim's heart. Modified rites for homicide pollution are required for killing two kinds of marsupials and the dog. The rule places these three animal kinds inside the set

Figure 19.2

for humans. Killed humans have full rites, killed animals have no rites, killed cassowary, dog, and marsupial have modified rites. Thus a bend is made in the line between man and nature to accommodate those beasts on the human side. When it comes to killing the cassowary, the rules require the hunter to club it with the butt of his spear, a risky enterprise. It is forbidden to shed its blood, so no sharp weapon is used. The same rule applies to killing dogs, should this be necessary. Apart from turning the hunt into a well-matched combat, this rule brings the cassowary and the dog further into the set of humans, for it also applies to a very small set of humans: sharp weapons may not be turned against kinsmen. Thus for all other humans and animals there is unrestricted killing. Only the dog, the cassowary, and the kinsman constitute the set in which bloodshed is forbidden. Then a further restriction locates the cassowary (without the dog this time) in a still smaller set of humans. When the Karam go to hunt the cassowary they must use a special language which avoids common names. For example, instead of the word for cassowary, it is referred to as 'mother of game mammals'. It is the language they use for speaking to their affines and cross-cousins. For all other humans and all other animals no special language is required: only for the cassowary and those close relatives by marriage, language is restricted. The answer to why the cassowary is identified with these affines and cross-cousins lies in the total system of animal and vegetable classification and the further application of analogous rules. The special language rule also applies when collecting pandanus nuts (see Figure 19.3). To explain this we need Bulmer's notion of 'special taxonomic status', which presupposes a system in which each major class in nature is represented by one species. The cassowary as a species is singled out from all the other game animals. Similarly, in the vegetable kingdom, the pandanus palm is treated as a prime wild crop, counterpoised against the prime cultivated crop, taro (see Figure 19.4). Rules create an avoidance situation between the game animals and the human food crops in a form that recalls the avoidance between in-laws. The cassowary must be kept out of the village when the taro is grown, and it must not be eaten in the taro planting and growing season. Otherwise (a causal connection) the taro will not grow. Karam believe that wild palms are propagated naturally by passing through the digestive system of wild game animals, including the cassowary. They do not plant pandanus palms and believe that they would not grow if they tried to do so. Thus the natural generation of forest species contrasts (thanks to these rules and beliefs) with the human planting and tending of crops and feeding of pigs and dogs. The game animals and wild plants are related by a system of natural affinity and descent. The cassowary is made to represent the natural affine, nature's sister and sister's child. It bestrides the boundary between vegetable and animal. It not only links up the descent groups of

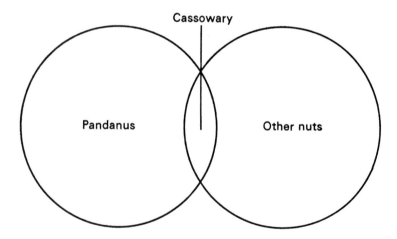

Figure 19.3 Karam: kinship model of wild nuts propagated by cassowary

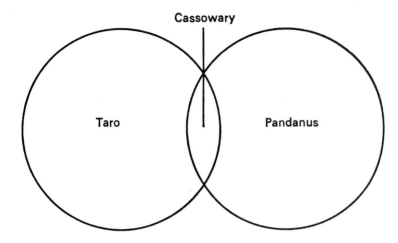

Figure 19.4 Karam: avoidance rules relate wild and cultivated crops to cassowary on model of human society

game animals (through being classed as their mother) with the wild nuts it propagates, but furthermore, it comes right out across the boundaries between wild and cultivated, animal and human, to be classed, on a kinship model, as an affinal link between man and nature. For it is made to relate to the prime cultivated crop by a replication of the avoidance rules for affines. The same representative of the wild animals bears the same relation to two contrasted systems of vegetable propagation, one natural, one cultivated. By these rules the cassowary becomes a kind of mediator but not unequivocally good. It is a mediator to be treated warily and honourably. This becomes clear when the tricky relation between Karam affines is known. I quote from Bulmer (1967: 18) that they depend on their sisters' children for help, but always fear that they will try to grab their land.

> Because of the dense population and the shortage of taro land in the mountainous country, the Karam, commuting between highland and valleys, depend on their affines for help in taro cultivation and the giving of feasts. The cousin relation is one which wavers between close dependence, risk that the cousin will try to take over the taro garden, and finally at worst, fear that he may be practising witchcraft and so become the enemy who has to be killed, but killed with a blunt instrument because he is a kinsman. Your cross-cousins are the people with moral claims on you which you are nevertheless sometimes quite reluctant to meet: and whose names you should not say. You cannot keep your real cross-cousins out of your inheritance, or out of your taro gardens, at least not unless and until you are beginning to suspect witchcraft and to consider homicide. How

appropriate that you should treat your metaphorical cross-cousins, the cassowaries, with due respect when you kill them, and make entirely sure that they never come anywhere near your taro.

Only by applying the kinship model and so drawing a series of homologies can the various rules yield sense (Figure 19.5). First, the Karam social world pivots between ego's agnates and ego's affines. My affines and sister's children, picked out by the special language avoidance, are related to me and also to other groups of agnates. I suspect them of trying to sequester my land, the basis of my social existence. The same picture applies to the wild vegetable world, represented by the prime wild nut, and its relation to other wild nut species, both propagated by the cassowary and other game animals. Any crossing or blurring of the boundary between cultivated and wild will have effects on the plants equivalent to the loss of its land for an agnatic unit. Both forms of plant life have to avoid the same creature, since the cassowary may not be eaten in their planting and gathering seasons respectively and the in-law avoidance language must be used. The logical picture of the avoidance rule manifests the cassowary and the affine or sister in the same form. Bulmer's rich material

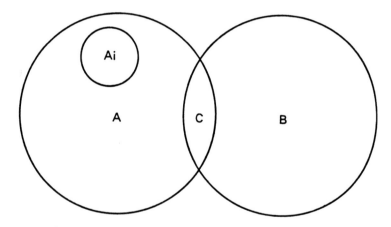

Figure 19.5 Karam social world

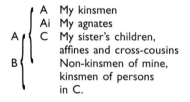

A   My kinsmen
Ai   My agnates
C   My sister's children,
      affines and cross-cousins
      Non-kinsmen of mine,
      kinsmen of persons
      in C.

Avoidance rules
Restricted weapons apply to A + C
Restricted speech applies to C only
A + C = ego's total range of relations by consanguinity and affinity

has encouraged him to emphasise the role that man-made rules play in setting up the causal system. He has thus thrown light on the force of habit by which causal connexions are imposed on nature. His notion of 'special taxonomic status' could be greatly developed. It has to be a status derived from a social category which it represents. It figures in a logical picture or formal pattern which is replicated over and over again. There must be many kinds of special taxonomic status according to the kinds of social pattern which the taxonomies depict. In this case, the two opposed social categories are agnates and affines. The agnates are seen as vulnerable to the encroaching demands of persons linked to them through females: their labour is very desirable but their greed for land is a menace. With such conflicting and intensely felt goals, Karam understandably would find anomalies in nature to show forth their dilemma. The cassowary is no saviour. Nor is it an abomination. Its status is exactly the honourable but untrustworthy one of the Karam affine. Here the interpretation of nature clearly reflects the dominant system of exchanges. The study of native taxonomic systems can never be the same after this cogent demonstration. But we are still in the stance of Lévy-Bruhl, looking from afar at a primitive mentality.

And what about the Lele pangolin and what about the pig in Judaism? Some big planks in the theoretical bridge are still missing. Bulmer's is a work of translation. He translates from the categories in which nature is thought to the categories in which social life is lived, the one into the other and back again. The next challenge is to go beyond the translation job to examining the properties of classification systems as such. My wish has always been to take seriously Durkheim's idea that the properties of classification systems derive from and are indeed properties of the social systems in which they are used. The questions Durkheim suggested were: How fuzzy are the boundaries of the categories? How well insulated the meanings they enclose? (1903: 6–7). How many categories are there? Are the principles relating them to each other systematic? If there is a system of thought, how stable is it? (1903: 35–41). These questions can be addressed to our own thought processes.

But the questions about classification systems have to be well matched by questions about the social systems that generate them. We cannot shirk the problem of finding a relevant classification of human societies.

Recall that the argument depends on a scale of readiness to do exchange. The boundaries of the categories of nature are expected to show a parallel with the inclusions and rejections permitted on social boundaries. Where society is based on the structuring of birth and marriage, the most significant exchanges will concern transfers of women. Ideally the thesis should be capable of being illustrated from those societies which anthropologists traditionally study and from which the puzzles of kinship theory derive. The examples I have to discuss clearly fall into each of the two recognised categories of kinship system. The Lele are in the class of elementary structures, since they enjoin marriage between the children of cross-cousins.[1]

The Karam are in the class of complex forms of kinship, since they only use the negative prohibition of incest to regulate their marriage alliances. Their rules, complicated by the distribution of bridewealth and land in each generation, end by ruling out many second cousins and third cousins.[2]

The Israelites fall also into the class of complex forms, but not in a way which is described or anticipated in alliance theory. For, on my reading of the list of prohibited degrees, they are an instance of those numerous peoples[3] who have no rule to ensure a wide network of alliance.

In all three cases we are interested in the extent to which the operation of the marriage rules allows for the incorporation of strangers into the circle of kinsmen. How the rules are worked is contingent on politics and practice. As I read it, the Lele are the most open to foreign alliance, the Israelites the least, and the Karam come somewhere in between. This interpretation goes beyond the basic rules to their mode of operation.

I have already summarised the case of the Karam. Now for the Lele: everything in the Lele working of their rules turns them to hope for sons-in-law or brides from distance places or along half-forgotten genealogical links going several generations back. Clan exogamy applies to the father's and to the mother's clan. Every village contains some members of four or five clans or more. Since every mother aims to keep her daughter by her side and every girl hopes to marry her first sweetheart in the village of her birth, the rules of exogamy by themselves would not frustrate their wishes. The village would become an endogamous unit. However, positive rules of exchange entitle a man to ask for his daughter's daughter in marriage, for himself or for another member of his clan.

His claim is based on the honour due to a son-in-law. All small populations are demographically vulnerable. The group that is recruited by matrilineal descent is doubly so (as I have argued elsewhere (1969: 121–35)). The Lele have written into their culture an awareness of demographic risk for the local section of the clan. For the Pangolin cult is a privileged membership open only to men who return to live in the village which their own clan founded. Its honours call them back and check the fractioning and disappearance of local clan units. Furthermore each clan honours the man who begets its female children. The affine then is counterpoised to ego's clan in a wholly positive sense, with none of the anxiety and suspicion which the Karam affines arouse. Once he has begotten a daughter, her clan owes him the right to dispose in marriage of his daughter's daughter. A man may make a similar claim on his son's daughter. The status of grandfather then becomes a permanent relation of alliance by marriage between the clans of three men who have a say in the allocation of a girl: her father's father's clan, her own clan, and her mother's father's clan. The tussle between these three and the use of girls for settling blood debts and other debts ensure that the women's preference, which I observed, for local and village endogamy, was overruled. Women were widely exchanged and links of permanent in-lawship established all over the country.

So much was the system committed to wide-ranging exchange that no one clan would have been stably associated with any one village were it not for other rules which gave cult and political privileges to members of founding clans and further privileges to offspring of their intermarriage. This widespread exchange of women did not of itself break down the political barriers between enemy villages. Marriage alliance did not make links freely through the entire society. Each small village was autonomous. It had its allies and traditional enemies. The movements of population normally flowed down sharply cut political grooves rather than across them. A girl demanded in payment for an offence against an enemy village would be less likely to be paid over than between friendly villages. Forcible abduction would be the rule in the case of the enemy village. But a girl stolen to settle a debt still had her clansmen. For them the rule of honouring the son-in-law was still valid; moreover, the right of her father to claim one of her daughters was still valid, though enmity between the villages would make it difficult to enforce. The Lele adjusted to this. A political abduction was made into a political marriage. The girl became the wife, not of one man, but of the age-set of her abductors. The whole village took on the legal role of husband and legal father to her children. Anyone who would claim her daughter in marriage would become the son-in-law of the whole village. His courtship and groom-service would be fittingly arduous; his marriage-payments appropriately splendid. The son-in-law of the village had diplomatic immunity, a role of political go-between and great honour, both in the village of his origin and in the village from which he had taken his wife. In due course, when his own daughter had grown up, his in-laws would claim the rights of a grandfather and demand for the village a girl in return. Thus the feud could be turned into an alliance, but not necessarily an effective one. Seen in this light and in the perspective of what has gone before, the Lele system of politics and marriage gave them experience of dangerous exchanges with hostile groups in which the first most precious bargain was to obtain a woman, and the next was the possibility of a continuing supply of daughter's daughters, and the last was the chance of a permanent alliance through generalised exchange of women. And all these prospects were mediated through the role of the son in-law, honoured in his own right, doubly honoured as the son-in-law of the sovereign village, trebly honoured as the third generation matrilineal descendant of a former son-in-law become grandfather.

Consistently, one should expect a role of double odium in the social system where double pollution is found in nature – and conversely. The Lele son-in-law of the village enjoyed double and treble honour since in him the system of exchange might profitably transcend all its boundaries. I would not go so far as to say that the son-in-law of the village was represented by the pangolin. But that the pangolin cult explicitly attracted back to the village sons-in-law who had been born in distant parts, and so reconstituted the relation of founding clan to village is an inescapable conclusion that I have put on record (1963). At most I am supposing that these rules of marriage with their political penalties and rewards are to be found imprinted upon the categories of nature. The same

Lele set up both the exchanges of women, the fragile patterning of villages and clans, and their own theory of causality. So I argue that their experience of mediation in marriage and political alliance allows them to imagine an effective religious mediator.

Figure 19.6 sums up their cosmological scheme. The first major contrast is between humans and animals. Humans are distinguished by their rules of shame and avoidance, their rules of exogamy, and their chronic infertility. The rules of avoidance apply to all polite intercourse. They are most stringently and typically required for the respect between in-laws. The rules of exogamy give the underlying structure to the exchanges of women. The infertility refers partly to the demographic instability of small matrilineal descent groups. Infertility is moreover a dominant concern for their ritual and medical practice. In each of these respects, animals are held in contrast: they are incestuous, shameless, and prolific. Certain humans and animals cross these boundaries and appear as members of the other set. Sorcerers take on the form of leopards; diviners do likewise to counteract sorcery. Other carnivorous animals are sorcerers' familiars who come into the village to do their treacherous work for them. Under one aspect the human world is divided between those who are vulnerable (women, babies, sterile men) and those who attack their fertility (sorcerers) and those who defend them against sorcery (the diviners). A neutral group are the men who have proof of their fertility, the initiated begetters. Their status is signalled by the rule that only they can safely eat the young of animals, the chest of animals, and carnivores, meat which would kill anyone else. Outside the class of living humans, the vicious spirits of dead sorcerers are opposed by the spirits

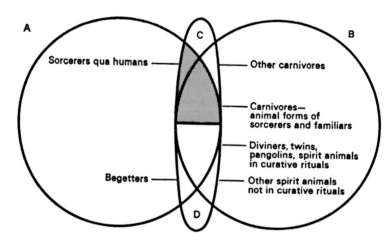

Figure 19.6 Lele:

A Humans (living)
B Animals
C Dead sorcerers   } non-
D Other dead humans and spirits } corporeal

of neutral dead humans and benevolent nature spirits (Figure 19.7). Likewise, the rules divide the animal world into three classes, ordinary animals, carnivorous animals, and spirit animals. The killing and ritual consumption of specific spirit animals is a central part of their prospering rituals. The category of spirit animals is constituted by two major criteria, non-predatory and water-inhabiting (fish and wild pig are prime examples) and two secondary criteria, burrowing and nocturnal. These classes sometimes overlap: nocturnal habits are a sign of spirit because the spirit world reverses the order of humans; burrowing suggests co-habitation with the dead; water means fertility. Some spirit animals are counted as dangerous food for all except the appropriate group of diviners; others are dangerous to pregnant women or to anyone undergoing treatment for infertility; others are prohibited in other curative rites. I would draw attention to another aspect of this classification. Whenever a species is allocated by its observed behaviour to one habitat or the other, if one of its subspecies by its behaviour strays into the class of spirit animals they pay special and favourable

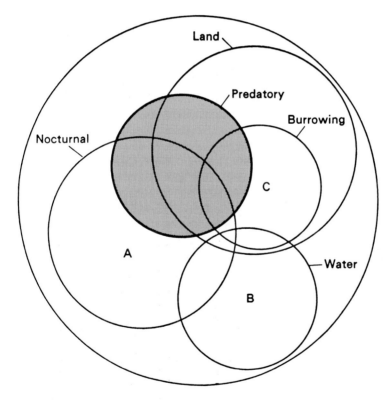

Figure 19.7 Lele: animals. Characteristics of spirit animals:
　　　　A　Nocturnal
　　　　B　Water
　　　　C　Burrowing

attention to the anomalous sub-class. This applies to cases of land animals who show water-loving habits. Wild pig is a spirit animal because (unlike other land mammals) it loves to wallow in the muddy sources of streams. Other primates avoid the water but the baboon loves to wash so it is counted a spirit animal. Antelopes are land animals, but one kind hides from the hunters by sinking deep into the water. Antelopes are mostly day feeders; one which feeds by night and sleeps by day is therefore a spirit animal. In sum, the Lele are extremely interested in boundary-crossing whenever they observe it. They associate it with good unless it bears the predatory mark of sorcery. Spirit species are specially favourable exceptions to the course of nature. Since squirrels with birds and monkeys are in the class of sky-creatures commonly prescribed for the diet of pregnant women, the flying squirrel does not cross any major classificatory boundary. An amphibian species of flying squirrel would be another matter. The most extraordinary boundary-crosser of their universe is the pangolin. A scaly fish-like tree-dweller, it bows its head like a man avoiding his mother-in-law. As a mammal which brings forth its young singly, it evidently does not share the fecundity which distinguishes animals from mankind. This anomaly mediates between humans and spirits and assures fertility. In human society the sexually potent son-in-law by his begetting is counterpoised against the destructive sorcerer. In nature the pangolin and the leopard have the special taxonomic status which this general vision of social life imposes. Thus Bulmer has helped me to complete my own translation of different levels of reality and to solve questions posed from my material by penetrating critics. I am now able to hear the meanings of Lele animal terms resonate with a more powerful charge through larger ranges of their experience than at first suspected.

For the more general problem of a taxonomy of classification systems I would like to think we now have two demonstration cases. The Lele expect to do well out of their system of exchanges: they have a welcome for the outsider who walks peacefully into their camp. The Karam have reason to be more pessimistic about their exchanges: their attitude to anomalies reflects their general caution. Both tribes allow the line between culture and nature to be crossed; the crossing places are guarded with rules. The rules represent theories of causality: either they ward off dangerous effects or they channel desirable ones.

Before turning to the Israelites, let me complete the accepted scheme of kinship structures by mentioning the Crow-Omaha which are distinguished from the elementary structures by using only the negative rules of incest and exogamy to organise their pattern of alliances, but using them so forcefully to define such a wide range of non-marriageable kin that the circulation of women through the entire system is ensured without setting up prescribed categories of partners (Lévi-Strauss, 1966: 19):

> the generalised definition of a Crow-Omaha system may best be formulated by saying that whenever a descent line is picked up to provide a mate, all individuals belonging to that line are excluded from the range of potential

mates from the first lineage, during a period covering several generations. Since this process repeats itself with each marriage, the system is kept in a state of permanent turbulence which is quite the reverse of that regularity of functioning and periodicity of returns which conform with the ideal model of an asymmetric marriage system.

Any such system, where a possibility of close intermarriage is very unlikely, has one result in common with the elementary structures with which it is contrasted in principle. Both structures of kinship allow the outsider to be brought in as a son-in-law to join the intimate circle of kinsmen. For the marriageable kin prescribed in the elementary structures are general categories which include distant classifications as well as close relations. On my argument it will be easier in both these types of structure (if they are worked as the Lele work theirs) to make identifications which go across the boundary separating human and animal. These are the tribes which marry their enemies, in which it makes sense to say that a man is a red parrot or a twin a bird. For it is argued that the greater the social distance between ego and marriageable persons, the stronger the sense of exchange between known and unknown. In such cases we predict a taxonomic system which draws a favourable attention to anomaly, since the offspring of the marriages are by birth half-known and half-unknown.

The Israelites' rules of marriage allowed them to marry their first cousins. Therefore the distinction between cross and parallel kinsmen, the one distinction which Lévi-Strauss takes to be fundamental to kinship (1966: 16) here is bereft of meaning. When the wife's brother is father's brother's son and in the class of husband's brothers, there is not exchange or alliance by marriage, but in-marrying, a denial of the value of exchange. Here again, as always, the rule itself says nothing without an account of how it is interpreted. Of this, more below, but note how different the ancient Israelite view of nature as shown in the final editing and interpreting of the Pentateuch. Here no anomalies are tolerated. Every living being that appears inconsistently across instead of within the lines of their classification is firmly marked anomalous and hustled into a special, excluded, sub-set.[4] In a paper which has to be treated as part of the evidence for the present argument, I have recently analysed the Israelite rules for altar and table as a particular type of classification system (Douglas, 1972). When its processes of inclusion and identification have been worked through, the result is a series of concentric circles, each larger boundary reinforcing the inner one, each inner one enclosing yet another. Everything that seems eligible to stand across any of the boundaries is picked out and put into the set of defilement. Our speculations about the kind of social intention which organises its universe in this way are straightforward. Here is a people who prefer their boundaries to remain intact. They reckon any attempt to cross them a hostile intrusion. They expect no good to come of external exchange and have no rules for facilitating it. When they think of their social organisation in spatial terms they set the holiest place within several concentric boundaries. The tribes of

Israel, when they camped, were to group on each side of the holy tent in which God revealed his presence. The closest area round the tent was occupied by Levites (Numbers 2: 17), Judah to the east, Ephraim to the west, on the north the camp of Dan, on the south the camp of Reuben (Ackroyd, 1970: 160). A similar concern to enclose the temple with triple boundaries shows in the geographical layout of Ezekiel's new land (Ackroyd, 1970: 103). The boundaries keep out the profane. The sons of Aaron were to avoid all strong drink, because they were 'to distinguish between the holy and the common, and between the unclean and the clean' (Leviticus 10: 10). Being holy means being set apart. The Israelites cherish their boundaries and want nothing better than to keep them strong and high.

> Blessed art thou, O Lord our God, King of the Universe, who makes a distinction between holy and profane, between light and darkness, between Israel and other nations, between the seventh day and the six working days. Blessed art thou, O Lord, who makest a distinction between holy and profane [from the Habdalah Service contemporary to our own day].

Inside the boundaries is a small political unit, a people surrounded by powerful, rapacious enemies. Defections and infiltrations are familiar in its history. Its boundaries are never strong enough. There is no rule requiring them to exchange their womenfolk, either with other lineages, or between their own tribes, still less with foreigners. The critical problems arise with the definition of a foreigner, especially of people who claim some of the criteria of common descent, but not all. Leach (1969: 47–9) has argued

> Even the formal rule book (Deuteronomy 23) equivocates about just how foreign is a foreigner. Edomites (and more surprisingly Egyptians) are not to be abhorred . . .
>   The children that are begotten of them shall enter into the congregation of the Lord in their third generation. Ammonites and Moabites, on the other hand, are absolutely tainted, 'even to their tenth generation they shall not enter the congregation of the Lord for ever'. Thus, even for the Patriarchs the distinction Israelite/foreigner was not a clear-cut matter of black and white but a tapering off through various shades of grey. The reason for this must be sought in later circumstances. The Jewish sectarians of the late historical Jerusalem were surrounded not only by foreigners, who were unqualified heathen, but also by semi-foreigners, such as the Samaritans who claimed to be Israelites like themselves. How strictly should the rules of endogamy apply in such cases?

If this is correct, it records a deep concern with the element which shows some but not sufficient criteria for membership of a class. The classification which counts abominable the beasts which either chew the cud or cleave the hoof but not both is isomorphic with the other classification of Israelites which does not object to intermarriage with female captives of far distant foes (Deuteronomy 20: 14–18) but worries about the prospect of intermarriage with half-blooded Israelites. The pig attracts, with the camel, the hare and rock-badger, the odium of half-eligibility for table and sacrifice. Worse, it is the only one of the four which cleaves the hoof. According to my analysis worked out in *Purity and Danger*, mode of locomotion is a major defining criterion. Edmund Leach (1969: 36) points out that Lévi-Strauss took the same view. By its cloven feet the pig nearly gets into the class of ungulates, hence a double odium. A further association with the undesirable marriage lies in the fact that the people of Israel, whether in exile, or before, or afterwards, were never living apart from foreigners and they must have frequently succumbed to the temptation to marry foreign girls. How else did the resident Canaanites come to be absorbed? In the relevant periods, betrothal to a foreigner was certain to be celebrated with feasting in breach of the Mosaic rules. But far more likely to appear on the table than the camel, the hare, and the rock-badger was the domesticated pig. So we move towards understanding its special taxonomic status.

In the Thailand animal system, the double pollution of sexual disorder is opposed to the double blessing of controlled virility. The Thai villagers treat the buffalo as a metaphor of ordered sexual energy. Tethered at night under the sleeping quarters, yoked for work in the day, the buffalo is reserved for the most important sacrifices. Rules which require it to be given for sacrifice in other households than its own echo the rules of marriage exchange. The noble buffalo is opposed in their thoughts to the ignoble dog: chased out of the sleeping quarters, its name used in sexual insults, the symbol of sex out of place and out of control. But more than the dog, the otter when it swims into the fields in flood time, as an invasive dog-like monster from the wild, appears as the full polar opposite of the domestic buffalo. A double anomaly, it incurs double odium. By the same arguments, the pig reared by Gentiles for food would seem to stand in the Hebrew taxonomy as doubly opposed to the perfect sacrificial victim, the beast without bodily blemish, and of equally perfect pedigree. I leave out the Thai villages from what follows. Their Buddhism involves them in importations and transactions with other cultures which place them beyond my limited comparisons.

Three social types, the Israelites, the Karam and the Lele, provide us with three types of classification system. In the first, exchange is not desired; all anomalies are bad and classed in a special sub-set expected to unleash disastrous chains of cause and effect. In the next, exchange is necessary but risky; anomalies are ambivalent, the rules that hedge them prevent dangerous effects. In the third, some exchange is reckoned clearly good, some is bad; anomalies likewise; the rules for approaching and avoiding them are the means for triggering off good effects. In this way the sociological specification for accepting a mediator is elucidated. A people who have nothing to lose by exchange and everything to gain will be predisposed towards the hybrid being, wearing the conflicting signs, man/god or man/beast. A people whose experience of foreigners is disastrous will cherish perfect categories, reject exchange, and refuse doctrines of mediation.

This admittedly speculative idea has implications for the history of religion. To justify putting it forth, the interpretation of the Israelite classifications needs to be located in historical time. What is agreed in Biblical scholarship needs to be separated from what is controversial. The only place and time to which I can safely refer is that assigned by the consensus on textual criticism to the editorial work of the so-called Priestly Code, known as P.[5] This starts in the period of Babylonian exile with energetic and scholarly reviewing of Israel's history. It continues to the end of the fifth century BC. P is generally agreed to be the latest source of material in the Pentateuch and later than the histories, Judges, Kings, and Samuel. P is identified by its distinctive style, exhortatory and repetitive, and by a concern for the regulations of the cult. The books which show no signs of the detailed provisions of P are by that fact dated before its promulgation and those which take them into account betray their later date. Likewise the distribution of historical information helps to establish the order of the sources that were collected together and established as the Hebrew Canon of the Bible (Rowley, 1950). P is the source to which is attributed the classification of clean and unclean animal kinds in which I am specially interested (Leviticus 11 and Deuteronomy 14). It suits my thesis well that small groups of learned exiles in Babylon, conscious of their unique historic mission, and conscious of the need to separate theirs from the culture of their conquerors, should have elaborated detailed rules of purity. Nowhere else in the world has such logic-chopping consistency been excelled. But alas for my thesis: the list of animals is not attributed to this source. Leviticus 11 and Deuteronomy 14 are believed to be a much older source, incorporated in the Priestly Code along with other obscure passages. The reason offered for their exception is that the list makes no sense. It is common for ancient law books to incorporate blocks of still more archaic rules, much as our own multiplication table included archaic measures, the rod, pole or perch. The block form is itself taken for evidence of separate origin. The argument assumes that the priestly editors, legalistic and rational though they were, occasionally admitted to the corpus old texts which made no sense to them but which piety forbade them to exclude. This might be convincing, had not great importance been attached to these very dietary laws. We are asked to believe that the people of Israel have been saddled with an irrational, undecipherable set of food-rules imposed on them by the most rigorously logical law-givers imaginable. It becomes even more implausible when the list of animals itself is examined. From the anthropologist's point of view the classifications appear admirably consistent with the rest of Leviticus and with the rest of the Priestly Code, and the Holiness Code to boot. It is hard to believe that the final Pentateuchal editors did not know what they were doing when they twice copied out the dietary rules in full. There seems no good reason for supposing that P stayed his editorial hand and left unsystematised little blocks, or 'balks' as the Scandinavian critic calls them, of uniformly formulated, nonsensical laws from ancient times. But this accounts for the paucity of comment on Leviticus 11. Either nothing is said about the animals which have become so important in Jewish life, or there is the crude medical materialism which I criticised in *Purity and Danger*, or there is this theory of unintelligible 'balks' which are not worth trying to decipher as they were probably quite as mystifying to the scholars of the fifth century BC (Noth, 1965).

My general argument requires P to be rehabilitated and cleared of the charge of inconsistency. In my view, he went on calmly applying the analogy of purity to the rules of the camp, the altar, the body, and also to animal kinds. P was never one to let piety override logic. In his theology there could be no conflict between logic and holiness. All this I have argued before. It may well be that these blocks are ancient sources, and so may be much else that was incorporated, indeed. But the strong evidence for the continuity and coherence of the interpretative tradition allows to the disparate origins of the text only limited interest. The provisions of P were promulgated by Ezra in the fourth century BC and were being followed by the Jewish community in the Christian era. By identifying the historical period in which I am concerned as that in which the Priestly source was edited I am committed to the fifth century. As to its early limits, I shall want to include the Deuteronomic source, and the history books which owe so much to it. The period, therefore, runs from the sixth century BC to the fifth, just before, during, and after the exile.

The next step is to establish that the people of Israel at that time did not practice lineage exogamy. At least there is no evidence that they did. Leach's arguments contribute to this result. What is at issue is the absence of any rule organising the internal exchange of women. Understandably, biblical scholars are often unaware of the implications of the list of prohibited degrees of kinship (Leviticus 18). The interpretation varies according to whether the list is taken to be illustrative of the category of forbidden kin, or exhaustive. By comparison with many tribal societies, if it is exhaustive, the list is extremely short. Certain close agnatic relations are not named. I would conclude that they are not prohibited for sex and marriage. Not only are these lineage endogamous marriages, but they are mandatory for the High Priest (Leviticus 21: 14–15).

If the case be conceded that the people who abhorred anomalies in the relevant period also did not accept any obligation to exchange their womenfolk beyond the range of a narrowly defined kindred, then I can proceed to speculate further about their attitude to animals in the light of other classification systems.

Comparative religion has often been a jousting-ground between rival beliefs. When social correlates of a religious response are revealed, the rationalists chalk up a point against the devout. The believers usually agree the score, sharing the doubtful assumption that a sacred doctrine must sprout in thin air and never be the product of social experience. In that debate, my particular thesis about mediators, though radically sociological, is neutral. If anything, it puts the thumb upon the other nose. If these connections hold good and if this is how classification systems are shaped to social ends, how could the extra-ordinary destiny of the Jewish people have been otherwise achieved? If you were God, could you devise a better plan? If you wanted to choose a people for yourself, reveal to them a monotheistic vision and give them a concept of holiness that they will know in their very bones, what would you do? Promise their descendants a fertile land and beset it with enemy empires. By itself that would almost be enough. A politically escalating chain would ensure the increasing hostility of their neighbours. Their mistrust of outsiders would ever be validated more completely. Faithful to your sanctuary and your law, it would be self-evident to them that no image of an animal, even a calf, even a golden one, could portray their god.

When two champions are in combat it is tempting for bystanders to guide their hands to more ammunition. Paul Ricoeur (1963) once challenged Lévi-Strauss to explain why his technique of structural analysis could be so splendidly demonstrated in exotic totemic tribes, but not for those ancient civilisations of Judah, Greece, and Rome on which our own history rests. The answer that a radical difference separates totemic and non-totemic cultures might have been damaging to Lévi-Strauss's claim to reveal a universal feature of the human mind. He himself has tried to avoid that reproach by proving that his myth analysis does apply to any culture whatsoever. And so it does. But in the course of the demonstration the technique became so pliable that it lost its claim to reveal the structures of any mind save its creator's. More effective, in reply to Ricoeur, would be to admit that there could be radically different types of society. Then the structural analysis of forms of kinship could be fitted to the analysis of classification. Curiosity would oblige us to seek out for study the most variant types of classification of nature and the most extreme variations of exchange of women. One notices that the array of marriage systems studied in his *Elementary Structures of Kinship* (1969) and those listed in 'The bear and the barber' (1963) do not include the type where there is no rule demanding exchange. And yet he has foreseen the case: 'A human group that considers itself a distinct species will see the rest of nature as constituted by separate, unrelated species.' Like an uncanny echo, Ecclesiasticus said: 'All living beings associate by species and man clings to one like himself; what fellowship has a wolf with a lamb?' (Ecclesiastes 13: 19–21).

In *La Pensée sauvage* Lévi-Strauss noted that the emphasis of a classification system may shift from the analogy between systems of relationships (which is characteristic of totemic systems) to the analogy between one item and another, for example, the single human group contemplating its likeness to a single animal species (1962: 116). This remarkable insight suggests that when the single human group sees itself thus there will be no room for a mediator in its theology. For surely a single group will only tend to see itself when high boundaries separate it from the rest of humanity. Thus isolated, it may understandably divide its constructed world of nature into separate and hostile species.

A group of humans that sees itself as a distinct species will not need to mirror in nature their society seen as a system of regulated transactions with other humans. Ideally they will not be engaged in such transactions. Here it is argued that the concept of wild nature can stand for the archetypal outsider at multiple levels, the outsider to the family, to the local unit, to the clan and the tribe. In the totemic system the outsider is entitled to a defined role in a regulated exchange. But if the priestly books tell the people to have no truck with the outsider, under any guise, then in those books we will except a different patterning of nature.

Throughout the Bible the close observation of natural life is full of comments on the tenderness of animals to their offspring. 'Even the jackals give the breast and suckle their young' (Lamentations). All creation reveals the glory of God. The Book of Job (4: 3) expresses intense awareness of wild nature. So observant, so sensitive to its metaphoric possibilities, these are the people whom Moses enjoined (Deuteronomy 4: 16–18):

> Beware lest you act corruptly by making a graven image for yourselves, in the form of any figure, the likeness of male or female, the likeness of any beast that is on the earth, the likeness of any winged bird that flies in the air, the likeness of anything that creeps on the ground, the likeness of any fish that is in the water under the earth.

The prohibition could weigh painfully. But on my argument one compelling reason for animal depiction is missing here in the Hebrew case. For they had no reason to use animals to represent the internal differentiation of their society. Animals represent God in general, humans in general, foreigners in general. As the High Priest and his kindred to the common people of the nation, as the clean to the unclean, as life to death, as humans are to animals, so were the Israelites as a whole to the rest of human kind. Such a situation may make it easier to accept a law against images of living beings and even account for the striking poverty of animal art forms left by the Israelites compared with the wealth of their literature and compared with the art of the expanding empires of their neighbours (Klingender, 1971).

Can we reverse the argument to consider the paintings of paleolithic man who left no other records of this thought? I risk the idea that if he painted animals at all it signifies something positive about his openness to commerce with his fellows. When he painted humans with antlers or animal masks it might say even more about his friendly relations with fellow humans of other groups. To see blasphemy in the idea of a baboon-god or a goat-footed one, or in the deification of bulls or cows, is to reject other people's certainty that gods in animal form are proper objects of adoration. It also rejects an attitude towards foreign human beings. The argument takes logic beyond the universal propensities of the human mind to the devious ways in which humans use logic to deal with one another. This is what Durkheim indicated when he argued against Hume and Kant that the origin of classification is neither in nature nor in the subjective constraints of the mind, but in society.

I started by considering the a priori in nature. My intention was to show how a guts reaction is founded. I argued that knowledge in the bones, a gut response, answers to a characteristic in the total pattern of classification. Something learnt for the first time can be judged instantly and self-evidently true or false. This flash of recognition would correspond to the split-second scanning of animal knowledge. The essence of my argument is that the stable points of reference for this kind of knowing are not particular external events, but the characteristics of the classification system itself. We are talking about the way the system has been set. It may be a setting that welcomes some anomalies and rejects others or one that rejects all anomalies. Using such a classification system there is no need to work out by slow deductive processes how to respond to a new anomaly that turns up. This argument is not developed in order to serve as an aid for interpreting the bizarre classifications of exotic civilisations. It relates to arguments between logicians about how relations of identity are constituted, not by primitives, but by ourselves.

The relation of the Karam cassowary to wild plants and animals has the same patterning of logical forms as the relation of the cassowary to human and non-human beings and this is of the same pattern as the relation between a woman's brothers and her children. For the Karam, all these these instances are true in the same unchallengeable way. For the Israelites the meaning of purity for table, bed, and altar is given in a single pattern of logically formed statements. But it is they themselves who have created the order of their universe so that the statements they make about it in this form are self-evidently true.

Religious doctrines of mediation have only afforded a field in which to develop an argument concerning self-evident statements about the world. The anthropologist does not hope to lead the logician out of the circle which the definition of synonymity encloses. Enough head-butting against that wall has proved its strength. Anthropology suggests, not a solution to a problem, but new problems with more hope of solution. Each category of thought has its place in a larger system. Its constituent elements are there because of rules which distinguish, bound, and fill the other categories. The rules and categories are generated in the processes of social intercourse. The drive of the fore-going argument is away from considering isolated categories and their application to particular series of events. Instead, consider the total universe in which the categories are used. Remembering that categories are for use, and remembering that each usage has implications for the rest of the system, and invoking some principle of economy or consistency within a system of classification, the problem of the a priori in nature can be probed in different terms. This essay has compared three classification systems with regard to their treatment of anomalous beings: one abhors, one respects, and one venerates them. Each happens to be remarkably homogeneous in its response to the anomalies it defines. Classification systems could similarly be compared along a dimension of homogeneity of principles for assigning events to classes. They could be compared along other dimensions.

Quine (1960: 78) has said:

> our theories and beliefs in general are under-determined by the totality of possible sensory evidence time without end . . . when two systems of analytical hypotheses fit the totality of verbal dispositions to perfection and yet conflict in their translations of certain sentences, the conflict is precisely a conflict of parts seen without wholes.

I have tried here to provide some clues about how our schemes of the world are determined by pointing to the logical patterning deployed in social behaviour. There are fewer possible varieties of social system than possible varieties of worlds to be known, but all possible universes do not have equal credibility for any one society. There is scope for semantic ascent by comparing the various social conditions for credibility. The comparative project shows how the structure of nature comes so satisfyingly to match the structure of mind, without blurring the fact that it is a different structure each time. Intuitional philosophies come to grief upon their failure to discover a list of intuitions or innate ideas common to the human race. Once beyond the simplest propositions of logic they are plunged deep into the artificial conventions of mathematics or paddling in trivial examples. A sociology of the uses of logic can do something to explain both the sense of certain knowledge and its erratically distributed content.[6]

NOTES

This lecture was given in a shorter version as the Henry Myers Lecture, on 4 May 1972, in University College, London. On 19 September in the same year I delivered it in an amended form at Barnard College, New York, as a lecture in honour of the late Virginia C. Gildersleeve. It still needs amendment but it has been a long time brewing already.

At least ten years ago Cyril Barrett and Ernest Gellner pointed out the relevance of Hume's philosophy to the arguments in *Purity and Danger*. Since then I owe further debts, apart from those acknowledged in the text, to colleagues in the Department of Anthropology of University College, London for criticism of parts of this paper as it took shape, and to Martin Hollis and I. Zaretsky who went through the whole argument. I am particularly grateful to Anne Akeroyd, Adam Kuper, Michael Thompson and James Urry, and Arthur Nead. For allowing me to try parts of the argument in other places, I thank Richard Parry, Bryan Wilson, R. Werbner, Professor C. Haimendorf, Professor Paul Stirling, Professor Roland Robertson and James Woodburn and Professor T. Luckmann. For advice on biblical sources I record my gratitude to Jacob Milgrom and J. Neusner.

1 I owe a debt of gratitutde to Luc de Heusch for clarifying the pattern of generalised exchange of women that the Lele followed (1964).

2 Lévi-Strauss expects the complex structures of kinship to parallel the elementary structures at the minimum point at which they are distinguished. 'All systems of kinship and marriage contain an "elementary" core which manifests itself in the incest prohibition . . . all systems have a "complex" aspect deriving from the fact that more than one individual can usually meet the requirements of even the most prescriptive systems, thus allowing for a certain freedom of choice . . .' and he goes on to characterise the complex structures, such as our own, as ones in which 'the incest prohibition that we deem sufficient to ensure a probability distribution of alliance links co-extensive with society itself still persists among us as a mechanical device . . . but a much lighter mechanical model, including only a few prohibited degrees' (1965: 1–19).

3 Rather the contrary: they supplement the rule of incest avoidance with a positive preference for marriage with the father's brother's daughter. Such a system, instead of achieving anything like a circulation of women through the entire society, encourages men to regard their womenfolk as part of their patrimony, to be held and shared exclusively within the narrow group of agnates. This is how the same rule is interpreted by the Marshdwellers of the Euphrates Delta (Salim, 1962) and by Fulani herdsmen (Stenning, 1954). If the case for interpreting the Israelites' custom in the same way may be admitted, then the contrast of Lele, Karam, and Israel is even better suited to demonstrate my thesis.

4 Living beings, not mythic beings are at issue. It is true that the cosmogony of the Israelites included hybrid beings such as the Cherubim and the extraordinary being of Ezekiel's dream, and that these were not judged adversely. But it was not expected that everyday life would bring a face-to-face encounter with such beings, and the rules of Leviticus 11 are concerned only with physical encounters. The arguments I have advanced against using myth material applies to rule out the relevance of Ezekiel's dream monster. In any case, no cult was paid to it.

5 In general it would suit my thesis to follow the minority view that takes P to be a very early source, since the unity and coherence of the Pentateuch in regard to purity laws supports this view, but obviously in such a technical matter I have no option but to follow the consensus.

6 To my knowledge no part of this essay has been discussed in anthropology. By showing that anomaly gets very different treatment in different social situations, and by insisting that classification is part of organisation, it contradicts Leach's attempt to have a universal theory of anomaly (1976). The social uses of logic have remained one of my central interests – as shown by the next essay, written twenty years later, on categories.

BIBLIOGRAPHY

ACKROYD, P.R. (1970), 'Israel under Babylon and Persia', in *New Clarendon Bible: Old Testament*, vol. 4. London, Oxford University Press.

ARDENER, E. (1967), Review of M. Douglas: *Purity and Danger*, *Man* (N.S.) 2, 139.

BULMER, R. (1967), 'Why is the cassowary not a bird? A problem of zoological taxonomy among the Karam of the New Guinea Highlands', *Man* (N.S.) 2, 5–25.

CAZENEUVE, J. (1972), *Lucien Lévy-Bruhl*, trans. P. Rivière, Oxford, Blackwell.

DOUGLAS, M. (1957), 'Animals in Lele religious symbolism', *Africa*, 27, 46–58.

DOUGLAS, M. (1963), *The Lele of the Kasai*, Oxford University Press for the International African Institute.

DOUGLAS, M. (1966), *Purity and Danger: an Analysis of Concepts of Pollution and Taboo*, London, Routledge & Kegan Paul.

DOUGLAS, M. (1969), 'Is matriliny doomed in Africa?', in *Man in Africa*, eds M. Douglas and P. Kaberry, London, Tavistock.

DOUGLAS, M. (1972), 'Deciphering a meal', *Daedalus, Journal of the American Academy of Arts and Sciences,* Winter 1972, *Myth, Symbol and Culture*, 68–81.

DURKHEIM, É. and MAUSS, M. (1903), 'De quelques formes primitives de classification' (*Année sociologique*, 1901–2). Translated: *Primitive Classification*, R. Needham, London, Cohen & West, 1963.

EVANS-PRITCHARD, E.E. (1956), *Nuer Religion*, Oxford, Clarendon Press.

GRICE, H.P. and STRAWSON, P.F. (1956), 'In defence of a dogma', *Phil. Rev.,* 65, 141–58.

HEUSCH, L. DE (1964), 'Structure et praxis sociales chez les Lele du Kasai', *Homme*, 4, 3, 87–109. Reprinted in *Pourquoi l'épouser? et autres essais*, Paris, Gallimard, 1971.

KLINGENDER, F. (1971), *Animals in Art and Thought to the End of the Middle Ages*, eds E. Antal and J. Harthan, London, Routledge & Kegan Paul.

LEACH, E.R. (1958), 'Trobriand clans and the kinship category *tabu*', in *The Development Cycle in Domestic Groups*, ed. J. Goody (*Camb. Pap. Social Anthrop., I*), Cambridge University Press.

LEACH, E.R. (1969), *Genesis as Myth and Other Essays*, London, Cape.

LÉVI-STRAUSS, C. (1958), 'La structure des mythes', in *Anthropologie structurale*, Paris, Plon. Originally: 'The structural study of myth, in *Myth, a Symposium (Journal of American Folklore*, 78, 270. 428–44: 1955).

LÉVI-STRAUSS, C. (1962). *La Pensée sauvage*, Paris, Plon.

LÉVI-STRAUSS, C. (1963), 'The bear and the barber', *Journal of the Royal Anthropological Institute, 93*, 1–11.

LÉVI-STRAUSS, C. (1966). 'The future of kinship studies', *Proceedings of the Royal Anthropological Institute 1965*, 13–22.

LÉVI-STRAUSS, C. (1969), *The Elementary Structures of Kinship*, London, Eyre & Spottiswoode.

LÉVY-BRUHL, L. (1910), *Les Fonctions mentales*, Paris, Alcan.

MALINOWSKI, B. (1935), *Coral Gardens and their Magic*, vol. 2, London, Allen & Unwin.

NOTH, M. (1965), *Leviticus: a Commentary*, London, SCM Press.

QUINE, W.V.O. (1943), 'Notes on existence and necessity', *Journal of Philosophy, 40*, 5, 113–27.

QUINE, W.V.O. (1960), *Word and Object*, Cambridge, Mass., MIT Press.

RICOEUR, P. (1963), 'Structure et herméneutique', *Ésprit*, 598–625.

ROWLEY, H.H. (1950), *The Growth of the Old Testament*, London, Hutchinson.

SALIM, S.M. (1962), *Marshdwellers of the Euphrates Delta*, London, Athlone Press.

STENNING, D. (1954), *Savannah Nomads: a Study of the Wodaabe Pastoral Fulani of Western Bornu Province, Northern Region, Nigeria*, London, Oxford University Press for the International African Institute.

TAMBIAH, S.J. (1969), 'Animals are good to think and good to prohibit', *Ethnology, 7*, 423–59.

Chapter 20

Rightness of categories

First published in Mary Douglas and David Hull (eds) (1993), *How Classification Works: Nelson Goodman among the Social Sciences*, Edinburgh, Edinburgh University Press

AGAINST SIMILARITY

Rival hypotheses compete, one hypothesis gets to be widely accepted and pushes out the others. How does this happen? If facts do not speak for themselves how is any particular piece of knowledge ever established? The different peoples that anthropologists study have different versions of the world. Very often the energy that drives the world in their version is theistic or spiritist, or magical. I suggested once that the world of the Lele, a Zairois people, was just as securely founded in knowledge as ours.[1] I did not mean that bows and arrows were more efficient artillery than guns, or that manual pounding of grain in wooden mortars was more efficient than an electric mill. I meant that the doctrines of the cult of the scaly anteater provided explanations of misfortune and success as satisfying intellectually as our best stochastic explanations can ever be. The latter are notoriously unsatisfying since they make a narrower sweep. Being told by the doctor that you are ill because there is a 90 per cent probability of being infected in the current flu epidemic may be sound but hardly explains anything at all and gives no guidance for future action. Being told that you are ill because you ate the wrong food at least confirms a dietary theory and tells you what to do. The problem of how theories get confirmation, why wrong theories get espoused, and what we mean by wrongness in a theory is still central to anthropology. Nelson Goodman's work on projection affords a number of leads for putting these questions on a better footing.

Most of the contemporary discussion of cognition takes place within an individualist theory. But anthropologists' questions need to be framed as questions about public knowledge, not about private ratiocination. Choosing the best hypothesis is a collective act, but the philosophy of knowledge makes little space for collective processes. There is an implicit though dubious assumption that individual knowledge comes first and that public knowledge is built up afterwards from combining the separate learning achievements of individuals.[2] Whereas for social animals, as Durkheim held,[3] learning is more likely to be a collective effort from the start.

So the question must shift to how the collective backing is mustered for one theory rather than another. This essay will search out the link between the system of knowledge (however fragmentary and unsystematic that may be) and the system of society (however unsolidary). Although successful hypotheses support sets of more or less reliable projections, in any instance several other hypotheses might have done as well. So how are the successful ones selected and entrenched? My perfectly conventional argument is that beliefs about the world will work if they support a working system of accountability. Holding other members of a community to account is one of the main uses to which knowledge is put (and for which it is sought in the first place).

For forty years or more I have puzzled about an unlikely set of projections from diet to health. An African people in Zaïre, the Lele, include young animals in the category of dangerous foods. In our Western culinary tradition the younger the animal, the more choice. Lele do not hold that young animals are dangerous for everyone, only for young humans. Carnivorous animals are also dangerous food for women and young people, but the case of the young forbidden to eat the young is my focus here. On Frazer's theory of 'sympathetic magic' the similarity between the two categories would be the reason. But sympathy is no explanation unless it is used consistently. In other projections to health from diet the Lele work similarity in the opposite direction: like must eat like, not avoid it. They regard the harnessed bush buck as a paragon of grace and elegance and since they greatly appreciate feminine beauty, on the principle of 'sweets to the sweet', they pay the harnessed bush buck the compliment of reserving its meat for women. We can see that young humans and young animals are similar in respect of age, and women and harnessed bush buck are similar in respect of beauty, but the first similarity indicates dangerous food and the second appropriate food.

Frazer was wrong about sympathetic magic, but wrong in good company. Images and metaphors, though they make a famously insecure basis for agreed categories, are constantly invoked. In 1987, in his book *Women, Fire and Dangerous Things, What Categories Reveal About the Mind*, published by Chicago University Press, George Lakoff has tried to go beneath the surface of discourse to uncover the prestructuring of experience on which abstract reasoning is based. His argument rests attractively on the idea that kinaesthetic image schemas are a source of abstract images. This is entirely plausible. A container scheme is universally available, with the associated concepts of interior, exterior, and boundary. There are also part–whole schemes, centre–periphery schemes, up–down, and front–back, and linear order schemes. Again, we can accept fully Lakoff's argument that such metaphorical projections are not arbitrary, artificial constructs, but natural to our condition (p. 275). He goes on to remark that each metaphor has a source domain, a target domain, and a source-to-target mapping. When we say, 'The crime rate keeps rising', the source domain is the experience of verticality; more of the crime wave is being mapped on to the up–down structure. Here again there can be no objection to his account of a usage. He has given us a list of physical experiences which provide sources of metaphors, and he does not claim that the list is complete. He must be right about these schemas being universally available. But to be really useful he would need to have a hypothesis about constraints on how the images are used in cognition. If the up/down arrow can be used in either direction, if anything can be the source domain, then his theory is of little help.

That metaphors can have a common spatio-kinetic basis is not a new idea and it does not explain why one projection wins over another. Suzanne Langer, in the steps of the German musicologists, has already plotted the kinetic basis for projection. Earlier, the linguist Edward Sapir considered how these experiences of space and gravity get taken up into speech. In the same tradition stands Robert Hertz's idea that right- and left-handedness provide world-wide models of complementary authority and subordination. Sometimes they do, but not always.[4] None of these seductive correlations proposed by esteemed scholars has so far been found to apply universally across cultures.[5]

If there were a limited number of schemes, and if they were always used in the same fashion, we would be on the way to charting the organisation of thought. But snags soon appear. For example, the bodily experience of verticality does not constrain in which direction the arrow of the metaphor will point. Accumulation can be mapped vertically, as Lakoff says, but not necessarily. 'More' can be a radial spreading out. Likewide, 'higher' in the vertical scale does not necessarily mean 'more'. 'Higher' can mean 'rarer' and so 'fewer', and 'less'. It is true that the reference point for low jokes is the nether part of the body, and presumably the same for low culture: the lower you go the more there is of it. Linguistic complexities are always there. Basic-level metaphors have to be jumbled up, though not so riotously as in the jingle:

> You've been very early of late,
> You were always behind, before.
> You'll end up first at last,
> If you go on like this any more.

A high cliff is also a deep ravine. In the 1960s, when generative grammars provided the theoretical model for many seminars on symbolism, speakers used to equate 'deep structure' with 'high' level of abstraction: deep could mean a property of the whole range, not a low position on it. Pondering why some musical notes are known as 'high', Goodman has suggested that it may be due to the prior entrenchment of the linguistic habit in mathematics whereby high frequency is associated with high numbers, a good instance of 'more' being 'higher'. But Leonard Meyer has suggested that the attributing of height to certain points in the musical scale has to do with the location of sound in the larynx.[6] Though both examples fit Lakoff's hypothesis they show that there is a lot of unpredictability in discovering the source experience and target metaphor. The identification of the source is quite open. Something else is needed to define the primal basic experience governing abstract reasoning. I shall argue that looking for the basis in physical experience is doomed. Only prejudice makes it plausible to hold that the physical basis is prior to or more basic than the social.

Lakoff does not claim that the list of metaphors projected from basic-level experience is exhaustive. But incompleteness is not a virtue: the unlimited possibilities of metaphors puts his theory on a par with other anthropological discoveries of isomorphic structures. We all have our favourite mappings of one idea or pattern upon another. We all face Lakoff's difficulty, in that there is no end to the number of metaphors. Donald Davidson's warnings against trustful attempts to recognise the meaning of a metaphor ought to be final:

> There are no instructions for devising metaphors; there is no manual for determining what a metaphor 'means' or 'says' . . . ('What metaphors mean' in Sheldon Sachs (ed.), *On Metaphor*, Chicago: Chicago University Press, 1979, p. 29.)

From the infinity of meanings of a metaphor there is an infinite range of choices. If we cannot explain how particular metaphors get picked out and start their career of established connections, we have not got a theory at all.

Like most other explanations of projection, Lakoff's depends explicitly on a perceived similarity between the source domain and the target. But alas, if the similarity is plausible to us, that can only be because we have become habituated to it, which means that it is entrenched in our own culture. Lakoff does not face the fact that his own favourite isomorphs derive their privileged status in his theory from being already privileged in his culture. Similarity does not inhere in objects, and in itself a similarity that we happen to perceive has no power to explain how similarity notions arise. All Lakoff can say is that some 'basic level' metaphors are universally available.

Frazer's *Golden Bough* is not the only book that would need to be rewritten if anthropologists took to heart the standard philosophers' criticism of similarity. Goodman's attack on isomorphism starts by saying that similarity gives no guarantee of right projection.[7] Similarity does not account for our predictive or inductive practice. Rather the other way round: inductive practice provides the basis for canons of similarity. He forces us to realise the implications of something often said before: any two things whatever can have properties in common. What significant properties they share depends on everyday practical organisation, and the assumptions and prejudices that go with it. Isomorphic images are two a penny.

EXEMPLIFICATION

So similarity is not the explanation of why the Lele believed that young must not eat young on pain of death. We still have to explain how the two kinds of young get classed together. How are classes of like things constituted? For this I turn to Nelson Goodman's teaching on exemplification. This is a primary mode of communication which does not depend on depiction. The sample of a class of objects does not represent the class. The sample is not an image of something else: it is simply an example. We can make a fresh start because the sample is not a depiction and ideas about similarity are not involved. Recognising a sample for what it is depends on a collectively learned habit. Though knowledge based on the sample will quickly have recourse to denotation and metaphor, in its initial stages such knowledge is not denotative or metaphorical. I shall argue below that collective belief is founded on exemplars. But the initial question is only transferred: can exemplars give better guarantees than metaphors? Yes, if the examples are used in regular procedures of accountability.

Collective beliefs are embodied in rules of behaviour. Rules are verified by the usual processes for verifying samples. Instances of following a rule are just instances, further examples of how the rule applies. Though there is matching to be done in recognising whether a new instance is an instance of the same rule, the matching is not by use of an image or metaphor: the applied context of a rule is a sample, a member of its own class. Rules are extended from the more general to the more particular, or back again, from particular to general, in one context after another. An argument about whether a rule applies or whether it has been correctly observed is not like an argument about how to interpret a metaphor. Argument about rules generally concerns legitimacy. The rules themselves do not come out of a picture-making faculty of individual minds, but out of a social process. Rules, I submit, are largely made to protect claims and to enforce accountability. The legitimacy of the rules depends on the general acceptability of the claims they support. A version of the world depends on the rules, and is guaranteed by the social system in which the mutual claims are honoured. Categories are right if they fit well with the relevant rules and claims, and wrong if they do not. This test of right categories does not apply to narrative or metaphor but it does apply to science, medicine, and technology. It is the test regularly applied by the Lele to the categories of their universe which are formulated by them in terms of rules about diet.

Goodman teaches that there must always be many versions of the world. But this does not imply that they should all be reducible to one. Any one version is correct or incorrect within its frame of reference. He insists that rightness is possible. It may be important to point this out, for some have read Goodman as a philosophical relativist for whom no version may be more right than another. In practical matters, as he himself says, mistakes can be calamitous. To muddle up the category of generals with the category of prisoners would be fatal: once the prisoners have been shot 'the penalty for using wrong categories is not merely an inconvenience'.[8] His own tentative answer to the question of what distinguishes right inductive categories from others (in his theory of projection[9]) is that rightness depends on the theory in which the categories serve and, in turn, the theory owes its value to the inductive categories that it establishes.

He adds that projection depends on prior entrenchment in the language, and entrenchment itself is largely a matter of habit; when otherwise equally well qualified hypotheses conflict, the decision normally goes to the one with the better entrenched predicates.

At first reading this seems to focus all the work of entrenchment on linguistic habit. Even if this is only a prudent demarcation of the bounds of philosophy it would be disappointing, either trivial or non-intuitive as Mary Hesse has suggested, unless we use the term to include much more than our everyday linguistic habits would justify.[10] Though it may be enough to say that theory uses and in itself justifies similarity notions, somehow the theory itself has to be justified. To explain its usefulness and acceptability by mere habit suggests fortuitousness, as if any other habit might have done as well, producing any other theory. Hence comes perhaps the idea that Goodman's philosophy is relativist in the bad sense of denying any difference between right and wrong versions of the world. But this interpretation ignores his sense of the world already given as the scene of action, the place where wrong categories will not work.

His own reply to the charge is in the form of a virtuous circle. He admits:

> This looks flagrantly circular. I have said that deductive inferences are justified by their conformity to valid general rules, and that general rules are justified by their conformity to valid inferences. But this circle is a virtuous one. The point is that rules and particular inferences alike are justified by being brought into agreement with each other. A rule is amended if it yields an inference we are unwilling to accept; an inference is rejected if it violates a rule we are unwilling to amend. The process of justification is the delicate one of making mutual adjustments between rules and accepted inferences; and in the agreement achieved lies the only justification needed for either.[11]

To defend against the charge of circularity by calling it a virtuous circle has a hint of special pleading. But remember that Goodman is always concerned with the knowledge of responsible, interested agents, people who interact in a world already old, and who are always bringing their practice and categories under review. Such a lively social world is quite alien to the existing philosophic discourse on cognition. Denotative in emphasis, linguistic in scope, it starts from an imaginary non-existent universe being interpreted by an imaginary isolated person with no prior experience or socialisation. In such a rarefied context it is easy to forget how logic and interaction are mutually interlocked, since the subject of knowing is defined to have nothing to do with interaction. In what follows I will not only imitate the argument of the virtuous circle, but extend it, make it denser, by showing why hypotheses have to be bought into agreement with acceptable rules, and rules into agreement with acceptable claims, and knowledge with the testing of claims. The practical use of exemplars for monitoring behaviour is the focus of this analysis. First, the subject of how exemplars work needs more attention.

EXEMPLARS, SIMILARS, AND NOTATION SYSTEMS

To denote is to depict or describe, to exemplify is to display.[12] In one sense, there is no denotation without classes or without knowing sample members of classes. In another, exemplification is the converse of denotation. A sample is an instance of a set of things which have a label. The sample exemplifies its own properties. It points from itself to the label, whereas denotation points from the label to the set of things it covers. The exemplar refers directly to itself. Interestingly, it does not refer to all of its properties: what it refers to as an exemplar has to be learned. This is where habit comes in, for the list of possible qualities any exemplar might exemplify is as limitless as the possible meanings of a metaphor. The relevant properties have to be learned. In short, it is necessary to insist that a thing can be an exemplar only if the exemplifying properties have been selected and agreed. The lady furnishing her room with new curtains looks at the swatch of materials from the shop; she chooses one sample and orders so many yards. The shopkeeper, receiving her order, does not cut up 30 yards into exactly the same size and shape as the sample; he knows that the size and shape of this sample is not relevant; the colour, texture, pattern, and everything that is conventionally exemplified in the bundle of swatches is known. For another example, when the gymnastics instructor does a knee bend and shouts 'Do as I do', the correct response of his class is not to shout 'Do as I do', but silently to bend their own knees. They have learnt what part of the action they are supposed to copy and what part is in parenthesis.[13] Shades of the late Erving Goffman seem to hover here, and intimations of ethnomethodology. Anthropologists are perforce very interested in tacit understandings, foregrounding of some meanings, backgrounding of others, weighting of some elements, implicit emendations. Goodman calls these the very processes of world-making.

The exemplar works like an analogy. Mary Hesse describes analogy as having positive elements that are recognised as the basis of a likeness, and also neutral elements that are discounted because they do not fit the model that is being used.[14] The neutral elements which were present, but not used, remain passively available as a potential source of new future theory. Recognising a sample is a selection process which does not depend on words. The fashion model is an exemplar without ever saying anything. However, the fact of being non-verbal is not the defining feature. The movements of the orchestra conductor are non-verbal representations of the music, but not samples of it. By such cases Goodman leads us to reflect on how we use exemplars. Because an exemplar refers directly to itself, and because it is not necessarily verbal, exemplification can be seen as more immediate than denotation. It derives directly from the most basic sorting into classes. Before that is done there can be no similars for us to recognise.

The next question is how anything gets selected and shaped to serve as an exemplar of a class. It is a question that can hardly be asked from the point of view of an individualist cognitive psychology. Goodman is unusual in having examined it in great detail. Any kind of denoting needs to make a match between bits of the world and the signs that refer to them. The chopping up is artificial, but it is not arbitrary. Denoting is not for its own sake, it has work to do in the making of worlds. For some purposes imprecision is acceptable, even desirable. For other purposes denoting needs to be very exact. Too often we think of communication as dependent on a one-off statement and its response. To trace the path of communication through a dialogue is to take the near view, conversation by conversation. Taking more distance, communication turns out to depend on repetition. Members of a class often have to be enumerated, the list checked, and the criteria for membership reviewed. This has to happen for similarities to be established. The more that denotation depends on repetition the more likely that a notation system will be developed. In art, apart from music and dance, there are not many well-developed notation systems. In mathematics, logic and science, precise notation improves communication. It is often important to know whether the allegedly repeated calculation is the same, whether the argument is the same, or whether the experiment is the same. The checking is done by examining exemplars and striving to eliminate ambiguity in their claims to be members of a set.

The object of a notation system is to reduce ambiguity. The less it is ambiguous, the better a notation system works. Our familiar alphabet is far from the ideal: it often allows two letters to refer to the same sound (ph- and f-), or one letter to two sounds (c-). No notation system has compliants which come naturally carved up, item by item, to match their appropriate inscriptions. The compliant set is as artificially constructed as the set of inscriptions.[15] The demand for accurate interpretation forces the creation of unambiguous exemplars. The more that precision is valued, the more the exemplars are carved into types that fulfil the requirements of the notation system. If the match were perfect, the notation system would guarantee recognition; there would be no interpretative choices to be made, but inevitably reducing the options impoverishes meaning. Consequently, symbolising moves between two poles: at one end is aesthetic interpretation with rich scope for alternative meanings, and at the other is the notation system in which the interpretative options are exhaustively coded. In between are all the other forms of notation.

When he has laid down the requirements of a notation system, Goodman points out that a map or scale diagram does not qualify because the reference is ambiguous. A digital pressure gauge qualifies because its dial shows unambiguous marks corresponding to uniquely identifiable states of pressure. But an analogue dial which makes no discontinuities between the marks is not a notation system in his strict sense. Yet there is notation going on, so he calls it a 'notation scheme'.

For some occasions, a 'notation scheme' will do, and on others nothing will serve but a strict 'notation system'.

EXEMPLIFICATION IN ANTHROPOLOGY

Several anthropologists have used exemplification in order to avoid a distinction between real and symbolic. When Clifford Geertz analysed political behaviour in nineteenth-century Bali he gave a succinct account of an ancient system of checks and countervailing checks in which no power can be sustained for long. In that system he concluded that the political struggle was manifestly not for power, and consequently it was not for the symbols of power either. The fierce rivalry of princes and lords could be completely described in its own right, without supposing that it symbolised something else. A competitive spectacle, bloody, violent and wildly extravagant, the dramatic displays of the court were the only political reality that counted. Rejecting representation, he fell back on saying that the display was the medium for competing for status. Display exemplified the status that it achieved by its splendour and lavishness. The display was an example of display: what it was was itself. In spite of the subtitle of Geertz's book, *The Theatre State in Nineteenth Century Bali*, which implies theatrical models of something else, the central theme is that by display the overlapping and competing social units *exemplify* the idea of the state. The argument was a theoretical *tour de force* in political philosophy, repudiating the assumption expounded by Bagehot that the theatrical functions of government are separate and external to its efficient workings.

> It has been the central argument of this work, displayed by the very divisions of its content and directive throughout the whole of its unfolding, that the life that swirled around the punggawas, perbekels, puris, and jeros of classical Bali comprised such an alternative conception of what politics is about and what politics comes to. A structure of action, now bloody, now ceremonious, the negara was also, and as such, a structure of thought. To describe it is to describe a constellation of enshrined ideas.[16]

Geertz's reason for using exemplars instead of images was a deliberate critical strategy for which he frequently cited Goodman. He rejected the language of images to avoid the distinction it imports between ideal and real, and between subjective and material. He was protesting against what Maurice Bloch has irreverently called[17] bouncing the ball of interpretation between two walls; one the functionalist, realist, practical, politico-socio-economic kind of interpretation and the other the symbolic, idealist, ideological, subjectivist kind. Thinking in terms of exemplars has the effect of drawing the same line without implying anything about relative reality. Because an exemplar is public property, every exemplar is an equally real result of world-making.

Maurice Bloch has also sought to understand rituals without counterpoising their symbolic meaning against some other more real reality. In his account of funeral rites among the Merino of Madagascar he wanted to interpret their custom of immuring the dried bones of the dead ancestors. He insists that the tombs are not symbols of continuity, but exemplars of resistance to the ravages of time. He has also allowed for some normative element for the tombs are also exemplars of the permanence of Merino moral teaching.

This is a step nearer to the use of exemplars for monitoring the world and the behaviour of people in it. Godfrey Lienhardt's sophisticated account of the religious experience of the Dinka develops this theme.[18] Against the intellectual fashion of thirty years ago he provided a model of cognition based on repeated enactment of exemplars. A Dinka rite mimes a wish, the miming articulates an intention. The community that has killed and eaten together the sacrificial ox has enacted some of its complex intentions about itself. It would be absurd to say that their ritual has represented a communion meal, when they have just eaten one. Their wish for the community to be possessed by divinity is realised (not represented) in the trance of their priests whom the spirit does possess. The quivering flesh of the dying victim is not symbolising something other than itself, it is an example of the same quivering in the flesh of the person in trance. The community is not depicting something but giving itself a sample of its idea of true community. Against this sample it measures its own achievement of the ideal. The sacrifice is a self-referencing enactment. In structuring the community's self-perception it structures its future behaviour: as Goodman says, the version of the world that has been adopted itself affects the world.

Geertz insisted that his choice of language did not put him with the subjectivists:

> Ideas are not, and have not been for some time, unobservable mental stuff. They are envehicled meanings, the vehicles being symbols (or in some usages, signs), a symbol being anything that denotes, describes, represents, exemplifies, labels, indicates, evokes, depicts, expresses – anything that somehow or other signifies. And anything that somehow or other signifies is intersubjective, and thus public, thus accessible to overt and corrigible *plein air* explication – arguments, melodies, formulas, maps, and pictures are not idealities to be stared at, but texts to be read; so are rituals, palaces, technologies, and social formations.[19]

He has deliberately jumbled together all kinds of symbols and signs in order to reject emphatically a distinction between material reality attributed to things signified and subjective immateriality attributed to symbols. He tells us to make no distinction between texts for reading and instructions for doing, or between such texts and the actual doing. He is warning us not to introduce degrees of reality between the reading of a musical score and the practical use of blueprints, jigs, and architectural drawings for making real, solid objects. He has used exemplification to create a frame of reference in which Goodman is not talking circular nonsense when he says that deductive inferences are justified by their conformity to valid general rules, and that general rules are justified by their conformity to valid inference. The argument is not circular in that the exemplars have been designed to refer to the world, to constitute a class of things in the world that can be denoted by signs. I would add that the things need to be denoted because the world needs to be monitored for living in.

Habit makes us look for a way of sorting out the jumble of different things being exemplified or the different ways of exemplifying. And indeed, pressure gauges, engineers' jigs, architects' models, blueprints are very different in their uses from scores for melodies and other written texts. It is safer to take it that the version of the world that counts as real is the version which is publicly accepted, albeit in process of scrutiny and emendation.

Public knowledge is central for anthropologists. Why do the Lele have their peculiar dietary ideas? To answer by saying that they are thinking magically, or mystically, or that they are just feeble-minded, is to stay at the level of individual cognition and to focus on denotation. From that standpoint their bizarre projections from religion to diet, and from diet to illness, have nothing to tell us about our own method of projection. But if we refuse the temptation to ethnic intellectual exceptionalism, and ask the question again starting from exemplars and classification, the answers are different. Exemplars are collectively constituted; their properties are collectively agreed; they work as public knowledge of the way the world is made. We can expect classes of exemplars to fit or match with other classes of exemplars, the system of classification being the whole construction of the inhabited world. Too easily the philosophy of cognition implies that the world is essentially uninhabited and that itself unaided justifies hypotheses about it. Reflection on exemplars gives us a different route for asking how hypotheses are justified, for everyday life, for science and for the Lele.

AUTHENTICITY

Though Goodman has written of exemplars in the context of aesthetics, the idea of exemplification is clearly fundamental to his criticism of theories of knowledge. As we have seen, anthropologists have been helped by his use of exemplification to attack representation theories of art, but the attack applies to any representation theories of knowledge. A picture is not a copy of nature. A picture can exemplify properties it has, such as greyness, or size, without depicting them. Once he has rejected truthfulness to nature as a criterion of painting, the art world gives him a new angle for approaching the idea of truth. Gratefully turning away from trying to think what a faithful reproduction of reality would entail, we now consider instead authenticity, fakes, and frauds. What replication, verification, and disproof are to philosophers of science, copying, authentication, and uncovering forgery are to the philosophy of art, but there are interesting differences. The theory of induction reaps a surprise benefit from leaving the science laboratories to visit the art galleries and concert halls. Comparing painting and music allow us to escalate the initial problem of projection through several stages of abstraction. We will find ourselves unhappy about treating verification of scientific theories by considering one theory at a time. Nor will it be enough to compare one set of theories with its one or two rival sets. In this inquiry the exact commensurability of concepts is beside the point: when the whole worlds are in process of being classified the issue is not particular meanings but a more general question of how the classifications are justified.

> Why then, can I no more make a forgery of Haydn's symphony or of Gray's poem than I can make an original of Rembrandt's painting or of his etching of *Tobit Blind*? (Goodman, *Languages of Art*, p. 115)

Of some art works it can be said that their justification lies in the performance. Repetition has been anticipated in their creation. Each new performance is another example of the work. It is not a copy or a forgery any more than a new writing of the letter B is a copy or forgery of other B's. The same applies to prints as well as to music, to chairs issuing from the Sheraton workshop, and to many other productions. A choir does not have to be able to trace its singing back to any original moment of composition. It is allowed to give encores. It can be reproached for a monotonous repertoire, but not charged with plagiarism. There could be a problem about the match between the programme notes and the performance, with some suggestion of wrongful attribution, but it is exceptional for the value of a musical work to be established solely on its unique historical origin. No one knows who composed folk music. On the other hand, in painting in the West the idea of forgery looms almost as large as it does in the issue of legal tender. Because of the linguistic habits of collectors, authenticity depends on tracing the history of the work from its inception. In the world of painting the notion of a genuine, original object excludes the copy. Anticipating the collector's concern for authenticity, even in the making of an engraving meant to reproduce many copies each copy is given its unique identity by its number. The creation of a genuine article is complementarily opposite to the possibility of fraud. A copy of a painting can have a lot of pejorative meaning, while in music even the word 'copy' may not apply between two performances.

Goodman distinguishes two processes of justification. One is authentication of an individual object, achieved by answering questions about its history. The other is a form of sampling, answering the question of whether it is a true member of its class. Although he does not say as much, the two forms of justification arise in two kinds of social process, the one developed by enhancing the competition of named individuals to own a piece of valuable property, the other by enhancing collaboration to reach a specified standard. The two sorts of social process are found in science. The first (which Goodman calls autographic, in which justification is by reference to a verified history of production) corresponds in science to the competition to be the first inventor of a useful idea, where success is crowned by having the name of the original author permanently attached to the method or discovery so that he has property rights in it. The second (which he calls allographic) corresponds to work done in the expectation of repeated anonymous performances of teams of teachers and researchers. In the latter case property rights are unimportant and the idea of a perfect reproduction is good, not pejorative. One of the side-advantages of paying attention to modes of justification is to discern two different social processes without suggesting that one (science) is more concerned with reality and the other (art) more concerned with representation – a notable advance.

The two processes of justifying are interdependent, in music as well as in science. The composer whose name is on the property depends for his reputation on the excellence of the performances. The career of the famous scientist who is here being compared to a famous painter much depends on whether an experiment that has been intended to replicate his own has been correctly carried out and can therefore be counted as an authentic example. Though the individual scientists may bitterly reproach one another for copying and plagiarism, the scientific community is more interested in replicability than in claims to priority. Some of the social implications of kinds of authentication have been developed by Israel Scheffler[20] with reference to ritual. The authority of valid orders based on a unique historical succession from the founder differs from the authority of a newly inspired prophet; sacraments whose efficacy depends on correctness of performance differ from the efficacy of charismatic hands laid on the sick. Many other examples come to mind and would repay study.

Goodman carries the distinction forward to elaborate upon another contrast which lies in the actual mode of authentication. It is in the nature of art not to be able to be submitted to notation. The impossibility of making a perfect copy of a painting is different from the circumstances of the Western art world in which even a perfect copy, totally indistinguishable from the original, has less value once its origin is known. (There are other art worlds in which perfect replication is desirable and even where something like painting by numbers if practised, but these products would probably escape Goodman's definition.) In the West the subtle density of inscriptions, rich repleteness of meaning, and resulting ambiguity which tend to make the painting unrepeatable, contrast with the absence of ambiguity imposed on products which have to be described by notation.

The two different ways of meaning are in stark contrast. Notation systems liberate the work from its history. In the case of music, made for repeated performance, the authentication is by means of the score. Goodman even goes so far as to say that the unique theoretical function of the musical score is authoritatively to identify a work.[21] Presumably the occasion arises when players disagree about the right way of playing a piece: they can resolve their dispute by looking at the score. This works up to a point. It does not mean that the musical score cannot perform any other function. As David Bloor has pointed out to me, that would be absurd. Being quite unmusical, I am not sure whether listening to a concert while following the score is a theoretical function at all. The idea of a unique theoretical function does not include using the score to light a fire, or for memorising the piece. As Goodman himself has said, a work of art can have various uses:

> A Rembrandt painting may cease to function as a work of art when used to replace a broken window, or as a blanket.[22]

Within his theory of verification the musical score makes the link between the present performance and the original that is made in the case of a painting by the unbroken historical record. Like the script for a play, like the jigs, diagrams, blueprints, and spirit levels that Geertz listed among other texts, the score is a model for performance. It is a basic analogy which describes in another medium what the performance is. Just as the sale room is not the regular situation for enjoying a painting, but is the regular situation for questioning authenticity, so in music and other activities questions of verification do not regularly arise. But for learning how to diagnose appendicitis, or cardiac disease, something equivalent to a score has to be used for checking on how this human body is constituted. For electrical or plumbing repairs the architect's drawing may be consulted: the question then is what sort of house is this? How is it made? The context of learning or checking is quite different from the aesthetic.

The theoretical functions of alphabets, pressure gauges, and musical scores are different. Having whetted our curiosity Goodman does not say nearly enough about the kinds of copies they respectively verify. In the context of production the musical score and the pressure gauge have a similar controlling function, but there are crucial differences in the context of identification. When the performance of the music is over, the manager of the concert hall may have an interest in checking the box office returns. The score was useful in rehearsal, for judging the performance of members of the orchestra, and in performance for co-ordination. In the next stage of appraisal there is no theory by which the manager can judge how to achieve a box office, or even a critical, success. He might turn from notation to the sound of clapping for a rough estimate.

In the other case, the dial of the pressure gauge is part of a well articulated theory about phenomena that it has been designed to monitor. Verifying the compliance has definite consequences: too much or too little pressure will be taken as a sign of an imminent explosion or leak. Something will certainly have to be done, and then the registration on the dial face will have to be checked again. Both the musicians and the engineers need to be justified. But the musician's score registers changes only within a narrowly defined context, while the engineer's pressure gauge enters a less segregated chain of explanations. Changes in its dial face register evidence for the theories that caused its code to be established. It functions to denote a particular connection between a theory and the samples of the world discriminated by the theory. The theory itself is part of a more comprehensive system of classification. The pressure gauge helps to establish the value of the whole classificatory system; regularly checking the dial face and adjusting the machinery establish it even more strongly.

Like a pioneer's road, Goodman's work on notation stops in the middle of a beautiful landscape. It is presented in the context of aesthetics, and has left in the background the application to the basic problems of projection which is one of his central concerns. Mentioning the pressure gauge reminds us that these regular checking processes are among the so-called 'linguistic habits' that justify the choice of a predicate. The pressure gauge tests the theory, and checking the dial face against how the world is behaving checks the value of the pressure gauge itself. It is at the centre of a whole flurry of reciprocal monitoring. Moreover, the notation defines the units of the world that are taken for exemplars in the categories that the theory is about. The results of repeated checking may require the classification to be adjusted. The task of monitoring the current version of the world by attention to the categories saves the logic from seeming to be circular because the authentication has a touchstone, the world that is being made. And if the dial face is right but has been read carelessly, someone is going to be fired. A demand for accountability has caused the dial face to be made so precisely.

EXEMPLARS CONSTITUTE COMMUNITIES

Goodman has given us the way that notation systems prepare exemplars, but we still lack the start of the process. We know that they are collectively constituted, that they are made in response to social needs, and that they need to be recognised by learning. But how are they learnt?

Thomas Kuhn takes us in the right direction by arguing that a community is constituted by shared exemplars. He argues not only that 'similarity perceptions' are learned by means of exemplars, but also that the learning of exemplars is part of the process of constituting a community.[23] He analyses the problem-solving exercises which are part of the training of science students and observes that they furnish their minds with exemplars; the shared process of learning to recognise what is exemplary about a particular item instils community-wide notions of similarity. He takes up the point we have already noted, that an exemplar is formed of richer and more variable materials than whatever it comes conventionally to exemplify. Exercises in standard questions and answers enable the students to go beyond the actual instances taught, because the exemplars stored in their minds are resources from which they can recognise entirely new problems and find new solutions. (This interestingly suggests that though notation schemes are attempts to control interpretation with some rigidity, their use does not inhibit innovation.)

It is a simple solution: to pay attention to standard questions and answers. Add the professional incentives to satisfy the examiners, and fill in the process of choosing the right questions to fit the candidate for emerging from the academy as a certificated member of the profession, and relate the choice of rightness of exam questions to the demands of the clients of the profession. With all this we are close to inserting the community's life into the description of exemplars. The questions must not be frivolously irrelevant, though they are sometimes allowed to be funny. Choosing good questions is a test of the examiner as well as of the candidate, hence the apparatus of external examining to provide self-monitoring. Failing the exam is a severe sanction for the student, but if they all were to fail it would be a severe sanction on the institution. Feelings run high in examination week. Classrooms and exams are kinds of public performances in which correct repetition is required. By drawing attention to puzzle-solving techniques in learning Kuhn has saved us from the charge of apparant frivolity that we might have incurred if we had considered exemplification in thin air. Exemplars are learnt in the course of mutual testing and defining and the emotional tension is why they are so well learnt. The puzzles are not minor issues, for much depends on the outcomes, which is why correctness of answers can sometimes be so crucial that nothing but a notation system will serve.

This insight allows us to embrace in one explanation the bizarre ideas of the Lele about their world, and the bizarre ideas of physicists about theirs. We have to ask how the Lele choose their equivalent of exam questions and what are the puzzle-solving techniques which they have to learn in order to answer them. We can ask what constitute right questions and what is the test for right answers, and what is the audience which monitors the proper conduct of the interrogation and the penalty of failing. All of their public religious occasions could be construed under this rubric of puzzle-solving performances because their religious practice is strongly directed to averting misfortune. Their central concern about health will illustrate the process of using exemplars to make and to contest claims. Regular rehearsal entrenches their medical categories through standard question-and-answer sessions which, since they have to do with life and death, are vitally important to them. The emotions roused by their medical consultations run very high. In public performances curing confirms and death disconfirms the classifications. In the long run the system to which their medical categories conform is the system of social relations. The rules which according to Lele knowledge apply to the world of animals are further exemplars of the rules that organise their own lives.

Before I realised the weakness of the metaphorical argument, I was content to say that the Lele projected their universe upon the animal world as a kind of picture. It was for long the standard right puzzle for anthropologists to consider why most people all over the world contrive to incorporate nature into the moral order.[24] The people that anthropologists traditionally study have never been reported as saying that their classifications mirror or reflect or depict their social relations, but structural analysis of their symbolism works because they do.[25] God and spirits and all the denizens of the earth and sky are classified by humans in a likeness of human classifications of themselves, by tribes, clans and lineages, families, elders and juniors. Why should that be? Appeal to linguistic habits is of no help here. Can it be attributed to some intuition that the parallelism will strengthen the moral order? The upholders of a particular order would be trying to support it by telling their children that it is written in the foundation of the universe. But this implies a community with no controversy on politics or morals, a complete and implausible stasis. We would still have to explain why one pattern of the moral order has prevailed over alternative patterns, the same question we asked about metaphor. The argument rests on the outside observers' perceiving a likeness. If the structure of society really gets projected on to nature, then we should be curious about some underlying cognitive process. How is it done? I am arguing that the process is by exemplification. Before the metaphors were the exemplars.

No sense could be had by asking the Lele the meaning of one food prohibition, or even of one class of prohibitions, for none was a solitary projection. The whole lot of animal prohibitions had to be seen as a single pattern. When I went to live among the Lele in 1949 I was struck by their extensive list of prohibited meats. Most animals were forbidden to some or other category of persons. In a true sense, as Tambiah has said,[26] the prohibited animals were used to codify their society. When I asked for a reason why one kind of person would die if they were to eat a particular animal kind they would start by saying they did not know, but went on to tell me about the territory and habits of the animal and then more about the particular vulnerabilities of the person. The dead live underground and burrowing animals are under their control. Fish live in the water and are under the sway of water spirits; water spirits control pregnant women. It was thought to be enough of an explanation that the bush rat lived in the bush, and to remind me that it belonged to the class of rats, and that rats lived in human habitations, which ruled them out as meat. No similarities or metaphors were ever invoked to explain the food prohibitions, only common habitat. It emerged that shared domicile set up a prohibition on eating: other tribes might eat dogs and cats, children were undiscriminating and might eat anything, but discerning Lele adults would never eat a domestic animal. Chickens were an awkward border-line case since women treated them as domestic animals, a case which they negotiated by ruling that no sensitive woman would eat domestic fowl. No man would eat an animal he reared, which ruled out domestic goats or pigs. The principle of shared domicile became a basis for classifying wild animals by habitats they shared, distinguished as sky, land and water; so squirrels went with birds; pigs with fish because they wallowed in the muddy sources of streams. These territories were qualified again into subterritories by nocturnal or diurnal habits of the animals. And right across the territorial distinctions ran the distinction between carnivores and all other animals.

Three underlying principles were being deployed for the animal categories, territory, overlordship and enmity, the prime principles of their own political relationships. Every Lele person would be a pawn to an overlord. 'Owner' might be the better translation since they used the word *kumu* for the chief of a village, the whole chiefly clan, for a senior male relative, for the elder brother, and descending again to straight proprietorship of a slave, or of a dog. These linguistic habits referred to clear relations of authority and subordination connected with territory. Only when a pawn came into his lord's territory did he have to pay him tribute of any game he kills; a father's curse (or an owner's curse) had power only within a limited geographical range, so it could be worthwhile to move away to avoid it. Everyone who was a follower would also own other followers.[27] The claims of an overlord were actually very weak, so he needed to be supported by other overlords to enforce them in case of dispute. At the same time the claims were very important to his status and influence, for the pawn's relation to his lord was half-way between slave and son. Above all, owning pawns gave a man rights to control the marriages of all their female descendants, the only real base of power in that society.

The relation of pawns of the same owner were the explicit model of the relations of animals inhabiting the same territory. The same word was used, the local spirits were the owner of the territory, and the animal locals subordinate. So pigs and fish came under the control of the water spirits, birds and squirrels came under the sky spirits, bush animals under bush spirits, forest animals under forest spirits. Humans, when they ventured into bush, forest or water, were going out of their territory (made safe for them by religion) and had to regard themselves as trespassers at risk, or as favoured visitors who kept the rules of their hosts. It was explicitly parallel to the case of going to visit another village.

Add to the principle of common territory the organisation of enmity and a vast range of food prohibitions are accounted for as extensions of rules from human life to animal life, each type being easy to recognise as exemplars. Enmity was incompatible with shared domicile. It was central to Lele religion that the human prosperity was punished by direct spirit action if members of the same village quarrelled. Diagnosis of illness sought out quarrels as the cause and required reconciliation or avoidance as the cure. Eating is an attack; therefore by extension, eating domestic animals incurs penalty, and likewise eating any animals whose territory one shares. So pregnant women must not attack fishes who are under the same water spirit. A barren woman thought to be cursed by her owner now deceased and buried had to avoid burrowing animals. Carnivorous animals respect no territory. Other animals prey on species different from their own, but carnivores were quite explicitly put in the class of enemies of their own kind, a class which included sorcerers.[28] Obviously, once we have got to know the system, we can see that it would be dangerous to eat carnivores without special protection.

By now it is clear that the counterpart to the coding of animal kinds was a parallel code for humans. The animal lore doubly underwrote health and hygiene, first because of dangers that it signalled and second because of immunities that could be obtained. The rules were made by God and God's favoured persons gained dispensations. It is hardly surprising that the persons that God singled out for special dietary privileges were those who were honoured in Lele culture. The result was a coding based on procreative achievements: for a man, to be sterile was to be forever insignificant, because all influence came from control of children. Three ranks of begetters distinguished the favoured men from the sterile: the lowest was the rank of first begetting, the next was the rank of begetting a male and female child in wedlock, the third was begetting twins. Each rank was organised into a set of initiates with exclusive ritual powers. And needless to say, the two systems, religious and secular, had a connection in that until a man begot a child he could not exercise the secular influence of a father.

This is where the elaboration of the codes sets in. Begetting defines male maturity; a sterile man, by virtue of the definition, is classed with children. The rule that forbids predation on one's own class stops children from eating young of animals, and the rule that separates adults from children by God's election allows adult men (not women ever) to eat young of animals. That is it. The rich cosmological metaphors of an animal order, a divine order of spirits, and the ever-fragile human order arise from the classifications. These conform to the way in which men class themselves for action in Lele villages. The value of the classifications is confirmed in meticulous questions and answers in public sessions to do with illness. The same rule articulates social claims at every level and claims to meat, somewhat as a claim of a scientist to be allowed to research within a dominant paradigm gives him a supplementary claim to laboratory space, experimental time and materials, and editorial attention when seeking to publish. This is how the exemplar constitutes the community. This is why the missions, by telling their converts that Christians could eat any meats they like, undermined the whole system of cults.

ANIMALS AS INSCRIPTIONS FOR NOTATION

The Lele coding of their animals turns the animals' existences into something like inscriptions in a notation system. Each adult animal counts as a true member of its class, whether old, blind, lame, sick or hale. It is unambiguously another instance of bushbuck, rat, civet cat or whatever. The inscriptions are discontinuous; one animal does not blend into another; there are spaces between them. The animals are well known, named, and clearly classified. Habits and habitat, which might easily produce overlapping or redundant inscriptions, are saved from ambiguity by rulings – for example, the preeminence of habitat as a classifier, which puts pigs and fish together but makes the water spirits the owners of the class. There is one major exception: no general ruling has been found to make it clear whether a small specimen is mature or young. At that point, in the old days any doubt was settled by a legitimate arbitrator: the decision of the Begetters' Association was final. They would declare the beast to be young and carry it off to eat at their communal feast. But since Christianity came to the Lele their authority is questioned; in default of legitimate arbitration the killing of a small animal in the hunt would trigger a violent row between the Begetters and the Christian hunters, not initiated into the cult and often not even qualified. The furious disputes about how to class an animal of uncertain age illustrates the bad consequences of ambiguity in a notation system.

Otherwise, the animal code is a perfect notation system. There can be no equivocation; there is no optional interpretation; recognition is guaranteed. As to the compliant set, the Lele matching social categories are also unambiguous. A person is a male or a female, a child or an adult. An adult woman is adult at first menstruation, then either pregnant, a mother or barren. A man is sterile, or adult, proved by begetting and initiation. The coding is activated at every hunt and whenever they sit down to eat. Somewhere at the back of the two codings stands an array of theories about the world, in which names of rituals and of spirits summarise complex diagnoses and standard remedies. To an enquiry about a sick member, the family might reply that the diviner says she has water-animal trouble, or burrowing animal problems. Everyone hearing such an answer can transpose it into dietary terms, or at meal times noticing a woman abstain from fish or burrowing animals can draw sound conclusions.

The theories are about the causes of illness and death. They are causal theories. But the immediate causes are efficient because there is a system in which they are all involved. The causal theories have considerable mutual compatibility. They have been worked out to fit in with established interests in a closely contested system of accountability. The rightness of the categories comes from the fit between the parts of the social system. The Lele have entrenched their theories about the forest and its fauna by embedding them in a given pattern of society. The system of thought in which the theories make sense is also a system of society. Their seemingly bizarre hypotheses about the relation of meat-eating and health depend on the enquiries they have made into empirically observed occurrences. Short-term illness is a sign that the patient has disregarded one of the categories for right eating. The sick room talk is about which local diviners and which familiar remedies to try. Chronic illness is a sign of sorcery and the talk then escalates to village quarrels and suspicions about who has ensorcelled whom and which foreign diviner to call in. The session with the diviner is conducted on standardised question-and-answer lines in standardised divinatory sessions. As Kuhn said, puzzle-solving practices directed to passionately important issues enhance the similarity perceptions of the community and entrench their theories.

The exemplary performances take place all the time. When dusk falls and the households prepare to eat, women and children go together, men group according to age. Particular animal foods will be served, which some are eating and others are refusing. Eating the right foods and abstaining from wrong ones publicly exemplifies the system of social categories. Every meal is ideally a performance of the right script. Some other performances are initiations, others are therapeutic rites. Each performance belongs to a known, named type, and is modelled on other exemplars. Judgments of correct or incorrect performance are not matters of booing or clapping of hands as at a concert, but more like deliberation upon a pressure gauge or medical diagnosis.

INTERESTS

Goodman's account of inductive categories being guaranteed by the theory which they serve and the theory being guaranteed by the rightness of the categories is illustrated by the Lele system of thought. Their coded animal kinds work less like a musical score and more like a pressure gauge. The proof is in the eating. The touchstone of rightness is the way the world reacts to their application of the categories. The villages create their world out of their own social rules, and they reinforce their social categories by the exemplars they make in the world of animals. There is nothing bizarre about the close attention they pay to one another's misfortunes. What else should they be concerned about? How else should they try to secure their hypotheses and convince one another, except by the effectiveness (as well as by the simplicity, economy, and elegance[29]) of their theories?

The members of a Lele village are engaged in a continual scrutiny of their own performances. When they ask whether the right performance has been prescribed to cure a grave trouble, it is as if they were worrying whether the dial of the pressure gauge has been correctly read, or whether anything is interfering with its correct registration. For their lives much hangs on the answer. Possible ambiguities in the animal inscriptions have to be checked and rechecked. The enquiries into what has gone wrong at earlier sick beds or post-mortems refer back to past exemplary diagnoses. Their system of thought works well for them because it is coordinated with their interest networks, extensive with their whole society.

Is this, then, an exotic instance of interest theory applied to the entrenchment of knowledge? Andy Pickering has a model[30] of theoretical change in high energy physics which focuses on the analogical role of an exemplar, and particularly on the scope it gives for referring back to established bodies of knowledge and practice.

> It is precisely the presence or absence of such 'referring back' which enables one to distinguish between exemplary achievements and those which I have called *ad hoc*. Finally, as the concrete embodiment of analogy, the aspect of exemplars which must be stressed is their multidimensional nature. It is only because exemplars are multidimensional constructs that one can

conceive of constellations of *related* bodies of practice based upon different exemplars – and the solidity of our knowledge is clearly dependent upon the extent of such constellations.[31]

From here Pickering goes on to ask how a piece of work becomes a classic which is referred to over and over again. How does anything become an exemplar? By what principles does one study get recognition and change the course of the whole development of the discipline, while another, apparently equally well set for success, is overlooked? For answer, he turns to the concept of interest as developed by Latour and Woolgar. This is basically a market model of scientific activity[32] in which scientists are busy accumulating their own private stock of credibility; they collaborate or work alone insofar as they expect a return on their investment in time and skill. There is a large agonistic element in their relationships modified by interdependence and mutual concern in the set of exemplars they have been using. As Pickering develops this viewpoint, scientists perceive their own interest in 'the deployment of their expertise in the articulation of the exemplar'. For Pickering the exemplar is a construct which intersects with the interests of some particular group or groups, and interest means the scientists' perception of the claims that they can make on behalf of their particular expertise by referring to the exemplar. A welcome aspect of this approach is the introduction of sociological and psychological factors into the discussion of cognition. At least this path of reasoning makes a place for Mary Hesse's point that 'the rules of argument and the criteria for truth are internal to a social system'.[33] Interests are not theories, they are expectations for personal fulfilment and claims on others for consideration. On this argument exemplars become defined and circulate because they intersect with interests rather than because of other grounds for rightness.

Does this imply that entrenchment is arbitrary and haphazard? Pickering's account of the controversy between physicists on the merits of 'charm' versus 'colour' theories in high energy physics is richly textured and depends on a less crude description of interests than I have provided. Even so, it encounters resistance among scientists, and it would not be fair to assume that in resisting his claims for an exemplary account in the philosophy of science they are merely looking out for their interests. There is resistance to the idea that scientists form little closed communities which communicate on the basis of a limited number of shared ideas. David Hull has shown that scientific communities are not so very homogeneous and that their members manage to communicate across them without agreeing on everything. His account of the institutions of science combines the self-interest of individual scientists with the mutual checking and questioning that assures the achievement of science's general goals.[34] In the history of science we find all kinds of cultural variation, entrepreneurial individualists, hierarchical control points, and small enclaves united in protest against some established mainstream. Goodman, Hesse, and Kuhn have been quoted above on the untapped richness in community variation. Scientists understandably reject sociologists' accounting for the success of one theory or another by cynical reduction to personal career interests. Lastly, there is an unacceptable hint of arbitrariness in the explanation by interests, as if a sufficiently powerful network of scientists could get anything established as an exemplar, regardless of merit.

However, in spite of these protests, the system of society must surely provide the justifications necessary for the system of knowledge that it goes by. In the course of world-making there are different sorts of justification, varying according to the kind of world inhabited at the particular time and place. Some kinds of world are like the market-place, where individual agents compete heavily and will not survive unless they look after their own and their allies' interests. This would correspond to the world for which Robert Merton has described the rage and despair of a scientist who finds some precursor has already invented his own invention.[35] It would be like the world of which Latour and Woolgar say that scientific activity 'is a fierce fight to *construct* reality'.[36] Theoretical physicisits may indeed inhabit a ferociously competitive world, and if so there will plausibly be moments when the fate of exemplars is settled mainly by considerations of interest.

But worlds are different. There is an *ad hominem* benefit in using cultural theory. For the sociologist with a theory about how scientific exemplars become established finds scientists themselves lined up in resistance. How can the sociological model be protected against attack? If it speaks from within one cultural bias the attacks are justified. Richard Rorty wrote that 'there is no way to step outside communities to a neutral standpoint'; this was in the context of explaining that for pragmatists there is no way of beating totalitarians by appealing to shared common premises.[37] But there is nothing to stop us from systematically setting up models of different communities based upon different premises, not beating our rivals but including their views as samples of what the world is like.

According to cultural theory a market model of science is not likely to be the only one. It can rest secure for those who believe that all worlds are organised as a market. They are more likely to go on believing this so long as their own world conforms to their expectations. Then their own experience gives their theories confirming exemplars. However, not all science worlds are organised on competitive principles with independent heroes expecting to put their names on valued property.[38] There are several kinds of science networks and well-tried criteria[39] for distinguishing the dominant organising principles of any community. Some cultural theory would help to protect sociology of science from the complaints of practising scientists. It may not be just cussedness on their part: their worlds might be really different.

To apply cultural theory to our original question (of how a hypothesis becomes established) we cannot do better than to follow Kuhn's idea that the production of the exemplar is part of the process of constituting the community. We would then become interested in how many kinds of community we can recognise. Though interest theory says little about the variety of scientific communities, the comparative project would not threaten but add to its explanatory power. Different kinds of community would be constituted on different kinds of exemplars. Kuhn's other idea is methodologically crucial, that puzzle-solving techniques are prime in the process of community creation. The example of the Lele community shows the serious testing that goes on for solving puzzles that deeply concern the community. If we still seem to be left with the initial question, why should exemplars be stronger than metaphors in entrenching knowledge? The answer depends on what we want the knowledge for. Through procedures of accountability in which they serve, exemplars found both the community and its knowledge. Richart Rorty's idea of the world of science is more like David Hull's than the unflattering one described by Merton, Latour and Woolgar, and Pickering. He even advocates it for a model:

> Human communities can only justify their existence by comparisons with other actual and possible human communities.
>
> Is the sort of community exemplified by groups of scientists and by democratic political institutions a means to an end, or is the formation of such a community the only goal we need? Dewey thought it was the only goal we needed, and I think he was right . . . any philosophical system is going to be an attempt to express the ideals of *some* community's way of life.[40]

ACKNOWLEDGMENTS

The problems which this chapter addresses have been present to me since my first fieldwork among the Lele, forty years ago. I am grateful to the Spencer Foundation for a grant which enabled me to return to Zaïre in 1987 to do further research on Lele principles of classification. I have been much helped by criticism from David Bloor, David Hull, Ian Hacking, Ngokwey Ndolamb, Quentin Skinner and Geoffrey Stout, who read early versions of the manuscript. An Italian version has been published under the title of 'Correttezza delle Categorie' in 1989, in *Rassegna di Sociologia*, a.XXX. n.2, pp. 207–38.

NOTES

1 See pp. x and xix of this book.
2 This may be another example of cultural bias forming both the empirical theory of how investigation should be conducted and a matching bias about how the world is. The parallel is suggested by Ian Hacking's account of two styles of statistics, the Prussian style, born of a collectivist political commitment, and the Western style, born of a commitment to individual freedom. Ian Hacking, *The Taming of Chance*, Cambridge, Cambridge University Press, 1990.

3 E. Durkheim, *The Elementary Forms of Religious Life* [1912], London, Allen and Unwin and New York, Macmillan, 1954.

4 Mary Douglas, 'The body of the world', *Tales of Cities, The Culture and Political Economy of Urban Spaces*, International Social Science Journal, Unesco/Blackwell, vol. 25, pp. 395–8.

5 Rodney Needham, *Right and Left: Essays on Dual Classification*, Chicago, University of Chicago Press, 1973. See also *Reconnaissances*, Toronto, University of Toronto Press, 1980, and *Circumstantial Deliveries*, California, University of California Press, 1981.

6 Leonard Meyer, *Emotion and Meaning in Music*, Chicago, Chicago University Press, 1957.

7 Nelson Goodman, 'Seven strictures against similarity', *Problems and Projects*, Indianapolis, The Bobbs Merrill Company, 1972.

8 Nelson Goodman, *Ways of Worldmaking*, Indianapolis, Hackett, 1978, pp. 127–8.

9 Nelson Goodman, *Fact, Fiction and Forecast*, Cambridge, Mass., Harvard University Press, 1979, 1983.

10 Mary Hesse, *The Structure of Scientific Inference*, London, Macmillan, 1979, pp. 80–5.

11 Goodman, *Fact, Fiction and Forecast*, p. 64.

12 Nelson Goodman, *Languages of Art*, Indianapolis, Hackett, p. 93.

13 *Ibid.* p. 63.

14 Hesse, *The Structure of Scientific Inference*.

15 Conventional theoretical lines between the elements have to be drawn for the purpose of matching the inscriptions; there ought to be theoretical neutral space between them and no redundancy or overlap.

16 Clifford Geertz, *Negara: The Theatre State in Nineteenth Century Bali*, Princeton, Princeton University Press, 1970, p. 135.

17 Maurice Bloch, *From Gift to Violence*, Cambridge, Cambridge University Press, 1986.

18 R.G. Lienhardt, *Divinity and Experience: The Religion of the Dinka*, Oxford, The Clarendon Press, 1961.

19 Geertz, *Negara*, p. 135.

20 Israel Scheffler, 'Symbolic aspects of ritual', *Inquiries, Philosophical Studies of Language, Science and Learning*, Indianapolis, Hackett, 1986, chapters 7, 8.

21 Goodman, *Languages of Art*, p. 128.

22 Goodman, *Ways of Worldmaking*, p. 128.

23 T.S. Kuhn, 'Second thoughts on paradigms', *The Structure of Scientific Theories*, ed. Frederick Suppes, Urbana, University of Illinois Press, 1974.

24 A.R. Radcliffe-Brown, 'The sociological theory of totemism', *Structure and Function in Primitive Society: Essays and Addresses*, London, Cohen and West, 1952.

25 Claude Lévi-Strauss, *The Savage Mind*, London, Weidenfeld and Nicolson, 1962.

26 S.J. Tambiah, 'Animals are good to think and good to prohibit', *Ethnology 8*, 4, 424–59.

27 Mary Douglas, *The Lele of the Kasai*, London, International African Institute, 1963, chapter 8, 'Blood debts'.

28 *Ibid.* Chapter 12, and 'Techniques of sorcery control in Central Africa', *Witchcraft and Sorcery in East Africa*, ed. John Middleton and E.H. Winter, London, Routledge & Kegan Paul, 1963, pp. 123–42.

29 Robin Horton, 'African traditional thought and Western science', *Africa*, *37*, 1 and 2, 1967, 50–71, 155–87.

30 Andy Pickering, 'The role of interests in high-energy physics: the choice between "charm" and "colour"', *Sociology*, *4*, 1980, 107–38.

31 *Ibid.* p. 130.

32 Bruno Latour and Steve Woolgar, *Laboratory Life: The Social Construction of Scientific Facts*, London, Sage, 1979.

33 Mary Hesse, *Revolutions and Reconstructions in the Philosophy of Science*, Hemel Hempstead, Harvester Wheatsheaf, 1980.
34 David Hull, *Science as a Process: An Evolutionary Account of the Social and Conceptual Development of Science*, Chicago, Chicago University Press, 1988, p. 357.
35 Robert K. Merton, 'Priorities in scientific discovery: a chapter in the sociology of science', *Proceedings, American Philosophical Society*, CV 471–87; and 'Resistance to multiple discoveries in science', *European Journal of Sociology* (Archives), 4, 1963, 237–82.
36 Latour and Woolgar, *Laboratory Life*, p. 243.
37 Richard Rorty, 'Science as solidarity', London, John Nelson, 1987, pp. 38–53.
38 Celia Bloor and David Bloor, 'Twenty industrial scientists: a preliminary exercise', *Essays in the Sociology of Perception*, ed. Mary Douglas, London, Routledge & Kegan Paul, 1982, pp. 83–102.
39 M. Thompson, R. Ellis and A. Wildavsky, *Cultural Theory*, Colorado, Westview Press, 1990.
40 Rorty, 'Science as solidarity', p. 49.

Chapter 21

Looking back on the 1970 essays

This section starts with the first essay I wrote on risk. 'Environments at risk', (Chapter 16, 1970). The late Aaron Wildavsky read it and immediately engaged me in an intense and exciting collaboration on risk and culture. He had already observed a discipline of risk analysis emerging and was looking out for a critical position to adopt. Since then risk studies have burgeoned into a huge and flourishing industry for policy analysts and health and safety engineers. I am glad to say that, thanks to the work of Wildavsky, Michael Thompson, Steve Rayner and others, a distinctively anthropological voice can be heard on the perception of risk and explanations of disaster.

I entered the field bearing arms for Evans-Pritchard's original 1937 study of Azande witch beliefs.[1] He had showed how belief relates to action: a system of accountability underpins the system of knowledge; if a belief does not legitimate any action, it is no longer interesting, it will lose support and eventually fade out. If certain interests are dissolved or removed, a corresponding section of beliefs loses its support. I am happy to be able to include (Chapter 17) a recent essay that was published in a volume in honour of Aaron Wildavsky, who died in 1993. An argument there against a bogus pretension to objectivity stands at the beginning of a strong move to bring anthropological criticism to bear on the social sciences.[2]

The essay on 'Self-evidence' (Chapter 19) makes a suggestion about how to discover where moral and political biases lurk within classification systems. All through the decades which this volume of essays represents I have been haunted by the 'abominations of Leviticus', the chapter of the Bible which came to my rescue when I was trying to understand the Lele prohibitions on animal foods. Some people are very pollution-conscious, very strict about preserving lines and boundaries, more xenophobic than others. This has always seemed to me to be an important variation in human society that should be studied and would lead to a better understanding of dissenting minorities and fundamentalist sects. But over the passage of time I have realised that the strong pollution consciousness that attaches to the forbidden animals in the Bible is a feature of Judaism rather than of the text of the Bible itself.

This is a very contentious claim, which it would be unsuitable to defend at any length in this volume.[3] But it is relevant to say that the organisation of land animals in Leviticus does project the organisation of human society. Like the Lele social and religious world projected upon animal life, the Bible uses the animals in each environment, sky, water, land, to lay out a projective screen on which the people of Israel saw their place in God's universe. They alone were consecrated and covenanted to be separated from the rest of the world as their consecrated and convenanted flocks and herds were separated from the rest of animal creation. I suggested something of this kind by Venn diagrams in the essay on 'Deciphering a meal' (Chapter 18), and inferred that it was on the right side of biblical scholarship when Jacob Milgrom proceeded to adopt similar diagrams in his Anchor Bible Commentary on Leviticus 1–16 (1991).

The other animals of God's creation are classified by Leviticus as not to be touched when dead. But take note that if their carcases cannot be touched, they cannot be skinned, or carved, or eaten. The rules of impure and abominable animals turn out to be about protecting them from human predation. The Levitical teaching thereby comes into line with the prophets and psalms which always present God as loving and caring for his creation. This makes a radical change in the reading of Leviticus, and it means that the general theory of pollution does not apply to its animals as I thought it did in the early 1960s. But the general theory of pollution would apply to the sages and later commentators who read aversion into the text.

The article on 'Self-evidence' (Chapter 19) is liberally sprinkled with references to philosophy and other learned disciplines. Do not mistake these references for pretension; they are actually desperate signals for help. The problem for anthropology is how to approach the processes of classification as an inherent part of the effort to organise. At that time, ideas about the relation of thought to society were beset by confusions. One is the picture theory of cognition which I have mentioned disparagingly several times in this book.

Graduate students in Oxford in the Institute of Social Anthropology soon after the Second World War were privileged to have in their company a distinguished scholar, Franz Steiner. A Jewish refugee from Nazi oppression, he was finishing a doctoral thesis as a student of Radcliffe Brown, and then of Evans-Pritchard.[4] He frequently warned us against problems with the verb 'to express'. Only recently have I recognised some of the background to this Wittgensteinian type of concern. Moshe Barasch's essay [5] on Conrad Fiedler's aesthetic philosophy shows how theories of representation in art were under attack from the turn of the century. Fiedler's own aesthetic theory was uniquely concerned with the artistic process, so it did nothing to reduce the prestige of sign and signifier in lingustics-based anthropology.

It was all very well to know that picture theories are often wrong and usually misleading. The case of anthropology called for a method of realism, a way to talk about knowledge that does not separate thing from its sysmbol, or distinguish between degrees of reality, thing-itself being real and symbol less so, or the other way round. Above all it is still important not to indulge in the idealism that separates the world of ideas from the world of action. Finally the cry for help was heard. Quentin Skinner guided me to a cognitive theory that does not need to assume some realism gap between thing and expression of the thing. This is the benefit of Nelson Goodman's approach.

When anthropologists use alleged pictorial similarities as the basis for explaining why two things are perceived as the same, they should be encouraged to read Goodman's *Seven Strictures against Similarity*.[6] Goodman bypasses the whole issue of expression, sign and signified, by focusing on a different process in the organising of thought, that is on classifying and sampling instead of perceiving similarity. Classification makes things synonymous by putting them in the same set. Any member of a set can symbolise the other members simply by virtue of shared membership. First it can stand as an exemplar, a sample of the other items in the set, and then, being able to exemplify, it is able to symbolise. This is illustrated in Chapter 20.

A classificatory system is made for use. How classes are made depends entirely on the classifiers' interests. Straight away this approach links knowledge to action. It allows no scope for a world of ideas to take to the air and balloon away without contact with the ground. My essay on Goodman refers explicitly to the Lele ethnography, since it applies his theories to the uses the Lele make

Figure 21.1 Railway Porter (to Old Lady travelling with a Menagerie of Pets). 'Station Master say, Mum, as Cats is "Dogs", and Rabbits is "Dogs", and so's Parrots; but this 'ere "Tortis" is a Insect, so there ain't no charge for it!' (*Punch*, March 6, 1869, vol. 56, p. 96)

of their classifications of animals. So it brings the book back to its starting point and allows me to ground my interpretations of dietary rules instead of leaving then unexplained as metaphors.

NOTES

1 E. Evans-Pritchard, *Witchcraft, Oracles and Magic among the Azande*, Clarendon Press, 1937.
2 Mary Douglas and Steve Ney, *Missing Persons*, California University Press, 1998.
3 See Mary Douglas, *Leviticus as Literature*, forthcoming 1999.
4 Franz Steiner, whose works are about to be published in English translation, died in 1952. Nearly fifty years later his scholarly stature and eminence as a German poet is being recognised. J. Adler ' An Oriental in the West, the originality of Franz Steiner as poet and anthropologist', *Times Literary Supplement*, 7 October 1994, pp. 16–17.
5 Moshe Barasch, *Modern Theories of Art, 2*, New York University Press, 1998, pp. 122–32.
6 Nelson Goodman, *Seven Strictures on Similarity*, New York, Bobbs Merrill, 1968.

Index